RACING
DIE-CAST
COLLECTIBLES

Mark Zeske

and the staff of *Beckett Racing and Motorsports Marketplace*

PRICING ANALYSIS BY DENNY PARSONS

BECKETT PUBLICATIONS

Published by
Beckett Publications
15850 Dallas Parkway
Dallas, Texas 75248

ISBN: 1-887432-81-7
Beckett® is a registered trademark of Beckett Publications.

This book is not licensed, authorized or endorsed by NASCAR, any driver or driver's association.

First Edition: May 2000

Beckett Corporate Sales and Information
(972) 991-6657

Contributors

Book design by David Timmons.

Thanks go to Bono Saunders of Bono's Race Place, George King of Hobby Maker, and Curtis Glass, Racing Champions collector extraordinaire, for lending us hundreds of die cast to be photographed.

PHOTOS

All photos courtesy of beckett.com unless otherwise noted.

Courtesy of Action Performance Companies, Inc.:
    15, 16, 17, 18 (top), 19 (bottom), 37, 58 (top), 62, 63, 64, 66, 68, 69, 70, 71 (top), 72, 77 (bottom), 78, 85
Dehoog/TDP: 123 (bottom)
Courtesy of Georgia Marketing & Promotions: 20
Don Grassman/CIA Stock Photography:
    74 (bottom)
Nigel Kinrade: 86, 120 (top)
Joyce Knoblach: 31
Dan Little: 29, 30
Courtesy of R.J. Reynolds: 77 (top), 89, 104 (top), 129
Courtesy of Sprint: 120 (bottom)
Courtesy of Texas Motor Speedway: 115
Courtesy of Upper Deck: 123 (top)

Contents

Collecting Racing Die-Cast Replicas

Driver Checklists

Racing Die-Cast Price Guide

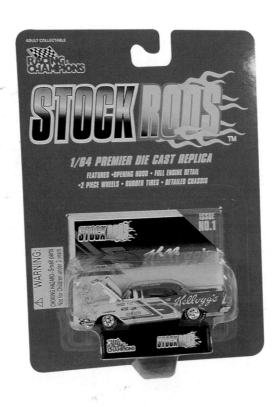

Collecting Racing Die-Cast Replicas

Why You Should Collect Die Cast

Victor Shaffer doesn't have to go far to understand why replica die-cast race cars have revved into high gear, booming into a business that could generate as much as $500 million in sales in 2000.

At home, Shaffer's two young daughters can't resist the miniature cars. No sooner do they get their hands on one, than the car goes zooming across the floor. At work, Shaffer is surrounded by a bunch of NASCAR fans, and they proudly display the colors of their favorite driver with 1:64 scale cars on top of their computers and 1:24 versions dominating the middle of their desks.

"There is just something that is inherently cool about the die-cast car, especially to a race fan," Shaffer says. "There is something magical about it,

kids—both little ones and big kids like me—always like to play with them. But for the race fan, the cars are a real badge of honor.

"Unlike other kinds of collectibles, die cast don't just get put away. People either have them out to display, or have them out to play with."

Not everyone has co-workers who are racing fanatics. Shaffer worked for years as an executive vice-president at Racing Champions, the company that started the market for racing replicas when it first came out with die-cast cars in 1989. Action Performance Companies Inc. has been going fender-to-fender with Racing Champions in the die-cast market since 1992, while toy giants Hasbro and Mattel have joined the NASCAR race in the last four years as the market boomed.

All four companies and hundreds of thousands of collectors seem to be

A variety of scales, paint jobs and variations multiply the sheer number of racing die-cast cars available to collectors.

winning. Action president Fred Wagenhals estimates that four years ago racing die-cast was just short of a $100 million business. He predicts the market in 2000 could reach $500 million.

People collect die-cast cars for a variety of reasons. Some people collect because they love cars and can't afford a 200-car garage, much less the cars to fill it. For many of us, these little vehicles are actually time machines. Many collectors enjoy collecting toy cars because it reminds them of the fun times and carefree joy of their youth. If you spent entire days of your childhood putting together Hot Wheels tracks, re-arranging the order of your

cars, putting together a village with Matchbox toys and testing the speeds of your cars against those of your best friend—you are a likely candidate to be a die-cast car collector.

Some of these reasons also apply to collectors who chase racing die-cast replicas, but the bottom line is simple. Most race collectors are big fans of the sport, and die-cast cars help them feel close to their heroes and the machines they drive on the race track. The bigger the fan's passion for racing, the bigger his collection.

Some just enjoy one form of racing and cheer for just one driver. So this casual collector, for example, might just have a few die-cast cars of

two-time Winston Cup champion Terry Labonte. Perhaps they collect just the replicas of Al Unser Jr., and only because they met the two-time Indianapolis 500 winner at a mall once and got his autograph.

Others, however, are die-hard fans and hard-nosed hobbyists. They eat, drink and sleep NASCAR, and want to get their hands on any stock car replica they can find. Or they worship all forms of racing, drive a Ford, and try to pick up every die-cast replica they can locate with the blue oval on it.

As the popularity of racing has grown in the 1990s, the hobby of collecting racing die-cast replicas has boomed. The growth in just the last three years is amazing.

Mattel has added several Pro Racing lines to its Hot Wheels brand and sponsors Kyle Petty's Winston Cup car to promote its replicas. The company has produced several racing sets, including a Daytona 500 game through a major licensing agreement with Daytona International Speedway, and even a NASCAR Barbie.

Racing Champions quadrupled its business in the past two years, with revenue of $234 million in 1999. The Illinois-based company increased its expansion in 1999 by buying Ertl,

Diecast cars are now available at toy stores, department stores, hobby shops, race trailers, grocery stores and even convenience stores.

another big manufacturer of die-cast replicas that focuses primarily on farm equipment and custom orders. Racing Champions is such a heavy hitter in the retail market that the Toys "R" Us chain named the company its 1998 vendor of the year.

Hasbro created its Winner's Circle line to produce racing replicas, reaching a deal to use Action's licenses with drivers. Hasbro's products are low-priced toys, while Action's products are higher cost, higher quality collectibles. The Winner's Circle 1:64 scale car was the top selling NASCAR-licensed item in 1998 and ranked as one of the nation's fifteen best-selling toys for 1999.

Action has benefited from the boom perhaps more than any other company. In April 1995, Action produced 70,000 die-cast pieces. In May of 1999, Wagenhals says Action produced two million cars in a month for the first time. Hasbro, through its licensing agreement with Action, produced another million cars. In other words, Action's licenses with race teams are producing more than forty times the number of cars that they were five years ago.

Denny Parsons is familiar with the success of all four of the major die-cast producers, plus several others on the fringe of the market. Parsons owns more than 2,000 1:64 scale NASCAR replicas. He used to work at one of the twenty-five Action distributors in the United States, but now tracks the die-

cast market for Beckett Publications, which produces the industry's top monthly price guide, *Beckett Racing & Motorsports Marketplace*.

Parsons believes one reason for the hobby's success is that the manufacturers have created something for everyone, from the collector who wants to get his hands on every piece to a youngster who just wants a single car of his favorite driver.

Increased demand and competition between manufacturers have given collectors more choices than ever. Inexpensive toy-grade replicas can be found at any Target or Eckerds, while there are a couple of highly detailed, limited edition mail-order new releases that cost more than $200. In addition, collectors can find unpainted, gold and chrome versions of their favorite drivers. Cars are available that make noises, have bodies that come off, serve as banks and have moving parts. There are commemorative cars to celebrate race wins and championships and even a Hot Wheels line called Swappin' Paint, where tire marks from an opponent have been left on the side of the car.

"You can get a top of the line Action Elite for about 100 bucks and you can get a $1.96 Racing Champions piece at Wal-Mart, plus virtually anything and everything in between," Parsons says.

For some collectors, the secondary market is important. They care not

A wide range of price points allows racing die-cast collectors to choose their budget.

only how much they pay for something, but also how much it is going to be worth when they turn it over. Some collectors have an even more serious motive: they hope to profit from buying low and selling high. Their plan calls for their collection to rise in value over a period of time, and then they can sell it for a profit. Sometimes just the act of assembling a collection will give additional value to the sum.

While many collectors have profited from their hobby, many others have never sold off even one piece of their collection. Veteran hobbyists will tell you to collect what you like, then no matter what happens, you'll be able to enjoy your collection. The key is to select whatever appeals to you the most.

But get ready. Once you get revved up about collecting die-cast race cars, you might not be able to stop.

"Racing collectors are among the most passionate sports fans there are," Parsons says. "A lot of the collectors are just plain addicted."

Where to Collect Your Replicas

Finding racing die-cast cars to collect can be as easy as going to a convenience store in your neighborhood. Collectors never know when or where they are going to have the next great find for their collection.

Your favorite department chain, drug store, grocery store and even convenience store routinely stock replica race cars. New cars and the latest releases of almost any brand are as close as the nearest mall. The Hot Wheels, Racing Champions and Winner's Circle brands can be found at almost any big toy chain, plus department stores such as Wal-Mart and Target.

Another great place to get your replica is your local hobby shop, which is usually operated by someone who knows a lot about die-cast collecting.

Many hobby shops will carry both new and vintage cars, but some shops may handle just new stock. Many of these types of dealers will often have a mail-order business as well, which can be valuable for a collector who lives in a rural area, has no hobby shops in his city or doesn't live close to a race track.

Racing collectibles can be found at two types of hobby shops. One is a general sports collectibles shop, the modern-day survivor of the old-fashioned baseball card shop. These shops will have some die-cast replicas sprinkled with their cards and their action figures. The other type of shop is an "everything racing" store, where die-cast cars usually vie for shelf space with T-shirts, hats and other racing apparel. Other collectibles include posters, signs, games and trading cards. NASCAR Thunder, a chain of stores licensed by NASCAR and oper-

ated by The Nashville Network, is one such shop.

Another version of these "everything racing" stories is the souvenir rig that travels from one race to another. These traveling trailers of souvenirs and memorabilia are often your best bet to find that latest and greatest die-cast car of your favorite driver.

Consequently, races can take on the characteristics of a collectibles show, another traditional spot to pick up a great piece.

Yet while racing is booming in popularity and brands such as Hot Wheels and Racing Champions have been staples of the biggest toy chains

for years, stock car racing has long been a regional sport.

There's no doubt that it is easier to get a hot, new release of a NASCAR legend such as Dale Earnhardt in North Carolina than in Oregon. Because of this, the racing hobby is full of mail-order dealers or collectors who buy and sell on the Internet.

Other collectors can also be a great source for die-cast cars. You can meet these brother and sister hobbyists by joining a club or collectors group, attending races or die-cast shows, and searching the Internet for discussion groups or on-line auctions.

Regional releases can provide collectors cross-country challenges when it comes to filling their collections.

NASCAR networks such as TNN have recognized the racing die-cast collectibles craze.

Collector club meetings will often turn into mini-shows. These meetings or major local shows usually offer a decent mix of both old and new cars. Because the crowds at these shows are primarily knowledgeable collectors, prices are reasonable.

Many great sources of non-racing toys cars aren't as good for the die-cast replicas of your favorite driver. The primary reason is that the racing market hasn't been in the mainstream long enough.

For example, collectors can frequently find a great deal on old Hot Wheels because a store or a chain is treating the cars like they are part of their toy inventory instead of a much

wanted and valuable collectible. Occasionally you can find cars that have been stored away in a warehouse for two or three years by the same retail shops that are selling the newest releases.

While some of these great deals include racing replicas, most of this discount die cast is non-racing. But some good racing bargains can be found at places that don't sell die-cast cars as their primary focus. Garage sales, swap meets, flea markets, thrift stores, antique dealers, estate sales and rummage sales often offer great opportunities. One of the major drawbacks to this approach is that you can stop at dozens and dozens of garage sales without even seeing a die-cast car.

Hard-to-find cars can pop up at garage sales or big-time hobby shops.

Networks such as QVC and the Home Shopping Network often enlist drivers to help sell collectible cars.

Of course, the more knowledge a collector has the better position they are to find a bargain. Beginning car collectors, on the other hand, should be wary. Just because a car looks old and the guy at the flea market says he has never seen one like it before, that doesn't mean the car is of any significant value. While buyers can benefit from a seller's unfamiliarity with the die-cast collectible market, they can also be hurt by it. A good strategy is to take a collector's guide such as this one or a monthly publication such as *Beckett Racing & Motorsports Marketplace* to help you determine prices and identify models.

Sometimes entire collections will be up for sale in auctions or estates sales. Many veteran collectors will advertise offers to buy die-cast collections in the classified section of local newspapers.

This can be a great way to significantly boost your collection at a low cost. With transactions such as these, you will often get duplicates of cars you already own. Collectors can turn this into a plus by then using these duplicates as trade bait at the next club meeting or die-cast show. Or perhaps collectors can sell these duplicates to other hobbyists, then use the cash to fill in holes in their collection.

From garage sales to trailers right outside the NASCAR garage at a Winston Cup race track, collectors need to keep their eyes open. There's no end to the places to snatch up that next great addition to a racing die-cast collection.

How to Collect Racing Die Cast

Even if a racing collector has hit it big in the lottery, there is simply no way to collect every die-cast replica produced. All beginning collectors come to the realization that their collection needs to have a focus point, a particular direction.

With the diversity of die-cast race cars available, the decision of what to collect is a difficult one. Scale can be an issue. For others, it's a particular brand, but even then most collectors need to narrow down their focus. Others possible factors in a collector's decision may be price or availability.

A beginning collector's best option is to start out with a particular criteria, then expand based on time, storage space and budget. Nobody can choose your game plan for you because it should be based on what makes you happy. You can even mix and match and, in fact, most collectors do. They'll

Beginning collectors should select a criteria such as Dale Earnhardt vehicles.

Collectors can show allegiance to sponsors such as Goodwrench . . .

Sponsor—Some collectors chase die-cast cars that carry the colors and logos of their favorite company. Coca-Cola, McDonald's, Anheiser-Busch, Miller Brewery, General Motors and Pennzoil are among the major corporations that have sponsored race cars for an extended period of time and in a variety of series.

collect every piece from the Winner's Circle line by Hasbro, but they'll also pick up all the replicas they can find of their favorite driver no matter the brand.

Here's some of the most common ways that car collectors approach the hobby:

Driver—By far the most common way to collect die cast is to chase the replicas piloted by a fan's favorite driver. Thanks to frequent changes of car makes and sponsors, drivers racing on multiple circuits and special paint jobs, a collector should have plenty of replicas to hunt down. The recent trend of die-cast makers produceing replicas from an earlier time in a driver's career has also increased the options. Many collectors have more than one favorite driver, so that can double or triple their fun. A good example of this would be fans of the Earnhardt family, who can chase replicas of both Dale and Dale Jr.

Series—The sport of auto racing is vast and varied. The type of cars range from dragsters that just race a quarter of a mile at a time to exotic sports cars that race 24 hours at a time. The most popular form of racing for die-cast collectors in the United States is the stock car circuits sanctioned by NASCAR. But Formula One, sprint cars, drag racing machines and Indy-style cars also are in strong demand.

Car Model—Race fans usually have a strong allegiance to one car make or

... or DuPont die-cast vehicles.

Budweiser vehicles are popular among NASCAR and beer brand collectors.

another. Consequently, many collectors will chase just replicas of Ford or Chevy. A Pontiac collector, for example, could have put together a collection of cars in 1999 for drivers such as Ernie Irvan, Bobby Labonte and Tony Stewart, all Pontiac drivers.

Promotional Cars—All sorts of companies involved in racing—from sponsors

Some collectors build their sets around NASCAR manufacturers such as Chevy, Ford and Pontiac.

such as Kellogg's to companies like Beckett Publications—will produce racing die cast to promote their company and its products. Many products, ranging from Country Time Lemonade to Jimmy Dean Sausage, have had mail-in die-cast offers on their packaging.

Support Vehicles or Team Machines

—Race fans also have a variety of support vehicles that they can collect as replicas. Among the many types of vehicles that have been sold in the colors of race teams are transporters, dually trucks, vans, Suburbans and pit wagons. In addition, die-cast planes and trains have been made with team colors and logos. A couple of real popular lines—Racing Champions Stock Rods and Winner's Circle Cool Customs—feature street cars from the past painted like a NASCAR racer.

Year—Many collectors will simply get one version of a car released from a certain year, then move to another year. Most often these collectors will limit themselves to one manufacturer. Often, beginning collectors will just chase the current releases, then work their way backward.

A variety of scales provide die-cast collectors options in detail, storage and price points.

Manufacturer—Some people try to collect as many replicas from one maker as possible. For instance, a Racing Champions collector would try to gather as many different drivers' replicas as possible made by the Illinois-based company. There are many variations on this theme, as a collector might limit himself to a certain manufacturer and scale (1:64 Hot Wheels) or a manufacturer's particular line (Action's Open Hood).

Variations—Many collectors just love those variations, created by changes in a die-cast car during its production run. Often the reasons for these changes have been long forgotten. Sometimes the plant will just run out of paint or a certain kind of wheel and switch to keep from shutting the factory down for the day. Other times a major change in the system, such as the latest innovation in robotic technology, will create a different look.

The changes could also have something to do with the packaging process. Many variations are easily explained as the result of cost-saving moves, while some are just the manufacturer fixing some mistake it made in the first version of the replica.

Series—Each manufacturer structures their series in different ways, so collecting by series can involve a wide variety of projects. A Racing Champions fan can chase just the Authentics line or an Action collector can buy just Elite models. An advantage of this type of collection is that usually each line will have a well-defined checklist.

Blister packs—Many variations are created when a die-cast car is packaged. Some collectors only want cars that are still in the original blister pack, thus ensuring they'll be in the best condition possible. While this is an easy way to collect current releases, it can get difficult for vintage models.

Scale—Scales are usually expressed as a ratio (1:64) or as a fraction (1/64). The larger the second number, or denominator, the smaller the scale. A 1:1 would be a regular sized car, while a 1:12 is twice the size of 1:24 car. In general, the larger the scale, the more the detail. A trend in recent years has been for large cars to be expensive collector's editions, not really toys at all

Sponsor race teams cross over from NASCAR to open-wheel die-cast collectibles.

Many new collections begin with 1:64 scale cars, but 1:18 scale collectibles are big sellers, too.

but more like a statue of a car. The larger scales can be a challenge to display.

The most popular scale for manufacturers and beginning collectors is 1:64, a size first made popular when Hot Wheels and Matchbox produced non-racing die cast in the 1950s and 1960s.

Another popular size is 1:43, primarily because this scale works with many of the popular train sets. Companies such as Danbury Mint and Franklin Mint frequently use a 1:24 scale, while 1:18 is popular with auto enthusiasts who collect the die-cast cars to reflect their love for real cars out there on the streets and highways. Racing die-cast makers also use these scales, plus Action produces 1:32 repli-

cas and Racing Champions has a line of 1:144 products. Many companies use a 1:87 scale to produce replicas of a race team's transporters.

Many collectors stick with the popular 1:64 size so they can buy more pieces. Other collectors chase fewer pieces, but want more detail and are willing to pay for it, so they grab the large scales. For some, staying with just one scale is enough, but others will collect replicas in all scales of their favorite driver.

No matter what the scale of car you collect or what criteria you chose to make your want list, make sure to have fun. Your collection should reflect your personality and the things that you enjoy.

Die-Cast Value Guide

How much is your racing die-cast car worth?

Two primary factors go into determining the value of your die-cast car: the supply versus demand equation, and its condition. And of all the variables involved in these two factors, the biggest is probably the popularity of the driver and team.

The supply of a certain car depends on a variety of items, but it is primarily set by the number of die-cast replicas produced by the manufacturer.

Also, attrition can be a factor. If a certain brand or line of cars get played with, while collectors tend to keep another manufacturer's pieces in their blister pack, the line that gets toyed with will likely have less cars in mint condition over a long period of time. Mattel's Pro Racing line of cars, for instance, work with the Hot Wheels line of toy tracks, so chances are good that some of them will get beaten up by children.

Time can also be a big factor. Simply, there will be more replicas from Racing Champions on the market from 1999 than there will be from 1989. Damage during shipping, licensing and production problems, legal battles and financial difficulties can all change the availability of a car.

For the most part, the rarer the car the better. Companies that limit their production have a better chance of their replicas becoming valuable collectibles. Consequently, rare variations can be worth 50 times more than the normal replica.

But of course, even a rare car has to be wanted by someone. If no one wants a particular variation, even if it is one of a kind, it is not going to be valuable in the marketplace. Trends

come and go, so it's hard to predict how long one trend might last. Many releases are in demand when they first come out, then interest wanes.

The popularity of the driver is probably the biggest factor in the demand. As a rule, the more a driver wins, the more popular his die-cast cars. But other factors also come in to play, including personality, team sponsor, hobby reputation among collectors, media exposure, commercials and age.

Bill Elliott, for example, has been winning the Winston Cup Most Popular Driver Award longer than Jeff Gordon has been competing in NASCAR. He's also had a string of marketing powerhouses such as Budweiser and

McDonald's as his sponsor. Consequently, even though he hasn't challenged for a championship the past few years, Elliott is in such demand that he's a spokesperson for Racing Champions. The flamboyant and popular Kyle Petty, who is sponsored by Hot Wheels and comes from a successful stock car racing family, is another example.

Funny Car legend John Force combines the best of everything, making him the most popular driver by far in the ranks of professional drag racing. Not only is Force perhaps the funniest and most spontaneous man in all of racing, but he also won eight NHRA titles in a nine-year stretch in the 1990s.

Since 1989, when Racing Champions began mass-producing racing die cast and for all practical purposes started the hobby, five drivers have won Winston Cup titles. All five have been popular with collectors—including 1992 champion Alan

Racing die-cast condition values are often separated between packaged and unpackaged collectibles.

Kulwicki, who died the following year in a plane crash—helping to drive replica sales.

During this time, two drivers have won multiple championships: Dale Earnhardt with four and Jeff Gordon with three. Not surprisingly, replicas of these two drivers are the most desired pieces on the market.

What racing circuit he drives on can also affect a driver's hobby popularity. In the 1990s, as the racing die-cast market has grown, the popularity of NASCAR and its Winston Cup circuit has rocketed. Consequently, a lesser Winston Cup star might still find his die-cast replicas in as much demand as a popular champion might in another form of racing. NASCAR drivers, for the most part, dominate the hobby.

The driver, however, is not the only reason a car can be in demand. Sometimes a team will have paint jobs featuring popular sponsors, such as Scooby Doo and Fred Flintstone schemes from the Cartoon Network Racing Team. The manufacturer can also create a product that will capture the fancy of collectors because of a new twist or high level of quality. Action's Hood Open and Elite series and Racing Champions' Stock Rods and NASCAR Rules are among the many lines that created strong buzz among collectors when they first came out.

Besides supply and demand, the condition of your die-cast car will go a long way in establishing its value. Even the rarest cars, if it is beat up and missing wheels, won't be in big demand.

Obviously, the better in condition your car, the more it will be valued by collectors. Condition isn't as important a factor with racing die-cast cars as it is for non-racing Hot Wheels and Matchbox. Collectors of racing die cast tend to keep their cars in mint condition, primarily because they don't play with them. The cars are often kept in the blister pack or are taken out of their package only to be displayed. Few issues have been released where there are not an abundant supply of racing die cast in mint condition.

One thing to watch out for, however, is that not even cars kept untouched in a blister pack can be automatically designated as mint. In fact, many toy cars already have blemishes before they leave the manufacturer. Mattel officials understand the distinction. In company literature, the toy maker defined four types of conditions just for cars in blister packs to help collectors.

A car "New in Blister" is the original package and has no visible flaws, with the package being undamaged. Flaws can't be found on the car even upon close examination.

A car with no visible flaws but in an original package that is distressed is called "New in Damaged Blister." A

close inspection of the car shows no flaws but the package has curls, creases, rips, discoloration, stains, cracks or a variety of other problems.

Mattel uses the "Almost New in Blister" tag for a car in the original packaging that has visible flaws. Possible flaws include discoloration,

the car can be spotted even though it is still in the package, while the blister pack also has visible signs of wear and tear.

But for the most part, these designations haven't caught on yet among the collectors of racing die-cast replicas. And they might not ever, if

The Cartoon Network has painted several characters on the hoods of NASCAR die-cast cars.

chips in the paint, flaking and a bubbling of the paint. These cars can even contain nicks, almost as if someone on the assembly line had accidentally dropped it on the floor before putting it in the blister pack. These designation means that the package is mint.

Finally, Mattel uses the designation of "Almost New in Damaged Blister" if both the car and the packaging have flaws. The imperfections on

the majority of collectors keep their cars in their original packaging or parked safely in a display case. If enough racing die-cast collectibles are kept in mint condition, any other condition will just be considered unacceptable.

On the other hand, the racing die-cast market is really just a decade old. Many of the early Racing Champions can still be found in their flat-bottom packages, but there are also many that

have been played with much like the original Hot Wheels of the late 1960s. Fifty years from now, when Jeff Gordon Jr. is about to retire from the Winston Cup circuit, many of the top die-cast pieces from the 1990s might well show their age.

The die-cast hobby as a whole hasn't adopted any one system of grading die-cast cars, even with the non-racing products such as Matchbox and Hot Wheels that have been around for decades.

Hot Wheels expert Michael Thomas Strauss and several Matchbox authors have published point systems of grading. While the details vary from one method to the other, the main ideas is that you can evaluate a car by adding up points for any defects found on the vehicle. Different defects have various point values.

Minor defects include:

- A small, barely noticeable scratch
- Slight wear on a decal
- Slightly tarnished base
- Minor wear on a wheel

More serious flaws, which commonly deduct twice or three times as many points as a minor defect, include:

- Up to three barely noticeable scratches
- Noticeable wear on decals
- Slightly crooked tampo or decal
- Substantial wear on decals

- A tarnished base
- Wheels show considerable wear

Major defects include:

- Small, but noticeable scratches
- More than one small dark spot
- A very noticeable dark spot
- Obvious scratches
- Paint missing
- Parts missing

Some scales are from 1 to 10, while others are up to 50. If no points are deducted, you might have a perfect 10, or a mint condition car. But most beginning collectors are quick to tag a car with a mint designation when it is far from being so.

Keeping up with all the changing variables that go into determining the value of your die-cast collection can be difficult, especially with millions of cars being made each month.

For many collectors, price guides are a must. *Beckett Racing & Motorsports Marketplace* (P.O. Box 7649, Red Oak, IA, 51591-0649) is one such price guide. The publication can help you find out what's new, what's hot in the hobby and whether or not that Jeff Gordon Star Wars car sitting on the dealer's table is really work the price tag. In addition, price guides can help you catalogue your current collection or create your hobby want list.

Maintaining and Displaying Die-Cast Cars

Collecting die-cast replicas of race cars can be addictive.

Before you know it, those first few have turned into a super-speedway field and there's not enough room to park all of your racing replica haulers on the corner of your desk.

Perhaps you've just hit the jackpot. You've picked up a big collection at a garage sale, yet the quality of the pieces vary from junkyard dogs to immaculate recent releases. How do you sort through this mess and what do you do with each car?

Most collectors try to keep their die-cast cars in their original packaging, since it adds value to the piece. What you do with your cars can be more important than how you find and acquire them. Here are some of the basics.

Storage and Display

Many veteran hobbyists and passionate race fans give their collection a room of its own. In addition, many of these collectors help their youngsters to start a collection of their own so the kids won't be tempted to play with mommy or daddy's cars.

Several manufacturers make plastic and wooden display cases just for die-cast cars. Most issues of collector magazines such as *Beckett Racing & Motorsports Marketplace* carry ads for such display cases. Of course, any carpenter can create a custom case to fit your own needs. Some collectors will buy display cases, often getting a good deal from stores going out of business, that were originally meant to house watches or jewelry.

Many collectors will use thumbtacks to hang blister packs to a bulletin board or wall. Regular book-

shelves can also be used and are quite popular with fans who want to put on display a wide variety of collectibles, mixing trading cards, autographed magazines, promotional pieces and other items with their die-cast cars.

If you are going to have fun collecting, displaying your collection is a priority.

"You just have to display some of your cars," says Mark Winkelman, a veteran hobbyist who is partial to Fords but collects a wide variety of die-cast cars. "If you keep them all in boxes stored away some place, you won't enjoy them as much. If you've got them displayed, just looking at them will get you excited about your collection.

"Sometimes I move them around in the case just to give them a different look, and I always get fired up about my collection."

Most race fans proudly display all or part of their collection, as often it serves as their pledge of allegiance to their favorite driver. These collector fans want every one to know exactly for whom they cheer. Also, changing your display occasionally also keeps the light from constantly hitting the cars from the same direction and fading them.

Caring for your cars is important

Supercollector Tom Henson of California doesn't hide any of his Earnhardt collection. "Everything I buy goes on display," Henson says.

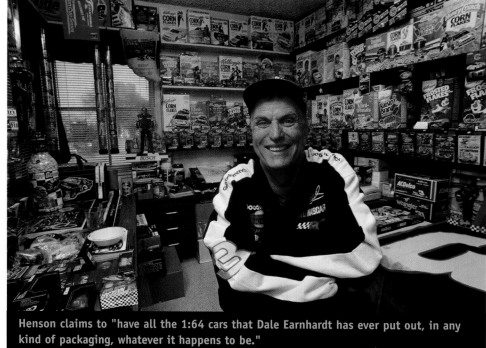

Henson claims to "have all the 1:64 cars that Dale Earnhardt has ever put out, in any kind of packaging, whatever it happens to be."

in retaining their value to you and for their future value to others. So no matter which route you go with a piece—display or storage—the less a car is handled, the better off it will be.

Some collectors use cotton gloves when they handle prized pieces. Always wash your hands thoroughly before touching your cars with your bare hands. Avoid touching bare die-cast metal with your fingers, as the oils, acids and salts from your skin will cause them to tarnish over time. Basically, the chemicals in your hand will do to your car what the salt placed on snowy and icy roads does to real cars. Decals are obviously easier damaged than the metal of a car, so try to avoid touching them if at all possible.

Some collectors have found that jewelry boxes make great transporta-

tion boxes, with one loose 1:64 car fitting nicely in each compartment. Cardboard boxes that new computer keyboards come packaged in are great for boxed 1:64 cars.

For the die-cast race cars that you are going to store away, spend a few dollars to protect them. Large-scale replicas, either 1:18 or 1:24, usually come in boxes with Styrofoam packaging inside. These boxes can usually be easily stacked inside larger cardboard boxes.

On the market are plastic clam shells for blister packs and small plastic boxes for even 1:64 scale loose cars. The clam shells and their blister packs store nicely in boxes that were originally meant for copier paper. If nothing else, collectors can use small plastic bags to help keep their loose cars safe.

Your collection needs to stay out of the attic. Cars need to be kept in a dry and dust-free environment, a place where the temperatures don't vary greatly. Dust can easily scratch or damage the toy's finish. Moisture and temperature changes can cause the metal in your cars to deteriorate.

Some types of die-cast cars might need special handling. Some lines of Hot Wheels and Johnny Lightning, for instance, have built-in batteries that should be removed. The batteries tend to corrode, and not only corrode the paint of the car they are in, but also the ones around them.

One issue that hasn't yet been addressed in the die-cast racing hobby is the storage of cars in their boxes, probably because the hobby is still

Indiana native Roger Moore dove into Jeff Gordon collectibles including the racer's early cars and tires.

young. Collectors of vintage Matchbox cars have found that they need to be separated from their original boxes, though they want to collect both. The very collectible boxes weren't built to stand the test of time and were printed on high-acidity card stock. The acid in paper will turn decals yellow and eventually even disintegrate rubber treads. One alternative is to use a small plastic bag as a liner, and keep the car in the box.

This might not be much of a problem in racing as the paper has changed considerably over the years. In addition, most of the large scale boxes would be helped by Styrofoam and bubble-wrap packaging.

Restoration

Because large volumes of die-cast race replicas have only hit the market in the past decade, most cars you add to your collection will be in mint condition. If you pick up any loose pieces, the situation may be different. Clearly something such as the Days of Thunder cars made by Racing Champions, originally available at Exxon stations and made as a toy, will be hard to find in mint condition.

Some cars will need cleaning, but collectors need to be careful. You don't really want to open a miniature car wash and be running your car through jet streams of water. Generally, the less water the better. Sometimes you'll pick up an older car that has been played

with and your only choice is to give it a quick bath. No matter how much water you use, soft bristle toothbrushes can be used to get into the cracks and crevices. The older the toothbrush, the better, as the bristles will get even softer with age and use. Keep your toothbrushes away from decals, however.

Many collectors will use a little bit of glass cleaner on their car, which will give their toy vehicles a new shine. Polishing compounds and even car wax—yes, the same polishing compound used on the car you drive to work each day—is also used by many collectors on their cars. The wax really does help restore die-cast cars to their original brilliance, though you might want to give a wax job to the least valuable pieces of your collection until you are satisfied with the process. Most collectors use a cotton swab to apply the wax, moving lightly and in a circular motion.

Collectors are free to go beyond cleaning and repairing, but it is important to keep your goals in mind when making decisions about major restoration.

For instance, cars can be touched up with a paint job, making small chips and nicks disappear. It can be expensive, but you can even give your die-cast car an entirely new paint job and make it look practically brand new. Of course, unless a collector is experienced at painting die-cast cars,

Handling their cars is important to some racing die-cast collectors who choose a hands-on display.

odds are their paint job will do more damage than good.

Collectors who are interested in eventually selling their collection should probably stay away from paint jobs. If they do try to sell or trade their cars, they need to let the potential new owner know of the restoration steps taken.

Customizing

Of course, collectors can do whatever they want to with their cars, especially if little consideration is given to reselling the vehicles. Some hobbyists demand even more details from their

race cars than the manufacturer and will paint additional logos or striping.

Some fans won't like how the maker of the replica matched the paint to the real vehicle, especially with some of the off-the-chart colors now being used by race teams, so they'll mix up their own batch of paint and try to do better. Collectors will even take apart die-cast cars and add details to the inside of the car. When it comes to restoration and customizing, anything that can be done with a big car can be done to a small car.

Other collectors elect to showcase their car collection under glass.

Insurance

No matter how big or small the size of your collection, you should think about insurance to cover your valuables in case of theft, fire, flood or any other kind of destruction. Cherished collectibles usually can't be replaced in the heart, but that doesn't mean the disaster has to be an entire loss.

Often, collectors can get a new lease on life if they have had the proper insurance on their collection. A well-funded collector can get right back in the hunt, often with a much better idea of chasing down all those items on the new want list.

Getting the proper insurance on your collection isn't difficult, especially if you house your collectibles at your home. Talk to your agent about the specifics of your collection. In many cases, a small collection will already be covered under your current homeowners insurance. But the bigger and more valuable the collection, the greater your insurance needs.

Many policies will insure specific categories of items, such as a racing die-cast collection, only up to a certain amount. If your collection's value is above that amount, you can "schedule" out specific items and insure those separately. Some companies even offer special collector's insurance, which might require a professional appraisal. But if your collection is big enough, going through this process can be well worth it.

Even if you have to get an addendum or rider added to your current policy, it is easily done and affordable. Renters who keep their collection at home should make sure they have renter's insurance.

Collectors should keep accurate records of their collection, including purchase prices and receipts. In addition, keep an inventory and photograph your collection. Keep these in a safe place, away from the collection, so that you will have your records if disaster strikes.

Collectors Clubs

Collector clubs have been around almost as long as die-cast cars. In fact, they've been around much longer than the mainstream market for racing die-cast collectibles, which have been produced on a large scale for only a decade.

Matchbox, for instance, had a club in the early 1960s before Mattel had even dreamed up their Hot Wheels line. But when Mattel did rev up its toy line, it also quickly introduced a club for kids of any age that wanted to be a part of the Hot Wheels phenomenon.

The clubs, in fact, provided special die-cast cars as a membership privilege. The chrome Hot Wheels cars of the late 1960s are some of the hobby's most desirable pieces. Both these trends continue today as Hot Wheels still has a collectors club, offering a

wide variety of benefits. These include a newsletter, exclusive merchandise, T-shirts, bumper stickers and more.

Hot Wheels was quick to modify its club for racing collectors when the line was extended to NASCAR and other racing series. During the 1999 NASCAR season, for instance, one of the exclusive offers for club members was a Pontiac replica similar to the one that Kyle Petty drives on the Winston Cup circuit. The car was from the 1:24 Hot Wheels Legends line but it had a different twist: a Hot Wheels 30th anniversary paint scheme.

Other racing die-cast manufacturers such as Action Performance Companies and Racing Champions were quick to imitate the Hot Wheels and Matchbox clubs.

The Racing Collectibles Club of America is a big part of Action's success. With more than 120,000 members, the club provides Action with

many of its strongest collectors. Action, in fact, produces many of its die-cast replicas just for its RCCA members, with complete RCCA lines.

But Action didn't just stop with one club. The company also offers membership in SelectNet, an on-line club. Members are offered racing replicas with an even more limited production than RCCA members. SelectNet also provides notification of cars for sale by e-mail with a three-week window of opportunity to buy. After the ordering period is over, Action makes the product, limiting the number made to the number ordered. Membership to Action's clubs is free.

Racing Champions also has more than one club. New for 1999 is the Platinum Club, formed to honor Racing Champions' 10th anniversary. For the $24.95 membership fee, you receive a Platinum 1:64 scale club car, a club collector pin and a membership card. The fee is only charged once and allows members to receive catalog offers that feature "members only" collectibles, which range from die-cast replicas to trading cards.

Johnny Lightning also offers a club—NewsFlash—with several levels of membership. The first NewsFlash car for members only was a 1954 Corvette Nomad.

Manufacturers often form clubs to help increase sales, but there are other types of clubs that aren't formed by manufacturers. If you have just a dozen members in your community interested in collecting cars, you can benefit from coming together as a club. Many of these clubs have established home pages on the Internet so they can share their tips and secrets with collectors not in their neighborhood.

Local collecting clubs help members keep abreast of the latest releases, share secrets of collecting, trade pieces and organize shows. These clubs are invaluable sources of information for the beginning collector.

Racing die-cast clubs haven't grown to the extent of the non-racing ones, primarily because people have been collecting Matchbox and Hot Wheels cars for much longer. The largest of these non-racing clubs have been around for a number of years and were founded by collecting experts. These large, international clubs provide something different than your local variety. Most of these large clubs publish newsletters written by veteran collectors with connections all over the world.

One such example is Matchbox USA, which was founded in 1977 by Charlie Mack. Another is Michael Thomas Strauss' club in San Carlos, Calif., which helps organize the Hot Wheels National Convention each year.

Collectors of racing replicas have a different kind of club they can turn to: drivers' fan clubs. Almost every driver at the top levels of professional

racing has a fan club. These clubs were formed to help the driver manage his fan mail, handle autograph requests and sell souvenirs.

These fan clubs can be a great resource for a racing die-cast collector, as almost every club will sell cars of their driver. Most of these die-cast cars will be the same kind that are available at your local hobby shop or retail toy store, but that doesn't mean the fan club doesn't provide a valuable service. If you've ever gone to your local Toys "R" Us week after week looking for that Johnny Benson piece, yet all you can ever find is the replica cars of Jeff Burton and Ricky Rudd, you'll know what we mean.

In addition, your favorite driver's fan club may give you collectible opportunities you just can't get anywhere else. Perhaps

you can get your hero to autograph your replica, or maybe the fan club will have a special die-cast piece made just for them. The Jeff Gordon National Fan Club, for instance, has offered an annual piece since it's inception. For the first couple of the years the cars were made by Racing Champions, but when Gordon signed an exclusive deal with Action a few years back, Jeff's fan club switched manufacturers. Most Gordon fans would be thrilled to have a complete run of these die-cast cars.

To see how closely fan clubs are involved in the die-cast market, you don't have to look any farther than Action Performance Companies. Action not only makes exclusive die-cast replicas for many fan clubs, it actually runs the clubs of five of

Racing fan clubs and collectors clubs often release exclusive models of die-cast collectible cars.

NASCAR's top drivers: Dale Earnhardt, Dale Earnhardt Jr., Bobby Labonte, Dale Jarrett and Rusty Wallace. Not surprisingly, each driver's club has special die-cast offers for members.

Action has even teamed up with stock car racing's top sanctioning body to form the NASCAR Fan Club. One of the benefits of membership is an exclusive NASCAR Fan Club die-cast car made by Action.

So if you are one of the thousands of fans discovering that you like collecting racing die-cast, join the club. You've got plenty to choose from, and membership does have its privileges.

Die-Cast Clubs

This is by no means an exhaustive list of car collectors clubs, but one that will help point you in the right direction. If you can't find a club close to your home, consider recruiting a couple of other collectors and creating your own.

Action
Racing Collectibles Club of America
1-800-952-0708
SelectNet
www.speedmall.com/selectnet/

Diecast Toy Collectors Association
(DTCA)
Dana Johnson
P.O. Box 1824
Bend, OR 97709-1824

Johnny Lightning Collector Club
1-800-MANTIS-8

Hot Wheels Collector Club
1-800-852-1075

Matchbox Club
1-800-524-TOYS

Matchbox Collectors Club
Everett Marshall
P.O. Box 977
Newfield, NJ 08344
609-697-2800

Matchbox International Collectors
Association (MICA)
North America Chapter
P.O. Box 28072
Waterloo, Ontario, Canada N2l 6J8
519-885-0529

Matchbox USA
Charlie Mack
62 Saw Mill Rd.
Durham, CT 06422
203-349-1655

National Hot Wheels Newsletter
Mike Strauss
26 Madera Ave.
San Carlos, CA 94070

Surfing the Internet

So, you're having trouble finding the Jeff Gordon Star Wars replica in the scale you want. You'd also like to go back and fill in a couple of gaps in your Winner's Circle collection, needing just a couple of common cars to have a complete run of the new Hasbro line. And you're really a Mark Martin collector, but you've also heard that Revell made some large-scale Scooby-Doo collectibles of the Cartoon Network Racing team a couple of years ago and you just have to get one for your kids.

In years past, collectors would let their fingers do the walking to find some of their prized possessions. A few minutes in the phone book, a couple of calls, and they'd be just a trip to the hobby shop away from finding that new Dale Earnhardt Jr. release with the Budweiser sponsorship.

And that method will still work, as will making the trip to your local racing collectibles show and actually letting your feet do the walking from table to table. But as the hobby heads into the next millennium, your fingers don't walk. They control your computer's mouse and head to the Internet. If you can't find what you want on the World Wide Web, then it's probably not on the market.

Of course, you need to have access to a computer that is wired to the Internet, but there's one as close as your local library. And the possibilities are almost endless. Any of the popular search engines will reveal thousands of Internet sites with information on die-cast cars. For instance, doing a search during the 1999 racing season on "Hot Wheels" with Alta Vista resulted in 13,564 matches, while "Racing Champions" came up with 3,273 and Action Performance Companies had a whopping 1,720,890.

Another effort on "Revell" with the Infoseek search engine produced 9,311 matches. Using Snap to look for "Racing Die Cast," collectors would have had 141,463 sites to explore.

Sure, not all of these matches will be good hits as you'll have to sort through the sites to find exactly what you want. The Action Performance search, for example, led us to many companies that dealt with performance enhancing products for real cars, not replicas. But you'll quickly learn how to pick out the good sites without wasting too much time. You'll quickly find hundreds of home pages trying to sell just the cars you were looking for, or perhaps a slight variation. Hard-to-find items will still be rare, but you'll have a better chance than the local hobby shop or that show at the VFW Hall.

For collectors, these virtual dealers offer several advantages to the local shop. First, hard-to-find pieces become a little easier to locate. Collectors can find a better inventory with a wider range of choices by visiting several stores, even if the stop is electronic. In addition, collectors get a chance to do comparison shopping, finding the best price in the World Wide Web.

Most large companies now have Internet sites to help them do business. But many collectors have also built home pages that can be great sources of information. To search for

bargains and buy supplies without leaving home, dealers and mail-order suppliers have also opened shop on the Web.

Now many drivers have homepages, with most of them offering special deals on their souvenirs. During the 1999 NASCAR season, for instance, driver Ernie Irvan had autographed die-cast replicas for sale on his Internet site.

As you surf, you'll find die-cast car collectors clubs that have sites. These are not only a great source of information, but can lead you to sources for the cars you are seeking. Many of these clubs will have bulletin boards where you can post information. There are also chat groups on the Internet that will not only allow you to ask questions and share your hobby, but can help you find collectors like yourself to trade with or buy from.

Before you know it, you'll be making online friends who can help you with your hobby. Of course, like with any purchase, the buyer should beware.

If you are going to make a trade or purchase with an e-mail pal, there are several steps to avoid getting burned. First, ask for at least three references. Most of these will be other collectors with e-mail accounts. Drop them a line and get a reading on the person you will be trading with.

Get a complete description, including condition, of the cars to be

traded. If it is a high-dollar or rare car, take the time to trade pictures. Get the complete address, not a post office box, of the person you are dealing with. Ask for a phone number and call up the person

As with any deal, don't be afraid to back out if you aren't comfortable with it.

Another great source for any collectible is the Beckett Publications site at www.beckett.com. Try the Beckett Collectibles Xchange feature, which offers three distinct services that make it easy for online users to buy, sell or trade their collectibles.

With Beckett Auction, Beckett employees do all the work in hosting online auctions. Collectors can bid on a variety of items in a low-risk and ethical environment. Or you can consign your collectibles to sell. Collector-to-

Collector Auction offers Beckett Collectibles Online members the opportunity to reach the same audience by hosting and maintaining their own auctions. The Beckett Buy/Sell/Trade area is the original Beckett marketplace for buying, selling and trading. Here, collectors post their own messages that can be read by the more than 270,000 members of Beckett Collectibles Online.

Another virtual collectibles show that is held 24 hours a day is eBay. This popular Internet auction site (www.ebay.com) holds continuous auctions for just about anything, including your favorite collectible car. A visit during the middle of the 1999 racing season found cars dating back from the 1940s to the latest Hot Wheels set, with a total of 44,871 die-cast cars up for auction. Not all of these were racing

replicas, but eBay does have two racing subcategories. The NASCAR division had 14,092 postings, while the NHRA section was holding 932 auctions. There were also 1,894 Johnny Lightning pieces for sale, plus die-cast cars from Corgi, Franklin Mint and Ertl. You can narrow your search among these items by key words. For example, searching on "Jeff Gordon" will produce items from the three-time Winston Cup champion for sale, while using "5" will help you find replicas of Terry Labonte's No. 5 cars.

Of course, you won't be able to go over these cars with a magnifying glass to be sure of their exact condition. First-time buyers should probably limit themselves to bidding on just items that have pictures online and don't expect everything you purchase to be in mint condition. In addition, most Internet auction services have feedback ratings on sellers, allowing buyers to judge just how happy they are with their purchases. If you see a seller with a history of unhappy transactions, stay away.

Almost all of the companies that produce die-cast cars have their own Internet sites. Not only can you find information about their products, but you can join a collectors club and even buy certain products directly from companies such as Hot Wheels (www.hotwheels.com), Racing Champions (www.racingchamps.com), Johnny Lightning (www.johnnylightning.com) and The American Racing Scene (www.racingscene.com).

Action Performance is a die cast producer that is dedicated to e-commerce. First, Action signed an exclusive agreement with NASCAR to handle the sanctioning body's sales of souvenirs. Then Action bought a company that had been producing a racing information site, creating a new division just for online commerce.

Action Interactive's next move was to open up SpeedMall, a virtual shopping center that includes hundreds of online stores, including the Action Collectibles Store, a shop for Chase Authentics and the Action Auction shop. The Action Auction shop, operated by the Beckett Online division of Beckett Publications, allows fans to sell and trade motorsports collectibles electronically.

So get out the mouse, grab your want list and put on your virtual wet suit. Time to go surfing. And if you can't find online that Action replica of the No. 30 Chevy Malibu that Dale Earnhardt drove in 1976 with Army sponsorship, odds are you aren't going to find it anywhere.

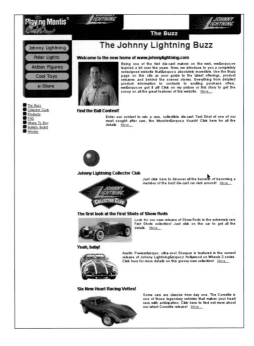

Going to the Races and Collectible Shows

So you finally made it to Florida for the Daytona 500, the Super Bowl of stock-car racing. You're ready for the total adventure—a huge race-day crowd, packed hotels lining the beaches and fast-food joints slowed to a crawl by long lines. But are you ready for the collectible shows, the souvenir trailers and the discount tents?

Perhaps you're not going to a NASCAR race, just taking a small plunge by hitting the show at your local Holiday Inn for your first big excursion. You're pumped, but are you ready?

To some collectors, attending a large show can be perhaps the most exciting part of their hobby. It provides the same thrills and chills that hit a driver behind the wheel of a 3,400-pound Winston Cup car blasting around the track at 200 mph. But for beginners and folks who are naturally shy, the experience can be difficult. Dealing with large crowds, the most knowledgeable die-cast experts in the world and a wide variety of collectibles can be an overwhelming task.

Questions shoot out like a replica Kyle Petty Hot Wheels car flying around the toy Daytona 500 track from Mattel:

- Am I prepared?
- What should I have brought?
- Is there a proper way to cover all the tables, to see all the dealers?
- How should I negotiate?
- What if I miss something?

Whether your goal for the event is a peaceful stroll down Memory Lane or a quick fix of wheelin' and dealin', you need to prepare before you go.

For some collectors, preparation means little more than packing a wallet full of cash. For others, more equipment is necessary: updated checklists, perhaps a supply of cars that you'd like to trade or sell, and the current *Beckett Racing & Motorsports Marketplace* magazine to help guide you through the maze of die-cast race cars that await you.

Just as your favorite driver and team spend many hours going through rituals of preparation before each race, you should be organized. Set some guidelines for yourself. What items am I going to look for? What is my goal? How much money can I spend?

Once the doors open, the race for top-notch collectibles is on. If you're after a rare Racing Champions that will be hard to find, you should have your buy-

ing price in mind before you get there. When you see the vehicle for that price, buy it right away. Sure, have some fun and try to negotiate. Maybe even walk a few tables away, but if you see that the rest of the tables are full of current Hot Wheels and an abundance of Winner's Circle replicas, beat it back to that first table in a hurry. If the piece is really that rare and the price is good, odds are it won't be around long.

If you're not sure what a fair price is, walk around and get a feel for the market. Keep in mind, however, that the show *is* the market. Price guides are just that—guides. If the car you want is listed in a couple of guides at $15 and there are none in the room for less than $25, it is up to you to determine just how bad you want that particular die-cast replica. The going rate

Racing die-cast collectors can find cars of their favorite drivers at the track.

Race team trailers also provide a selection of race-day t-shirts, mugs, flags and other collectibles.

Many collectors arrive at the track early to allow for easier pre-race shopping.

is obviously more than $15, no matter what it says in black and white.

Oh, you can refuse to pay more than the guide price that day, but be prepared to deal with your emotions if that car is listed higher in the next guide. Did you do the right thing by passing?

Don't forget about regional premiums and discounts. Many drivers' items are worth more in the market in which they come from. For example, an Ernie Irvan piece might carry a higher price tag in the driver's home state of California than it does in North Carolina. And even though Rusty Wallace comes from St. Louis, the prices for his cars might be lower in Missouri if dealers there have spent years stocking up on Wallace's issues.

Sometimes the premium can come

from some other factor. Bobby Labonte's No. 18 Interstate Batteries might be hard to find in Dallas, for instance, because not only is Labonte a native Texan, but his sponsor is based in the city. It is not always easy to determine the ratio of supply to demand.

The key is to base your purchases on what you like. How bad do you want it? After all, collecting is a hobby. A collectible's value is different for each collector. Let your own sense of value be the determining factor.

The winner in many races is the team that knows when to pit or how to squeeze extra mileage out of his fuel. Just like a crew chief, a collector needs to have a plan.

One way to get the first crack at that desired piece is to attack the

Collectors should consider the logistics of storing large collectibles on race day.

Race team trailers sometimes offer hard-to-find collectibles.

show in a different way than the crowd. Odds are—especially if the show is at a local recreation or civic center, a small hotel or something like a VFW Hall—that the traffic has a pattern.

Many collectors seem to take the same general path through the show—starting at the entrance and moving counterclockwise. Try going the other way. Or instead of starting at the door and working your way back, start at the back and work your way to the door.

If you're lucky, you'll find a variety of items that are on your want list. Here's where you need to have set limits for the amount of time and money you're willing to spend. If not, you might be finding yourself hobby rich

but running out of gas on your way back home.

If you plan to search for some unique items, say a large-scale Ertl piece or a flat-bottom Racing Champions blister pack, try to be at the show when it opens on the first day. Your odds of finding that rare gem clearly improve the earlier you start looking.

As you're walking the showroom floor, you might overhear talk about a particular car or perhaps even a certain dealer. Maybe you'll see a collector and a dealer in animated negotiations. You can feel it. Something's up. Something's hot. Something's got everybody on edge.

Collectors call it a "buzz."

Most of the big shows seem to

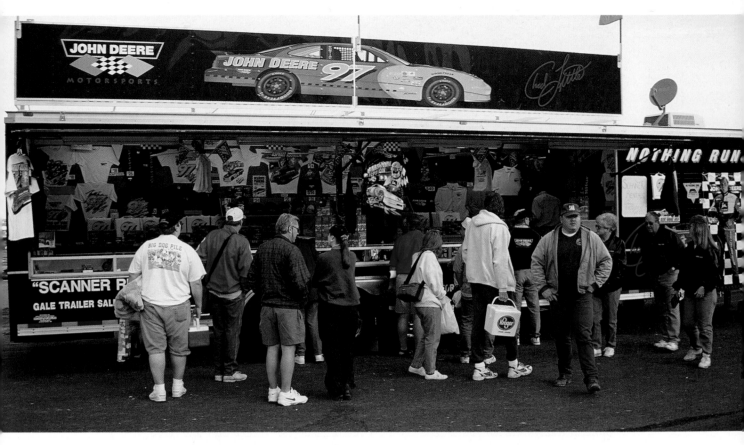

have it. Sometimes you know before hand what is going to be the star attraction of the show, perhaps an out-of-town dealer with a large selection of Dale Earnhardt replicas or a complete run of Winner's Circle pieces. However, usually there are no indicators before the show what will be the hot product.

You want to get to the point that within a few hours of watching and listening, perhap even a few minutes, you will be able to recognize some trends.

Maybe an Action distributor has large number of 1:64 scale cars that he wants to take out of his inventory. Perhaps a table is blowing out a bunch of common cars from middle-of-the-

pack drivers at cut-rate prices that are just too good to pass up.

Watch for dealer-to-dealer transactions, but also beware of getting sucked up into the hype. Cars will start selling for more than their guide prices, and before you know it, no more are left in the room. Or perhaps you wind up with the hotly traded commodity, but it doesn't even fit into your collection.

Sometimes by the end of the show's last day, as dealers are packing up, you may be able to get offers they balked at earlier. A dealer who specializes in the tough-to-get vintage vehicles won't care about taking his stuff home and saving it for a future show. But someone stocking cases of the lat-

Trailers provide excellent opportunities for filling out driver-specific collections.

est product that didn't sell too well might be willing to lighten his load before he leaves.

Be respectful of the merchant and his merchandise and know what is and what is not being discounted.

As you negotiate, never offer your cars for sale without knowing how much you want. When a dealer is selling replicas at his table, it is his responsibility to say what he wants for them. When you offer to sell to him, it is your responsibility to say how much you want. You can shop around some, but don't be surprised if the original dealer isn't in a buying mood when you get back.

Buying die-cast replicas at a NASCAR track during a Winston Cup race can be just like shopping at a large collectibles show, but it can also be similar to buying a die-cast piece at Target or Wal-Mart discount stores.

Show Checklist

1. Be prepared. Get your want list and any of your trade bait organized. Don't wait until you get to the show to plan your strategy.

2. List your top 10 wants and what you expect to pay for each particular item.

3. Plan how you are going to cover the show. Try to set up a route that lets you cover as many tables as possible without repeating any.

4. Take a notepad. Write down where you saw a particular piece, and your collectible will be easier to find later.

5. Take supplies. Pack plenty of storage bags or cases for your purchases.

6. Talk to dealers. They are helpful and knowledgeable about the products they sell. If you have questions, ask them.

7. Stay alert to trends and listen for the "buzz." Read between the lines when a dealer talks about different products.

8. Check with the promoter or some of the dealers ahead of time. You are looking for an edge, any edge. See if anything unusual is being planned. Perhaps a heavy-hitting dealer with a large and unique inventory is coming, or maybe it is just a part-time shower who happens to have the same interests that you do.

9. Dress comfortably. A good, comfortable pair of tennis shoes is a must.

10. Have fun. After all, collecting is a hobby, not a job.

There are two types of sellers at these big races.

One is a corporate seller, and these are the guys who run the official souvenir trailers. These haulers are usually painted in the colors of the team and offer merchandise, ranging from $2 stickers to $1,000 leather jackets. Many of these trailers are operated for the teams by Action and Racing Champions, the two biggest makers of racing die cast. While these trailers do have the latest merchandise, the prices are non-negotiable and often on the high side.

The process is relatively simple. Find the trailer of your favorite driver, see if it has that die-cast piece of your hero you've been looking for, then determine if the marked price is within your budget.

The other type of die-cast seller at a race is the same kind of dealer that shows up at your local racing or die-cast car show. He gets his replicas from a variety of sources that include other dealers, manufacturers, distributers and even collectors. Conse-

quently, his die-cast inventory will be all over the map.

These dealers will sometimes set up in trailers that look much like the team rigs, except that there won't be any team paint scheme or logos. Most will be a solid white or black. Sometimes a group of these dealers will band together and set up a big tent or take over a parking lot a mile or two from the track, setting up a virtual road show for racing collectibles. These type of dealers you can negotiate with just like someone at a die-cast show at your local recreation center.

But no matter who the dealer is and what type of operation he has, you are the one in charge. Collecting die-cast race replicas is your hobby, and you can approach it any way you want. Chasing cars should be a stress-free experience, no matter how big the show is. Be prepared to walk away from any deal, unless it is a good one for you.

Make sure your accomplish your main goal—to have fun.

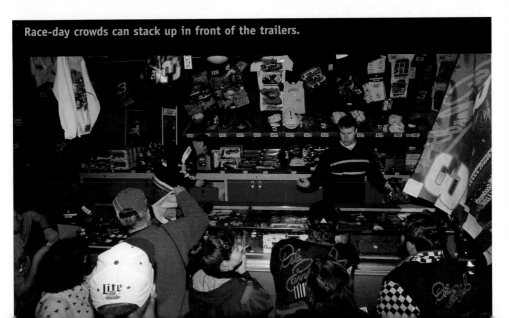

Race-day crowds can stack up in front of the trailers.

NASCAR Driver Fan Clubs

Blaise Alexander
36 Teakwood Dr.
Tiffin, OH 448-1950

Glenn Allen
P.O. Box 2247
Cornelius, NC 28031

Bobby Allison
6616 Walmsley Blvd.
Richmond, Va. 23224

John Andretti
2416 Music Valley Dr,
Suite 161
Nashville, TN 37214

Ron Barfield
P.O. Box 1508
Dawsonville, GA 30534

Johnny Benson
3102 Bird St. NE
Grand Rapids, MI 49505

Joe Bessey
2004 Renaissance Blvd.
King of Prussia, PA 19406

Rich Bickle
7365 Elwood Dr.
Charlotte, NC 28227

Dave Blaney
P.O. Box 470142
Tulsa, OK 74147-0142

Brett Bodine
304 Performance Rd.
Mooresville, NC 28115

Geoff Bodine
P.O. Box 1790
Monroe, NC 28111-1790

Todd Bodine
P.O. Box 2427
Cornelius, NC 28031

Jeff Burton
P.O. Box 1160
Halifax, VA 24558

Ward Burton
3475 Myer Lee Dr. NE
Winston-Salem, NC 27101

Rick Carelli
2009 Market St.
Denver, CO 80205

Rodney Combs
2601 Forsythe Lane
Concord, NC 28025

Stacy Compton
P.O. Box 637
Hurt, VA 24563

Delma Cowart
6134 Scott Lake Rd.
Lakeland, FL 33813

Ricky Craven
P.O. Box 472
Concord, NC 28026

Mike Dillon
P.O. Box 30414
Winston-Salem, NC 27130

Dale Earnhardt
1-888-332-5823

Dale Earnhardt Jr.
1-877-CLUB-E-JR

Bill Elliott
P.O. Box 248
Dawsonville, GA 30534

Tim Fedewa
P.O. Box 428
Terrell, NC 28682

Jeff Fuller
103 Commercial Park Dr.
Concord, NC 28025

Jeff Gordon
P.O. Box 515
Williams, AZ 86046-0515

David Green
P.O. Box 4821
Archdale, NC 27263-4821

NASCAR DRIVER FAN CLUBS cont.

Jeff Green
P.O. Box 268
Cornelius, NC 28031

Mark Green
P.O. Box 5735
Concord, NC 28207

Steve Grissom
P.O. Box 989
Statesville, NC 28687-0989

Bobby Hillin
110 Knob Hill Rd.
Mooresville, NC 28115

Lance Hooper
P.O. Box 903323
Palmdale, CA 93590-3323

Ron Hornaday
P.O. Box 870
Kannapolis, NC 28082-0870

Jimmy Horton
P.O. Box 4425,
Bethlehem, PA 18018

Tommy Houston
P.O. Box 5250
Conover, NC 28613

Ernie Irvan
703 Performance Rd.
Mooresville, NC 28115

Dale Jarrett
1-888-324-3527

Buckshot Jones
P.O. Box 1612
Duluth, GA 30136

Jason Keller
P.O. Box 14748
Greenville, SC 29610

Matt Kenseth
10 Water St.
Cambridge, WI 53523

Tammy Jo Kirk
743 Peek Rd.
Dalton, Ga. 30721

Bobby Labonte
1-877-4-Bobbyl

Terry Labonte
P.O. Box 843
Trinity, NC 27370

Randy LaJoie
P.O. Box 3478
Westport, CT 06880

Kevin Lepage
159 Bevan Dr.
Mooresville, NC 28115

Chad Little
P.O. Box 562323
Charlotte, NC 28256

Curtis Markham
433 Bostwick Lane
Gaithersburg, MD 20878

Sterling Marlin
1116 W. 7th St. Suite 62
Columbia, TN 38401

Mark Martin
P.O. Box 68
Ash Flat, AR 72513

Rick Mast
Rt. 6 Box 224-A
Lexington, VA 24450

Jeremy Mayfield
P.O. Box 2365
Cornelius, NC 28031

Ted Musgrave
P.O. Box 1089
Liberty, NC 27298

Jerry Nadeau
P.O. Box 1358
Harrisburg, NC 28075

Joe Nemechek
P.O Box 1131
Mooresville, NC 28115

Steve Park
P.O. Box 172
E Northport, NY 11731

Kyle Petty
135 Longfield Dr.
Mooresville, NC 28115

NASCAR DRIVER FAN CLUBS cont.

Richard Petty
1028 East 22nd St.
Kannapolis, NC 28083

Robert Pressley
P.O. Box 46361
Washington, DC 20050

Stevie Reeves
200 Rolling Hill Rd., Suite 113
Mooresville, NC 28115

Ricky Rudd
P.O. Box 7586
Richmond, VA 23231

Hermie Sadler
P.O. Box 871
Emporia, VA 28847

Andy Santerre
P.O. Box 994
Harrisburg, NC 28075

Jay Sauter
P.O. Box 278
516-D River Hwy.
Mooresville, NC 28115

Patty Moise
Elton Sawyer
P.O. Box 77919
Greensboro, NC 27417

Ken Schrader
P.O. Box 1227
Kannapolis, NC 28082

Dennis Setzer
P.O. Box 214897
Auburn Hills, MI 48326

Morgan Shepherd
P.O. Box 1456
Stow, OH 44224-0456

Lake Speed
P.O. Box 499
Danville, WV 25053

Jimmy Spencer
P.O. Box 1626
Mooresville, NC 28115

Jack Sprague
280 Hwy 29 S.
Suite 120 Box 173
Concord, NC 28027

Billy Standridge
1521 Sulphur Springs Rd.
Shelby, NC 28152

Tim Steele
11433 24th Ave.
Marne, MI 49435-9716

Mike Stefanik
200 Myrtle St. 7th floor
New Britain, CT 06053

Tony Stewart
5777 W. 74th St.
Indianapolis, IN 46278

Randy Tolsma
610 Performance Rd.
Mooresville, NC 28115

Dick Trickle
5415 Vesuvius-Furnace Rd.
Iron Station, NC 28080

Bill Venturini
7621 Texas Trail
Boca Raton, FL 33487

Kenny Wallace
P.O. Box 3050
Concord, NC 28025

Mike Wallace
224 Rolling Hill Rd.
Suite 9A
Mooresville, NC 28115

Rusty Wallace
1-877-787-8992

Darrell Waltrip
P.O. Box 381
Harrisburg, NC 28075

Michael Waltrip
P.O. Box 339
Sherrills Ford, NC 28673

Rick Wilson
P.O. Box 304
Mulberry, FL 33860

Getting Your Die Cast Signed

When it comes to racing autographs, a die-cast car can be a perfect canvas for a driver's signature. To many racing fans, there is no better way to form a complete collectible package than by putting the autograph of the driver together with his car.

Getting started with your autographed die-cast collection is easy, with plenty of replica cars and transporters available. From the packaging of a 1:64 scale truck to the deck lid of a 1:18 car, anything is fair game for a signature. Drivers are also among the most accessible pro athletes when it comes to signing, either in person or via the mail.

Most people begin with 1:64 scale cars because of their availability and price. This is especially true of collec-

tors who plan to mail their die-cast replicas to drivers to be signed, because not everything mailed finds its way back home. Collectors who get all their autographs in person don't have that problem, but they do have to lug their cars to the track, shopping mall or wherever else their favorite driver is making a personal appearance.

With smaller cars, you probably want to ask the driver to sign the packaging. There just isn't enough room on a 1:64 replica to get a driver's signature. The bigger the replica a collector wants to get signed, the more room the driver actually has to scribble on the die-cast car. But the collection belongs to you and you can do anything you want, including having drivers sign the packaging that came with your 1:18 or 1:24 scale car.

Even if you are sending your die-cast piece off in the mail to get signed, it is all right to ask the driver

A driver can usually produce a better signature when seated at a table.

to sign on a certain place: the hood, the roof, the packaging, etc. Just be polite. Some collectors will even mail a pen that they would like the driver to use. Drivers so often receive requests in the mail that they almost always have their own supply of Sharpies. In fact, many will keep a Sharpie in their pocket at all times. But that doesn't mean you don't want to have a special pen with you when you get that signature on your die-cast replica, especially if you want a certain color to be used that matches either the paint scheme of the car or the packaging.

If you are going to be mailing your die cast to drivers, be sure to have the proper packaging materials. For a 1:64 scale die-cast, two bubble-lined 8-by-11.5 inch envelopes will

work great. One will be used to send the car to the driver. Collectors need to address the second envelope to themselves, and include proper postage so their replica can be returned at no cost to the driver.

The bubble-lined envelopes should help to keep the car in good condition on its journey to the driver and back. The envelopes are available at most post offices, mail stores, drug stores and supermarkets. These envelopes will also house 1:24 scale size cars that are out of their packaging.

Spend some time on your letter requesting the autograph. Your letter should politely ask for the signature of the driver and if you have a specific place where you would like that car or package to be signed, be sure to

include that information. This doesn't insure that the memorabilia will get signed where you want it, but it will increase your odds. As always be sure to use the words "please" and "thank you." Once your letter is done, enclose it with your die-cast piece and your self-addressed stamped envelope and head to the mailbox.

A frequent question from beginning collectors is, "How much more valuable is my collectible item now that I have it signed?" While collecting racing die-cast cars is a relatively new hobby, collectors have been chasing trading cards of sports figures for a century.

One of the biggest debates in the collecting hobby is what happens to the value of a trading card when it gets signed. To many, getting a card signed is defacing the card. To others,

there is no better item to get signed. Usually, having a card autographed will add value to the card but will decrease the number of people that would normally be interested in obtaining the card. This decrease can be significant, which obviously makes it harder to sell the signed card, especially if the holder of the prize now believes it is worth more.

One good rule of thumb is to avoid having expensive cards signed, unless you plan to keep them in your collection. Cheaper cards are normally the best items to get signed, especially if you might want to trade or sell them in the future. A card valued at five cents, once it is signed, usually can carry a value of $1-$2. A $20 card that is signed will often be held in lower regard by many card collectors, and the few that are interested may

not be willing to pay a premium for the autograph.

Most of this also holds true for getting your die-cast cars signed. The biggest difference is that the vast majority of die-cast pieces are common enough that they would be suitable for getting signed. In addition, the majority of die-cast collectors aren't thinking to sell when they buy their pieces.

Collecting autographs is always more fun if done for enjoyment and entertainment rather than financial reward. The value is in the experience: The story behind every signature collected makes them priceless.

How Die Cast is Made

Few dictionaries even attempt to define the term "die-cast," while many collectors have just a vague idea of the way their prized cars are made.

A die-cast car was originally molten metal, which is given its shape by a mold and then allowed to harden. The cars are then painted and decals are applied to give them the appearance of the race cars that take to the track each week.

But Fred Wagenhals, one of the driving forces behind the racing die-cast market as the president of Action Performance Companies, doesn't mind going beyond the basics. Not only does Wagenhals know the process well, but he also enjoys sharing the details with collectors. Wagenhals believes race fans crave detail in their replicas and that the more they know about production, the better the collector they become.

Action has produced a wide variety of die-cast replicas, including pit wagons, banks, trucks, cars, pedal cars, haulers and cars made of pewter and crystal, in almost every scale.

Wagenhals will spell out the number of components in each product, the labor hours required for production, the number of logos and graphics and the dimensions of each die cast. For example, five years ago Action made a replica of Dale Earnhardt's 1/64 scale dually and show trailer that required 44 separate pieces and 13-plus hours to assemble.

According to Wagenhals, the attention to detail pays off in the long run. The better the product produced, the more collectible it will become. And the more a stock car miniature resembles the real-life original, the more want lists it will make.

Racing die-cast cars even resemble real cars prior to assembly.

Of the effort involved in each Action die cast, most sweat revolves around tampo painting. "Suppose you're doing a Budweiser car," Wagenhals says. "The base color, red, would be baked on." Then, the die cast enters the tampo room, where dies are applied. "It's like a printing press, kind of a rubber stamp effect," he explains. "It puts different colors down in layers." A four-color sponsor's insignia would require four separate passes or applications.

Although the tampo process eliminates the need for hand painting, it requires that machine operators keep

A racing die-cast truck awaits a tampo paint process.

the replicas in the same position within the painting apparatus to ensure each application registers properly.

One reason the paint job is so important is that much of the racing die-cast products are actually from the same mold or "tool," as they are called. Almost all of the Winston Cup replicas of the Ford Taurus come from the same tool, with only the tampo painting distinguishing Rusty Wallace's car from those of Mark Martin, Ricky Rudd or Jeff Burton.

Peachstate Motorsports, which produces primarily transporters, used just two models—a Ford AeroMax sleeper cab and a Kenworth T600—to produce the first 13 models in their line. Again, only the colors and logos painted on the transporters distinguish the different teams.

But don't think making Peachstate's line of haulers is simple. The average Peachstate transporter uses 80 to 100 components and the company has continued to expand its tooling. From the beginning, owner Tom Long worked with experienced companies such as Racing Collectibles Inc., Revell and Ertl on the production of his 1/64 scale transporters.

Long is constantly developing new tools, having started die-cast lines as diverse as replica golf carts and vintage muscle cars. Beginning work on a new project is one of Long's biggest challenges. With any new project, work begins when "the concept is explained to a tooling engineer at the plant through discussions, photographs and drawings," Long explains. "Then, the engineer will quote you the tooling cost for the sample."

The difference between an ordinary Chevy truck . . .

traceability," he says, talking about rare, early samples of certain projects. "Some would be of great value to collectors, but they aren't for sale."

Long says the process for starting up a new line of tools isn't for the faint of heart or for those without staying power. "It can take one year," he says. "If you believe you'll release a new die cast is less than nine months, you're fooling yourself. The gestation period is about the same as a baby."

Once production cranks up for any motorsports die cast, Long says most manufacturing techniques are the same with any company. "It's all basic materials, zinc and plastic, bought by the ton and injection molded," he explains.

"Then, you draw it down," Long continues. "Just like a photograph, this is simpler than a blown-up example being reduced. The production piece is pliable, made of a plastic material. It's shipped back to you. That's when you make changes, and it goes back and forth, maybe for months."

The process isn't the same for each company. Long's engineers produce an initial production piece that is as big as two times the size of the desired die cast, providing more and larger details for this stage of development. Action, on the other hand, creates prototypes that are the same size as the eventual die-cast piece.

Long is hesitant to use the word "prototype" within earshot of hobbyists. "We have good

. . . and a Goodwrench collectible is the paint.

The Making of a Hot Wheel

Mattel has made more than one billion Hot Wheels since the first vehicle was produced in 1968. More than 3,500 variations have been made. Mattel officials say that making a die-cast car, from concept to shipping, takes from 10 to 12 months. The company breaks down the process into eight steps.

1. The vehicle begins life in the imagination of Mattel's designers. To keep up with the latest trends, the designers visit auto shows and races.

2. The ideas are then sketched onto an artist's drawing board. The designers may create hundreds of versions. The best drawings are then test-marketed with focus groups, ultimately selecting one design.

3. If the vehicle already exists, as in the case of the race cars, the original is photographed. Details—including interior and exterior, close-ups of the grill, etc.—are captured on film. Often the manufactures and owners are consulted.

4. Precise measurements of the original are taken. The photographs and "specs" are sent to the engineering department, which translates the data into mechanical drawings.

5. The drawings are then sent to a pattern maker, who makes a wooden model of the car four times larger than an actual Hot Wheels car. The models must faithfully reproduce the details of the cars, including emblems, logos, door handles, shape of headlight and instrumental panel.

6. Molds are made from the models. The die-cast is injected into the molds, and the body of the vehicle emerges.

7. The body is then polished, washed and then spray-painted. Letters, logos, and other details such as pin striping are then printed on.

8. Finally, all of the parts including wheels, chassis and engine are assembled.

Collectors might be surprised at the high level of technology used in diecast production.

Most difficulties in producing die-cast products stems from the fact that almost all of the replicas are produced overseas. Long has followed production throughout the Orient and names China, Korea, Taiwan and Vietnam as primary die-cast producers.

Generally, offices are based in Hong Kong, but manufacturing plants often are in China, one to two hours away for modern travelers, but an entirely different world.

Getting from the office to the plant is like "going from one planet to another," Long says. "Travel can be hazardous."

A major problem, of course, is that workers who speak English there aren't likely to speak NASCAR. "There is a language barrier," Long agrees. "Many workers don't understand fully what they are replicating. However, they are experts at duplicating exactly any request you have. Therefore, you don't put down anything you don't want on the finished product."

For instance, if a yellow post-it note of instructions is included on a drawing, chances are the same colored rectangle will be painted on the die cast.

Because manufacturing occurs outside North America, Action tries to eliminate miscommunication with foreign factories. "Our designs are on computer. Engineers receive the entire package off of a disk," Wagenhals says.

In the past, some die-cast flaws from facilities in the Orient could be traced to miscommunication between divisions. A plant hours away from office headquarters might lack constant supervision of production. Now, Long says companies such as Peachstate can call upon independent, third-party monitors hired to enter factories and provide additional quality control.

Action's Wagenhals wonders if collectors take stock of the technology his and other companies continue to employ in die-cast improvements. "I don't think they care how we do it," he says of collectors. "They just want better quality."

Specialty Paint Jobs

Two-time Winston Cup champion Terry Labonte found out the hard way how important one-time, special paint jobs are to NASCAR fans.

"You'd think I'd know better," says the driver of the No. 5 Kellogg's Corn Flakes Chevy. "The fans just love them. During appearances that's all I hear from fans. 'You got any special paint schemes this year?' "

But Labonte slipped during a two-hour collectibles show televised live from the Phoenix headquarters of Action Performance Companies in 1998. The show was selling collectibles and souvenirs featuring Terry's Iron Man II paint job, which he was driving that week at Phoenix International Raceway to celebrate his record 600th consecutive Winston Cup start.

And Terry paid for the mistake for months.

"It's hard to sit on QVC for two hours and not daydream," Labonte explains. "I made the mistake of saying that I didn't think we were going to have any [special paint schemes in 1999]. I didn't know it at the time, but we [had] two planned. But the fans went crazy. They called the shop, wrote and wrote and wrote. They spent all winter trying to get us to change our minds."

"I'm still getting letters about it."

Collectors don't need to worry. The practice of teams using a special paint job, then producing die-cast cars and other collectibles in the new scheme, won't be going away any time soon. The trend not only increases sales, but provides sponsors with additional exposure. Without a doubt, the practice of producing special paint schemes is the biggest development in

Sponsors have realized the benefits of special paint job promotions.

the die-cast market since Racing Champions became the first company to mass produce NASCAR replicas in 1989.

Fred Wagenhals, the president of Action, helped pioneer the special scheme program. He and his shareholders are included among those who love the practice. Just the Coca-Cola program in late 1998 that featured Dale Earnhardt and Dale Earnhardt Jr. sold more than $20 million worth of collectibles. In fact specialty schemes accounted for 25 percent of Action's sales in 1998.

"That's a pretty big number. Every time we offer a special paint scheme, it does really well," Wagenhals says. "The collectors are hooked on them."

Shop owners are another hobby element that appreciates the one-time paint jobs. They help Wagenhals get rid of his inventory.

"It has been wonderful," says Linda Roberts, co-owner of Ike's Cards & Diecast in Tennessee. " It brings

people into our shop looking for that special color scheme, then there's no telling what they are going to buy. A lot of people still like the regular paint jobs—especially the black Earnhardt and the rainbow-striped Jeff Gordon— but they *love* those special paint jobs."

Wagenhals was at a meeting trying to figure out how to sell more of those black Earnhardt cars when he helped come up with the idea for a special paint scheme. He was with Don Hawk, the president of Dale Earnhardt Inc., and Joe Mattes, who was the president of Sports Image Inc., which handled Dale's souvenir sales. It was December of 1994, and the three were talking at a Charlotte-area restaurant called the Rainbow Deli.

Wagenhals said, "Wouldn't it be something if Dale could just run in another color car for just one race?"

Hawk hopped on the idea, calling Richard Childress, Dale's car owner, from the restaurant. Richard quickly signed off on the idea, and so did

Dale. Even before the group left the restaurant, it had selected the Winston, a NASCAR non-points all-star race held each year in May in Charlotte, as the race.

The result was Dale's silver car, which he raced the next May as a tribute to RJ Reynolds and its 25-year sponsorship of NASCAR under its Winston brand. The effort was a huge success, with Action's silver Earnhardt car quickly finding its way to the top of everybody's want list.

The one-time paint job picked up steam later in 1995 with Bill Elliott's Thunderbat, done by McDonald's to promote their in-store promotion of a Batman movie. In 1996, Earnhardt wore an Olympic paint job at the Winston. And by 1997, specialty paint jobs were standard operating procedures for NASCAR teams.

By the end of the 1999 season, the number of special paint schemes will be reaching the 200 mark. Some drivers, such as Labonte and Elliott, have raced as many as 10 times with a limited edition paint job.

Most of the special schemes race at special events. The Winston has produced the most, including the top programs from Earnhardt and Gordon. The Bud Shootout in Daytona, another non-points event, has also been popular for one-time paint jobs. Indy's Brickyard 400 and the second Charlotte race in October also seem to have a variety of special paint schemes. Last year's Pepsi 400, the first NASCAR night race at Daytona

Special paint jobs turn NASCARs into effective high-profile billboards.

Looks like Dale caught him a big 'un with the Bass Pro Shops paint job.

International Speedway, drew the biggest field of one-time paint jobs in 1998.

For the 1999 Winston, Mark Martin drove a black car with a paint job advertising Eagle One products. Gordon raced with a Superman scheme, while Earnhardt used a retro Wrangler Jeans paint job that resembled one from early in his career. Dale Jarrett, his team and sponsors (Ford Quality Care Service and Ford Credit) kept the same colors but reversed the paint job to draw attention to the Susan G. Komen Breast Cancer Foundation. Labonte promoted the new K-Sentials program from Kellogg's.

Teams use most of the special paint schemes in conjunction with a promotion or celebration, and the timing involves a milestone, anniversary or sponsorship program. A movie paint scheme, for example, would be used close to the film's release. Several paint schemes in the past couple of years have involved charities, with some of the proceeds going to such groups as cancer research foundations.

Collectors love the special schemes, primarily for the Wagenhals' original vision. It is great to pick up something special of their hero.

But not all paint jobs are created equal. With the dramatic increase of special paint jobs, it was bound to produce too much of a good thing.

Action hasn't missed with any special paint jobs featuring Earnhardt and Gordon, and the company isn't likely to any time soon. But several other teams on the Winston Cup circuit have had specialty schemes fall flat.

Tyler Rodgers, who worked for

The Intimidator doesn't always wear black. Neither does his car.

several years as the buyer for the NASCAR Thunder chain of specialty stores, wishes for a perfect stock car world in which all of the special paint jobs feature superstar drivers, major sponsorship promotions, and a legitimate racing reason to celebrate.

"For the drivers that already move souvenirs, the special paint schemes are great," Rodgers says. "But not all of the special paint schemes have been great. Their success usually goes back to who the driver is and what event the paint job is tied in to. I want big drivers and big events."

Wagenhals agrees. You can't just change the paint job to sell more die-cast cars. Collectors will feel used.

"We think it is better if the program is tied into something, and anniversaries and big races are great," Fred says. "Just

changing the paint job to just change the paint job or just to sell souvenirs doesn't really work."

Bill Korbus, McDonald's motor-sports manager, enjoys the special paint schemes as much as any fan. The fast-food chain and driver Bill Elliott have had some of NASCAR's best success with the practice, helping to pioneer the program with the Thunderbat in 1995 and before enjoying a four-scheme Happy Meal series in 1998.

Korbus says sponsors can't justify the special paint schemes just to sell

Jeff Gordon's paint job helped promote a thrilling prehistoric ride.

souvenirs. Their slice of the licensing pie isn't that big.

"We have to tie it into some promotion we are doing in our stores or it doesn't make sense," Bill says. "The money we make in die-cast cars and T-shirts doesn't even cover the costs of changing the paint on the car and buying everybody on the crew a new uniform that matches. But it sure helps get people interested in what's going on at McDonald's, and that's what we want."

Roberts says she doesn't see collectors or dealers tiring of the promotions, their special paint schemes and collectibles any time soon.

Dealers who buy large quantities of special schemes will frequently find themselves with some unmovable pieces, but these duds are more than justified by the hot paint jobs. And most of her customers collect primarily die-casts cars of just a driver or two, so the number of paint schemes they wind up chasing is limited. Occasionally she'll hear a gripe, but these are from collectors who try to

Clark Kent didn't get behind the wheel.

chase every paint job released.

"There are a few people that give some negative vibes about having to chase still another paint job, but not many," Roberts says.

Wagenhals talks to collectors all the time. And he listens. His company was involved with more than two dozen special paint schemes in 1999, though Wagenhals tried to spread them out among different series while sticking to legitimate programs with big-name drivers such as Earnhardt, Gordon, Rusty Wallace and Jeremy Mayfield. He also tried to make sure every player involved was a big one, leading to Superman, Star Wars characters and Harley-Davidson motorcycles appearing on NASCAR hoods.

"Collectors still want them," Fred says. "The best way I know to gauge their interest is to see what sells. And they're still buying them."

And if Fred has any doubts, he can go ask Labonte. Terry's got a few letters he could show him.

Driver Checklists

Jeff Burton

Hometown:
South Boston, VA

Birthdate:
June 29, 1967

Personal:
Jeff's brother, Ward, is also a Winston Cup driver. Jeff caught the racing bug at age 5 while watching Ward race go-karts. Jeff was an outstanding athlete at Halifax County (Virginia) Senior High, playing basketball and soccer, where he was varsity team captain. He still enjoys sports, especially boating and basketball. His favorite sports team is the Duke University basketball team and coach Mike Krzyzewski is his favorite sports personality. Jeff also describes himself as a cat person.

Hobby:
Jeff is not only a promising young driver on the Winston Cup circuit, but also in the hobby. His best seasons and collectibles still lie in the future. He has had only a few special paint schemes, although he raced with a Bruce Lee paint job at the Japan exhibition race in 1998 and with a NASCAR Rocks scheme in 1999. As a Roush driver, Racing Champions has produced most of his most recent die-cast replicas. His Exide paint job was produced by Revell in 1996 and Action in 1997.

Career Highlights
- Began racing full-time in NASCAR Winston Cup Series in 1994 with Stavola Brothers.
- Spent two years with Stavola Brothers team and won 1994 NASCAR Winston Cup Rookie of the Year award before moving to Roush Racing.
- Won first career NASCAR Winston Cup pole at second Michigan race in 1996, a season in which he finished 13th in Winston Cup points, despite missing one race.
- Quickly developed into a title contender at Roush. He earned his first win in 1997 at the first Winston Cup race held at Texas Motor Speedway.
- Career-best fourth in NASCAR Winston Cup Standings in 1997, winning three races. He then finished fifth in the 1998 standings.
- Won six races in 1999, upping his career total to 11.
- Has developed a rivalry with another Jeff, three-time Winston Cup champion Jeff Gordon. Several times the two have battled to the finish. In addition, he has continued his lifelong battle with his brother, Ward. Three times in 1999, the two brothers finished first and second in a Winston Cup race, with Jeff winning each time.

SCALE	MANUFACTURER	SPONSOR

1990–92

SCALE	MANUFACTURER	SPONSOR
1:64	Matchbox White Rose Super Stars	TIC Financial '92 BX

1993–94

| 1:87 | Racing Champions Transporters | Raybestos Yellow box hobby only |

1993–98

| 1:18 | Ertl 1:18 | Raybestos |

1993

1:64	Matchbox White Rose Super Stars	Baby Ruth BX
1:64	Matchbox White Rose Super Stars	TIC Financial BX
1:87	Matchbox White Rose Transporters Super Star Series	Baby Ruth
1:87	Matchbox White Rose Transporters Super Star Series	TIC Financial

1994

1:64	Ertl White Rose Transporters BGN Promos	Baby Ruth BGN
1:64	Matchbox White Rose Super Stars	Raybestos BX
1:64	Matchbox White Rose Super Stars	TIC Financial Future Cup Stars BX
1:24	Racing Champions	Raybestos w/ Goodyear tires
1:24	Racing Champions	Raybestos w/ Hoosier tires
1:64	Racing Champions	Raybestos
1:64	Racing Champions Hobby	Raybestos
1:64	Racing Champions Premier	Raybestos
1:64	Racing Champions Transporters	Raybestos

1995

1:64	Matchbox White Rose Super Stars	Raybestos
1:64	Matchbox White Rose Super Stars	Raybestos Super Star Awards
1:80	Matchbox White Rose Transporters Super Star Series	Raybestos
1:24	Racing Champions	Raybestos
1:64	Racing Champions	Raybestos
1:64	Racing Champions	Raybestos w/ Blue numbers
1:24	Racing Champions Banks	Raybestos
1:64	Racing Champions Premier	Raybestos
1:64	Racing Champions Premier Transporters	Raybestos
1:64	Racing Champions To the Maxx	Raybestos
1:64	Racing Champions Transporters	Raybestos

1996

1:64	Matchbox White Rose Super Stars	Exide
1:24	Racing Champions	Exide
1:64	Racing Champions	Exide
1:24	Revell	Exide
1:64	Revell	Exide

SCALE	MANUFACTURER	SPONSOR
1:24	Revell Collection	Exide
1:64	Revell Collection	Exide

1997

1:24	Action Racing Collectables	Exide
1:64	Action Racing Collectables	Exide
1:64	Action Racing Collectables	Track Gear
1:24	Action Racing Collectables Banks	Track Gear
1:24	Action/RCCA	Track Gear
1:64	Action/RCCA	Track Gear
1:24	Action/RCCA Banks	Exide
1:24	Action/RCCA Elite	Exide
1:24	Action/RCCA Elite	Track Gear
1:64	Hot Wheels Collector Edition	Exide
1:64	Hot Wheels Collector Edition/Short Track	Exide
1:64	Hot Wheels Collector Edition/Speedway Edition	Exide
1:64	Hot Wheels Pro Racing	Exide
1:24	Racing Champions	Exide
1:24	Racing Champions	Track Gear
1:64	Racing Champions	Exide
1:64	Racing Champions	Track Gear
1:64	Racing Champions Pinnacle Series	Exide
1:64	Racing Champions Premier w/Medallion	Exide
1:64	Racing Champions Previews	Exide
1:64	Racing Champions Silver Chase	Exide
1:64	Racing Champions Stock Rods	Exide
1:64	Racing Champions Stock Rods	Exide
1:64	Racing Champions Stock Rods	Exide
1:24	Racing Champions SuperTrucks	Exide
1:64	Racing Champions SuperTrucks	Exide
1:64	Racing Champions Transporters	Exide
1:64	Racing Champions Transporters	Track Gear
1:64	Racing Champions Transporters	Exide
1:64	Racing Champions Transporters	Track Gear
1:24	Revell Collection	Exide
1:24	Revell Collection	Exide Texas Motor Speedway
1:43	Revell Collection	Exide
1:24	Revell Hobby	Exide
1:24	Revell Retail	Exide

1998

1:64	Hot Wheels Collector Edition/Preview Edition	Exide
1:64	Hot Wheels Collector Edition/Test Track	Exide
1:64	Hot Wheels Collector Edition/Track Edition	Exide
1:64	Hot Wheels Collector Edition/Trading Paint	Exide
1:24	Racing Champions	Exide
1:24	Racing Champions	Track Gear
1:64	Racing Champions	Exide
1:64	Racing Champions	Track Gear
1:24	Racing Champions Authentics	Bruce Lee

SCALE	MANUFACTURER	SPONSOR
1:24	Racing Champions Authentics	Exide
1:24	Racing Champions Authentics Banks	Exide
1:64	Racing Champions Chrome Chase	Exide
1:64	Racing Champions Chrome Chase	Track Gear
1:24	Racing Champions Gold	Exide
1:24	Racing Champions Gold	Track Gear
1:24	Racing Champions Gold Banks	Exide
1:24	Racing Champions Gold Hood Open	Exide
1:24	Racing Champions Gold Hood Open Banks	Exide
1:64	Racing Champions Gold w/Medallion	Exide
1:64	Racing Champions Gold w/ Medallion	Track Gear
1:64	Racing Champions Pinnacle Series	Track Gear
1:64	Racing Champions Press Pass Series	Exide
1:64	Racing Champions Press Pass Series	Track Gear
1:24	Racing Champions Reflections of Gold	Exide
1:64	Racing Champions Reflections of Gold	Exide
1:64	Racing Champions Reflections of Gold	Track Gear
1:24	Racing Champions Signature Series	Track Gear
1:64	Racing Champions Signature Series	Exide
1:64	Racing Champions Signature Series	Track Gear
1:24	Racing Champions Stock Rods	Exide
1:24	Racing Champions Stock Rods	Exide
1:24	Racing Champions Stock Rods	Exide Gold
1:24	Racing Champions Stock Rods	Track Gear
1:64	Racing Champions Stock Rods	Exide
1:64	Racing Champions Stock Rods	Exide
1:64	Racing Champions Stock Rods	Exide Gold
1:64	Racing Champions Stock Rods	Exide Gold
1:64	Racing Champions Stock Rods	Exide Gold
1:64	Racing Champions Stock Rods	Track Gear
1:64	Racing Champions Stock Rods	Track Gear
1:24	Racing Champions Stock Rods Reflections of Gold	Exide
1:64	Racing Champions Stock Rods Reflections of Gold	Exide
1:64	Racing Champions Toys 'R Us Gold	Exide
1:64	Racing Champions Transporters	Exide
1:64	Racing Champions Transporters	Exide w/ car

1999

SCALE	MANUFACTURER	SPONSOR
1:64	Hot Wheels Collector Edition	Exide
1:64	Hot Wheels Collector Edition/Pit Crew	Exide
1:64	Hot Wheels Collector Edition/Pit Crew Gold	Exide
1:64	Hot Wheels Collector Edition/Test Track	Exide
1:64	Hot Wheels Collector Edition/Track Edition	Caterpillar
1:24	Racing Champions	Exide
1:24	Racing Champions	Exide Bruce Lee
1:64	Racing Champions	Exide

SCALE	MANUFACTURER	SPONSOR
1:64	Racing Champions	Exide Bruce Lee
1:24	Racing Champions 24K Gold	Exide
1:24	Racing Champions 24K Gold	Track Gear
1:64	Racing Champions 24K Gold	Exide
1:64	Racing Champions 24K Gold	Track Gear
1:24	Racing Champions Gold	Exide
1:24	Racing Champions Gold	Exide Bruce Lee
1:64	Racing Champions Gold w/Medallion	Exide
1:64	Racing Champions NASCAR RULES	Exide
1:64	Racing Champions NASCAR RULES	Bruce Lee
1:64	Racing Champions NASCAR RULES	Track Gear
1:24	Racing Champions Platinum	Exide
1:24	Racing Champions Platinum	Track Gear
1:64	Racing Champions Platinum	Exide
1:64	Racing Champions Platinum	Track Gear
1:64	Racing Champions Press Pass Series	Track Gear
1:64	Racing Champions Press Pass Series	Exide
1:24	Racing Champions Signature Series	Exide
1:64	Racing Champions Signature Series	Exide
1:24	Racing Champions Stock Rods	Bruce Lee
1:24	Racing Champions Stock Rods	Exide
1:64	Racing Champions Stock Rods	Exide
1:64	Racing Champions Stock Rods	Exide Gold
1:64	Racing Champions Toys R Us Chrome Chase	Exide
1:64	Racing Champions Transporters	Exide
1:64	Racing Champions Transporters 24K Gold	Exide
1:64	Racing Champions Transporters Gold	Exide
1:64	Racing Champions Transporters Platinum	Exide
1:64	Racing Champions Transporters Signature Series	Exide
1:24	Racing Champions Under the Lights	Exide
1:64	Racing Champions Under the Lights	Exide

2000

SCALE	MANUFACTURER	SPONSOR
1:64	Hot Wheels Deluxe Scorchin Scooter	Exide
1:64	Racing Champions NASCAR RULES	Exide
1:64	Racing Champions Premier Preview	Exide
1:24	Racing Champions Preview	Exide
1:64	Racing Champions Previews	Exide
1:64	Racing Champions Stock Rods	Exide
1:24	Racing Champions Time Trial 2000	Exide
1:64	Racing Champions Time Trial 2000	Exide

Dale Earnhardt

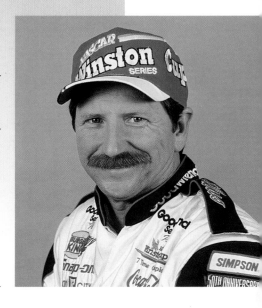

Hometown:

Kannapolis, NC

Birthdate:

April 29th, 1951

Personal:

Earnhardt is an avid hunter and fisherman. He not only owns a farm, but horses, dogs, cats, cows, bulls and chickens. Among his favorite things are the Atlanta Braves, the Outlaw Josey Wales movie and steak. He owns two jets and two boats that are better than 50 feet long. Dale was inspired by his father, Ralph, who was the 1956 NASCAR Sportsman champion and named one of NASCAR's top 50 drivers in 1998.

Hobby:

Richard Petty may be the king of stock car racing, but Earnhardt is the king of stock car collectibles. His popularity and business savvy helped turn the die-cast hobby into the huge business it is today. He created the practice of wearing special paint schemes, then producing replicas of the one-time paint jobs. He started off with a silver anniversary car for Winston, then quickly followed with a red-white-and-blue Olympics paint job and an orange Wheaties version. Earnhardt also had a big impact on the hobby when he signed an exclusive deal with Action Performance Companies, Inc. This relationship has allowed Action to go back and create replicas from Earnhardt's past.

Career Highlights

- Seven-time Winston Cup Champion (1980, '86, '87, '90, '91, '93, '94). Tied with Richard Petty for most Winston Cup titles.
- Ranks sixth on all-time Winston Cup win list, with his 75th victory coming in the fourth race of the 2000 season in Atlanta.
- First driver to top $30 million in career earnings.
- Biggest career victories include the 1995 Brickyard 400 and the 1998 Daytona 500.
- 1979 Winston Cup rookie of the year.
- First win came in 16th start, Southeastern 500 in April of 1979 at Bristol. First pole came in 24th attempt, NAPA 400 in June of 1979 at Riverside.
- First three-time winner of The Winston all-star race.
- Won 125-mile qualifier at Daytona 12 times, including one each year of the 1990s.
- Won more IROC titles and races than any other driver.

SCALE	MANUFACTURER	SPONSOR

1989–90

| 1:87 | Matchbox White Rose Transporters Super Star Series | Goodwrench '89 |
| 1:87 | Matchbox White Rose Transporters Super Star Series | Goodwrench '90 |

1989

| 1:64 | Racing Champions Flat Bottom | Goodwrench |

1990–92

1:64	Matchbox White Rose Super Stars	GM '90 BX
1:64	Matchbox White Rose Super Stars	GM Parts '91 BX
1:64	Matchbox White Rose Super Stars	Goodwrench '92 BL
1:64	Matchbox White Rose Super Stars	Mom-n-Pop's '92 poly bag

1990

| 1:64 | Racing Champions | GM Performance Parts |
| 1:64 | Racing Champions | Goodwrench |

1991–92

| 1:24 | Racing Champions | Goodwrench w/ Fender Stickers |
| 1:24 | Racing Champions | Goodwrench w/ Tampo Decals |

1991

1:64	Action/RCCA 1983-86 T-Bird Series	Wrangler
1:87	Matchbox White Rose Transporters Super Star Series	Goodwrench
1:64	Racing Champions	Lumina EB
1:64	Racing Champions	Lumina NP
1:64	Racing Champions	Lumina PB

1992–94

1:24	Racing Champions Banks	Goodwrench BGN car
1:24	Racing Champions Banks	Goodwrench w/ numbered box
1:24	Racing Champions Banks	Goodwrench w/ unnumbered box
1:24	Racing Champions Banks	Goodwrench with Snap On
1:24	Racing Champions Banks	Mom-n-Pop's

1992–95

1:64	Action/RCCA Transporters	D.Earnhardt/ Wrangler 85
1:64	Action/RCCA Transporters	D.Earnhardt/ Wrangler
1:64	Action/RCCA Transporters	Goodwrench BGN Dale Earnhardt Inc.
1:64	Action/RCCA Transporters	Goodwrench RCR
1:64	Action/RCCA Transporters	RCCA Club Only w/ cars

SCALE	MANUFACTURER	SPONSOR

1992–96

1:24	Brookfield Collectors Guild Suburbans	7-Time Champion 1995
1:24	Brookfield Collectors Guild Suburbans	AC-Delco
1:24	Brookfield Collectors Guild Suburbans	Brickyard Winner
1:24	Brookfield Collectors Guild Suburbans	Goodwrench 1992
1:24	Brookfield Collectors Guild Suburbans	Goodwrench Silver 1995
1:24	Brookfield Collectors Guild Suburbans	Olympic
1:24	Brookfield Collectors Guild Suburbans	Richard Petty 7-Time Champion 1995 paint scheme split half 3 half 43 tampos are reversed
1:24	Brookfield Collectors Guild Suburbans	Richard Petty 7-Time Champion 1995 paint scheme split half 3 half 43
1:24	Brookfield Collectors Guild Suburbans	Richard Petty 7-Time Champion 2 pack '95

SCALE	MANUFACTURER	SPONSOR
	1992	
1:87	Matchbox White Rose Transporters	1992 Super Star Series
1:43	Racing Champions	Goodwrench
1:64	Racing Champions	Goodwrench
1:64	Racing Champions Premier	Goodwrench
1:64	Racing Champions Transporters	Goodwrench
1:64	Winross Transporters	Goodwrench in Wooden box
1:64	Winross Transporters	Goodwrench produced for White Rose Collectibles
	1993–94	
1:87	Racing Champions Transporters	Goodwrench
	1993–95	
1:24	Action Racing Collectables	Goodwrench 1988 Monte Carlo
1:24	Action Racing Collectables	Goodwrench 1995 Monte Carlo Black Windows Promo
1:24	Action Racing Collectables	Goodwrench 1995 Monte Carlo Brickyard Special
1:24	Action Racing Collectables	Goodwrench 1995 Monte Carlo Promo
1:24	Action Racing Collectables	Brickyard Special
1:24	Action Racing Collectables	Richard Petty 7 and 7 Special
1:24	Action Racing Collectables	Wrangler 1981 Pontiac
1:24	Action Racing Collectables	Wrangler 1981 Pontiac
1:24	Action Racing Collectables	Wrangler 1983 Thunderbird
1:24	Action Racing Collectables	Wrangler 1985 Monte Carlo
1:24	Action Racing Collectables	Wrangler 1987 Monte Carlo
1:64	Action Racing Collectables	1985 Camaro ASA Platinum Series
1:64	Action Racing Collectables	Goodwrench 1988 Monte Carlo Platinum Series
1:64	Action Racing Collectables	Goodwrench 1994 Lumina Platinum Series
1:64	Action Racing Collectables	Goodwrench 1995 Monte Carlo Brickyard Special
1:64	Action Racing Collectables	Goodwrench 1995 Monte Carlo Platinum Series
1:64	Action Racing Collectables	Goodwrench Silver Car Blister w/out card package
1:64	Action Racing Collectables	Goodwrench Silver Car Platinum Series
1:64	Action Racing Collectables	Goodwrench Silver Car Race World Promo
1:64	Action Racing Collectables	Goodwrench AC Racing Promo
1:64	Action Racing Collectables	Dual package Brickyard Special
1:64	Action Racing Collectables	Dual package Kellogg's Promo
1:64	Action Racing Collectables	Richard Petty 7 and 7 Special
1:64	Action Racing Collectables	Wrangler 1981 Pontiac Platinum Series
1:64	Action Racing Collectables	Wrangler 1984 Monte Carlo Platinum Series
1:24	Action Racing Collectables Banks	Goodwrench 1994 Lumina
1:24	Action Racing Collectables Banks	Goodwrench 1995 Monte Carlo Sports Image
1:24	Action Racing Collectables Banks	Goodwrench 1995 Monte Carlo w/ headlights
1:24	Action Racing Collectables Banks	Goodwrench 1995 Monte Carlo w/out headlights
1:24	Action Racing Collectables Banks	Goodwrench Silver Car Black Wheels
1:24	Action Racing Collectables Banks	Goodwrench Silver Car Red Wheels
1:24	Action Racing Collectables Banks	Wrangler 1984 Monte Carlo
1:24	Action/RCCA	Goodwrench 1988 Monte Carlo Fast Back
1:24	Action/RCCA	Goodwrench 1994 Lumina

SCALE	MANUFACTURER	SPONSOR
1:24	Action/RCCA	Goodwrench 1995 Monte Carlo
1:24	Action/RCCA	Goodwrench Silver Car Black Wheels
1:24	Action/RCCA	Goodwrench Silver Car Red Wheels
1:24	Action/RCCA	Richard Petty 7 and 7 Special
1:24	Action/RCCA	Wrangler 1984 Monte Carlo Blue & Yellow
1:24	Action/RCCA	Wrangler 1984 Monte Carlo Blue Sides
1:24	Action/RCCA	Wrangler 1987 Monte Carlo
1:64	Action/RCCA	Goodwrench 1994 Lumina
1:64	Action/RCCA	Goodwrench 1994 Lumina Hood Open
1:64	Action/RCCA	Goodwrench 1995 Monte Carlo Hood Open
1:64	Action/RCCA	Goodwrench Club Only
1:64	Action/RCCA	Goodwrench Silver Car Hood Open
1:64	Action/RCCA	Wrangler 1981 Pontiac
1:64	Action/RCCA	Wrangler 1985 Monte Carlo Notchback
1:64	Action/RCCA	Wrangler 1987 Monte Carlo Fastback
1:64	Action/RCCA	Wrangler Revell
1:24	Action/RCCA Banks	Goodwrench 1994 Lumina
1:24	Action/RCCA Banks	Wrangler 1981 Pontiac
1:24	Action/RCCA Banks	Wrangler 1981 Pontiac
1:24	Action/RCCA Banks	Wrangler 1982 Thunder Bird
1:24	Action/RCCA Banks	Wrangler 1985 Monte Carlo
1:24	Action/RCCA Banks	Wrangler 1987 Monte Carlo
1:24	Revell	Goodwrench 1994 Sports Image
1:24	Revell	Goodwrench 6-Time Champion

SCALE	MANUFACTURER	SPONSOR
1:24	Revell	Goodwrench Black Wheels Sports Image car
1:24	Revell	Goodwrench Kellogg's Promo
1:24	Revell	Goodwrench Silver Wheels

1993–98

SCALE	MANUFACTURER	SPONSOR
1:24	Action Dually Trucks	Goodwrench
1:24	Action Dually Trucks	Goodwrench 1996 Bank
1:24	Action Dually Trucks	Goodwrench Bank 7-Time Champion
1:24	Action Dually Trucks	Wheaties Bank
1:18	Ertl	Goodwrench 7-Time
1:18	Ertl	Goodwrench '93 Lumina
1:18	Ertl	Goodwrench '95 Monte Carlo
1:18	Ertl	Goodwrench Silver Car
1:18	Ertl	Richard Petty 7-time Champions

1993–99

SCALE	MANUFACTURER	SPONSOR
1:64	Action Dually w/Chaparral Trailer	Goodwrench 1996
1:64	Action Dually w/Chaparral Trailer	Goodwrench 1996 w/out the trailer
1:64	Action Dually w/Chaparral Trailer	Goodwrench '95
1:64	Action Dually w/Chaparral Trailer	Goodwrench Bass Pro
1:64	Action Dually w/Chaparral Trailer	Goodwrench w/out Trailer
1:64	Action Dually w/Chaparral Trailer	Wheaties
1:64	Action Dually w/Chaparral Trailer	Wheaties w/out trailer
1:64	Action Dually w/Chaparral Trailer	Dale Earnhardt's Kids Mom-n-Pop's
1:16	Action Racing Collectables Pit Wagon Banks	Goodwrench
1:16	Action Racing Collectables Pit Wagon Banks	Goodwrench 1996
1:16	Action Racing Collectables Pit Wagon Banks	Goodwrench 25th
1:16	Action Racing Collectables Pit Wagon Banks	Goodwrench 7-Time Champion
1:16	Action Racing Collectables Pit Wagon Banks	Goodwrench '99
1:16	Action Racing Collectables Pit Wagon Banks	Goodwrench Plus Bass Pro
1:16	Action Racing Collectables Pit Wagon Banks	Wheaties

1993

Scale	Manufacturer	Sponsor
1:24	Racing Champions	Goodwrench Goodyear in White
1:24	Racing Champions	Goodwrench Goodyear in Yellow
1:24	Racing Champions	Goodwrench Mom-n-Pop's
1:43	Racing Champions	Goodwrench
1:64	Racing Champions	Goodwrench
1:64	Racing Champions	Goodwrench Mom-n-Pop's
1:43	Racing Champions Premier	Goodwrench
1:64	Racing Champions Premier	Dale Earnhardt Inc.
1:64	Racing Champions Premier	Goodwrench
1:64	Racing Champions Premier Transporters	Goodwrench
1:87	Racing Champions Premier Transporters	Goodwrench
1:87	Racing Champions Premier Transporters	Goodwrench Dale Earnhardt Inc.
1:64	Racing Champions PVC Box	Back in Black
1:64	Racing Champions PVC Box	Busch Clash Win
1:64	Racing Champions PVC Box	Darlington Win
1:64	Racing Champions PVC Box	Twin 125 Win
1:64	Racing Champions Transporters	Goodwrench
1:64	Racing Champions Transporters	Goodwrench Promo

1994–96

Scale	Manufacturer	Sponsor
1:96	Action/RCCA Transporters	Goodwrench '96
1:96	Action/RCCA Transporters	Goodwrench
1:96	Action/RCCA Transporters	Wrangler 85
1:96	Action/RCCA Transporters	Wrangler 87

1994

Scale	Manufacturer	Sponsor
1:64	Ertl White Rose Transporters Past and Present	Goodwrench
1:64	Ertl White Rose Transporters Past and Present	Wrangler
1:64	Matchbox White Rose Super Stars	Gold Lumina Super Star Awards
1:80	Matchbox White Rose Transporters Super Star Series	Goodwrench

Scale	Manufacturer	Sponsor
1:24	Racing Champions	Goodwrench
1:43	Racing Champions Premier	Goodwrench
1:64	Racing Champions Premier	Goodwrench
1:64	Racing Champions Premier Brickyard 400	Goodwrench
1:64	Racing Champions Premier Transporters	Goodwrench
1:87	Racing Champions Premier Transporters	Goodwrench
1:64	Racing Champions Transporters	Goodwrench Promo

1995

Scale	Manufacturer	Sponsor
1:64	Action/RCCA Transporters	Richard Petty 7 and 7 Champion special
1:64	Matchbox White Rose Super Stars	Gold 7-Time Champion Super Star Awards
1:64	Matchbox White Rose Super Stars	Goodwrench
1:80	Matchbox White Rose Transporters Super Star Series	Goodwrench
1:80	Matchbox White Rose Transporters Super Star Series	Snap On

1996

Scale	Manufacturer	Sponsor
1:24	Action Racing Collectables	AC-Delco
1:24	Action Racing Collectables	Goodwrench 1996 Monte Carlo
1:24	Action Racing Collectables	Olympic Car
1:24	Action Racing Collectables	Olympic Food City Promo
1:24	Action Racing Collectables	Olympic Goodwrench Box
1:24	Action Racing Collectables	Olympic Green Box
1:24	Action Racing Collectables	Olympic Green Box No Trademark on Hood of Car
1:24	Action Racing Collectables	Olympic Sports Image
1:24	Action Racing Collectables	Olympic w/ Mom-n-Pop's decal
1:24	Action Racing Collectables	Wrangler
1:64	Action Racing Collectables	16-car set
1:64	Action Racing Collectables	AC-Delco
1:64	Action Racing Collectables	Goodwrench
1:64	Action Racing Collectables	Goodwrench Blister w/ card package
1:64	Action Racing Collectables	Olympic Car Blister w/ card package

SCALE	MANUFACTURER	SPONSOR
1:64	Action Racing Collectables	Olympic Hood Open Car
1:64	Action Racing Collectables	Olympic Hood Open in Green Box
1:24	Action Racing Collectables Banks	Olympic
1:24	Action/RCCA	Wrangler 1982 Thunderbird
1:64	Action/RCCA	AC Delco
1:64	Action/RCCA	Goodwrench
1:64	Action/RCCA	Wrangler 1982 Thunderbird
1:24	Action/RCCA Banks	AC-Delco
1:24	Action/RCCA Banks	Goodwrench
1:64	Peachstate Transporters	Goodwrench
1:24	Revell	Goodwrench
1:24	Revell	Olympic car
1:64	Revell	Goodwrench
1:64	Revell	Olympic
1:64	Revell	Olympic Small Box
1:24	Revell Collection	Olympic
1:64	Revell Collection	Olympic

1997–98

SCALE	MANUFACTURER	SPONSOR
1:24	Winner's Circle	AC Delco 1996 Monte Carlo
1:24	Winner's Circle	Goodwrench
1:24	Winner's Circle	Goodwrench Plus
1:24	Winner's Circle	Goodwrench Plus Bass Pro
1:24	Winner's Circle	Goodwrench Silver
1:24	Winner's Circle	Wheaties
1:64	Winner's Circle	Coke
1:64	Winner's Circle	Goodwrench '88 MC
1:64	Winner's Circle	"10,000 RPM 1975 Dodge"
1:64	Winner's Circle	1978 MC
1:64	Winner's Circle	AC Delco
1:64	Winner's Circle	Bass Pro
1:64	Winner's Circle	Dayvault's
1:64	Winner's Circle	Goodwrench
1:64	Winner's Circle	Goodwrench 1994 Lumina

SCALE	MANUFACTURER	SPONSOR
1:64	Winner's Circle	Goodwrench 1995 Monte Carlo
1:64	Winner's Circle	Goodwrench 1990 Lumina
1:64	Winner's Circle	Goodwrench Camaro ASA
1:64	Winner's Circle	Goodwrench Plus
1:64	Winner's Circle	Goodwrench Plus Daytona
1:64	Winner's Circle	Goodwrench Silver
1:64	Winner's Circle	Lowes Foods
1:64	Winner's Circle	Mike Curb 1980 Olds
1:64	Winner's Circle	Wheaties
1:64	Winner's Circle	Wrangler 1981 Pontiac
1:64	Winner's Circle	Wrangler 1982 TB
1:64	Winner's Circle	Wrangler 1984 Monte Carlo
1:64	Winner's Circle	Wrangler 1985 Monte Carlo
1:64	Winner's Circle	Wrangler 1986 Monte Carlo
1:64	Winner's Circle	Wrangler 1987 Monte Carlo Fast Back

1997

SCALE	MANUFACTURER	SPONSOR
1:24	Action Racing Collectables	Goodwrench Brickyard Special
1:24	Action Racing Collectables	Wheaties
1:24	Action Racing Collectables	Wheaties Mail-In
1:24	Action Racing Collectables	Wheaties Snap-On
1:24	Action Racing Collectables	Wheaties Sports Image
1:64	Action Racing Collectables	AC Delco
1:64	Action Racing Collectables	AC Delco Black Window Blister Pack
1:64	Action Racing Collectables	Goodwrench
1:64	Action Racing Collectables	Goodwrench Brickyard Special
1:64	Action Racing Collectables	Goodwrench Plus
1:64	Action Racing Collectables	Goodwrench Plus Box
1:64	Action Racing Collectables	Wheaties
1:64	Action Racing Collectables	Wheaties Hood Open Sports Image

SCALE	MANUFACTURER	SPONSOR
1:64	Action Racing Collectables	Wheaties Mail-In
1:64	Action Racing Collectables	Wheaties Black Window Blister Pack
1:24	Action Racing Collectables Banks	AC Delco
1:24	Action Racing Collectables Banks	Goodwrench
1:24	Action Racing Collectables Banks	Goodwrench Plus
1:24	Action Racing Collectables Banks	Lowes Food
1:24	Action Racing Collectables Banks	Wheaties Snap-On
1:24	Action Racing Collectables Banks	Wrangler 1984 Monte Carlo Daytona
1:24	Action/RCCA	AC Delco
1:24	Action/RCCA	Goodwrench
1:24	Action/RCCA	Goodwrench Plus
1:24	Action/RCCA	Lowes Food
1:24	Action/RCCA	Wrangler 1984 Monte Carlo Daytona
1:64	Action/RCCA	AC Delco
1:64	Action/RCCA	Goodwrench
1:64	Action/RCCA	Goodwrench Plus
1:64	Action/RCCA	Wheaties
1:24	Action/RCCA Banks	Goodwrench Plus
1:24	Action/RCCA Banks	Wheaties
1:24	Action/RCCA Elite	AC Delco
1:24	Action/RCCA Elite	Goodwrench
1:24	Action/RCCA Elite	Goodwrench Plus
1:24	Action/RCCA Elite	Wheaties Gold number plate
1:24	Action/RCCA Elite	Wheaties Pewter number plate
1:18	Revell Collection	Wheaties

1998–99

SCALE	MANUFACTURER	SPONSOR
1:18	Action Racing Collectables	Budweiser
1:18	Action Racing Collectables	Bass Pro
1:18	Action Racing Collectables	Coke
1:18	Action Racing Collectables	Goodwrench 1999
1:18	Action Racing Collectables	Goodwrench Plus Daytona
1:18	Action Racing Collectables	Goowrench Silver
1:18	Action Racing Collectables	Wheaties
1:18	Action Racing Collectables	Wrangler '99

1998

SCALE	MANUFACTURER	SPONSOR
1:24	Action Racing Collectables	"10,000 RPM '78 Dodge"
1:24	Action Racing Collectables	Coke

SCALE	MANUFACTURER	SPONSOR
1:24	Action Racing Collectables	Dayvault's
1:24	Action Racing Collectables	Goodwrench Plus
1:24	Action Racing Collectables	Goodwrench Plus Bass Pro
1:24	Action Racing Collectables	Goodwrench Plus Daytona
1:32	Action Racing Collectables	Goodwrench Plus Bass Pro
1:32	Action Racing Collectables	Goodwrench Plus Daytona
1:64	Action Racing Collectables	"10,000 RPM 1978 Dodge"
1:64	Action Racing Collectables	Coke
1:64	Action Racing Collectables	Dayvault's
1:64	Action Racing Collectables	Dayvault's All Pink
1:64	Action Racing Collectables	Goodwrench Plus
1:64	Action Racing Collectables	Goodwrench Plus Bass Pro
1:64	Action Racing Collectables	Goodwrench Plus Blister Pack
1:64	Action Racing Collectables	Goodwrench Plus Daytona
1:64	Action Racing Collectables	Wrangler
1:24	Action Racing Collectables Banks	"10,000 RPM 1975 Dodge"
1:24	Action Racing Collectables Banks	Coke
1:24	Action Racing Collectables Banks	Dayvault's
1:24	Action Racing Collectables Banks	Goodwrench Plus Bass Pro
1:24	Action Racing Collectables Banks	Goodwrench Plus Daytona
1:24	Action Racing Collectables Banks	Goodwrench Plus w/Coke
1:24	Action Racing Collectables Banks	Goodwrench Plus w/o Coke
1:64	Action/RCCA	Coke
1:64	Action/RCCA	Dayvault's
1:64	Action/RCCA	Goodwrench Plus
1:64	Action/RCCA	Goodwrench Plus Bass Pro
1:64	Action/RCCA	RPM 1978 Dodge

SCALE	MANUFACTURER	SPONSOR
1:24	Action/RCCA Banks	"10,000 RPM 1978 Dodge"
1:24	Action/RCCA Banks	Coke
1:24	Action/RCCA Banks	Dayvault's
1:24	Action/RCCA Banks	Goodwrench Plus
1:24	Action/RCCA Banks	Goodwrench Plus Bass Pro
1:24	Action/RCCA Banks	Goodwrench Plus Daytona
1:24	Action/RCCA Elite	" 10,000 RPM 1978 Dodge"
1:24	Action/RCCA Elite	Coke
1:24	Action/RCCA Elite	Dayvault's
1:24	Action/RCCA Elite	Goodwrench Plus
1:24	Action/RCCA Elite	Goodwrench Plus Bass Pro
1:24	Action/RCCA Elite	Goodwrench Plus Daytona
1:24	Action/RCCA Elite	Goodwrench Silver
1:32	Action/RCCA Gold	Goodwrench Plus Bass Pro
1:18	Revell Club	Coke
1:18	Revell Club	Goodwrench Plus
1:18	Revell Club	Goodwrench Plus Bass Pro
1:18	Revell Club	Goodwrench Plus Daytona
1:24	Revell Club	Coke
1:24	Revell Club	Goodwrench Plus
1:24	Revell Club	Goodwrench Plus Bass Pro
1:24	Revell Club	Goodwrench Plus Daytona
1:18	Revell Collection	Coke
1:18	Revell Collection	Goodwrench Plus
1:18	Revell Collection	Goodwrench Plus Bass Pro
1:18	Revell Collection	Goodwrench Plus Brickyard Special
1:24	Revell Collection	Wrangler
1:24	Revell Collection	Coke
1:24	Revell Collection	Goodwrench Plus
1:24	Revell Collection	Goodwrench Plus Bass Pro
1:24	Revell Collection	Goodwrench Plus Brickyard Special
1:43	Revell Collection	Coke
1:43	Revell Collection	Goodwrench Plus

SCALE	MANUFACTURER	SPONSOR
1:43	Revell Collection	Goodwrench Plus Bass Pro
1:64	Revell Collection	Coke
1:64	Revell Collection	Goodwrench Plus
1:64	Revell Collection	Goodwrench Plus Bass Pro
1:64	Revell Collection	Goodwrench Plus Brickyard Special
1:24	Revell Hobby	Goodwrench Plus
1:24	Revell Hobby	Goodwrench Plus Bass Pro
1:43	Winner's Circle	Goodwrench Plus
1:43	Winner's Circle	Goodwrench Plus Bass Pro
1:64	Winner's Circle Pit Row	Bass Pro
1:64	Winner's Circle Pit Row	Coke
1:64	Winner's Circle Pit Row	Goodwrench

1999

SCALE	MANUFACTURER	SPONSOR
1:24	Action Racing Collectables	Budweiser
1:24	Action Racing Collectables	Army '76 Malibu
1:24	Action Racing Collectables	Hy-Gain '76
1:24	Action Racing Collectables	Wrangler
1:24	Action Racing Collectables	Goodwrench 25th Anniversary
1:64	Action Racing Collectables	Army '76 Malibu
1:64	Action Racing Collectables	Goodwrench
1:64	Action Racing Collectables	Goodwrench 25th Anniversary
1:64	Action Racing Collectables	Wrangler
1:24	Action Racing Collectables Banks	Budweiser
1:24	Action Racing Collectables Banks	Gargoyles '97 MC
1:24	Action Racing Collectables Banks	Sikkens 1997 Monte Carlo White
1:24	Action Racing Collectables Banks	Goodwrench
1:24	Action Racing Collectables Banks	Wrangler
1:64	Action/RCCA	Army '76 Malibu

SCALE	MANUFACTURER	SPONSOR
1:64	Action/RCCA	Hy-Gain '76 Malibu
1:64	Action/RCCA	Wrangler
1:64	Action/RCCA	Goodwrench
1:64	Action/RCCA	Goodwrench 25th Anniversary
1:24	Action/RCCA Banks	Wrangler
1:24	Action/RCCA Banks	Goodwrench 25th Anniversary
1:24	Action/RCCA Elite	Army '76 Malibu
1:24	Action/RCCA Elite	Goodwrench
1:24	Action/RCCA Elite	Hy-Gain '76 Malibu
1:18	Revell Club	Goodwrench
1:24	Revell Club	Goodwrench
1:18	Revell Collection	Budweiser
1:18	Revell Collection	Goodwrench
1:24	Revell Collection	Budweiser
1:24	Revell Collection	Sikkens Blue
1:24	Revell Collection	Goodwrench
1:24	Revell Collection	Goodwrench 25th
1:43	Revell Collection	Goodwrench
1:64	Revell Collection	AC Delco
1:64	Revell Collection	Budweiser
1:64	Revell Collection	Sikkens Blue
1:64	Revell Collection	Superman
1:64	Revell Collection	Wrangler
1:64	Revell Collection	Goodwrench
1:64	Revell Collection	Goodwrench 25th

SCALE	MANUFACTURER	SPONSOR
1:24	Revell Collection Banks	Budweiser
1:24	Winner's Circle	AC Delco
1:64	Winner's Circle	Coke
1:64	Winner's Circle	AC Delco
1:64	Winner's Circle	Sikkens
1:64	Winner's Circle	Coke
1:64	Winner's Circle	Goodwrench
1:64	Winner's Circle	Crane Cams 1979 Monte Carlo
1:64	Winner's Circle	Goodwrench 1995 Brickyard Winner
1:64	Winner's Circle Pit Row	Goodwrench 25th
1:43	Winner's Circle Speedweeks	Goodwrench
1:64	Winner's Circle Speedweeks	Goodwrench
1:64	Winner's Circle Tech Series	AC Delco
1:64	Winner's Circle Tech Series	Goodwrench

2000

SCALE	MANUFACTURER	SPONSOR
1:18	Action Racing Collectables	Taz No Bull
1:24	Action Racing Collectables	Goodwrench
1:24	Action Racing Collectables	GW Taz
1:64	Action Racing Collectables	Goodwrench
1:64	Action Racing Collectables	Taz No Bull
1:24	Action Racing Collectables Banks	GM Goodwrench
1:24	Action Racing Collectables Banks	Taz No Bull
1:24	Action/RCCA Elite	Goodwrench.
1:24	Revell Collection	Taz No Bull
1:64	Revell Collection	Test Car
1:64	Winner's Circle Preview	GM Goodwrench
1:64	Winner's Circle Preview	GM Goodwrench

Dale Earnhardt Jr.

Hometown:
Concord, NC

Birthdate:
October 10th, 1974

Personal:
Dale Jr. likes his music, spending much of his time building a large CD collection and buying just the right stereo systems for his home and personal vehicles. His favorite bands include Pearl Jam and Third Eye Blind. His favorite song is Joe Cocker's "A Little Help From My Friends." Other Earnhardt favorites include the TV show *Seinfeld*, actor Cuba Gooding Jr., actress Cameron Diaz, Irish Setter dogs and red Corvettes.

Hobby:
The two-time Busch champion is following in his father's footsteps. Bursting on the scene in 1998, Dale Jr. soared to the top of the collectibles market. But because the third-generation driver hasn't been racing long, "Little E" doesn't have that many paint schemes on the market. Most on the market have been produced in large quantities. Earnhardt signed a long-term deal with Action Performance Companies before the start of the 1999 season. His Budweiser paint schemes, for his Winston Cup cars, have been popular since they debuted in May of 1999.

Career Highlights
- In his first two years of racing full-time on a NASCAR touring circuit, 1998 and 1999, Earnhardt won Busch Grand National titles both seasons.
- Earnhardt is one of just four drivers to win multiple Busch titles. The others are Jack Ingram, Sam Ard and Randy LaJoie.
- Earnhardt is 10th on the all-time Busch victory list, winning 13 races in 1998 and 1999.
- Earnhardt owns the single-season record for money winnings on the Busch circuit with $1,680,598. He is one of two drivers with more than $3 million in career Busch earnings.
- Made Winston Cup debut in the 1999 Coca-Cola 600.
- First led a Winston Cup race in the November of 1999 Atlanta event.
- In April of 2000, in the seventh race of his rookie season, won his first Winston Cup race. He won at Texas Motor Speedway, which was also the site of his first Busch victory. Dale Jr. needed just 12 Winston Cup starts to reach victory lane.

1993–95

Scale	Manufacturer	Sponsor
1:64	Action/RCCA	Mom-n-Pop's

1997–98

Scale	Manufacturer	Sponsor
1:24	Winner's Circle	AC Delco
1:64	Winner's Circle	AC Delco

1998-99

Scale	Manufacturer	Sponsor
1:18	Action Racing Collectables	AC Delco
1:18	Action Racing Collectables	Coke
1:18	Action Racing Collectables	Sikkens
1:18	Action Racing Collectables	Wrangler

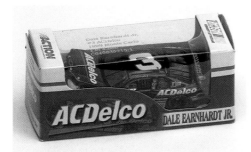

1998

Scale	Manufacturer	Sponsor
1:24	Action Racing Collectables	AC Delco
1:24	Action Racing Collectables	Coke
1:24	Action Racing Collectables	Sikkens
1:24	Action Racing Collectables	Wrangler
1:32	Action Racing Collectables	AC Delco
1:64	Action Racing Collectables	AC Delco
1:64	Action Racing Collectables	AC Delco Blister Pack
1:64	Action Racing Collectables	Coke
1:64	Action Racing Collectables	Sikkens
1:24	Action Racing Collectables Banks	AC Delco
1:24	Action Racing Collectables Banks	AC Delco Snap-On
1:24	Action Racing Collectables Banks	Coke
1:24	Action Racing Collectables Banks	Sikkens
1:24	Action Racing Collectables Banks	Wrangler
1:64	Action/RCCA	AC Delco
1:64	Action/RCCA	Coke
1:64	Action/RCCA	Sikkens
1:24	Action/RCCA Banks	AC Delco
1:24	Action/RCCA Banks	Coke
1:24	Action/RCCA Banks	Sikkens
1:24	Action/RCCA Banks	Wrangler
1:24	Action/RCCA Elite	AC Delco
1:24	Action/RCCA Elite	Coke
1:24	Action/RCCA Elite	Sikkens
1:32	Action/RCCA Gold	AC Delco
1:18	Revell Club	AC Delco
1:18	Revell Club	Coke

Scale	Manufacturer	Sponsor
1:24	Revell Club	AC Delco
1:24	Revell Club	Coke
1:18	Revell Collection	AC Delco
1:18	Revell Collection	Coke
1:18	Revell Collection	Wrangler
1:24	Revell Collection	AC Delco Dealer Issued
1:24	Revell Collection	AC Delco Trackside Issued
1:24	Revell Collection	Coke
1:43	Revell Collection	Coke
1:43	Revell Collection	Wrangler
1:64	Revell Collection	AC Delco
1:64	Revell Collection	Coke
1:24	Revell Collection Banks	Coke
1:24	Revell Collection Banks	Wrangler
1:24	Revell Hobby	AC Delco
1:64	Revell Hobby	AC Delco
1:43	Winner's Circle	AC Delco
1:64	Winner's Circle Pit Row	AC Delco
1:64	Winner's Circle Pit Row	Coke

1999

Scale	Manufacturer	Sponsor
1:24	Action Racing Collectables	AC Delco
1:24	Action Racing Collectables	Gargoyles 1997 Monte Carlo
1:24	Action Racing Collectables	Sikkens 1997 Monte Carlo White

SCALE	MANUFACTURER	SPONSOR
1:64	Action Racing Collectables	AC Delco
1:64	Action Racing Collectables	AC Delco Black Window Blister Pack
1:64	Action Racing Collectables	Budweiser
1:64	Action Racing Collectables	Gargoyles
1:64	Action Racing Collectables	Sikkens White
1:24	Action Racing Collectables Banks	AC Delco
1:64	Action/RCCA	AC Delco
1:64	Action/RCCA	Gargoyles 1997 Monte Carlo
1:64	Action/RCCA	Sikkens White 1997 Mote Carlo
1:24	Action/RCCA Banks	AC Delco
1:24	Action/RCCA Banks	Budweiser

SCALE	MANUFACTURER	SPONSOR
1:24	Action/RCCA Banks	Gargoyles
1:24	Action/RCCA Elite	Budweiser
1:24	Action/RCCA Elite	AC Delco
1:24	Action/RCCA Elite	Sikkens White
1:18	Revell Club	Gargoyles
1:24	Revell Club	Gargoyles 1997 Monte Carlo
1:24	Revell Club	Sikkens White 1997 Monte Carlo
1:18	Revell Collection	Gargoyles

SCALE	MANUFACTURER	SPONSOR
1:18	Revell Collection	Sikkens White 1997 Monte Carlo
1:24	Revell Collection	Gargoyles 1997 Monte Carlo
1:24	Revell Collection	Sikkens White 1997 Monte Carlo
1:43	Revell Collection	AC Delco
1:64	Revell Collection	Gargoyles
1:64	Revell Collection	Sikkens 1997 Monty Carlo
1:43	Winner's Circle Speedweeks	AC Delco

2000

SCALE	MANUFACTURER	SPONSOR
1:24	Action Racing Collectables	Budweiser
1:64	Action Racing Collectables	Budweiser
1:64	Action/RCCA	Budweiser
1:24	Action/RCCA Elite	2000 Test Car
1:24	Revell Collection	Test Car
1:24	Revell Collection	Budweiser
1:64	Revell Collection	Budweiser
1:43	Winner's Circle Preview	Superman '9

Bill Elliott

Hometown:

Dawsonville, GA

Birthdate:

October 8, 1955

Personal:

Racing is a family business for Elliott, with more than a half-dozen close relatives involved in the sport. Outside of racing and his family, Elliott's two greatest loves are snow skiing and flying. He owns several aircraft that he uses for both personal and business use. If his Winston Cup career had never panned out, Elliott would have either been a pilot or a truck driver for his good friend Curtis Colwell in Blairsville, Georgia. Elliott considers David Pearson and Jody Ridley his racing heroes and Burt Reynolds as his favorite actor.

Hobby:

Elliott remains popular in the hobby despite struggling on the track for the past few years since becoming an owner-driver. He had Budweiser and Coors as sponsors early in his career, with die-cast replicas carrying the beer brands that are hard to come by. His latest sponsor, McDonald's, has helped him stay on collectors' want lists. He's had several popular paint schemes, many of them involving a promotion done by McDonald's. When Elliott drove his black ThunderBat car to promote a Batman movie, he helped make the special paint scheme a lasting part of die-cast collecting. Most of his die-cast replicas have been made by Hot Wheels or Racing Champions

Career Highlights

- 1988 Winston Cup Champion.
- In 1998, won Winston Cup's Most Popular Driver award for an unprecedented 13th time.
- Won inaugural Winston Million in 1985 by winning three of four "crown jewel" events (Daytona 500, Winston 500, Southern 500).
- Made Winston Cup debut in 1976. First full NASCAR Winston Cup season was 1983.
- First win came in 117th start, Winston Western 500 in 1983 at Riverside. First pole came in 56th attempt, at '81 Rebel 500 at Darlington.
- Three-time Winston Cup runner-up (1985, 1987, 1992).
- American Driver of the Year in 1985 and 1988.
- NMPA Driver of the Year in 1985.
- Won four consecutive races in 1992 to tie modern-era record.
- Won single-season record, 11 superspeedway races in '85.
- Owns fastest official time in a stock car, going 212.809 mph in qualifying for '87 Winston 500 at Talladega.

SCALE	MANUFACTURER	SPONSOR
1987–90		
1:64	Winross Transporters	Coors '90
1989–90		
1:87	Matchbox White Rose Transporters Super Star Series	Melling '90
1989		
1:64	Racing Champions Flat Bottom	Motorcraft Melling Ford
1990–92		
1:64	Matchbox White Rose Super Stars	Amoco '92 BL
1990		
1:64	Racing Champions	Orange and Blue Stripe No Melling on the car
1:64	Racing Champions	Orange and Blue Stripe w/ Melling on the car
1:64	Racing Champions	Red and Blue Stripe w/ Melling on the car
1991–92		
1:24	Racing Champions	Amoco
1:24	Racing Champions	Melling
1991		
1:64	Action/RCCA 1983-86 T-Bird Series	Melling
1:87	Matchbox White Rose Transporters Super Star Series	Melling w/ Ford cab
1:87	Matchbox White Rose Transporters Super Star Series	Melling w/ Mack cab
1:43	Racing Champions	Melling
1:64	Racing Champions	Ford EB Car is 1/2 blue
1:64	Racing Champions	Ford EB Car is 3/4 blue
1:64	Racing Champions	Ford PB
1:64	Racing Champions	Old Ford body style EB Orange and White paint scheme
1:64	Racing Champions	Old Ford body style NP Orange and White paint scheme
1:64	Racing Champions Transporters	Melling w/ Red paint scheme
1:64	Winross Transporters	Coors Light
1:64	Winross Transporters	Fan Club
1:64	Winross Transporters	Museum w/ Blue Paint scheme
1992–94		
1:24	Racing Champions Banks	Amoco
1:24	Racing Champions Banks	Budweiser
1:24	Racing Champions Banks	Budweiser Hardy Boys car
1992–95		
1:64	Action/RCCA Transporters	Bud 1993
1:64	Action/RCCA Transporters	Bud 1994
1:64	Action/RCCA Transporters	McDonald's
1:64	Action/RCCA Transporters	Melling RCCA
1992–97		
1:24	Raceway Replicas	Budweiser 1992
1992		
1:43	Funstuf Pit Row	Amoco
1:64	Funstuf Pit Row	Amoco on the Deck Lid
1:64	Funstuf Pit Row	Amoco on the Hood
1:87	Matchbox White Rose Transporters 1992 Super Star Series	Melling
1:43	Racing Champions	Amoco
1:64	Racing Champions	Amoco
1:64	Racing Champions	Melling
1:64	Racing Champions Premier	Amoco
1:64	Racing Champions Transporters	Amoco
1:64	Racing Champions Transporters	Melling w/ Blue paint scheme
1:64	Winross Transporters	Fan Club
1:64	Winross Transporters	Museum w/ red paint scheme
1993–94		
1:87	Racing Champions Transporters	Amoco
1993–95		
1:24	Action Racing Collectables	Budweiser
1:24	Action Racing Collectables	McDonald's
1:64	Action Racing Collectables	Budweiser 1994 Platinum Series
1:64	Action Racing Collectables	McDonald's 1995 Platinum Series
1:64	Action Racing Collectables	Thunderbat Platinum Series
1:24	Action Racing Collectables Banks	Budweiser
1:24	Action Racing Collectables Banks	McDonald's
1:24	Action Racing Collectables Banks	McDonald's Thunderbat
1:24	Action/RCCA	McDonald's 1995
1:24	Action/RCCA	McDonald's Thunderbat
1:64	Action/RCCA	Budweiser Hood Open
1:64	Action/RCCA	McDonald's Hood Open
1:64	Action/RCCA	McDonald's Thunderbat Hood Open
1:64	Action/RCCA	Melling Club Only

SCALE	MANUFACTURER	SPONSOR
1993–98		
1:24	Action Dually Trucks	Budweiser Bank
1:24	Action Dually Trucks	Mac Tonight Bank
1:24	Action Dually Trucks	McDonald's Bank
1:18	Ertl	MT Prestige Series
1:18	Ertl	Budweiser
1:18	Ertl	McDonald's
1:18	Ertl	McDonald's 1996
1:18	Ertl	McDonald's 1997
1:18	Ertl	McDonald's Thunderbat
1993–99		
1:64	Action Dually w/Chaparral Trailer	Budweiser
1:64	Action Dually w/Chaparral Trailer	Mac Tonight
1:64	Action Dually w/Chaparral Trailer	McDonald's
1:16	Action Racing Collectables Pit Wagon Banks	Budweiser
1:16	Action Racing Collectables Pit Wagon Banks	Mac Tonight
1:16	Action Racing Collectables Pit Wagon Banks	McDonald's
1993		
1:24	Racing Champions	Amoco
1:24	Racing Champions	True Value IROC car
1:43	Racing Champions	Amoco
1:64	Racing Champions	Amoco
1:43	Racing Champions Premier	Amoco
1:43	Racing Champions Premier	Budweiser
1:64	Racing Champions Premier	Budweiser Promo
1:64	Racing Champions Premier Transporters	Budweiser
1:87	Racing Champions Premier Transporters	Amoco
1:87	Racing Champions Premier Transporters	Budweiser
1:64	Racing Champions Transporters	Amoco
1:64	Winross Transporters	Fan Club
1994–96		
1:96	Action/RCCA Transporters	McDonald's
1994		
1:64	Ertl White Rose Transporters BGN Promos	Budweiser in Wooden case Promo
1:64	Racing Champions Transporters	Amoco
1:64	Winross Transporters	Budweiser
1995–96		
1:18	Racing Champions	McDonald's Monopoly

SCALE	MANUFACTURER	SPONSOR
1995		
1:64	Matchbox White Rose Super Stars	Gold Thunderbird Super Star Awards
1:64	Matchbox White Rose Super Stars	McDonald's
1:64	Matchbox White Rose Super Stars	McDonald's Thunderbat
1:80	Matchbox White Rose Transporters Super Star Series	McDonald's
1:24	Racing Champions	McDonald's
1:24	Racing Champions	McDonald's Thunderbat
1:64	Racing Champions	McDonald's
1:64	Racing Champions	McDonald's Thunderbat
1:24	Racing Champions Banks	McDonald's
1:24	Racing Champions Banks	McDonald's Thunderbat
1:64	Racing Champions Premier	McDonald's
1:64	Racing Champions Premier Transporters	McDonald's
1:24	Racing Champions Previews	McDonald's
1:64	Racing Champions Previews	McDonald's
1:64	Racing Champions To the Maxx	McDonald's
1:64	Racing Champions Transporters	McDonald's
1:64	Racing Champions Transporters	McDonald's Thunderbat
1:64	Winross Transporters	McDonald's
1996		
1:64	Action Racing Collectables	McDonald's
1:64	Action/RCCA	McDonald's
1:24	Action/RCCA Banks	McDonald's
1:64	Matchbox White Rose Super Stars	McDonald's
1:80	Matchbox White Rose Transporters Super Star Series	McDonald's
1:64	Peachstate Transporters	McDonald's
1:24	Racing Champions	McDonald's
1:24	Racing Champions	McDonald's Hood Open
1:24	Racing Champions	McDonald's Monopoly
1:24	Racing Champions	McDonald's Monopoly Hood Open
1:64	Racing Champions	10-Time Most Popular Driver Silver car
1:64	Racing Champions	McDonald's
1:64	Racing Champions	McDonald's Monopoly
1:24	Racing Champions Banks	McDonald's
1:24	Racing Champions Banks	McDonald's Monopoly
1:24	Racing Champions Chrome Banks	McDonald's
1:24	Racing Champions Hobby Banks	McDonald's Hobby

SCALE	MANUFACTURER	SPONSOR
1:24	Racing Champions Hood Open Banks	McDonald's Monopoly Hood Open
1:64	Racing Champions Premier Transporters	McDonald's
1:64	Racing Champions Premier w/ Medallion	McDonald's Hood Open
1:64	Racing Champions Premier w/ Medallion	McDonald's Monopoly Hood Open
1:24	Racing Champions Previews	McDonald's
1:64	Racing Champions Previews	McDonald's
1:64	Racing Champions Silver Chase	McDonald's
1:64	Racing Champions Transporters	McDonald's
1:64	Racing Champions Transporters	McDonald's Monopoly
1:64	Racing Champions Transporters	McDonald's Monopoly w/ one car or two cars
1:64	Racing Champions Transporters	McDonald's w/ one car or two cars

1997

SCALE	MANUFACTURER	SPONSOR
1:24	Action Racing Collectables	Mac Tonight
1:64	Action Racing Collectables	Mac Tonight
1:64	Action Racing Collectables	McDonald's
1:24	Action Racing Collectables Banks	McDonald's
1:24	Action/RCCA	McDonald's
1:64	Action/RCCA	Mac Tonight
1:64	Action/RCCA	McDonald's
1:24	Action/RCCA Banks	Mac Tonight
1:24	Action/RCCA Elite	Mac Tonight
1:24	Action/RCCA Elite	McDonald's
1:64	Hot Wheels Collector Edition	McDonald's
1:64	Hot Wheels Collector Edition/Short Track	MacTonight
1:64	Hot Wheels Collector Edition/Short Track	McDonald's
1:64	Hot Wheels Collector Edition/ Speedway Edition	McDonald's
1:64	Hot Wheels Pro Racing	McDonald's
1:64	Matchbox White Rose Super Stars	McDonald's
1:64	Matchbox White Rose Transporters	Mac Tonight in acrylic case
1:64	Matchbox White Rose Transporters	McDonald's in acrylic case
1:18	Racing Champions	McDonald's Gold
1:18	Racing Champions	McDonald's Hobby
1:24	Racing Champions	Mac Tonight
1:24	Racing Champions	Mac Tonight 3-car set
1:24	Racing Champions	McDonald's
1:64	Racing Champions	Mac Tonight

SCALE	MANUFACTURER	SPONSOR
1:64	Racing Champions	McDonald's
1:24	Racing Champions Banks	Mac Tonight
1:64	Racing Champions Gold	McDonald's
1:24	Racing Champions Gold Banks	McDonald's Gold
1:64	Racing Champions Hobby	McDonald's
1:24	Racing Champions Hobby Banks	McDonald's Hobby
1:24	Racing Champions Hood Open Banks	McDonald's Hood Open
1:64	Racing Champions Pinnacle Series	McDonald's
1:64	Racing Champions Premier Preview w/ Medallion	McDonald's
1:64	Racing Champions Premier w/ Medallion	Mac Tonight
1:24	Racing Champions Previews	McDonald's
1:64	Racing Champions Previews	McDonald's
1:24	Racing Champions Stock Rods	MacTonight
1:64	Racing Champions Stock Rods	Mac Tonight
1:64	Racing Champions Stock Rods	Mac Tonight
1:64	Racing Champions Stock Rods	McDonald's
1:64	Racing Champions Stock Rods	McDonald's
1:64	Racing Champions Stock Rods	McDonald's
1:24	Racing Champions SuperTrucks	Team ASE
1:64	Racing Champions SuperTrucks	Team ASE
1:64	Racing Champions Transporters	McDonald's
1:87	Racing Champions Transporters	McDonald's
1:18	Revell Collection	Mac Tonight
1:18	Revell Collection	McDonald's
1:24	Revell Collection	Mac Tonight
1:24	Revell Collection	McDonald's
1:43	Revell Collection	Mac Tonight
1:24	Revell Hobby	Mac Tonight
1:24	Revell Hobby	McDonald's
1:64	Revell Hobby	McDonald's

1998

SCALE	MANUFACTURER	SPONSOR
1:64	Hot Wheels Collector Edition/Pit Crew	McDonald's
1:64	Hot Wheels Collector Edition/ Preview Edition	McDonalds
1:64	Hot Wheels Collector Edition/ Track Edition	McDonald's
1:24	Racing Champions	Happy Meal
1:24	Racing Champions	Mac Tonight

SCALE	MANUFACTURER	SPONSOR
1:24	Racing Champions	McDonald's
1:64	Racing Champions	McDonald's
1:64	Racing Champions Chrome Chase	McDonald's
1:24	Racing Champions Driver's Choice Banks	McDonald's
1:24	Racing Champions Gold	Happy Meal
1:24	Racing Champions Gold	McDonald's
1:24	Racing Champions Gold Banks	McDonald's
1:24	Racing Champions Gold Hood Open	Happy Meal
1:24	Racing Champions Gold Hood Open	McDonald's
1:64	Racing Champions Gold w/Medallion	Happy Meal
1:64	Racing Champions Gold w/ Medallion	McDonald's
1:64	Racing Champions Pinnacle Series	McDonald's
1:64	Racing Champions Press Pass Series	Happy Meal
1:64	Racing Champions Press Pass Series	McDonald's
1:24	Racing Champions Reflections of Gold	McDonald's
1:64	Racing Champions Reflections of Gold	McDonald's
1:24	Racing Champions Signature Series	McDonald's
1:64	Racing Champions Signature Series	Happy Meal
1:64	Racing Champions Signature Series	McDonald's
1:24	Racing Champions Stock Rods	McDonald's
1:24	Racing Champions Stock Rods	McDonald's
1:24	Racing Champions Stock Rods	McDonald's Gold
1:24	Racing Champions Stock Rods	McDonald's Gold
1:24	Racing Champions Stock Rods	McDonald's Gold
1:24	Racing Champions Stock Rods	McDonald's Gold
1:64	Racing Champions Stock Rods	McDonald's
1:64	Racing Champions Stock Rods	McDonald's
1:64	Racing Champions Stock Rods	McDonald's
1:64	Racing Champions Stock Rods	McDonald's
1:64	Racing Champions Stock Rods	McDonald's
1:64	Racing Champions Stock Rods	McDonald's
1:64	Racing Champions Stock Rods	McDonald's Gold
1:64	Racing Champions Stock Rods	McDonald's Gold
1:24	Racing Champions Stock Rods Reflections of Gold	McDonald's
1:64	Racing Champions Stock Rods Reflections of Gold	McDonald's
1:24	Racing Champions SuperTrucks	Team ASE
1:64	Racing Champions SuperTrucks	Team ASE
1:64	Racing Champions Toys 'R Us Gold	Happy Meal
1:64	Racing Champions Transporters	Happy Meal w/ car
1:64	Racing Champions Transporters Gold	Happy Meal
1:64	Racing Champions Transporters Gold	Mac Tonight
1:64	Racing Champions Transporters Gold	McDonald's
1:64	Racing Champions Transporters Signature Series	Happy Meal

1999

SCALE	MANUFACTURER	SPONSOR
1:64	Hot Wheels Collector Edition	Drive Thru
1:64	Hot Wheels Collector Edition/Pit Crew	McDonalds
1:64	Hot Wheels Collector Edition/Pit Crew Gold	Drive Thru
1:64	Hot Wheels Collector Edition/Track Edition	Drive Thru
1:24	Hot Wheels Pro Racing	Drive Thru
1:43	Hot Wheels Pro Racing	McDonald's
1:43	Hot Wheels Track Edition	Drive Thru
1:24	Racing Champions	Drive Thru
1:64	Racing Champions	McDonald's
1:64	Racing Champions 24K Gold Stock Rods	Drive Thru
1:64	Racing Champions 3-D Originals	Drive Thru
1:64	Racing Champions Chrome Chase	Drive Thru
1:24	Racing Champions Chrome Signature Series	Drive Thru
1:64	Racing Champions Chrome Signature Series	Drive Thru
1:24	Racing Champions Gold	McDonald's
1:64	Racing Champions Gold w/ Medallion	Drive Thru
1:64	Racing Champions NASCAR RULES	Drive Thru
1:24	Racing Champions Platinum	Drive Thru
1:64	Racing Champions Platinum	Drive Thru
1:64	Racing Champions Platinum Stock Rods	Drive Thru
1:64	Racing Champions Press Pass Series	Drive Thru
1:64	Racing Champions Radio Controled Die Cast	Drive Thru
1:24	Racing Champions Signature Series	Drive Thru
1:64	Racing Champions Signature Series	Drive Thru
1:24	Racing Champions Stock Rods	Drive Thru
1:24	Racing Champions Stock Rods	Drive Thru Gold
1:64	Racing Champions Stock Rods	Drive Thru
1:64	Racing Champions Stock Rods	Drive Thru Gold
1:64	Racing Champions Toy's R Us Chrome Chase	Drive Thru
1:64	Racing Champions Trackside	Drive Thru
1:64	Racing Champions Transporters	Drive Thru
1:64	Racing Champions Transporters 24K Gold	Drive Thru
1:64	Racing Champions Transporters Gold	Drive Thru
1:64	Racing Champions Transporters Signature Series	Drive Thru
1:24	Racing Champions Under the Lights	Drive Thru
1:64	Racing Champions Under the Lights	Drive Thru

2000

SCALE	MANUFACTURER	SPONSOR
1:64	Hot Wheels Deluxe Scorchin Scooter	McDonald's

Jeff Gordon

Hometown:
Pittsboro, Indiana

Birthdate:
August 4, 1971

Personal:
Jeff Gordon began racing go-karts and quarter-midgets at age five. In 1979 and 1981, Jeff was the quarter-midget national champion. He was inspired by stepfather, John Bickford, who moved family to Midwest to give Jeff, then a 13-year old, better racing opportunity. Jeff's wife, Brooke, served as Miss Winston in 1993. They met when Jeff visited victory lane at Daytona after his victory in Gatorade 125s. Enjoys skiing (both water and snow), video games, golf and racquetball.

Hobby:
Jeff's die-cast cars constantly sell out. Though he has had an exclusive deal with Action Performance Companies for the past several years, he has had cars produced by Ertl and Racing Champions. Since joining the Winston Cup circuit, he has battled Dale Earnhardt annually for the top spot on collectors' want lists. Among his most popular paint schemes have been Star Wars, Superman, Chromalusion, Jurassic Park and Pepsi.

Career Highlights

- Three-time Winston Cup champion, winning titles in 1995 and 1997-98.
- In 1999, once again led Winston Cup series in victories to become the first driver in NASCAR history to top circuit in wins for five consecutive seasons.
- Became the youngest champion in Winston Cup's modern era (since 1972) when he won 1995 title at age 24. Second youngest champion ever behind 23-year-old Bill Rexford in 1950.
- One of only two drivers (Bill Elliott is the other) to capture Winston Million. Gordon claimed that prize by winning Daytona 500, Coca-Cola 600 and Southern 500 in 1998.
- Named NMPA Driver of the Year for 1995.
- 1990 USAC midget champion.
- 1991 USAC Silver Crown champion.
- 1991 Busch Grand National Rookie of the Year.
- Posted more than 500 short-track wins.
- Won record 11 Busch Grand Nationals poles in 1992.
- At 21 in 1993, became youngest driver ever to win 125-mile qualifying race for Daytona 500 and first rookie since Johnny Rutherford in 1963. He was named 1993 Winston Cup Rookie of the Year.

SCALE	MANUFACTURER	SPONSOR

1990–92

| 1:64 | Matchbox White Rose Super Stars | Baby Ruth Orange Lettering '92 BX |
| 1:64 | Matchbox White Rose Super Stars | Baby Ruth Red Lettering '92 BX |

1991–92

| 1:24 | Racing Champions | Baby Ruth |

1992–94

1:24	Racing Champions Banks	DuPont
1:24	Racing Champions Banks	DuPont Brickyard Special
1:24	Racing Champions Banks	DuPont Coca-Cola 600 Winner
1:24	Racing Champions Banks	DuPont Snickers

1992–95

| 1:64 | Action/RCCA Transporters | Baby Ruth produced for Peachstate |
| 1:64 | Action/RCCA Transporters | DuPont produced for GMP |

1992–96

1:24	Brookfield Collectors Guild Suburbans	DuPont Silver 1996
1:24	Brookfield Collectors Guild Suburbans	DuPont 1996
1:24	Brookfield Collectors Guild Suburbans	DuPont Rookie of the Year 1993

1992

1:43	Funstuf Pit Row	Baby Ruth
1:64	Funstuf Pit Row	Baby Ruth
1:87	Matchbox White Rose Transporters 1992 Super Star Series	Baby Ruth
1:43	Racing Champions	Baby Ruth
1:64	Racing Champions	Baby Ruth
1:64	Racing Champions Transporters	Baby Ruth

1993–94

| 1:87 | Racing Champions Transporters | DuPont |
| 1:87 | Racing Champions Transporters | DuPont Yellow box hobby only |

1993–95

1:64	Action Racing Collectables	DuPont 1995 Champion
1:64	Action Racing Collectables	DuPont Valvoline Team Promo
1:64	Action Racing Collectables	DuPont 1994 Lumina Platinum Series

SCALE	MANUFACTURER	SPONSOR
1:64	Action Racing Collectables	DuPont 1995 Monte Carlo Platinum Series
1:64	Action Racing Collectables	DuPont AC Racing Promo
1:24	Action Racing Collectables Banks	DuPont 1995 Champion
1:24	Action Racing Collectables Banks	DuPont 1995 Monte Carlo
1:24	Action/RCCA	DuPont 1995 Monte Carlo
1:64	Action/RCCA	Baby Ruth Revell
1:64	Action/RCCA	DuPont 1993 Lumina HO
1:64	Action/RCCA	DuPont 1994 Lumina Hood Open
1:64	Action/RCCA	DuPont 1995 Monte Carlo Hood Open
1:24	Revell	Baby Ruth produced for RCI

1993–98

1:24	Action Dually Trucks	DuPont 1996
1:24	Action Dually Trucks	DuPont 1998
1:24	Action Dually Trucks	DuPont Bank
1:24	Action Dually Trucks	DuPont Coca-Cola Bank
1:18	Ertl	Baby Ruth
1:18	Ertl	DuPont '94 Lumina
1:18	Ertl	DuPont '95 Buck Fever
1:18	Ertl	DuPont '95 GMP
1:18	Ertl	DuPont White Rose Collectibles Bank
1:18	Ertl	DuPont White Rose Collectibles Bank No serial number on bottom

1993–99

1:64	Action Dually w/Chaparral Trailer	DuPont
1:64	Action Dually w/Chaparral Trailer	DuPont 1996
1:64	Action Dually w/Chaparral Trailer	DuPont 1996 w/out the trailer
1:64	Action Dually w/Chaparral Trailer	DuPont 1998
1:64	Action Dually w/Chaparral Trailer	DuPont Chromalusion
1:64	Action Dually w/Chaparral Trailer	DuPont w/out Trailer

SCALE	MANUFACTURER	SPONSOR
1:16	Action Racing Collectables Pit Wagon Banks	DuPont
1:16	Action Racing Collectables Pit Wagon Banks	DuPont '96
1:16	Action Racing Collectables Pit Wagon Banks	Lost World

1993

SCALE	MANUFACTURER	SPONSOR
1:64	Matchbox White Rose Super Stars	DuPont BL
1:87	Matchbox White Rose Transporters Super Star Series	DuPont
1:24	Racing Champions	DuPont
1:43	Racing Champions	DuPont
1:64	Racing Champions	DuPont
1:43	Racing Champions Premier	DuPont
1:64	Racing Champions Premier	DuPont
1:64	Racing Champions Premier Transporters	DuPont
1:87	Racing Champions Premier Transporters	DuPont
1:64	Racing Champions PVC Box	DuPont
1:64	Racing Champions PVC Box	DuPont Daytona
1:64	Racing Champions PVC Box	DuPont Fan Club
1:64	Racing Champions PVC Box	DuPont Twin 125 Win
1:64	Racing Champions Transporters	DuPont
1:64	Winross Transporters	DuPont

1994–96

SCALE	MANUFACTURER	SPONSOR
1:96	Action/RCCA Transporters	DuPont

1994

SCALE	MANUFACTURER	SPONSOR
1:64	Ertl White Rose Transporters BGN Promos	Baby Ruth BGN
1:64	Ertl White Rose Transporters Past and Present	DuPont
1:64	Matchbox White Rose Super Stars	DuPont BX
1:80	Matchbox White Rose Transporters Super Star Series	DuPont
1:24	Racing Champions	Coca-Cola Winner
1:24	Racing Champions	DuPont
1:24	Racing Champions	DuPont Snickers
1:24	Racing Champions	DuPont Brickyard Special Purple Box
1:43	Racing Champions	DuPont
1:43	Racing Champions	DuPont Coca-Cola 600 Winner
1:64	Racing Champions	DuPont
1:64	Racing Champions	DuPont Brickyard special
1:64	Racing Champions Hobby	DuPont

SCALE	MANUFACTURER	SPONSOR
1:43	Racing Champions Premier	DuPont Snickers
1:64	Racing Champions Premier	DuPont
1:64	Racing Champions Premier	DuPont 1993 Rookie of the Year
1:64	Racing Champions Premier Brickyard 400	DuPont
1:64	Racing Champions Premier Transporters 1994	DuPont Winston Select special
1:64	Racing Champions To the Maxx	DuPont
1:64	Racing Champions Transporters	DuPont
1:24	Revell Hobby	DuPont

1995–96

SCALE	MANUFACTURER	SPONSOR
1:18	Racing Champions	DuPont
1:18	Racing Champions	DuPont Signature Series

1995–98

SCALE	MANUFACTURER	SPONSOR
1:24	Action Sprint Cars	Hap's
1:24	Action Sprint Cars	Stanton
1:64	Action Sprint Cars	Stanton

1995

SCALE	MANUFACTURER	SPONSOR
1:64	Matchbox White Rose Super Stars	DuPont
1:80	Matchbox White Rose Transporters Super Star Series	DuPont
1:24	Racing Champions	DuPont
1:24	Racing Champions	DuPont Signature Series
1:24	Racing Champions	DuPont Signature Series Hood Open
1:64	Racing Champions	DuPont
1:64	Racing Champions	DuPont Coca-Cola
1:64	Racing Champions	DuPont Signature Series
1:64	Racing Champions	DuPont Signature Series combo w/ SuperTruck
1:24	Racing Champions Banks	DuPont

1:24	Racing Champions Banks	DuPont Signature Series HO 1995 Champion
1:24	Racing Champions Banks	DuPont Signature Series Hood Open
1:64	Racing Champions Matched Serial Numbers	DuPont
1:43	Racing Champions Premier	Brickyard Win
1:64	Racing Champions Premier	DuPont
1:64	Racing Champions Previews	DuPont
1:24	Racing Champions Sprint Cars	JG Motorsports
1:24	Racing Champions SuperTrucks	DuPont Signature Series
1:64	Racing Champions SuperTrucks	No Driver Association DuPont w/ Gordon on the card
1:64	Racing Champions SuperTrucks To the Maxx	DuPont
1:64	Racing Champions To the Maxx	DuPont
1:64	Racing Champions Transporters	DuPont
1:64	Racing Champions Transporters	DuPont Signature Series
1:87	Racing Champions Transporters	DuPont '95
1:64	Racing Champions Transporters Previews	DuPont
1:24	Revell	DuPont

1996–99

| 1:18 | GMP Sprint Cars | Molds Unlimited |

1996

1:64	Action Racing Collectables	DuPont Monte Carlo Blister package
1:64	Action Racing Collectables	DuPont Monte Carlo
1:24	Action Racing Collectables Banks	DuPont 1996 Monte Carlo w/ Quaker State decal
1:24	Action/RCCA	DuPont Monte Carlo
1:64	Action/RCCA	DuPont
1:64	Matchbox White Rose Super Stars	DuPont
1:64	Matchbox White Rose Super Stars	DuPont SSA
1:80	Matchbox White Rose Transporters Super Star Series	DuPont
1:24	Racing Champions	DuPont
1:24	Racing Champions	DuPont 1995 Champion

1:24	Racing Champions	DuPont 1995 Champion Hood Open
1:64	Racing Champions	DuPont
1:24	Racing Champions Chrome Banks	DuPont
1:64	Racing Champions Hobby	DuPont
1:24	Racing Champions Hobby Banks	DuPont Hobby
1:64	Racing Champions Premier Transporters	DuPont
1:64	Racing Champions Premier w/Medallion	DuPont
1:64	Racing Champions Premier w/Medallion	DuPont 1995 Champion
1:64	Racing Champions Premier w/Medallion	DuPont Hood Open
1:24	Racing Champions Previews	DuPont
1:64	Racing Champions Previews	DuPont
1:64	Racing Champions Silver Chase	DuPont
1:64	Racing Champions Sprint Cars	JG Motorsports
1:64	Racing Champions Transporters	DuPont w/ one car or two cars
1:87	Racing Champions Transporters	DuPont Premier Transporter
1:24	Revell	DuPont
1:64	Revell	DuPont
1:24	Revell Collection	DuPont

1997–98

1:24	Winner's Circle	DuPont
1:24	Winner's Circle	Dupont Million Dollar Date
1:24	Winner's Circle	DuPont Premier
1:24	Winner's Circle	Lost World
1:64	Winner's Circle	1985 Pro Sprint
1:64	Winner's Circle	Baby Ruth
1:64	Winner's Circle	Carolina Ford
1:64	Winner's Circle	Challenger Sprint
1:64	Winner's Circle	DuPont
1:64	Winner's Circle	Dupont Million Dollar Date
1:64	Winner's Circle	DuPont 1993 Lumina
1:64	Winner's Circle	DuPont 1994 Lumina
1:64	Winner's Circle	DuPont 1997 Champion Gordon on Roof of Car
1:64	Winner's Circle	DuPont ChromaPremier
1:64	Winner's Circle	Lost World

1997

| 1:24 | Action Racing Collectables | DuPont |
| 1:24 | Action Racing Collectables | DuPont Brickyard Special |

SCALE	MANUFACTURER	SPONSOR
1:24	Action Racing Collectables	DuPont Mac Tools
1:24	Action Racing Collectables	DuPont Premier Promo
1:24	Action Racing Collectables	DuPont Premier Sports Image
1:24	Action Racing Collectables	Lost World Sports Image
1:64	Action Racing Collectables	DuPont
1:64	Action Racing Collectables	DuPont Bickyard Special
1:64	Action Racing Collectables	DuPont Chroma Premier
1:64	Action Racing Collectables	DuPont Million Dollar Date
1:64	Action Racing Collectables	DuPont Million Dollar Date Black Window
1:64	Action Racing Collectables	Lost World
1:64	Action Racing Collectables	Lost World Black Window Blister Pack
1:64	Action Racing Collectables	Lost World Hood Open Sports Image
1:24	Action Racing Collectables Banks	DuPont Chroma Premier
1:24	Action Racing Collectables Banks	DuPont Million Dollar Date
1:24	Action Racing Collectables Banks	DuPont Million Dollar Date Mac Tools
1:24	Action Racing Collectables Banks	Lost World
1:24	Action/RCCA	DuPont ChromaPremier
1:24	Action/RCCA	DuPont Million Dollar Date
1:24	Action/RCCA	Lost World
1:64	Action/RCCA	DuPont
1:64	Action/RCCA	DuPont ChromaPremier
1:64	Action/RCCA	DuPont Million Dollar Date
1:64	Action/RCCA	Lost World
1:24	Action/RCCA Banks	DuPont
1:24	Action/RCCA Elite	Dupont
1:24	Action/RCCA Elite	Dupont Million Dollar Date
1:24	Action/RCCA Elite	Dupont Premier
1:24	Action/RCCA Elite	Lost World
1:24	Racing Champions	DuPont
1:64	Racing Champions	DuPont
1:64	Racing Champions Premier Preview w/ Medallion	DuPont
1:87	Racing Champions Preview Transporters	DuPont
1:24	Racing Champions Previews	DuPont
1:64	Racing Champions Previews	DuPont
1:64	Racing Champions Transporters	DuPont
1:87	Racing Champions Transporters	DuPont
1:64	Racing Champions Transporters Previews	DuPont
1:18	Revell Collection	Lost World

1998–99

SCALE	MANUFACTURER	SPONSOR
1:18	Action Racing Collectables	Chromalusion
1:18	Action Racing Collectables	Pepsi
1:18	Action Racing Collectables	Superman

1998

SCALE	MANUFACTURER	SPONSOR
1:24	Action Racing Collectables	DuPont
1:24	Action Racing Collectables	DuPont Brickyard Winner
1:24	Action Racing Collectables	DuPont Chromalusion
1:24	Action Racing Collectables	DuPont Chromalusion Mac Tools
1:24	Action Racing Collectables	DuPont Mac Tools
1:24	Action Racing Collectables	DuPont No Bull
1:24	Action Racing Collectables	Baby Ruth
1:32	Action Racing Collectables	DuPont
1:64	Action Racing Collectables	DuPont
1:64	Action Racing Collectables	DuPont Brickyard Winner
1:64	Action Racing Collectables	DuPont Chromalusion
1:64	Action Racing Collectables	DuPont No Bull
1:24	Action Racing Collectables Banks	Baby Ruth '92 TB
1:24	Action Racing Collectables Banks	DuPont
1:24	Action Racing Collectables Banks	DuPont Chromalusion
1:24	Action Racing Collectables Banks	DuPont No Bull
1:64	Action/RCCA	Baby Ruth
1:64	Action/RCCA	DuPont
1:64	Action/RCCA	DuPont Chromalusion
1:64	Action/RCCA	DuPont No Bull
1:24	Action/RCCA Banks	Baby Ruth
1:24	Action/RCCA Banks	DuPont
1:24	Action/RCCA Banks	DuPont Chromalusion

SCALE	MANUFACTURER	SPONSOR
1:24	Action/RCCA Elite	Baby Ruth
1:24	Action/RCCA Elite	DuPont
1:24	Action/RCCA Elite	DuPont Chromalusion
1:32	Action/RCCA Gold	DuPont
1:18	Revell Club	DuPont
1:18	Revell Club	DuPont Chromalusion
1:24	Revell Club	DuPont
1:24	Revell Club	DuPont Chromalusion
1:18	Revell Collection	DuPont
1:18	Revell Collection	DuPont Brickyard Special
1:18	Revell Collection	DuPont Chromalusion
1:24	Revell Collection	DuPont
1:24	Revell Collection	DuPont Brickyard Special
1:24	Revell Collection	DuPont Chromalusion
1:43	Revell Collection	DuPont
1:43	Revell Collection	DuPont Chromalusion
1:64	Revell Collection	DuPont
1:64	Revell Collection	DuPont Brickyard Special
1:64	Revell Collection	DuPont Chromalusion
1:24	Revell Hobby	DuPont
1:64	Revell Hobby	DuPont
1:43	Winner's Circle	DuPont
1:64	Winner's Circle Pit Row	DuPont

1999

SCALE	MANUFACTURER	SPONSOR
1:24	Action Racing Collectables	Pepsi Star Wars
1:24	Action Racing Collectables	Carolina Ford
1:24	Action Racing Collectables	Dupont
1:24	Action Racing Collectables	Pepsi
1:24	Action Racing Collectables	Superman
1:64	Action Racing Collectables	DuPont Superman
1:64	Action Racing Collectables	Star Wars
1:64	Action Racing Collectables	Baby Ruth 1992 Thunderbird

SCALE	MANUFACTURER	SPONSOR
1:64	Action Racing Collectables	Carolina Ford
1:64	Action Racing Collectables	DuPont
1:64	Action Racing Collectables	Pepsi
1:24	Action Racing Collectables Banks	Star Wars
1:24	Action Racing Collectables Banks	Carolina Ford
1:24	Action Racing Collectables Banks	DuPont
1:24	Action Racing Collectables Banks	Pepsi
1:64	Action/RCCA	DuPont
1:64	Action/RCCA	Star Wars
1:64	Action/RCCA	Superman
1:64	Action/RCCA	Carolina Ford
1:64	Action/RCCA	Pepsi
1:24	Action/RCCA Banks	DuPont
1:24	Action/RCCA Banks	Carolina Ford
1:24	Action/RCCA Banks	Pepsi
1:24	Action/RCCA Elite	Carolina '91 TB
1:24	Action/RCCA Elite	Pepsi Star Wars
1:24	Action/RCCA Elite	Superman
1:24	Action/RCCA Elite	DuPont
1:24	Action/RCCA Elite	Pepsi
1:18	Revell Club	Pepsi
1:18	Revell Club	Superman
1:24	Revell Club	DuPont
1:24	Revell Club	Pepsi
1:18	Revell Collection	DuPont
1:18	Revell Collection	Star Wars
1:18	Revell Collection	Pepsi
1:24	Revell Collection	DuPont
1:24	Revell Collection	DuPont Daytona
1:24	Revell Collection	Pepsi
1:24	Revell Collection	Superman
1:43	Revell Collection	Star Wars
1:43	Revell Collection	Superman
1:43	Revell Collection	DuPont
1:43	Revell Collection	Pepsi
1:64	Revell Collection	DuPont Daytona
1:64	Revell Collection	Superman
1:64	Revell Collection	DuPont
1:64	Revell Collection	Pepsi
1:24	Winner's Circle	Pepsi
1:64	Winner's Circle	Pepsi
1:64	Winner's Circle Pit Row	Pepsi
1:64	Winner's Circle Pit Row	Dupont No Bull 5 Winner
1:43	Winner's Circle Speedweeks	DuPont
1:64	Winner's Circle Speedweeks	Dupont
1:64	Winner's Circle Tech Series	DuPont

2000

SCALE	MANUFACTURER	SPONSOR
1:24	Action Racing Collectables	DuPont
1:64	Action Racing Collectables	DuPont Millennium
1:24	Revell Collection	DuPont
1:64	Revell Collection	Test Car
1:43	Winner's Circle Preview	DuPont
1:64	Winner's Circle Preview	DuPont

Dale Jarrett

Hometown:
Conover, North Carolina

Birthdate:
November 26, 1956

Personal:
Dale Jarrett grew up racing at Hickory Motor Speedway where his father, two-time Winston Cup champion Ned Jarrett, was once track promoter. He was all-conference in football, basketball and golf at Newton-Conover High School. Jarrett is nearly a scratch golfer and would have attempted professional golf if he hadn't gotten into racing. He spends a great deal of time and energy doing charity work, with hospitals, cancer research and Motor Racing Outreach being among his favorite organizations. Enjoys outdoors and spending time with his children.

Hobby:
Strong enough in the marketplace to have an exclusive deal with Action, Jarrett should benefit even more from winning the 1999 Winston Cup championship and having Ricky Rudd join him at Yates Racing. His best special paint schemes have been his Batman car from 1998 and his 1999 reverse paint job that benefited cancer research.

Career Highlights
- First Winston Cup victory came in his 129th start, at the 1991 Champion 400 at Michigan Speedway.
- Won the 1993 Daytona 500 with car owner Joe Gibbs, spending three successful years with the former NFL coach's team.
- Started driving for Robert Yates Racing in 1995 as replacement for Ernie Irvan in the No. 28 car while Irvan recovered from 1994 crash injuries.
- First driver to win Daytona 500 and Brickyard 400 in same season (1996). Lists first win in 1991 and 1996 Brickyard 400 as most memorable races.
- 1999 Winston Cup Champion.

SCALE	MANUFACTURER	SPONSOR
1990–92		
1:64	Matchbox White Rose Super Stars	Interstate Batteries '92 BL
1991–92		
1:24	Racing Champions	Citgo
1:24	Racing Champions	Interstate Batteries
1991		
1:43	Racing Champions	Citgo
1:64	Racing Champions	Ford EB
1:64	Racing Champions	Ford PB
1992–94		
1:24	Racing Champions Banks	Interstate Batteries
1992–95		
1:64	Action/RCCA Transporters	Havoline
1992		
1:43	Funstuf Pit Row	Interstate Batteries
1:64	Funstuf Pit Row	Citgo
1:64	Funstuf Pit Row	Citgo w/ Winston Decal on Fender
1:64	Funstuf Pit Row	Interstate Batteries
1:87	Matchbox White Rose Transporters 1992 Super Star Series	Interstate Batteries
1:43	Racing Champions	Interstate Batteries
1:64	Racing Champions	Citgo
1:64	Racing Champions	Interstate Batteries
1:64	Racing Champions Transporters	Interstate Batteries
1993–94		
1:87	Racing Champions Transporters	Interstate Batteries
1:87	Racing Champions Transporters	Interstate Batteries Yellow box hobby only
1993–95		
1:64	Action Racing Collectables	Havoline Platinum Series
1:24	Action Racing Collectables Banks	Havoline
1:24	Action/RCCA	Havoline
1:24	Action/RCCA	Interstate Batteries
1:64	Action/RCCA	Havoline Hood Open
1:64	Action/RCCA	Interstate Batteries 1994 Hood Open

SCALE	MANUFACTURER	SPONSOR
1:64	Action/RCCA	Interstate Batteries Revell
1:24	Revell	Interstate Batteries
1:24	Revell	Mac Tools
1993–98		
1:24	Action Dually Trucks	Havoline Bank
1:24	Action Dually Trucks	Interstate Batteries Bank
1:24	Action Dually Trucks	Quality Care Bank
1:18	Ertl	Havoline
1:18	Ertl	Interstate Batteries
1:18	Ertl	Mac Tools
1:18	Ertl	Quality Care
1993–99		
1:64	Action Dually w/Chaparral Trailer	Havoline
1:64	Action Dually w/Chaparral Trailer	Havoline w/out Trailer
1:64	Action Dually w/Chaparral Trailer	Interstate Batteries
1:64	Action Dually w/Chaparral Trailer	Interstate Batteries w/out Trailer
1:16	Action Racing Collectables Pit Wagon Banks	Interstate Batteries
1:16	Action Racing Collectables Pit Wagon Banks	Quality Care Batman
1993		
1:64	Matchbox White Rose Super Stars	Pic-N-Pay BX
1:24	Racing Champions	Interstate Batteries
1:64	Racing Champions	Interstate Batteries
1:64	Racing Champions Premier	Interstate Batteries
1:87	Racing Champions Premier Transporters	Interstate Batteries
1:64	Racing Champions PVC Box	Interstate Batteries
1:64	Racing Champions Transporters	Interstate Batteries
1:64	Winross Transporters	Interstate Batteries
1994–96		
1:96	Action/RCCA Transporters	Havoline
1994		
1:64	Ertl White Rose Transporters Past and Present	Interstate Batteries
1:64	Matchbox White Rose Super Stars	Pic-N-Pay BX
1:80	Matchbox White Rose Transporters Super Star Series	Pic-N-Pay Shoes
1:24	Racing Champions	Interstate Batteries

SCALE	MANUFACTURER	SPONSOR
1:64	Racing Champions	Interstate Batteries
1:64	Racing Champions Hobby	Interstate Batteries
1:64	Racing Champions Premier	Interstate Batteries
1:64	Racing Champions Premier Brickyard 400	Interstate Batteries
1:87	Racing Champions Premier Transporters	Shoe World
1:64	Racing Champions Transporters	Interstate Batteries
1:64	Racing Champions Transporters	Interstate Batteries Yellow box hobby only

1995–96

1:18	Racing Champions	Quality Care

1995

1:64	Matchbox White Rose Super Stars	Havoline
1:80	Matchbox White Rose Transporters Super Star Series	Havoline
1:24	Racing Champions	Havoline
1:64	Racing Champions	Havoline
1:24	Racing Champions Banks	Havoline Hood Open
1:24	Racing Champions Banks	Mac Tools
1:64	Racing Champions Premier	Havoline
1:64	Racing Champions Previews	Havoline
1:64	Racing Champions To the Maxx	Havoline
1:64	Racing Champions Transporters	Ernie Irvan Havoline both signatures on trailer
1:87	Racing Champions Transporters	Ernie Irvan Havoline both signatures on trailer
1:24	Revell	Mac Tools Promo by American Miniatures
1:64	Winross Transporters	Mac Tools

SCALE	MANUFACTURER	SPONSOR

1996

1:24	Action Racing Collectables	Quality Care
1:64	Action Racing Collectables	Quality Care
1:64	Action/RCCA	Quality Care
1:24	Action/RCCA Banks	Quality Care
1:64	Matchbox White Rose Super Stars	Quality Care
1:80	Matchbox White Rose Transporters Super Star Series	Quality Care
1:24	Racing Champions	Quality Care
1:24	Racing Champions	Quality Care Hood Open
1:64	Racing Champions	Band-Aid Promo
1:64	Racing Champions	Quality Care
1:24	Racing Champions Banks	Band-Aid
1:24	Racing Champions Chrome Banks	Quality Care
1:24	Racing Champions Hobby Banks	Quality Care Hobby
1:24	Racing Champions Hood Open Banks	Quality Care Hood Open
1:64	Racing Champions Premier Transporters	Quality Care
1:64	Racing Champions Premier w/Medallion	Quality Care
1:64	Racing Champions Silver Chase	Quality Care
1:64	Racing Champions Transporters	Band-Aid w/one car or two cars
1:64	Racing Champions Transporters	Quality Care
1:64	Racing Champions Transporters	Quality Care w/one car or two cars
1:24	Revell	Quality Care
1:24	Revell Collection	Quality Care
1:64	Revell Collection	Quality Care

1997–98

1:24	Winner's Circle	Quality Care
1:64	Winner's Circle	Quality Care

1997

1:24	Action Racing Collectables	Quality Care
1:24	Action Racing Collectables	Quality Care Brickyard Special
1:24	Action Racing Collectables	Quality Care Mac Tools

SCALE	MANUFACTURER	SPONSOR
1:64	Action Racing Collectables	Quality Care
1:64	Action Racing Collectables	Quality Care Brickyard Special
1:24	Action Racing Collectables Banks	White Rain
1:24	Action/RCCA	White Rain
1:64	Action/RCCA	Quality Care
1:64	Action/RCCA	White Rain
1:24	Action/RCCA Banks	Quality Care
1:24	Action/RCCA Elite	Ford Credit
1:24	Action/RCCA Elite	White Rain
1:24	Racing Champions	Gillette
1:24	Racing Champions	White Rain
1:64	Racing Champions	White Rain
1:64	Racing Champions Transporters	Gillette
1:64	Racing Champions Transporters	Gillette w/ one or two cars
1:64	Racing Champions Transporters	White Rain
1:64	Racing Champions Transporters 1997	Gillette
1:64	Racing Champions Transporters 1997	White Rain
1:18	Revell Club	Quality Care
1:18	Revell Collection	Ford Credit
1:24	Revell Collection	White Rain
1:43	Revell Collection	Ford Credit
1:64	Revell Hobby	White Rain
1:24	Revell Retail	Quality Care

1998

SCALE	MANUFACTURER	SPONSOR
1:24	Action Racing Collectables	Quality Care
1:24	Action Racing Collectables	Quality Care Batman
1:24	Action Racing Collectables	White Rain
1:32	Action Racing Collectables	Quality Care Batman
1:64	Action Racing Collectables	Quality Care
1:64	Action Racing Collectables	Quality Care Batman
1:64	Action Racing Collectables	White Rain
1:24	Action Racing Collectables Banks	Quality Care
1:24	Action Racing Collectables Banks	Quality Care Batman
1:64	Action/RCCA	Quality Care
1:64	Action/RCCA	Quality Care Batman
1:64	Action/RCCA	White Rain
1:24	Action/RCCA Banks	Quality Care
1:24	Action/RCCA Banks	Quality Care Batman
1:24	Action/RCCA Banks	Quality Care No Bull
1:24	Action/RCCA Banks	White Rain
1:24	Action/RCCA Elite	Quality Care
1:24	Action/RCCA Elite	Quality Care Batman
1:24	Action/RCCA Elite	Quality Care No Bull

SCALE	MANUFACTURER	SPONSOR
1:32	Action/RCCA Gold	Quality Care
1:18	Revell Club	Quality Care
1:18	Revell Club	Quality Care Batman
1:24	Revell Club	Quality Care
1:24	Revell Club	Quality Care Batman
1:18	Revell Collection	Quality Care
1:24	Revell Collection	Quality Care
1:24	Revell Collection	Quality Care Batman
1:43	Revell Collection	Quality Care
1:43	Revell Collection	Quality Care Batman
1:64	Revell Collection	Quality Care
1:64	Revell Collection	Quality Care Batman
1:24	Revell Collection Banks	Quality Care Batman
1:24	Revell Hobby	Quality Care
1:43	Winner's Circle	Quality Care
1:64	Winner's Circle Pit Row	Batman
1:64	Winner's Circle Pit Row	Quality Care

1999

SCALE	MANUFACTURER	SPONSOR
1:24	Action Racing Collectables	Quality Care White
1:24	Action Racing Collectables	Rayovac
1:24	Action Racing Collectables	Quality Care
1:64	Action Racing Collectables	Quality Care White
1:64	Action Racing Collectables	Rayovac
1:64	Action Racing Collectables	Quality Care
1:24	Action Racing Collectables Banks	QC White
1:24	Action Racing Collectables Banks	Quality Care
1:64	Action/RCCA	QC White
1:24	Action/RCCA Elite	QC White
1:24	Revell Collection	QC White
1:24	Revell Collection	Quality Care
1:64	Revell Collection	Quality Care
1:64	Winner's Circle	Quality Care No Bull 5 Winner
1:64	Winner's Circle Speedweeks	Quality Care
1:64	Winner's Circle Tech Series	Quality Care

Bobby Labonte

Hometown:

Corpus Christi, Texas

Birthdate:

May 8, 1964

Personal:

Became interested in racing watching his older brother Terry race. Bobby Labonte lists his biggest break in racing as when he was fired from crew job at Hagan Racing in 1986, which resulted in pursuing a driving career. Enjoys standup comedians and has a dry sense of humor. Big fan of the Dallas Cowboys, despite his car owner, Joe Gibbs, being a former Super Bowl winning coach with the Washington Redskins. Likes singer Bob Seger. If not for racing he'd like to be an airplane pilot.

Hobby:

Bobby Labonte has been a rising hobby star, with his popularity growing every season. With 1999 Winston Cup rookie of the year Tony Stewart, Labonte makes a dynamic one-two collectibles team for Joe Gibbs Racing. Labonte has been involved in several successful one-time promotions, including a Hall of Fame car when Gibbs was inducted into the Pro Football Hall of Fame, a promotional piece for the movie *Small Soldiers*, a flame-filled *Hot Rod* magazine special and a Lone Star scheme for the first race at Texas Motor Speedway. In addition to being a top die-cast attraction, Labonte is also in big demand among card collectors.

Career Highlights

- Finished second to Jeff Gordon in 1993 NASCAR Winston Cup rookie of the year standings.
- NASCAR Busch series champion in 1991 and runner-up by three points to Joe Nemecheck for 1992 Busch title. Also won Busch title in 1994 as car owner with David Green as driver.
- His first NASCAR Winston Cup start was at Dover in 1991. First career pole came at Richmond in fall 1993 in his 24th start.
- Has done extremely well in Winston Cup racing at Charlotte, Michigan and Atlanta tracks.
- Has won at least one race in each of the past five Winston Cup seasons.
- Enjoyed the best year of his career in 1999, finishing second in the Winston Cup points standings.

1990–92

Scale	Manufacturer	Sponsor
1:64	Matchbox White Rose Super Stars	Penrose '92 BX
1:64	Matchbox White Rose Super Stars	Slim Jim '92 BX

1991

Scale	Manufacturer	Sponsor
1:64	Action/RCCA Oldsmobile Series	Penrose

1992–94

Scale	Manufacturer	Sponsor
1:24	Racing Champions Banks	Dentyne
1:24	Racing Champions Banks	Maxwell House

1992–95

Scale	Manufacturer	Sponsor
1:64	Action/RCCA Transporters	Maxwell House produced for Peachstate
1:64	Action/RCCA Transporters	Penrose

1992

Scale	Manufacturer	Sponsor
1:87	Matchbox White Rose Transporters 1992 Super Star Series	Slim Jim

1993–94

Scale	Manufacturer	Sponsor
1:87	Racing Champions Transporters	Maxwell House

1993–95

Scale	Manufacturer	Sponsor
1:64	Action Racing Collectables	Interstate Batteries

1993–98

Scale	Manufacturer	Sponsor
1:24	Action Dually Trucks	Interstate Batteries
1:24	Action Dually Trucks	Maxwell House B

1993

Scale	Manufacturer	Sponsor
1:64	Matchbox White Rose Super Stars	Maxwell House BL
1:87	Matchbox White Rose Transporters Super Star Series	Maxwell House
1:24	Racing Champions	Maxwell House
1:64	Racing Champions	Maxwell House
1:87	Racing Champions Premier Transporters	Maxwell House
1:64	Racing Champions Transporters	Maxwell House

1994

Scale	Manufacturer	Sponsor
1:24	Racing Champions	Dentyne
1:24	Racing Champions	Maxwell House
1:64	Racing Champions	Maxwell House
1:43	Racing Champions Premier	Maxwell House
1:64	Racing Champions Premier	Dentyne
1:64	Racing Champions Transporters	Maxwell House

1995–96

Scale	Manufacturer	Sponsor
1:18	Racing Champions	Interstate Batteries

1995

Scale	Manufacturer	Sponsor
1:64	Matchbox White Rose Super Stars	Interstate Batteries
1:24	Racing Champions	Interstate Batteries

Scale	Manufacturer	Sponsor
1:64	Racing Champions	Interstate Batteries w/ roof flaps
1:64	Racing Champions	Interstate Batteries w/out roof flaps
1:64	Racing Champions Matched Serial Numbers	Interstate Batteries
1:64	Racing Champions Premier	Interstate Batteries
1:64	Racing Champions To the Maxx	Interstate Batteries
1:64	Racing Champions Transporters	Interstate Batteries
1:24	Revell	Interstate Batteries

1996

Scale	Manufacturer	Sponsor
1:24	Action Racing Collectables	Interstate Batteries
1:64	Action/RCCA	Interstate Batteries
1:24	Action/RCCA Banks	Interstate Batteries
1:64	Peachstate Transporters	Interstate Batteries
1:64	Press Pass Transporter 1996	Interstate Batteries
1:24	Racing Champions	Interstate Batteries
1:24	Racing Champions	Shell
1:64	Racing Champions	Interstate Batteries
1:64	Racing Champions	Shell
1:24	Racing Champions Chrome Banks	Interstate Batteries Chrome
1:64	Racing Champions Hobby	Interstate Batteries
1:24	Racing Champions Hobby Banks	Interstate Batteries Hobby
1:64	Racing Champions Premier w/ Medallion	Interstate Batteries

SCALE	MANUFACTURER	SPONSOR
1:64	Racing Champions Premier w/ Medallion	Interstate Batteries Hood Open
1:64	Racing Champions Premier w/ Medallion	Shell
1:24	Racing Champions Previews	Interstate Batteries
1:64	Racing Champions Previews	Interstate Batteries
1:64	Racing Champions Silver Chase	Interstate Batteries
1:64	Racing Champions Transporters	Shell
1:87	Racing Champions Transporters	Interstate Batteries
1:87	Racing Champions Transporters	Shell
1:24	Revell	Interstate Batteries
1:64	Revell	Interstate Batteries
1:24	Revell Collection	Interstate Batteries
1:64	Revell Collection	Interstate Batteries

1997–98

SCALE	MANUFACTURER	SPONSOR
1:24	Winner's Circle	Interstate Batteries
1:24	Winner's Circle	Interstate Batteries Small Soldiers
1:64	Winner's Circle	Interstate Batteries
1:64	Winner's Circle	Interstates Batteries Small Soldiers

1997

SCALE	MANUFACTURER	SPONSOR
1:24	Action Racing Collectables	Interstate Batteries
1:24	Action Racing Collectables	Interstate Batteries Hall of Fame
1:24	Action Racing Collectables	Interstate Batteries Mac Tools
1:64	Action Racing Collectables	Interstate Batteries

SCALE	MANUFACTURER	SPONSOR
1:64	Action Racing Collectables	Interstate Batteries Hall of Fame
1:64	Action/RCCA	Interstate Batteries Hall of Fame
1:64	Action/RCCA	Interstate Batteries
1:24	Action/RCCA Banks	Interstate Batteries
1:24	Action/RCCA Banks	Interstate Batteries Hall of Fame
1:24	Action/RCCA Elite	Interstate Batteries
1:18	Racing Champions	Interstate Batteries Gold
1:18	Racing Champions	Interstate Batteries Hobby
1:24	Racing Champions	Interstate Batteries
1:64	Racing Champions	Interstate Batteries
1:64	Racing Champions Gold	Interstate Batteries
1:24	Racing Champions Gold Banks	Interstate Batteries Gold
1:64	Racing Champions Hobby	Interstate Batteries
1:24	Racing Champions Hobby Banks	Interstate Batteries Hobby
1:64	Racing Champions Pinnacle Series	Interstate Batteries
1:64	Racing Champions Premier Preview w/ Medallion	Interstate Batteries
	Racing Champions Premier w/ Medallion	Interstate Batteries
1:64	Racing Champions Premier w/ Medallion Silver Chase	Interstate Batteries
1:24	Racing Champions Previews	Interstate Batteries
1:64	Racing Champions Previews	Interstate Batteries
1:64	Racing Champions Stock Rods	Interstate Batteries
	Racing Champions Transporters 1997	Interstate Batteries
1:24	Revell Club	Interstate Batteries Texas Motor Speedway
1:18	Revell Collection	Interstate Batteries
1:24	Revell Collection	Interstate Batteries

SCALE	MANUFACTURER	SPONSOR

SCALE	MANUFACTURER	SPONSOR
1:24	Revell Collection	Interstate Batteries Texas Motor Speedway
1:64	Revell Collection	Bobby and Interstate Batteries and Kellogg's 2-car Tin Set
1:24	Revell Collection Banks	Interstate Batteries Texas Motor Speedway
1:24	Revell Hobby	Interstate Batteries
1:24	Revell Hobby	Interstate Batteries Texas Motor Speedway
1:64	Revell Hobby	Interstate Batteries
1:64	Revell Hobby	Interstate Batteries Texas Motor Speedway
1:64	Revell Retail	Interstate Batteries
1:64	Revell Retail	Interstate Batteries Texas Motor Speedway

1998

SCALE	MANUFACTURER	SPONSOR
1:24	Action Racing Collectables	Interstate Batteries
1:24	Action Racing Collectables	Interstate Batteries Hot Rod
1:24	Action Racing Collectables	Interstate Batteries Small Soldiers
1:64	Action Racing Collectables	Interstate Batteries
1:64	Action Racing Collectables	Interstate Batteries Hot Rod
1:64	Action Racing Collectables	Interstate Batteries Small Soldiers
1:24	Action Racing Collectables Banks	Interstate Batteries Hot Rod
1:24	Action Racing Collectables Banks	Interstate Batteries Small Soldiers
1:64	Action/RCCA	Interstate Batteries
1:64	Action/RCCA	Interstate Batteries Hot Rod
1:64	Action/RCCA	Interstate Batteries Small Soldiers
1:24	Action/RCCA Banks	Interstate Batteries
1:24	Action/RCCA Banks	Interstate Batteries Small Soldiers
1:24	Action/RCCA Elite	Interstate Batteries Small Soldiers
1:32	Action/RCCA Gold	Interstate Batteries
1:18	Revell Club	Interstate Batteries Hot Rod
1:18	Revell Club	Interstate Batteries Small Soldiers

SCALE	MANUFACTURER	SPONSOR
1:24	Revell Club	Interstate Batteries Hot Rod
1:24	Revell Club	Interstate Batteries Small Soldiers
1:18	Revell Collection	Interstate Batteries Hot Rod
1:18	Revell Collection	Interstate Batteries Small Soldiers

SCALE	MANUFACTURER	SPONSOR
1:24	Revell Collection	Interstate Batteries
1:24	Revell Collection	Interstate Batteries Hot Rod
1:24	Revell Collection	Interstate Batteries Small Soldiers
1:43	Revell Collection	Interstate Batteries
1:43	Revell Collection	Interstate Batteries Hot Rod
1:43	Revell Collection	Interstate Batteries Small Soldiers
1:64	Revell Collection	Interstate Batteries
1:64	Revell Collection	Interstate Batteries Hot Rod
1:64	Revell Collection	Interstate Batteries Small Soldiers
1:24	Revell Hobby	Interstate Batteries
1:24	Revell Hobby	Interstate Batteries Hot Rod
1:64	Revell Hobby	Interstate Batteries
1:64	Winner's Circle Pit Row	Interstate Batteries

SCALE	MANUFACTURER	SPONSOR
1:64	Winner's Circle Pit Row	Small Soldiers

1999

SCALE	MANUFACTURER	SPONSOR
1:24	Action Racing Collectables	Interstate Batteries
1:64	Action Racing Collectables	Interstate Batteries
1:64	Action Racing Collectables	Kellogg's
1:24	Action Racing Collectables Banks	Interstate Batteries
1:64	Action/RCCA	Interstate Batteries
1:24	Action/RCCA Elite	Interstate Batteries
1:24	Revell Club	Interstate Batteries
1:24	Revell Collection	Interstate Batteries
1:64	Revell Collection	Interstate Batteries
1:64	Winner's Circle	Interstate Batteries
1:43	Winner's Circle Speedweeks	Interstate Batteries
1:64	Winner's Circle Speedweeks	Interstate Batteries
1:64	Winner's Circle Tech Series	Interstate Batteries

2000

SCALE	MANUFACTURER	SPONSOR
1:24	Action Racing Collectables	Interstate Batteries
1:64	Revell Collection	Interstate Batteries
1:43	Winner's Circle Preview	Interstate Batteries
1:64	Winner's Circle Preview	Interstate Batteries

Terry Labonte

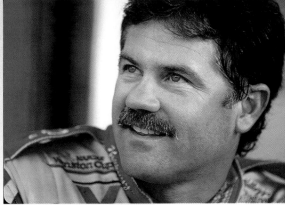

Hometown:

Corpus Christi, Texas

Birthdate:

November 16, 1956

Personal:

Racing is a family affair for the Labontes. Not only does Terry's brother, Bobby, also race on the Winston Cup circuit, but their father has served as team manager for Busch teams owned by both sons. Terry's son Justin is now trying his hand at the sport, sharing a Busch ride with his father and uncle in 1999. Terry is quiet and low-keyed off the track. The native Texan is a big fan of the NFL's Dallas Cowboys. He is married and has two children.

Hobby:

Terry Labonte might have more pieces, from more die-cast makers, than any other NASCAR driver. While he has had several replicas created by Action Performance Companies, he has never had an exclusive deal with the company. Consequently, Terry Labonte also has a wide variety of replicas from companies such as Hot Wheels and Racing Champions. His sponsor, Kellogg's, has been very aggressive in using special paint schemes to promote its products. In addition, Kellogg's has implemented several promotions on its product boxes that have allowed collectors to purchase die-cast cars through the mail. His largest promotion was his Iron Man replica cars, which commemorated his record-breaking streak of consecutive starts.

Career Highlights

- NASCAR Winston Cup Champion in 1984 and 1996.
- Tied Richard Petty's mark of 513 consecutive Winston Cup starts at North Wilkesboro on April 14, 1996 and broke it the next week at Martinsville. He has made more than 600 consecutive starts, breaking the NASCAR record with each new race.
- Won his second career championship in 1996 by 37 points over teammate Jeff Gordon and made NASCAR Winston Cup history with the longest time between titles. His first title came 12 years earlier.
- Started with quarter-midgets in Texas in 1964.

- Finished fourth in his first NASCAR Winston Cup race — 1978 Southern 500.
- Member of the 1979 rookie class, with Dale Earnhardt and Harry Gant.
- First career win came in 59th start, 1980 Southern 500. First pole came in 72nd attempt, 1981 Coca-Cola 500 at Atlanta.
- Won 1989 IROC championship.
- Considers his victory at Texas Motor Speedway in 1999 as the biggest race win of his career.

SCALE	MANUFACTURER	SPONSOR

1990

1:64	Racing Champions	Oldsmobile

1991–92

1:24	Racing Champions	Sunoco
1:24	Racing Champions	Sunoco Arrow on decal points at tire

1991

1:64	Racing Champions	Buick PB
1:64	Racing Champions	Oldsmobile EB
1:64	Racing Champions	Oldsmobile NP
1:64	Racing Champions	Oldsmobile PB
1:64	Racing Champions	Oldsmobile PB
1:64	Winross Transporters	Sunoco

1992–94

1:24	Racing Champions Banks	Kellogg's
1:24	Racing Champions Banks	MW Windows

1992–95 .

1:64	Action/RCCA Transporters	Kellogg's produced for Peachstate

1992–96

1:24	Brookfield Collectors Guild Suburbans	Kellogg's 1996
1:24	Brookfield Collectors Guild Suburbans	Kellogg's Silver 1996

1992

1:64	Funstuf Pit Row	Sunoco
1:64	Funstuf Pit Row	Sunoco w/ Busch decal
1:64	Racing Champions	Suncoo w/ Yellow bumper
1:64	Racing Champions	Sunoco w/ Blue bumper
1:64	Racing Champions Transporters	Sunoco
1:64	Winross Transporters	Sunoco

1993–94

1:87	Racing Champions Transporters	Kellogg's
1:87	Racing Champions Transporters	Kellogg's Yellow box hobby only

1993–95

1:64	Action Racing Collectables	Dual package Kellogg's Promo
1:64	Action Racing Collectables	Kellogg's Platinum Series
1:24	Action Racing Collectables Banks	Kellogg's
1:64	Action/RCCA	Kellogg's 1994 Lumina HO
1:24	Revell	Sunoco

1993–98

1:24	Action Dually Trucks	Kellogg's '96 Bank
1:24	Action Dually Trucks	Kellogg's Bank

SCALE	MANUFACTURER	SPONSOR
1:18	Ertl	Honey Crunch distributed by GMP
1:18	Ertl	Kellogg's
1:18	Ertl	Kellogg's Silver car

1993

1:64	Matchbox White Rose Super Stars	MW Windows BX
1:64	Matchbox White Rose Super Stars	Sunoco BL
1:87	Matchbox White Rose Transporters Super Star Series	MW Windows
1:87	Matchbox White Rose Transporters Super Star Series	Sunoco
1:24	Racing Champions	Kellogg's
1:43	Racing Champions	Kellogg's
1:64	Racing Champions	Kellogg's
1:64	Racing Champions Premier	Kellogg's
1:87	Racing Champions Premier Transporters	Kellogg's
1:64	Racing Champions Transporters	Kellogg's

1994

1:64	Ertl White Rose Transporters Past and Present	Kellogg's
1:64	Matchbox White Rose Super Stars	Kellogg's BX
1:80	Matchbox White Rose Transporters Super Star Series	Kellogg's
1:24	Racing Champions	Kellogg's
1:24	Racing Champions	MW Windows
1:43	Racing Champions	Kellogg's
1:64	Racing Champions	Kellogg's
1:64	Racing Champions Hobby	Kellogg's
1:64	Racing Champions Hobby	MW Windows
1:43	Racing Champions Premier	Kellogg's
1:64	Racing Champions Premier	Kellogg's
1:87	Racing Champions Premier Transporters	Kellogg's
1:64	Racing Champions To the Maxx	Kellogg's
1:64	Racing Champions Transporters	Kellogg's
1:64	Racing Champions Transporters	Kellogg's Yellow box hobby only
1:24	Revell Hobby	Kellogg's
1:64	Winross Transporters	Kellogg's

1995–96

1:18	Racing Champions	Bayer

1995

1:64	Matchbox White Rose Super Stars	Kellogg's
1:24	Racing Champions	Kellogg's
1:64	Racing Champions	Kellogg's
1:64	Racing Champions	MW Windows
1:24	Racing Champions Banks	Kellogg's
1:64	Racing Champions Matched Serial Numbers	Kellogg's
1:64	Racing Champions Previews	MW Windows
1:64	Racing Champions To the Maxx	MW Windows

SCALE	MANUFACTURER	SPONSOR
1:64	Racing Champions Transporters	Kellogg's
1:64	Racing Champions Transporters Previews	MW Windows

1996

SCALE	MANUFACTURER	SPONSOR
1:64	Action Racing Collectables	Kellogg's Iron Man
1:64	Action Racing Collectables	Kellogg's Japan
1:24	Action Racing Collectables Banks	Kellogg's Japan
1:24	Action Racing Collectables Banks	Kellogg's Silver Car
1:24	Action/RCCA	Kellogg's Japan
1:24	Action/RCCA	Kellogg's Silver car
1:64	Action/RCCA	Kellogg's Ironman
1:64	Action/RCCA	Kellogg's Japan
1:64	Matchbox White Rose Super Stars	Kellogg's
1:24	Press Pass	Kellogg's Silver car
1:24	Racing Champions	Bayer Hood Open
1:24	Racing Champions	Kellogg's
1:24	Racing Champions	Kellogg's Hood Open
1:24	Racing Champions	Kellogg's Silver car
1:24	Racing Champions	Kellogg's Silver Hood Open
1:64	Racing Champions	Kellogg's
1:64	Racing Champions	Kellogg's Silver car
1:64	Racing Champions	Kellogg's w/ Iron Man card
1:24	Racing Champions Chrome Banks	Kellogg's Silver Hood Open
1:24	Racing Champions Hobby Banks	Kellogg's Hobby
1:24	Racing Champions Hood Open Banks	Kellogg's Silver Hood Open
1:64	Racing Champions Premier w/ Medallion	Bayer Hood Open
1:64	Racing Champions Premier w/Medallion	Kellogg's Silver car Hood Open
1:24	Racing Champions Previews	Bayer
1:24	Racing Champions Previews	Kellogg's
1:64	Racing Champions Previews	Kellogg's

SCALE	MANUFACTURER	SPONSOR
1:64	Racing Champions Silver Chase	Kellogg's
1:64	Racing Champions Transporters	Kellogg's w/ one car or two cars
1:87	Racing Champions Transporters	Kellogg's
1:64	Racing Champions Transporters Previews	Kellogg's
1:24	Revell	Kellogg's
1:64	Revell	Kellogg's
1:24	Revell Collection	Honey Crunch
1:24	Revell Collection	Kellogg's
1:24	Revell Collection	Kellogg's Silver
1:64	Revell Collection	Honey Crunch
1:64	Revell Collection	Kellogg's 2 car set

1997

SCALE	MANUFACTURER	SPONSOR
1:64	Hot Wheels Collector Edition	Kellogg's
1:64	Hot Wheels Collector Edition/Short Track	Kellogg's
1:64	Hot Wheels Collector Edition/Short Track	Kellogg's Tony
1:64	Hot Wheels Collector Edition/ Speedway Edition	Kellogg's
1:64	Hot Wheels Pro Racing	Kellogg's
1:64	Matchbox White Rose Super Stars	Kellogg's
1:64	Matchbox White Rose Super Stars	Kellogg's SSA Gold
1:64	Matchbox White Rose Transporters	Kellogg's in acrylic case
1:24	Racing Champions	Bayer
1:24	Racing Champions	Kellogg's
1:24	Racing Champions	Kellogg's 1996 Champion
1:24	Racing Champions	Kellogg's 1996 Champion Hood Open
1:24	Racing Champions	Tony the Tiger
1:64	Racing Champions	Bayer
1:64	Racing Champions	Kellogg's 1996 Champion
1:64	Racing Champions	Kellogg's 2-car set
1:64	Racing Champions	Tony the Tiger
1:24	Racing Champions Banks	Kellogg's 1996 Champion
1:24	Racing Champions Banks	Kellogg's Champion Chrome
1:24	Racing Champions Hood Open Banks	Kellogg's Hood Open
1:64	Racing Champions Pinnacle Series	Kellogg's
1:64	Racing Champions Premier Preview w/ Medallion	Kellogg's
1:64	Racing Champions Premier Transporters	Kellogg's
1:64	Racing Champions Premier w/ Medallion	Tony the Tiger
1:64	Racing Champions Premier w/	Kellogg's

SCALE	MANUFACTURER	SPONSOR
	Medallion Silver Chase	
1:87	Racing Champions Preview Transporters	Kellogg's
1:24	Racing Champions Previews	Kellogg's
1:64	Racing Champions Previews	Kellogg's
1:64	Racing Champions Silver Chase	Kellogg's 1996 Champion
1:24	Racing Champions Stock Rods	Kellogg's
1:24	Racing Champions Stock Rods	Spooky Loops
1:24	Racing Champions Stock Rods	Spooky Loops
1:64	Racing Champions Stock Rods	Kellogg's
1:64	Racing Champions Stock Rods	Kellogg's
1:64	Racing Champions Stock Rods	Spooky Loops
1:64	Racing Champions Stock Rods	Spooky Loops
1:64	Racing Champions Stock Rods	Spooky Loops
1:64	Racing Champions Stock Rods	Spooky Loops
1:64	Racing Champions Stock Rods	Spooky Loops Chrome
1:64	Racing Champions Transporters	Kellogg's
1:64	Racing Champions Transporters	Kellogg's 1996 Winston Cup Champion
1:87	Racing Champions Transporters	Kellogg's
1:64	Racing Champions Transporters Previews	Kellogg's
1:18	Revell Club	Spooky Loops
1:18	Revell Club	Tony the Tiger
1:24	Revell Club	Kellogg's
1:24	Revell Club	Spooky Loops
1:24	Revell Club	Spooky Loops Bank
1:24	Revell Club	Tony the Tiger
1:24	Revell Club	Tony the Tiger Bank
1:18	Revell Collection	Kellogg's
1:18	Revell Collection	Spooky Loops
1:18	Revell Collection	Tony the Tiger
1:24	Revell Collection	Kellogg's
1:24	Revell Collection	Kellogg's 1996 Champion
1:24	Revell Collection	Kellogg's Texas Motor Speedway
1:24	Revell Collection	Kellogg's distributed by Mac Tools
1:24	Revell Collection	Spooky Loops
1:24	Revell Collection	Tony the Tiger
1:43	Revell Collection	Spooky Loops
1:43	Revell Collection	Tony The Tiger
1:64	Revell Collection	Bobby and Interstate Batteries and Kellogg's 2-car Tin Set
1:64	Revell Collection	Kellogg's Tony HO

SCALE	MANUFACTURER	SPONSOR
1:64	Revell Collection	Kellogg's
1:64	Revell Collection	Kellogg's 1996 Champion
1:64	Revell Collection	Spooky Loops
1:24	Revell Collection Banks	Tony the Tiger
1:24	Revell Hobby	Kellogg's
1:24	Revell Hobby	Kellogg's Texas Motor Speedway
1:24	Revell Hobby	Spooky Loops
1:24	Revell Hobby	Tony the Tiger
1:64	Revell Hobby	Kellogg's
1:64	Revell Hobby	Spooky Loops
1:64	Revell Hobby	Tony the Tiger
1:24	Revell Retail	Kellogg's Texas Motor Speedway
1:24	Revell Retail	Spooky Loops
1:24	Revell Retail	Tony The Tiger packaged in Food City box
1:64	Revell Retail	Kellogg's Texas Motor Speedway
1:64	Revell Retail	Spooky Loops

1998

SCALE	MANUFACTURER	SPONSOR
1:24	Action Racing Collectables	Blasted Fruit Loops
1:24	Action Racing Collectables	Kellogg's
1:24	Action Racing Collectables	Kellogg's Corny
1:24	Action Racing Collectables	Kellogg's Ironman
1:64	Action Racing Collectables	Blasted Fruit Loops
1:64	Action Racing Collectables	Kellogg's
1:64	Action Racing Collectables	Kellogg's Corny
1:64	Action Racing Collectables	Kellogg's Ironman
1:24	Action Racing Collectables Banks	Blasted Fruit Loops
1:24	Action Racing Collectables Banks	Kellogg's
1:24	Action Racing Collectables Banks	Kellogg's Corny
1:24	Action Racing Collectables Banks	Kellogg's Ironman
1:64	Action/RCCA	Blasted Fruit Loops

SCALE	MANUFACTURER	SPONSOR
1:64	Action/RCCA	Kellogg's
1:64	Action/RCCA	Kellogg's Corny
1:64	Action/RCCA	Kellogg's Ironman
1:24	Action/RCCA Banks	Blasted Fruit Loops
1:24	Action/RCCA Banks	Kellogg's
1:24	Action/RCCA Banks	Kellogg's Corny
1:24	Action/RCCA Banks	Kellogg's Ironman
1:24	Action/RCCA Elite	Blasted Fruit Loops
1:24	Action/RCCA Elite	Kellogg's
1:24	Action/RCCA Elite	Kellogg's Corny
1:24	Action/RCCA Elite	Kellogg's Ironman
1:32	Action/RCCA Gold	Kellogg's
1:64	Hot Wheels Collector Edition/Pit Crew	Kellogg's
1:64	Hot Wheels Collector Edition/Preview Edition	Kellogg's
1:64	Hot Wheels Collector Edition/Test Track	Kellogg's
1:64	Hot Wheels Collector Edition/Track Edition	Kellogg's
1:43	Hot Wheels Pro Racing	Kellogg's
1:24	Racing Champions	Blasted Fruit Loops
1:24	Racing Champions	Kellogg's
1:24	Racing Champions	Kellogg's Corny
1:64	Racing Champions	Kellogg's
1:64	Racing Champions	Kellogg's Corny
1:64	Racing Champions Chrome Chase	Kellogg's
1:64	Racing Champions Chrome Chase	Kellogg's Corny
1:24	Racing Champions Driver's Choice Banks	Kellogg's
1:24	Racing Champions Gold	Blasted Fruit Loops
1:24	Racing Champions Gold	Kellogg's
1:24	Racing Champions Gold	Kellogg's Corny
1:18	Racing Champions Gold Hood Open	Kellogg's
1:24	Racing Champions Gold Hood Open	Blasted Fruit Loops
1:24	Racing Champions Gold Hood Open	Kellogg's
1:24	Racing Champions Gold Hood Open	Kellogg's Corny
1:24	Racing Champions Gold Hood Open Banks	Blasted Fruit Loops
1:24	Racing Champions Gold Hood Open Banks	Kellogg's Corny
1:64	Racing Champions Gold w/ Medallion	Kellogg's
1:64	Racing Champions Gold w/ Medallion	Blasted Fruit Loops
1:64	Racing Champions Gold w/ Medallion	Kellogg's Corny
1:64	Racing Champions Pinnacle Series	Kellogg's
1:64	Racing Champions Press Pass Series	Kellogg's
1:24	Racing Champions Reflections of Gold	Kellogg's
1:64	Racing Champions Reflections of Gold	Kellogg's
1:24	Racing Champions Signature Series	Kellogg's
1:64	Racing Champions Signature Series	Kellogg's
1:24	Racing Champions Stock Rods	Kellogg's
1:24	Racing Champions Stock Rods	Kellogg's
1:24	Racing Champions Stock Rods	Kellogg's Corny
1:24	Racing Champions Stock Rods	Kellogg's Gold
1:64	Racing Champions Stock Rods	Blasted Fruit Loops
1:64	Racing Champions Stock Rods	Kellogg's
1:64	Racing Champions Stock Rods	Kellogg's
1:64	Racing Champions Stock Rods	Kellogg's
1:64	Racing Champions Stock Rods	Kellogg's
1:64	Racing Champions Stock Rods	Kellogg's
1:64	Racing Champions Stock Rods	Kellogg's
1:64	Racing Champions Stock Rods	Kellogg's
1:64	Racing Champions Stock Rods	Kellogg's Corny
1:64	Racing Champions Stock Rods	Kellogg's Corny
1:64	Racing Champions Stock Rods	Kellogg's Corny Gold
1:64	Racing Champions Stock Rods	Kellogg's Corny Gold
1:64	Racing Champions Stock Rods	Kellogg's Gold
1:64	Racing Champions Stock Rods	Spooky Loops
1:24	Racing Champions Stock Rods Reflections of Gold	Kellogg's
1:24	Racing Champions Stock Rods Reflections of Gold	Kellogg's
1:64	Racing Champions Stock Rods Reflections of Gold	Kellogg's
1:64	Racing Champions Toys 'R Us Gold	Blasted Fruit Loops
1:64	Racing Champions Toys 'R Us Gold	Kellogg's Corny
1:64	Racing Champions Transporters	Kellogg's
1:64	Racing Champions Transporters	Kellogg's Corny
1:64	Racing Champions Transporters	Kellogg's Corny w/ car
1:64	Racing Champions Transporters	Kellogg's w/ car
1:87	Racing Champions Transporters	Kellogg's
1:64	Racing Champions Transporters Gold	Kellogg's
1:64	Racing Champions Transporters Gold	Kellogg's Corny
1:64	Racing Champions Transporters Reflections of Gold	Kellogg's
1:64	Racing Champions Transporters Signature Series	Kellogg's
1:18	Revell Club	Blasted Fruit Loops
1:18	Revell Club	Kellogg's Corny
1:24	Revell Club	Blasted Fruit Loops
1:24	Revell Club	Kellogg's
1:24	Revell Club	Kellogg's Corny

SCALE	MANUFACTURER	SPONSOR
1:24	Revell Club	Kellogg's Corny Bank
1:24	Revell Club	Kellogg's Ironman Bank
1:18	Revell Collection	Blasted Fruit Loops
1:18	Revell Collection	Kellogg's Corny
1:24	Revell Collection	Blasted Fruit Loops
1:24	Revell Collection	Kellogg's
1:24	Revell Collection	Kellogg's Corny
1:43	Revell Collection	Blasted Fruit Loops
1:43	Revell Collection	Kellogg's
1:43	Revell Collection	Kellogg's Corny
1:43	Revell Collection	Kellogg's Ironman
1:64	Revell Collection	Blasted Fruit Loops
1:64	Revell Collection	Kellogg's
1:64	Revell Collection	Kellogg's Corny
1:64	Revell Collection	Kellogg's Ironman
1:24	Revell Collection Banks	Kellogg's
1:24	Revell Collection Banks	Kellogg's Corny
1:24	Revell Hobby	Kellogg's
1:24	Revell Hobby	Kellogg's Corny
1:64	Revell Hobby	Kellogg's Corny

1999

SCALE	MANUFACTURER	SPONSOR
1:24	Action Racing Collectables	K-Sentials
1:24	Action Racing Collectables	Kellogg's
1:64	Action Racing Collectables	K-Sentials
1:24	Action Racing Collectables Banks	Kellogg's
1:64	Action/RCCA	K-Sentials
1:64	Hot Wheels Collector Edition	Kellogg's
1:64	Hot Wheels Collector Edition/Pit Crew	Kellogg's
1:64	Hot Wheels Collector Edition/Pit Crew Gold	Kellogg's
1:64	Hot Wheels Collector Edition/Track Edition	Kellogg's
1:64	Hot Wheels Collector Edition/ Trading Paint	Kellogg's
1:24	Hot Wheels Pro Racing	Kellogg's

SCALE	MANUFACTURER	SPONSOR
1:43	Hot Wheels Pro Racing	Kellogg's
1:24	Racing Champions	Kellogg's
1:64	Racing Champions	Kellogg's
1:24	Racing Champions 24K Gold	Kellog's
1:64	Racing Champions 24K Gold	Kellog's
1:64	Racing Champions 24K Gold Stock Rods	Kelloggs
1:64	Racing Champions 3-D Originals	Kellogg's
1:24	Racing Champions Chrome Chase	Kellogg's
1:64	Racing Champions Chrome Chase	Kellogg's
1:24	Racing Champions Chrome Signature Series	Kellogg's
1:24	Racing Champions Gold	Kellogg's
1:64	Racing Champions Gold w/Medallion	Kellogg's
1:24	Racing Champions Platinum	Kellog's
1:64	Racing Champions Platinum	Kellogg's
1:64	Racing Champions Platinum Stock Rods	Kellogg's
1:64	Racing Champions Press Pass Series	Kellogg's
1:24	Racing Champions Signature Series	Kellogg's
1:64	Racing Champions Signature Series	Kellogg's
1:24	Racing Champions Stock Rods	Kellogg's
1:24	Racing Champions Stock Rods	Blasted Fruit Loops
1:24	Racing Champions Stock Rods	Kellogg's Iron Man
1:24	Racing Champions Stock Rods	Kellogg's Iron Man
1:64	Racing Champions Stock Rods	Kellogg's
1:64	Racing Champions Stock Rods	Kellogg's Corny
1:64	Racing Champions Stock Rods	Kellogg's Iron Man
1:64	Racing Champions Stock Rods	Kellogg's Iron Man
1:64	Racing Champions Stock Rods	Iron Man Gold
1:64	Racing Champions Toy's R Us Chrome Chase	Kellogg's
1:64	Racing Champions Transporters	Kellogg's
1:64	Racing Champions Transporters 24K Gold	Kellogg's
1:64	Racing Champions Transporters Gold	Kellogg's
1:64	Racing Champions Transporters Platinum	Kellogg's
1:64	Racing Champions Transporters Signature Series	Kellogg's
1:64	Racing Champions Under the Lights	Kellogg's
1:24	Revell Collection	Kellogg's
1:64	Revell Collection	Kellogg's
1:64	Revell Collection	K-Sentials

2000

SCALE	MANUFACTURER	SPONSOR
1:64	Hot Wheels Deluxe	Kellogg's
1:64	Hot Wheels Deluxe Scorchin Scooter	Kellogg's

Mark Martin

Hometown:
Batesville, Arkansas

Birthdate:
January 9, 1959

Personal:
A very religious, family man, Martin's main hobby is enjoying time with his family. He is also a devoted body builder, who can often be found in the gym working out before sunrise. While Martin keeps a strict diet and emphasizes eating healthy foods, his favorite meal is "a cheeseburger and fries." Enjoys flying, movies by Arnold Schwarzenegger and Jodie Foster, and music from Melissa Etheridge, Bonnie Raitt and Stevie Nicks.

Hobby:
Martin, Bill Elliott and Terry Labonte are the top names in the NASCAR hobby not locked up into an exclusive deal with Action Performance Companies. Martin did sign a deal with the company in 1999 for Action to produce some replicas from early in his career, but he's no longer under contract. Martin is one of the top Ford drivers in the hobby. His sponsor, Valvoline, has been aggressive in creating several special paint schemes.

Career Highlights
- Top six of the final Winston Cup standings each of past 11 seasons.
- Martin is the winningest driver in Busch Grand National history, breaking Jack Ingram's record of 31 career victories in 1998.
- Four-time ASA champion.
- Started Winston Cup in 1981, running five races and winning two poles that season. First pole came in third attempt, at Nashville in July.
- Finished second to Geoff Bodine for 1982 NASCAR Winston Cup Rookie of the Year.
- First victory came in 113th start, 1989 AC Delco 500 at Rockingham, after six second-place finishes.
- Voted NMPA Driver of the Year in 1989.

SCALE	MANUFACTURER	SPONSOR

1989–90

| 1:87 | Matchbox White Rose Transporters Super Star Series | Folgers '90 |

1991

1:87	Matchbox White Rose Transporters Super Star Series	Folgers w/ Ford cab
1:87	Matchbox White Rose Transporters Super Star Series	Folgers w/ Mack cab
1:43	Racing Champions	Valvoline

#6 Valvoline Thunderbird

1992–97

| 1:24 | Raceway Replicas | Valvoline 1994 |

1992

1:43	Funstuf Pit Row	Valvoline
1:64	Racing Champions Transporters	Valvoline
1:64	Racing Champions Transporters	Winn Dixie

1993–94

| 1:87 | Racing Champions Transporters | Valvoline |
| 1:87 | Racing Champions Transporters | Valvoline Yellow box hobby only |

1993–95

1:24	Action Racing Collectables	Valvoline
1:24	Action Racing Collectables	Valvoline 1995 Brickyard Special
1:64	Action Racing Collectables	Folgers Platinum Series
1:64	Action Racing Collectables	Miller 1985 ASA
1:64	Action Racing Collectables	Valvoline Brickyard Special Platinum Series
1:64	Action Racing Collectables	Valvoline Brickyard Special Blister package
1:64	Action Racing Collectables	Valvoline Platinum Series
1:64	Action Racing Collectables	Valvoline Valvoline Team Promo
1:24	Action Racing Collectables Banks	Folgers
1:24	Action Racing Collectables Banks	Miller 1984 ASA
1:24	Action Racing Collectables Banks	Valvoline 1995

SCALE	MANUFACTURER	SPONSOR
1:24	Action/RCCA	Folgers
1:64	Action/RCCA	Folgers Promo
1:64	Action/RCCA	Miller Acrylic
1:64	Action/RCCA	Stroh's Light 2 car combo

1993–95

1:64	Action/RCCA	Valvoline 1995 Thunderbird Hood Open
1:64	Action/RCCA	Valvoline Hood Open Brickyard Special
1:64	Action/RCCA	Valvoline Revell
1:24	Action/RCCA Banks	Valvoline 1995
1:24	Action/RCCA Banks	Valvoline Brickyard Special
1:24	Revell	Valvoline
1:24	Revell	Winn Dixie produced for GMP

1993–98

1:24	Action Dually Trucks	Valvoline Bank
1:18	Ertl	Valvoline
1:18	Ertl	Valvoline 1996
1:18	Ertl	Valvoline 1997
1:18	Ertl	Winn Dixie GMP

1993

1:87	Matchbox White Rose Transporters Super Star Series	Valvoline
1:64	Racing Champions	Valvoline
1:64	Racing Champions	Winn Dixie
1:43	Racing Champions Premier	Valvoline
1:43	Racing Champions Premier	Winn Dixie
1:64	Racing Champions Premier	Valvoline
1:64	Racing Champions Premier	Valvoline Four in a Row Promo
1:64	Racing Champions Premier	Winn Dixie
1:87	Racing Champions Premier Transporters	Valvoline
1:87	Racing Champions Premier Transporters	Winn Dixie
1:64	Racing Champions PVC Box	Winn Dixie
1:64	Racing Champions Transporters	Valvoline
1:64	Racing Champions Transporters	Winn Dixie

1994

1:64	Matchbox White Rose Super Stars	Valvoline BX
1:64	Matchbox White Rose Super Stars	Winn Dixie BX
1:24	Racing Champions	Valvoline Reese's
1:24	Racing Champions	Winn Dixie
1:43	Racing Champions	Winn Dixie
1:64	Racing Champions	Valvoline
1:64	Racing Champions	Winn Dixie
1:64	Racing Champions Hobby	Valvoline
1:43	Racing Champions Premier	Valvoline
1:43	Racing Champions Premier	Winn Dixie

SCALE	MANUFACTURER	SPONSOR
1:64	Racing Champions Premier	Valvoline
1:64	Racing Champions Premier	Valvoline four in a row special
1:64	Racing Champions Premier	Winn Dixie
1:64	Racing Champions Premier Brickyard 400	Valvoline
1:87	Racing Champions Premier Transporters	Winn Dixie
1:64	Racing Champions To the Maxx	Valvoline
1:64	Racing Champions Transporters	Valvoline
1:64	Racing Champions Transporters	Winn Dixie

1995

SCALE	MANUFACTURER	SPONSOR
1:64	Matchbox White Rose Super Stars	Valvoline
1:80	Matchbox White Rose Transporters Super Star Series	Valvoline
1:80	Matchbox White Rose Transporters Super Star Series	Winn Dixie
1:24	Racing Champions	Valvoline
1:24	Racing Champions	Winn Dixie
1:64	Racing Champions	Valvoline
1:64	Racing Champions	Winn Dixie
1:24	Racing Champions Banks	Valvoline
1:24	Racing Champions Banks	Winn Dixie
1:64	Racing Champions Matched Serial Numbers	Bayer
1:43	Racing Champions Premier	Winn Dixie
1:64	Racing Champions Premier	Valvoline
1:64	Racing Champions Premier	Winn Dixie
1:24	Racing Champions Previews	Valvoline
1:64	Racing Champions Previews	Valvoline
1:64	Racing Champions To the Maxx	Valvoline
1:64	Racing Champions Transporters	Valvoline
1:64	Racing Champions Transporters	Winn Dixie
1:24	Revell	Valvoline

1996

SCALE	MANUFACTURER	SPONSOR
1:24	Action Racing Collectables	Miller ASA '85
1:64	Action Racing Collectables	Valvoline
1:24	Action Racing Collectables Banks	Miller 1985 ASA
1:24	Action Racing Collectables Banks	Valvoline
1:24	Action/RCCA	Valvoline Thunderbird
1:64	Action/RCCA	Valvoline
1:64	Matchbox White Rose Super Stars	Valvoline
1:64	Peachstate Transporters	Valvoline
1:24	Racing Champions	Valvoline
1:24	Racing Champions	Valvoline Hood Open
1:24	Racing Champions	Winn Dixie
1:24	Racing Champions	Winn Dixie Hood Open
1:64	Racing Champions	Roush Box Promo
1:64	Racing Champions	Valvoline
1:64	Racing Champions	Valvoline Dura Blend
1:64	Racing Champions	Winn Dixie Promo

SCALE	MANUFACTURER	SPONSOR
1:24	Racing Champions Banks	Valvoline
1:24	Racing Champions Chrome Banks	Valvoline Chrome
1:64	Racing Champions Hobby	Valvoline
1:24	Racing Champions Hobby Banks	Valvoline Hobby
1:24	Racing Champions Hood Open Banks	Winn Dixe Hood Open
1:64	Racing Champions Premier Transporters	Valvoline
1:64	Racing Champions Premier w/ Medallion	Valvoline Dura Blend Hood Open
1:24	Racing Champions Previews	Valvoline
1:64	Racing Champions Previews	Valvoline
1:64	Racing Champions Silver Chase	Valvoline
1:64	Racing Champions Transporters	Winn Dixie
1:64	Racing Champions Transporters	Winn Dixie w/ one car or two cars
1:87	Racing Champions Transporters	Valvoline
1:64	Racing Champions Transporters Previews	Valvoline
1:24	Revell	Valvoline
1:64	Revell	Valvoline
1:24	Revell Collection	Valvoline
1:64	Revell Collection	Valvoline
1:64	Revell Collection	Valvoline Dura Blend

1997

SCALE	MANUFACTURER	SPONSOR
1:24	Action Racing Collectables	Valvoline
1:24	Action Racing Collectables	Valvoline Mac Tools
1:64	Action Racing Collectables	Valvoline
1:64	Action Racing Collectables	Winn Dixie
1:24	Action Racing Collectables Banks	Winn Dixie
1:24	Action/RCCA	Winn Dixie
1:64	Action/RCCA	Valvoline
1:64	Action/RCCA	Winn Dixie
1:24	Action/RCCA Banks	Valvoline
1:24	Action/RCCA Elite	Valvoline
1:24	Action/RCCA Elite	Winn Dixie
1:64	Hot Wheels Collector Edition	Valvoline
1:64	Hot Wheels Collector Edition/Short Track	Valvoline
1:64	Hot Wheels Collector Edition/ Speedway Edition	Valvoline
1:64	Hot Wheels Pro Racing	Valvoline
1:18	Racing Champions	Valvoline Gold
1:18	Racing Champions	Valvoline Hobby
1:24	Racing Champions	Valvoline
1:24	Racing Champions	Winn-Dixie Promo
1:64	Racing Champions	Valvoline
1:64	Racing Champions	Winn Dixie
1:24	Racing Champions Banks	Winn Dixie

SCALE	MANUFACTURER	SPONSOR
1:64	Racing Champions Gold	Valvoline
1:24	Racing Champions Gold Banks	Valvoline Gold
1:64	Racing Champions Hobby	Valvoline
1:24	Racing Champions Hobby Banks	Valvoline Hobby
1:24	Racing Champions Hood Open Banks	Valvoline Hood Open
1:64	Racing Champions Pinnacle Series	Valvoline
1:64	Racing Champions Premier Preview w/ Medallion	Valvoline
1:64	Racing Champions Premier Transporters	Winn Dixie
1:64	Racing Champions Premier w/ Medallion	Valvoline
1:87	Racing Champions Preview Transporters	Valvoline
1:24	Racing Champions Previews	Valvoline
1:64	Racing Champions Previews	Valvoline
1:64	Racing Champions Stock Rods	Valvoline
1:64	Racing Champions Stock Rods	Valvoline
1:64	Racing Champions Stock Rods	Valvoline
1:64	Racing Champions Stock Rods	Valvoline
1:24	Racing Champions SuperTrucks	Exide
1:64	Racing Champions SuperTrucks	Exide
1:64	Racing Champions Transporters	Valvoline
1:64	Racing Champions Transporters	Valvoline w/ one car or two cars
1:64	Racing Champions Transporters	Winn Dixie
1:64	Racing Champions Transporters	Winn Dixie Promo
1:87	Racing Champions Transporters	Valvoline
1:87	Racing Champions Transporters	Winn Dixie
1:64	Racing Champions Transporters Previews	Valvoline
1:18	Revell Collection	Valvoline
1:18	Revell Collection	Winn Dixie
1:43	Revell Collection	Valvoline
1:64	Revell Collection	Valvoline/Winn Dixie 2 car set
1:24	Revell Hobby	Valvoline
1:64	Revell Hobby	Valvoline
1:24	Revell Retail	Valvoline

1998

SCALE	MANUFACTURER	SPONSOR
1:64	Hot Wheels Collector Edition/Pit Crew	Valvoline
1:64	Hot Wheels Collector Edition/ Preview Edition	Eagle One
1:64	Hot Wheels Collector Edition/ Preview Edition	Syntec
1:64	Hot Wheels Collector Edition/ Preview Edition	Valvoline
1:64	Hot Wheels Collector Edition/Test Track	Valvoline
1:64	Hot Wheels Collector Edition/Track Edition	Eagle One
1:64	Hot Wheels Collector Edition/Track Edition	Synpower

SCALE	MANUFACTURER	SPONSOR
1:64	Hot Wheels Collector Edition/Track Edition	Valvoline
1:64	Hot Wheels Collector Edition/ Trading Paint	Valvoline
1:43	Hot Wheels Pro Racing	Valvoline
1:24	Racing Champions	Eagle One
1:24	Racing Champions	Kosei
1:24	Racing Champions	Synpower
1:24	Racing Champions	Valvoline
1:64	Racing Champions	Eagle One
1:64	Racing Champions	Kosei
1:64	Racing Champions	Valvoline
1:64	Racing Champions	Winn Dixie
1:64	Racing Champions	Winn Dixie Promo
1:24	Racing Champions Authentics	Eagle One
1:24	Racing Champions Authentics	Synpower
1:24	Racing Champions Authentics	Valvoline
1:24	Racing Champions Authentics Banks	Eagle One
1:24	Racing Champions Authentics Banks	Synpower
1:24	Racing Champions Authentics Banks	Valvoline
1:64	Racing Champions Chrome Chase	Eagle One
1:64	Racing Champions Chrome Chase	Valvoline
1:64	Racing Champions Chrome Chase	Winn Dixie
1:24	Racing Champions Driver's Choice Banks	Valvoline
1:24	Racing Champions Gold	Eagle One
1:24	Racing Champions Gold	Syntec
1:24	Racing Champions Gold	Valvoline
1:24	Racing Champions Gold	Winn Dixie
1:24	Racing Champions Gold Banks	Valvoline
1:24	Racing Champions Gold Hood Open	Syntec
1:24	Racing Champions Gold Hood Open	Valvoline
1:24	Racing Champions Gold Hood Open Banks	Eagle One
1:24	Racing Champions Gold Hood Open Banks	Synpower
1:24	Racing Champions Gold Hood Open Banks	Valvoline
1:64	Racing Champions Gold w/Medallion	Eagle One
1:64	Racing Champions Gold w/Medallion	Syntec
1:64	Racing Champions Gold w/Medallion	Valvoline
1:64	Racing Champions Gold w/Medallion	Winn Dixie
1:64	Racing Champions Pinnacle Series	Valvoline
1:64	Racing Champions Press Pass Series	Eagle One
1:64	Racing Champions Press Pass Series	Valvoline
1:64	Racing Champions Press Pass Series	Winn Dixie
1:24	Racing Champions Reflections of Gold	Valvoline
1:24	Racing Champions Reflections of Gold	Winn Dixie
1:64	Racing Champions Reflections of Gold	Valvoline
1:64	Racing Champions Reflections of Gold	Winn Dixie
1:24	Racing Champions Signature Series	Valvoline
1:64	Racing Champions Signature Series	Valvoline
1:24	Racing Champions Stock Rods	Valvoline

SCALE	MANUFACTURER	SPONSOR
1:24	Racing Champions Stock Rods	Valvoline
1:24	Racing Champions Stock Rods	Valvoline
1:64	Racing Champions Stock Rods	Valvoline
1:64	Racing Champions Stock Rods	Valvoline
1:64	Racing Champions Stock Rods	Valvoline
1:64	Racing Champions Stock Rods	Valvoline
1:64	Racing Champions Stock Rods	Valvoline
1:64	Racing Champions Stock Rods	Winn Dixie
1:64	Racing Champions Stock Rods	Winn Dixie
1:64	Racing Champions Stock Rods	Winn Dixie
1:24	Racing Champions Stock Rods Reflections of Gold	Valvoline
1:64	Racing Champions Stock Rods Reflections of Gold	Valvoline
1:64	Racing Champions Toys 'R Us Gold	Eagle One
1:64	Racing Champions Toys 'R Us Gold	Valvoline
1:64	Racing Champions Toys 'R Us Gold	Winn Dixie
1:64	Racing Champions Transporters	Eagle One
1:64	Racing Champions Transporters	Eagle One w/ car
1:64	Racing Champions Transporters	Winn Dixie
1:64	Racing Champions Transporters	Winn Dixie Promo w/ car
1:64	Racing Champions Transporters	Winn Dixie w/ car
1:87	Racing Champions Transporters	Valvoline
1:64	Racing Champions Transporters Gold	Eagle One
1:64	Racing Champions Transporters Gold	Valvoline
1:64	Racing Champions Transporters Reflections of Gold	Valvoline
1:64	Racing Champions Transporters Reflections of Gold	Winn Dixie
1:64	Racing Champions Transporters Signature Series	Valvoline

1999

SCALE	MANUFACTURER	SPONSOR
1:64	Hot Wheels Collector Edition	Valvoline
1:64	Hot Wheels Collector Edition/ Pit Crew	Valvoline
1:64	Hot Wheels Collector Edition/ Pit Crew Gold	Valvoline

SCALE	MANUFACTURER	SPONSOR
1:64	Hot Wheels Collector Edition/ Track Edition	Valvoline
1:64	Hot Wheels Collector Edition/ Trading Paint	Valvoline
1:24	Hot Wheels Pro Racing	Hot Wheels
1:24	Racing Champions	Valvoline
1:64	Racing Champions	Valvoline
1:64	Racing Champions	Winn Dixie
1:24	Racing Champions 24K Gold	Valvoline
1:64	Racing Champions 24K Gold	Valvoline
1:24	Racing Champions Chrome Chase	Valvoline
1:64	Racing Champions Chrome Chase	Valvoline
1:64	Racing Champions Chrome Chase	Winn Dixie
1:24	Racing Champions Chrome Signature Series	Valvoline
1:64	Racing Champions Chrome Signature Series	Valvoline
1:24	Racing Champions Gold	Valvoline
1:64	Racing Champions Gold w/Medallion	Valvoline
1:64	Racing Champions Gold w/Medallion	Winn Dixie
1:64	Racing Champions NASCAR RULES	Valvoline
1:24	Racing Champions Platinum	Valvoline
1:64	Racing Champions Platinum	Valvoline
1:64	Racing Champions Press Pass Series	Valvoline
1:24	Racing Champions Signature Series	Valvoline
1:64	Racing Champions Signature Series	Valvoline
1:64	Racing Champions Signature Series	Winn-Dixie
1:24	Racing Champions Stock Rods	Valvoline
1:64	Racing Champions Stock Rods	Valvoline
1:64	Racing Champions Toy's R Us Chrome Chase	Valvoline
1:64	Racing Champions Transporters	Valvoline
1:64	Racing Champions Transporters 24K Gold	Valvoline
1:64	Racing Champions Transporters Chrome Chase	Valvoline
1:64	Racing Champions Transporters Gold	Valvoline
1:64	Racing Champions Transporters Platinum	Valvoline
1:64	Racing Champions Transporters Signature Series	Valvoline

2000

SCALE	MANUFACTURER	SPONSOR
1:24	Action Racing Collectables	Activision '83 Monte Carlo
1:24	Action Racing Collectables	Jim Magill '83 Monte Carlo
1:64	Hot Wheels Deluxe Scorchin Scooter	Valvoline
1:64	Racing Champions NASCAR RULES	Valvoline
1:64	Racing Champions Pit Crew	Valvoline
1:64	Racing Champions Premier Preview	Valvoline
1:24	Racing Champions Preview	Valvoline
1:64	Racing Champions Previews	Valvoline
1:64	Racing Champions Stock Rods	Valvoline
1:24	Racing Champions Time Trial 2000	Valvoline
1:64	Racing Champions Time Trial 2000	Valvoline
1:64	Racing Champions Transporters Previews	Valvoline

Richard Petty

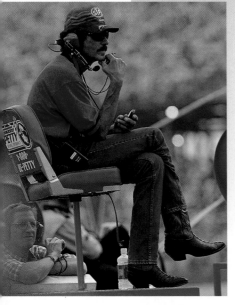

Hometown
Level Cross, North Carolina

Birthdate
July 2, 1937

Personal:
Richard Petty is one of the main cogs of NASCAR's first family. His father, Lee Petty, won three Winston Cup championships and the first Daytona 500 in 1959. Richard's son, Kyle, has raced on the Winston Cup circuit for more than two decades. Kyle's son, Adam, is a regular on the Busch circuit and makes his Winston Cup debut in 2000. Richard Petty is a stock car racing icon, always wearing his trademark cowboy hat and shades. He might have signed more autographs than anyone in history as he credits fans for his long career. Petty received the Medal of Freedom, the highest U.S. civilian award, in 1992. He is a good old Southern boy and likes the simple pleasures in life.

Hobby:
Petty retired from driving in 1992, but because he continues to own his No. 43 car his popularity has continued in the hobby. In addition, Petty Enterprises has fielded NASCAR entries since the beginning of sanctioned stock car races. Adam, Richard's grandson, is a promising driver on the Busch circuit so it is likely that a Petty will be on NASCAR want lists for years to come. Most die-cast makers have had some dealings with Richard Petty, though he no longer has a licensing agreement with Action Performance Companies. He currently has major deals with Hot Wheels and Racing Champions. He's also had cars replicated by high-dollar manufacturers such as the Franklin Mint. Has had virtually every car he drove on the Winston Cup circuit turned into a die-cast replica.

Career Highlights
* Won seven Winston Cup championships, a record he shares with Dale Earnhardt.
* Won a Winston Cup record 200 races, almost twice as many as any other driver.
* Won a record seven Daytona 500s.
* 1959 NASCAR Rookie of the Year.
* Won a record 27 races in 1967, including 10 in a row.
* Won 200 of 1,156 Winston Cup starts for a winning percentage of 17.3 percent
* Named Most Popular Winston Cup Series Driver nine times.
* Raised in Winston Cup from 1959 to 1992.
* Member of almost every motorsports hall of fame that exists. Also a member of the North Carolina Athletic Hall of Fame.
* Owns the No. 43 Winston Cup team, with John Andretti as driver.

SCALE	MANUFACTURER	SPONSOR

1989–90

1:87	Matchbox White Rose Transporters Super Star Series	Richard Petty STP '89
1:87	Matchbox White Rose Transporters Super Star Series	Richard Petty STP '90

1990–92

1:64	Matchbox White Rose Super Stars	Richard Petty STP '92 BL

1990

1:64	Racing Champions	Richard Petty Pontiac

1991–92

1:24	Racing Champions	Richard Petty STP w/ Blue Wheels

1991

1:87	Matchbox White Rose Transporters Super Star Series	Richard Petty STP 20th Anniversary
1:43	Racing Champions	Richard Petty STP
1:64	Racing Champions	Richard Petty Pontiac EB
1:64	Racing Champions	Richard Petty Pontiac NP
1:64	Racing Champions	Richard Petty Pontiac PB
1:64	Winross Transporters	Richard Petty STP

1992–94

1:24	Racing Champions Banks	Richard Petty STP

1992–95

1:64	Action/RCCA Transporters	Richard Petty STP RCCA

1992

1:64	Funstuf Pit Row	Richard Petty STP
1:64	Funstuf Pit Row	Richard Petty STP w/ Winston Decal on Fender
1:87	Matchbox White Rose Transporters 1992 Super Star Series	Richard Petty STP
1:64	Racing Champions	Richard Petty STP w/ Black wheels
1:64	Racing Champions	Richard Petty STP w/ Blue wheels
1:64	Racing Champions Premier	Richard Petty STP
1:64	Racing Champions Transporters	Richard Petty STP
1:64	Racing Champions Transporters	Richard Petty STP Fan Appreciation Tour
1:64	Winross Transporters	Richard Petty STP Fan Appreciation Tour

1993–95

1:64	Action/RCCA	Richard Petty STP 1991 Grand Prix Revell

1993–98

1:18	Ertl	Richard Petty STP
1:18	Ertl	Richard Petty STP 7-Time Champion

1994

1:64	Ertl White Rose Transporters BGN Promos	Richard Petty Petty Anniversary Tour Promo

1999

1:24	Racing Champions Petty Collection	Richard Petty '70 Superbird
1:64	Racing Champions Petty Collection	Richard Petty Ford Torino
1:64	Racing Champions Petty Collection	Richard Petty Pepsi Roadrunner
1:64	Racing Champions Petty Collection	Richard Petty Plymouth Barracuda
1:64	Racing Champions Petty Collection	Richard Petty Plymouth Belvedere
1:64	Racing Champions Petty Collection	Richard Petty Plymouth Fury
1:64	Racing Champions Petty Collection	Richard Petty Plymouth Fury
1:64	Racing Champions Petty Collection	Richard Petty Plymouth Plaza
1:64	Racing Champions Petty Collection	Richard Petty Plymouth Roadrunner
1:64	Racing Champions Petty Collection	Richard Petty Plymouth Savoy
1:64	Racing Champions Petty Collection	Richard Petty Plymouth Savoy
1:64	Racing Champions Petty Collection	Richard Petty Plymouth Superbird
1:64	Racing Champions Petty Collection	Richard Petty STP Buick Regal
1:64	Racing Champions Petty Collection	Richard Petty STP Dodge Charger
1:64	Racing Champions Petty Collection	Richard Petty STP Dodge Charger
1:64	Racing Champions Petty Collection	Richard Petty STP Dodge Charger
1:64	Racing Champions Petty Collection	Richard Petty STP Dodge Charger
1:64	Racing Champions Petty Collection	Richard Petty STP Dodge Charger
1:64	Racing Champions Petty Collection	Richard Petty STP Grand Prix
1:64	Racing Champions Petty Collection	Richard Petty STP Roadrunner

Rusty Wallace

Hometown:
St. Louis, Mo.

Birthdate:
Aug. 14, 1956

Personal:
Rusty's father was 30-time track champion in the St. Louis area and his younger brothers Kenny and Mike are both NASCAR drivers. Wallace is infatuated with airplanes and flying. In fact he owns and pilots his own jet and helicopter. Rusty also loves rock music and considers NASCAR driver Bobby Allison his hero.

Hobby:
He has a long-term deal with Action Performance Companies that gives the company exclusive rights to make his die-cast replicas. His replica cars are partly prized because he has had tobacco and alcohol sponsors for more than a decade. For many years, collectors shied away from putting these sponsors' logos on cars to keep from influencing children. Wallace had four paint schemes in each of the 1998 and 1999 seasons, including popular special paint schemes that featured Elvis, Harley-Davidson motorcycles and the Adventures of Rusty, a Miller Brewery ad campaign.

Career Highlights

- Winston Cup champion in 1989
- Winston Cup Rookie of the Year in 1984
- NMPA Driver of the Year in 1988 and 1993
- USAC Rookie of the Year in 1979 and ASA National Champion in 1983
- 1991 IROC champion
- The Winston winner in 1989
- $1 million or more in earnings in eight seasons
- Runner-up to Bill Elliott for 1988 Winston Cup title by 24 points and runner-up to Dale Earnhardt for 1993 title by 80 points
- Considered one of best Winston Cup road racers of all-time
- In 1998, won a race for the 13th season in a row and finished in the top 10 in points for the sixth consecutive year

SCALE	MANUFACTURER	SPONSOR
1990–92		
1:64	Matchbox White Rose Super Stars	Penske '92 BL
1990		
1:64	Racing Champions	Old Pontiac Miller Genuine Draft
1:64	Racing Champions	Oldsmobile
1:64	Racing Champions	Pontiac Miller
1:64	Racing Champions	Pontiac Miller Genuine Draft
1:64	Racing Champions	Pontiac w/ Silver Decals
1991–92		
1:24	Racing Champions	AC Delco
1:24	Racing Champions	Pontiac Excitement
1991		
1:43	Racing Champions	Pontiac Excitement
1:64	Racing Champions	Pontiac EB
1:64	Racing Champions	Pontiac Miller EB
1:64	Racing Champions	Pontiac Miller Genuine Draft EB
1:64	Racing Champions	Pontiac Miller Genuine Draft NP
1:64	Racing Champions	Pontiac no MGD EB
1:64	Racing Champions	Pontiac PB
1:64	Racing Champions Transporters	Penske Racing
1992–94		
1:24	Racing Champions Banks	Ford Motorsports
1:24	Racing Champions Banks	Pontiac Excitement
1992–95		
1:64	Action/RCCA Transporters Platinum Series	Delco Remy
1:64	Action/RCCA Transporters	Miller
1992		
1:87	Matchbox White Rose Transporters 1992 Super Star Series	Penske
1:64	Racing Champions	Pontiac Excitement
1:64	Racing Champions Transporters	Penske
1993–94		
1:87	Racing Champions Transporters	Penske
1:87	Racing Champions Transporters	Penske Yellow box hobby only
1993–95		
1:64	Action Racing Collectables	Ford Motorsports Platinum Series
1:64	Action Racing Collectables	Miller Geniune Draft Platinum Series Acrylic display case

SCALE	MANUFACTURER	SPONSOR
1:64	Action Racing Collectables	Pontiac Excitement AC Racing Promo
1:64	Action Racing Collectables	Pontiac Excitement Delco Remy Promo
1:24	Action Racing Collectables Banks	Ford Motorsports
1:24	Action Racing Collectables Banks	Kodiak
1:24	Action Racing Collectables Banks	Miller Geniune Draft
1:24	Action/RCCA	Ford Motorsports
1:24	Action/RCCA	Miller Genuine Draft 1995 Thunderbird
1:64	Action/RCCA	Kodiak 1989 Pontiac HO Acrylic
1:64	Action/RCCA	Miller Genuine Draft 1995 Hood Open in acrylic case
1:64	Action/RCCA	Miller Genuine Draft Club Only
1:64	Action/RCCA	Pontiac Excitement Revell
1993–98		
1:24	Action Dually Trucks	Miller Genuine Draft 1996 Bank
1:24	Action Dually Trucks	Miller Genuine Draft Bank
1:24	Action Dually Trucks	Miller Genuine Draft Silver Bank
1:24	Action Dually Trucks	Miller Lite Bank
1:18	Ertl	Kodiak
1:18	Ertl	Miller Genuine Draft
1:18	Ertl	Miller Genuine Draft
1:18	Ertl	Miller Silver car
1993–99		
1:64	Action Dually w/Chaparral Trailer	Miller Genuine Draft
1:64	Action Dually w/Chaparral Trailer	Miller Genuine Draft w/out the trailer
1:64	Action Dually w/Chaparral Trailer	Miller Lite
1:16	Action Racing Collectables Pit Wagon Banks	Ford Motorsports
1:16	Action Racing Collectables Pit Wagon Banks	Miller Genuine Draft
1:16	Action Racing Collectables Pit Wagon Banks	Miller Lite
1:16	Action Racing Collectables Pit Wagon Banks	Miller Lite 1998

SCALE	MANUFACTURER	SPONSOR
1993		
1:24	Racing Champions	Pontiac Excitement
1:43	Racing Champions	Pontiac Excitement
1:64	Racing Champions	Pontiac Excitement
1:64	Racing Champions Premier	Pontiac Excitement
1:64	Racing Champions Premier Transporters	Ford Motorsports
1:87	Racing Champions Premier Transporters	Penske
1:64	Racing Champions Transporters	Penske
1994–96		
1:96	Action/RCCA Transporters	Miller Geniune Draft
1994		
1:64	Matchbox White Rose Super Stars	Ford Motorsports BX
1:24	Racing Champions	Ford Motorsports Black Ford Oval
1:24	Racing Champions	Ford Motorsports Blue Ford Oval
1:64	Racing Champions	Ford Motorsports
1:64	Racing Champions	Ford Motorsports w/ no Blue
1:64	Racing Champions Hobby	Ford Motorsports
1:43	Racing Champions Premier	Ford Motorsports
1:64	Racing Champions Premier	Mac Tools
1:64	Racing Champions Premier	Miller Genuine Draft
1:64	Racing Champions To the Maxx	Ford Motorsports
1:64	Racing Champions Transporters	Penske
1:64	Racing Champions Transporters	Penske Yellow box hobby only
1995–96		
1:18	Racing Champions	MGD
1995		
1:64	Action/RCCA Transporters	Miller Genuine Draft Platinum Series
1:24	Racing Champions	Ford Motorsports
1:64	Racing Champions	Ford Motorsports
1:24	Racing Champions Banks	Ford Motorsports
1:64	Racing Champions Matched Serial Numbers	Ford
1:64	Racing Champions Premier	Ford Motorsports
1:64	Racing Champions Premier Transporters	Miller Genuine Draft in acrylic case

SCALE	MANUFACTURER	SPONSOR
1:64	Racing Champions Premier Transporters	Penske Bank
1:24	Racing Champions Previews	Ford Motorsports
1:64	Racing Champions Previews	Ford Motorsports
1:64	Racing Champions To the Maxx	Ford Motorsports
1:64	Racing Champions Transporters	Penske
1:87	Racing Champions Transporters	Miller Genuine Draft in acrylic case
1:64	Racing Champions Transporters Previews	Penske
1996		
1:24	Action Racing Collectables	Miller Genuine Draft
1:24	Action Racing Collectables	Miller Genuine Draft Silver Anniversary
1:64	Action Racing Collectables	Miller Genuine Draft Silver
1:64	Action Racing Collectables	Miller Splash Paint Acrylic
1:24	Action Racing Collectables Banks	Miller Genuine Draft
1:24	Action/RCCA	Kodiak
1:24	Action/RCCA	Miller Genuine Draft
1:64	Action/RCCA	Kodiak 1989 Grand Prix Acrylic
1:64	Action/RCCA	Miller Genuine Draft
1:64	Action/RCCA	Miller Genuine Draft Silver car in Acrylic Case
1:24	Action/RCCA Banks	Miller Genuine Draft
1:24	Action/RCCA Banks	Miller Genuine Draft Silver Anniversary Car
1:24	Press Pass	Miller Silver car
1:24	Racing Champions	Miller Genuine Draft
1:24	Racing Champions	Miller Genuine Draft Hood Open
1:24	Racing Champions	Penske Racing
1:64	Racing Champions	Miller Genuine Draft
1:64	Racing Champions	Penske Racing
1:24	Racing Champions Chrome Banks	Penske Chrome
1:24	Racing Champions Hobby Banks	Penske Hobby
1:24	Racing Champions Hood Open Banks	Miller Genuine Draft Hood Open
1:64	Racing Champions Premier Transporters	Penske
1:64	Racing Champions Premier w/Medallion	Miller Genuine Draft Hood Open In Miller Package

SCALE	MANUFACTURER	SPONSOR
1:24	Action Racing Collectables Banks	Miller Genuine Draft 1990 Grand Prix
1:24	Action Racing Collectables Banks	Miller Lite Texas Motor Speedway
1:24	Action/RCCA	Miller Genuine Draft 1990 Grand Prix
1:24	Action/RCCA	Miller Lite Texas Motor Speedway
1:64	Action/RCCA	Miller Lite
1:64	Action/RCCA	Miller Lite Japan
1:64	Action/RCCA	Miller Lite Texas Motor Speedway
1:24	Action/RCCA Banks	Miller Lite
1:24	Action/RCCA Banks	Miller Lite Japan
1:24	Action/RCCA Elite	Miller Lite
1:24	Action/RCCA Elite	Miller Lite Texas Motor Speedway
1:64	Matchbox White Rose Super Stars	Miller Lite packaged in a bottle
1:64	Matchbox White Rose Transporters	Miller Lite in acrylic case
1:18	Racing Champions	Miller Lite Gold
1:18	Racing Champions	Miller Lite Hobby
1:24	Racing Champions	Miller Lite distributed by Matco
1:24	Racing Champions	Penske
1:64	Racing Champions	Miller Lite Matco
1:64	Racing Champions	Penske Racing
1:24	Racing Champions Banks	Miller Lite Matco
1:24	Racing Champions Banks	Miller Lite Matco Chrome
1:64	Racing Champions Gold	Miller Lite
1:24	Racing Champions Gold Banks	Miller Lite Gold
1:64	Racing Champions Hobby	Miller Lite
1:24	Racing Champions Hobby Banks	Miller Lite Hobby
1:64	Racing Champions Premier w/Medallion	Penske
1:24	Racing Champions Stock Rods	Penske
1:64	Racing Champions Stock Rods	Miller Lite
1:64	Racing Champions Stock Rods	Penske
1:64	Racing Champions Stock Rods	Penske
1:64	Racing Champions Transporters	Penske
1:87	Racing Champions Transporters	Penske
1:24	Revell Club	Miller Lite
1:18	Revell Collection	Miller Lite
1:24	Revell Collection	Miller Lite
1:24	Revell Collection	Miller Lite Japan

SCALE	MANUFACTURER	SPONSOR
1:64	Racing Champions Silver Chase	Miller Genuine Draft
1:64	Racing Champions Transporters	Miller Genuine Draft
1:64	Racing Champions Transporters	Penske
1:64	Racing Champions Transporters	Penske w/ one car or two cars
1:87	Racing Champions Transporters	Penske
1:24	Revell	Penske Motorsports
1:64	Revell	Miller Genuine Draft Promo
1:64	Revell	Miller Genuine Draft Silver car
1:64	Revell	Penske Racing
1:24	Revell Collection	MGD Silver
1:24	Revell Collection	Miller Genuine Draft Silver SuperTruck
1:24	Revell Collection	Miller Genuine Draft SuperTruck
1:24	Revell Collection	Penske
1:64	Revell Collection	Miller
1:64	Revell Collection	Miller Genuine Draft 2 car set
1:64	Revell Collection	Miller Genuine Draft Silver

1997–98

1:24	Winner's Circle	Penske Elvis
1:64	Winner's Circle	Penske Elvis

1997

1:24	Action Racing Collectables	Miller Lite
1:24	Action Racing Collectables	Miller Lite Japan
1:64	Action Racing Collectables	Miller Genuine Draft 1990 Grand Prix
1:64	Action Racing Collectables	Miller Lite
1:64	Action Racing Collectables	Miller Lite Japan
1:64	Action Racing Collectables	Miller Lite Texas Motor Speedway

SCALE	MANUFACTURER	SPONSOR
1:24	Revell Collection	Miller Lite Texas Motor Speedway
1:24	Revell Collection	Miller Suzuka
1:43	Revell Collection	Miller Lite
1:64	Revell Collection	Miller Lite
1:64	Revell Collection	Miller Lite Texas Special
1:24	Revell Hobby	Miller Lite
1:64	Revell Hobby	Miller Lite
1:24	Revell Retail	Penske
1:64	Revell Retail	Penske

1998

SCALE	MANUFACTURER	SPONSOR
1:24	Action Racing Collectables	Adventures of Rusty
1:24	Action Racing Collectables	Miller Lite
1:24	Action Racing Collectables	Miller Lite Elvis
1:24	Action Racing Collectables	Miller Lite TCB
1:64	Action Racing Collectables	Adventures of Rusty
1:64	Action Racing Collectables	Miller Lite
1:64	Action Racing Collectables	Miller Lite Elvis
1:64	Action Racing Collectables	Miller Lite TCB
1:64	Action Racing Collectables	Rusty Wallace/ Jeremy Mayfield on Pit Wall Base
1:24	Action Racing Collectables Banks	Miller Lite
1:24	Action Racing Collectables Banks	Miller Lite Elvis
1:64	Action/RCCA	Adventures of Rusty
1:64	Action/RCCA	Miller Lite
1:64	Action/RCCA	Miller Lite Elvis
1:64	Action/RCCA	Miller Lite TCB
1:24	Action/RCCA Banks	Adventures of Rusty
1:24	Action/RCCA Banks	Miller Lite
1:24	Action/RCCA Banks	Miller Lite Elvis
1:24	Action/RCCA Banks	Miller Lite TCB
1:24	Action/RCCA Elite	Adventures of Rusty
1:24	Action/RCCA Elite	Miller Lite
1:24	Action/RCCA Elite	Miller Lite Elvis
1:32	Action/RCCA Gold	Miller Lite
1:64	Johnny Lighting Stock Car Legends	Gatorade 1984 Grand Prix
1:18	Revell Club	Adventures of Rusty
1:18	Revell Club	Miller Lite Elvis
1:24	Revell Club	Adventures of Rusty
1:24	Revell Club	Miller Lite

SCALE	MANUFACTURER	SPONSOR
1:24	Revell Club	Miller Lite Elvis
1:24	Revell Club	Miller Lite TCB Bank
1:18	Revell Collection	Adventures of Rusty
1:18	Revell Collection	Miller Lite
1:18	Revell Collection	Miller Lite Elvis
1:18	Revell Collection	Miller Lite TCB
1:24	Revell Collection	Adventures of Rusty
1:24	Revell Collection	Miller Lite
1:24	Revell Collection	Miller Lite Elvis
1:24	Revell Collection	Miller Lite TCB
1:43	Revell Collection	Adventures of Rusty
1:43	Revell Collection	Miller Lite Elvis
1:64	Revell Collection	Miller Lite
1:64	Revell Collection	Adventures of Rusty
1:64	Revell Collection	Miller Lite Elvis
1:64	Revell Collection	Miller Lite TCB
1:24	Revell Collection Banks	Miller Lite
1:24	Revell Hobby	Adventures of Rusty
1:24	Revell Hobby	Miller Lite Elvis
1:43	Winner's Circle	Miller Lite Elvis
1:64	Winner's Circle Pit Row	Elvis
1:64	Winner's Circle Pit Row	Rusty

1999

SCALE	MANUFACTURER	SPONSOR
1:24	Action Racing Collectables	Harley-Davidson
1:24	Action Racing Collectables	Miller Texas
1:24	Action Racing Collectables	Miller Lite
1:64	Action Racing Collectables	True to Texas
1:64	Action Racing Collectables	Miller Lite
1:24	Action Racing Collectables Banks	Harley-Davidson
1:24	Action Racing Collectables Banks	Miller Lite
1:24	Action/RCCA Banks	True to Texas
1:24	Revell Club	Miller Lite
1:18	Revell Collection	Miller Lite
1:24	Revell Collection	Miller Lite
1:43	Revell Collection	Miller Lite Harley Davidson
1:64	Revell Collection	Harley-Davidson
1:64	Revell Collection	Miller Lite
1:64	Winner's Circle	Rusty
1:64	Winner's Circle Pit Row	Rusty
1:64	Winner's Circle Speedweeks	Rusty
1:64	Winner's Circle Tech Series	Rusty Wallace

Darrell Waltrip

Hometown:
Franklin, Tenn.

Birthdate:
Feb. 5, 1947

Personal:
Waltrip owns several animals, including multiple dogs, a rabbit, a cat and a couple of registered Tennessee Walking Horses. Waltrip ran track and played basketball in high school, holding the Kentucky state record for the 880-yard dash for several years. He is a big fan of the University of Kentucky basketball team and admires former NFL quarterback Joe Montana. Waltrip says his favorite food is chicken and that if he weren't a Winston Cup driver he'd like to be a trial lawyer.

Hobby:
Should get a big boost from his retirement tour, as the veteran driver has announced that 2000 will be his last season behind the wheel. Waltrip enjoyed similar attention when he celebrated his 25th season as a Winston Cup driver in 1997. Many of his older paint schemes were used on die-cast replicas during his 25th season including a special chrome scheme that was popular with collectors. Waltrip die-cast cars were already on the market before the boom in NASCAR in the 1990s, giving him as many vintage replicas as any driver. Darrell will stay in the spotlight as he moves to the broadcasting booth for 2001.

Career Highlights

- Owns 84 victories (most of modern era), tying him with Bobby Allison for third on all-time win list.
- Three-time Winston Cup champion, winning in 1981, 1982 and 1985.
- Seventh in all-time superspeedway victories with 37 and fourth in all-time Winston Cup poles with 59.
- National Motorsports Press Association's Driver of the Year in 1977, 1981 and 1982.
- Only five-time winner of Coca-Cola 600.
- Won modern-era record eight races from pole in 1981 and tied all-time record of four consecutive wins.
- Won 1989 Daytona 500 in 17th try, his most memorable race.
- Winner of inaugural The Winston in 1985.
- Voted Driver of the Decade for the 1980s.
- In February of 1990, Waltrip became the first Winston Cup driver to win more than $10 million.
- Won NASCAR's Most Popular Driver Award in 1989 and 1990.

127

SCALE	MANUFACTURER	SPONSOR

1991–92

| 1:24 | Racing Champions | Western Auto w/ Fender Stickers |
| 1:24 | Racing Champions | Western Auto w/ Tampo Decals |

1991

| 1:87 | Matchbox White Rose Transporters Super Star Series | Western Auto |

1992–94

1:24	Racing Champions Banks	Tide Orange paint scheme
1:24	Racing Champions Banks	Tide Primer gray car
1:24	Racing Champions Banks	Western Auto

1992–95

| 1:64 | Action/RCCA Transporters | Delco Remy Platinum Series |
| 1:64 | Action/RCCA Transporters | Western Auto RCCA |

1992

1:43	Racing Champions	Western Auto
1:43	Racing Champions	Western Auto Promo
1:64	Racing Champions	Western Auto
1:64	Racing Champions Premier	Western Auto
1:64	Racing Champions Transporters	Western Auto
1:64	Racing Champions Transporters	Western Auto Promo
1:64	Winross Transporters	Western Auto
1:64	Winross Transporters	Western Auto w/ Red paint scheme

1993–94

| 1:87 | Racing Champions Transporters | Western Auto |

1993–95

1:24	Action Racing Collectables	Budweiser 1984 Monte Carlo
1:24	Action Racing Collectables	Mountain Dew
1:64	Action Racing Collectables	Budweiser 1985 Monte Carlo 1994 Platinum Series
1:64	Action Racing Collectables	Gatorade 1980 Olds Platinum Sieries
1:64	Action Racing Collectables	Mountain Dew 1982 Buick 1995 Platinum Series
1:64	Action Racing Collectables	Pepsi Camaro ASA Platinum Series
1:64	Action Racing Collectables	Superflo

SCALE	MANUFACTURER	SPONSOR
		Camaro Platinum Series
1:64	Action Racing Collectables	Tide Camaro Platinum Series
1:64	Action Racing Collectables	Western Auto 1995 Monte Carlo Platinum Series
1:64	Action Racing Collectables	Western Auto AC Racing Promo
1:64	Action Racing Collectables	Western Auto Delco Remy Promo
1:24	Action Racing Collectables Banks	Budweiser 1986 Monte Carlo
1:24	Action Racing Collectables Banks	Gatorade Oldsmobile
1:64	Action/RCCA	Budweiser 1984 Monte Carlo
1:64	Action/RCCA	Gatorade
1:64	Action/RCCA	Superflo Camaro
1:64	Action/RCCA	Western Auto 1994 Lumina Hood Open
1:64	Action/RCCA	Western Auto 1995 Monte Carlo Hood Open
1:64	Action/RCCA	Western Auto Revell Club Only
1:24	Action/RCCA Banks	Budweiser 1986 Monte Carlo

SCALE	MANUFACTURER	SPONSOR
1:24	Action/RCCA Banks	Gatorade Monte Carlo
1:24	Action/RCCA Banks	Mountain Dew
1:24	Revell	Western Auto

1993–98

SCALE	MANUFACTURER	SPONSOR
1:24	Action Dually Trucks	Parts America Chrome Bank
1:18	Ertl	Parts America
1:18	Ertl	Western Auto

1993–99

SCALE	MANUFACTURER	SPONSOR
1:64	Action Dually w/Chaparral Trailer	Parts America Chrome

1993

SCALE	MANUFACTURER	SPONSOR
1:24	Racing Champions	Western Auto
1:43	Racing Champions	Western Auto
1:64	Racing Champions	Western Auto
1:43	Racing Champions Premier	Western Auto
1:64	Racing Champions Transporters	Western Auto
1:64	Racing Champions Transporters	Western Auto Promo

1994

SCALE	MANUFACTURER	SPONSOR
1:64	Ertl White Rose Transporters Past and Present	Western Auto
1:64	Matchbox White Rose Super Stars	Western Auto BX
1:80	Matchbox White Rose Transporters Super Star Series	Western Auto
1:24	Racing Champions	Western Auto
1:64	Racing Champions	Western Auto
1:64	Racing Champions Hobby	Western Auto
1:87	Racing Champions Premier Transporters	Western Auto
1:64	Racing Champions Transporters	Western Auto
1:24	Racing Champions	Western Auto
1:64	Racing Champions	Western Auto
1:64	Racing Champions To the Maxx	Western Auto

1995–96

SCALE	MANUFACTURER	SPONSOR
1:18	Racing Champions	Western Auto

1996

SCALE	MANUFACTURER	SPONSOR
1:24	Action/RCCA	Parts America
1:24	Action/RCCA	Tide
1:64	Action/RCCA	Tide 1988 Monte Carlo

SCALE	MANUFACTURER	SPONSOR
1:24	Action/RCCA Banks	Budweiser 1984 Monte Carlo
1:24	Action/RCCA Banks	Western Auto
1:24	Racing Champions	Parts America
1:64	Racing Champions	Parts America
1:24	Racing Champions Chrome Banks	Parts America Chrome
1:24	Racing Champions Hobby Banks	Parts America Hobby
1:24	Racing Champions Previews	Western Auto
1:64	Racing Champions Previews	Western Auto
1:64	Racing Champions Silver Chase	Parts America
1:18	Racing Champions SuperTrucks	Western Auto
1:64	Racing Champions SuperTrucks	Die Hard
1:64	Racing Champions SuperTrucks	Western Auto
1:64	Racing Champions Transporters	Parts America
1:87	Racing Champions Transporters	Parts America
1:64	Racing Champions Transporters Previews	Western Auto
1:24	Revell	Parts America
1:64	Revell	Parts America
1:24	Revell Collection	Parts America
1:64	Revell Collection	Parts America

1997

SCALE	MANUFACTURER	SPONSOR
1:64	Action Racing Collectables	Parts America 7 Car set
1:24	Action Racing Collectables Banks	Parts America
1:24	Action Racing Collectables Banks	Parts America 7 Car Bank set
1:24	Action/RCCA	Parts America 7 Car set
1:24	Action/RCCA	Parts America Chrome
1:64	Action/RCCA	Parts America 7 Car set
1:64	Action/RCCA	Parts America Chrome
1:24	Action/RCCA Elite	Parts America
1:24	Action/RCCA Elite	Parts America Chrome
1:18	Racing Champions	Parts America Chrome
1:24	Racing Champions	Parts America
1:24	Racing Champions	Parts America Chrome
1:24	Racing Champions	Parts America Chrome Promo

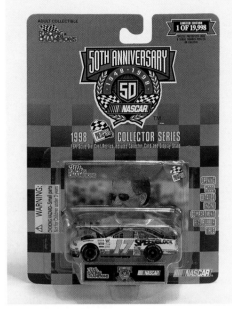

SCALE	MANUFACTURER	SPONSOR
1:64	Racing Champions	Parts America
1:64	Racing Champions	Parts America Chrome
1:64	Racing Champions Premier w/ Medallion	Parts America
1:64	Racing Champions Premier w/ Medallion	Parts America Chrome
1:24	Racing Champions Stock Rods	Parts America
1:64	Racing Champions Stock Rods	Parts America
1:64	Racing Champions Stock Rods	Parts America
1:64	Racing Champions Transporters	Parts America
1:64	Racing Champions Transporters	Parts America w/ one car or two cars
1:87	Racing Champions Transporters	Parts America
1:24	Revell Collection	Parts America
1:24	Revell Hobby	Parts America
1:64	Revell Hobby	Parts America
1:64	Revell Hobby	Parts America 7 Car Set
1:24	Revell Retail	Parts America
1:24	Revell Retail	Parts America 6 Car set

1998

SCALE	MANUFACTURER	SPONSOR
1:24	Action Racing Collectables	Flock Special
1:24	Action Racing Collectables	Pennzoil
1:64	Action Racing Collectables	Flock Speical
1:64	Action Racing Collectables	Pennzoil
1:24	Action Racing Collectables Banks	Pennzoil
1:24	Action Racing Collectables Banks	Tim Flock Special
1:64	Action/RCCA	Pennzoil
1:64	Action/RCCA	Tim Flock Special

SCALE	MANUFACTURER	SPONSOR
1:24	Action/RCCA Banks	Flock Special
1:24	Action/RCCA Banks	Pennzoil
1:24	Action/RCCA Elite	Pennzoil
1:24	Action/RCCA Elite	Tim Flock Special
1:64	Johnny Lighting Stock Car Legends	Gatorade 1979 Monte Carlo
1:64	Johnny Lighting Stock Car Legends	Pepsi 1983 Monte Carlo
1:24	Racing Champions	Darrell Waltrip Tim Flock Special
1:24	Racing Champions	Builders' Square
1:64	Racing Champions	Flock Special
1:64	Racing Champions	Speedblock
1:24	Racing Champions Gold	Builders' Square
1:24	Racing Champions Gold	Flock Special
1:24	Racing Champions Gold Hood Open	Builders' Square
1:64	Racing Champions Gold w/ Medallion	Flock Special
1:64	Racing Champions Press Pass Series	Builders Square
1:64	Racing Champions Toys 'R Us Gold	Builders' Square
1:64	Racing Champions Toys 'R Us Gold	Flock Special

1999

SCALE	MANUFACTURER	SPONSOR
1:64	Hot Wheels Collector Edition	Big-K
1:64	Hot Wheels Collector Edition/Track Edition	Big K
1:64	Hot Wheels Transporters	Big-K
1:24	Racing Champions	Big K
1:64	Racing Champions	Big K
1:24	Racing Champions Gold	Big K
1:64	Racing Champions Gold w/ Medallion	Big K
1:64	Racing Champions Press Pass Series	Big K
1:64	Racing Champions Stock Rods	Big K
1:64	Racing Champions Stock Rods	Big K
1:64	Racing Champions Stock Rods	Big K Gold
1:64	Racing Champions Transporters Gold	Big K
1:24	Revell Collection	Big K

2000

SCALE	MANUFACTURER	SPONSOR
1:64	Hot Wheels Crew's Choice	Route 66

Racing Die-Cast
Price Guide

How To Use This Price Guide

Only A Guide

Beckett listings are to be used only as a guide. The prices do not represent an offer to buy or sell on the part of any party.

How Pieces Are Listed

This die-cast price guide is organized by manufacturer, scale, year, car number, driver and sponsor. Banks are listed under the appropriate manufacturer.

Under each manufacturer the primary grouping is scale. Die-cast listings are by scale in order from largest to smallest. For example, RACING CHAMPIONS 1:24, RACING CHAMPIONS 1:43, etc. Within each grouping, the die casts are listed in chronological order.

Sample of Scale Order

The smaller the bottom number of the fraction, the larger the piece. (From Largest to Smallest) Cars: 1/18, 1/24, 1/43, 1/64.

CONDITION GUIDE

Most die-cast products are sold in their original packaging. Due to variations and descriptions, packaging is sometimes as important as the die-cast piece itself.

Mint prices listed are for unblemished die-cast products in their original, undamaged packaging.

Here are some guidelines to determine conditions:

Mint (MT) — A piece and package that has no blemishes is considered Mint. The item looks like it just rolled off the manufacturing line. Die casts are valued in this guide in Mint.

Near Mint (NRMT) — This is a piece with one very minor flaw. Any one of the following would lower a Mint piece to NRMT: decals on the piece being slightly smudged, barely noticeable scratches on the packaging, a small bend in the packaging. NRMT die casts are also featured in this guide.

Excellent (EX) — This is a piece with noticeable defects or wear. Any of the following would be characteristics of an EX die-cast piece: wrinkled decals, paint smudges, packaging with easily noticeable scratches or wear. EX die casts are valued at 45–75% of this guide's Mint price.

Good (G) — This is a piece with major defects or wear. All of the following would lower a piece to G: Faded decals, a loose wheel, scratches on the die cast, packaging with several creases. G die casts are valued at 20–40% of this guide's Mint price.

Poor (P) — This is a piece that has been well-used or abused. A piece in this condition usually has been taken out of the packaging and been played with. Characteristics of P are: scratched off decals, dents in the die cast, scratches all over the die cast, unattractive and mutilated boxes. P die casts are valued at 5–15% of this guide's Mint price.

Die casts without original packaging and in Mint condition are valued at 25–50% of this guide.

1993-99 Action Racing Collectables Pit Wagon Banks 1:16

These 1:16 scale replicas of Pit Wagons were produced by Action Racing Collectibles. ARC began producing them in 1994 and they are a coin bank. The teams in Winston Cup racing have these Pit Wagons in which they tote from the garage area to the pits.

Car / Driver / Sponsor	MINT	NRMT
2 Rusty Wallace Ford Motorsports	40.00	18.00
2 Rusty Wallace Miller Genuine Draft	60.00	27.00
2 Rusty Wallace Miller Lite 1997	60.00	27.00
2 Rusty Wallace Miller Lite 1998	60.00	27.00
3 Dale Earnhardt Goodwrench	70.00	32.00
3 Dale Earnhardt Goodwrench 1996	65.00	29.00
3 Dale Earnhardt Goodwrench 7-Time Champion	70.00	32.00
3 Dale Earnhardt Wheaties	70.00	32.00
3 Dale Earnhardt Goodwrench Plus Bass Pro	70.00	32.00
3 Dale Earnhardt Goodwrench '99	60.00	27.00
3 Dale Earnhardt Goodwrench 25th	60.00	27.00
11 Bill Elliott Budweiser	40.00	18.00
16 Ted Musgrave Family Channel	30.00	13.50
18 Dale Jarrett Interstate Batteries	30.00	13.50
24 Jeff Gordon DuPont	100.00	45.00
24 Jeff Gordon DuPont '96	65.00	29.00
24 Jeff Gordon Lost World	60.00	27.00
28 Davey Allison Havoline	50.00	22.00
28 Davey Allison Havoline Mac Tools	50.00	22.00
28 Ernie Irvan Havoline	45.00	20.00
28 Ernie Irvan Mac Tools	35.00	16.00
28 Kenny Irwin Havoline Joker	60.00	27.00
30 Michael Waltrip Pennzoil	30.00	13.50
41 Joe Nemechek Meineke	30.00	13.50
42 Kyle Petty Mello Yello	30.00	13.50
51 Neil Bonnett Country Time	60.00	27.00
88 Dale Jarrett Quality Care Batman	60.00	27.00
94 Bill Elliott Mac Tonight	60.00	27.00
94 Bill Elliott McDonald's	35.00	16.00

1998-99 Action Racing Collectables 1:18

These 1:18 scale cars were distributed by Action through their distributor network.

Car / Driver / Sponsor	MINT	NRMT
1 Dale Earnhardt Jr. Coke	125.00	55.00

Car / Driver / Sponsor	MINT	NRMT
1 Steve Park Pennzoil	80.00	36.00
1 Steve Park Pennzoil Shark	90.00	40.00
2 Rusty Wallace Miller Lite	90.00	40.00

3 Dale Earnhardt Goowrench Silver	130.00	57.50

3 Dale Earnhardt Wheaties	100.00	45.00
3 Dale Earnhardt Goodwrench Plus Daytona	100.00	45.00
3 Dale Earnhardt Bass Pro	125.00	55.00
3 Dale Earnhardt Coke	100.00	45.00

3 Dale Earnhardt Goodwrench 1999	100.00	45.00
3 Dale Earnhardt GM Goodwrench Sign	100.00	45.00
3 Dale Earnhardt Wrangler '99	110.00	50.00

3 Dale Earnhardt Jr. AC Delco	110.00	50.00

Car / Driver / Sponsor	MINT	NRMT
3 Dale Earnhardt Jr. AC Delco Superman	125.00	55.00
5 Terry Labonte K-Sentials	100.00	45.00
5 Terry Labonte NASCAR Racers	100.00	45.00
8 Dale Earnhardt Jr. Budweiser	125.00	55.00
10 Ricky Rudd Tide Kid's Car	150.00	70.00
18 Bobby Labonte NASCAR Racers	120.00	55.00

20 Tony Stewart Home Depot	160.00	70.00
20 Tony Stewart Habitat for Humanity	125.00	55.00
24 Jeff Gordon Chromalusion	160.00	70.00
24 Jeff Gordon DuPont '99	120.00	55.00
24 Jeff Gordon Superman	125.00	55.00
24 Jeff Gordon NASCAR Racers	125.00	55.00
24 Jeff Gordon Pepsi	150.00	70.00
24 Jeff Gordon Star Wars	125.00	55.00
27 Casey Atwood Castrol	125.00	55.00

31 Dale Earnhardt Jr. Wrangler	125.00	55.00

31 Dale Earnhardt Jr. Sikkens Blue	125.00	55.00
31 Dale Earnhardt Jr. Sikkens White	125.00	55.00
36 Ernie Irvan M&M's Countdown	120.00	55.00

CAR / DRIVER / SPONSOR	MINT	NRMT
36 Ernie Irvan M&M's	120.00	55.00
36 Ernie Irvan M&M's Millennium	100.00	45.00
88 Dale Jarrett Quality Care	125.00	55.00

2000 Action Racing Collectables 1:18

These 1:18 scale cars were distributed by Action through their distributor network.

CAR / DRIVER / SPONSOR	MINT	NRMT
3 Dale Earnhardt Goodwrench	125.00	55.00
3 Dale Earnhardt Taz No Bull	125.00	55.00

CAR / DRIVER / SPONSOR	MINT	NRMT
20 Tony Stewart Home Depot	125.00	55.00

1993-95 Action Racing Collectables 1:24

These 1:24 scale replicas were produced by Action Racing Collectables. Most pieces were packaged in a blue box and have the Action Racing Collectables logo or the Racing Collectibles Inc. logo on the box.

CAR / DRIVER / SPONSOR	MINT	NRMT
1 Rick Mast Skoal Acrylic Case	60.00	27.00
1 Winston Show Car	60.00	27.00
2 Ricky Craven DuPont	90.00	40.00
2 Dale Earnhardt Wrangler 1981 Pontiac	300.00	135.00
Feb-43 Dale Earnhardt Richard Petty 7 and 7 Special	200.00	90.00
3 Dale Earnhardt Wrangler 1985 Monte Carlo	250.00	110.00
3 Dale Earnhardt Goodwrench 1988 Monte Carlo	400.00	180.00
3 Dale Earnhardt Goodwrench 1995 Monte Carlo Black Windows Promo	100.00	45.00

CAR / DRIVER / SPONSOR	MINT	NRMT
3 Dale Earnhardt Goodwrench 1995 Monte Carlo Brickyard Special	100.00	45.00
3 Dale Earnhardt Goodwrench 1995 Monte Carlo Promo	100.00	45.00

CAR / DRIVER / SPONSOR	MINT	NRMT
3 Dale Earnhardt Wrangler 1981 Pontiac	250.00	110.00

CAR / DRIVER / SPONSOR	MINT	NRMT
3 Dale Earnhardt Wrangler 1987 Monte Carlo	400.00	180.00
3 Jeff Green Goodwrench	45.00	20.00
3 Richard Childress Black Gold	45.00	20.00
24-Mar Dale Earnhardt Jeff Gordon Brickyard Special	125.00	55.00
4 Sterling Marlin Kodak	40.00	18.00
6 Mark Martin Valvoline 1995 Brickyard Special	125.00	55.00
6 Mark Martin Valvoline	90.00	40.00
7 Geoff Bodine Exide	30.00	13.50
7 Alan Kulwicki Hooter's	100.00	45.00
7 Alan Kulwicki Zerex	100.00	45.00
11 Bill Elliott Budweiser	160.00	70.00
11 Darrell Waltrip Budweiser 1984 Monte Carlo	75.00	34.00
11 Darrell Waltrip Mountain Dew	80.00	36.00
12 Neil Bonnett Budweiser 1984 Monte Carlo	75.00	34.00

CAR / DRIVER / SPONSOR	MINT	NRMT
15 Dale Earnhardt Wrangler 1983 Thunderbird	200.00	90.00

CAR / DRIVER / SPONSOR	MINT	NRMT
15 Lake Speed Quality Care	20.00	9.00
16 Ted Musgrave Primestar	30.00	13.50
28 Ernie Irvan Havoline	60.00	27.00
41 Joe Nemechek Meineke	30.00	13.50
42 Kyle Petty Coors Light	60.00	27.00
42 Kyle Petty Mello Yello	90.00	40.00
94 Bill Elliott McDonald's	45.00	20.00
98 Derrike Cope Fingerhut	25.00	11.00

1996 Action Racing Collectables 1:24

These 1:24 scale replicas were produced by Action Racing Collectables. Most pieces were packaged in a blue box and have the Action Racing Collectibles logo or the Racing Collectibles Inc. logo on the box.

CAR / DRIVER / SPONSOR	MINT	NRMT
2 Mark Martin Miller ASA '85	60.00	27.00
2 Rusty Wallace Miller Genuine Draft	120.00	55.00
2 Rusty Wallace Miller Genuine Draft Silver Anniversary	80.00	36.00

CAR / DRIVER / SPONSOR	MINT	NRMT
3 Dale Earnhardt AC-Delco	60.00	27.00
3 Dale Earnhardt Goodwrench 1996 Monte Carlo	60.00	27.00
3 Dale Earnhardt Olympic Car	60.00	27.00
3 Dale Earnhardt Olympic Food City Promo	100.00	45.00
3 Dale Earnhardt Olympic Goodwrench Box	80.00	36.00

CAR / DRIVER / SPONSOR	MINT	NRMT
3 Dale Earnhardt Olympic Green Box	150.00	70.00
3 Dale Earnhardt Olympic Green Box No Trademark on Hood of Car	100.00	45.00
3 Dale Earnhardt Olympic with Mom-n-Pop's decal	100.00	45.00
3 Dale Earnhardt Olympic Sports Image	60.00	27.00

CAR / DRIVER / SPONSOR	MINT	NRMT
10 Ricky Rudd Tide	60.00	27.00
14 Jeff Green Racing For Kids	50.00	22.00
15 Dale Earnhardt Wrangler	125.00	55.00
18 Bobby Labonte Interstate Batteries 1996	80.00	36.00
21 Michael Waltrip Citgo	50.00	22.00
29 No Driver Association Scooby-Doo	60.00	27.00
31 Mike Skinner Snap-On	120.00	55.00
31 Mike Skinner Snap-On Promo	125.00	55.00
42 Kyle Petty Coors Light 1996	60.00	27.00
43 Bobby Hamilton STP Silver car with Clear Windows	100.00	45.00
43 Bobby Hamilton 5 Car set with Clear Windows	300.00	135.00
57 Jason Keller Halloween Havoc	50.00	22.00
88 Ernie Irvan Havoline	50.00	22.00
88 Dale Jarrett Quality Care	60.00	27.00
98 Jeremy Mayfield RCA	60.00	27.00

1997 Action Racing Collectables 1:24

These 1:24 scale replicas were produced by Action Racing Collectibles. Most pieces were packaged in a blue box and have the Action Racing Collectibles logo or the Racing Collectibles Inc. logo on the box.

CAR / DRIVER / SPONSOR	MINT	NRMT
2 Rusty Wallace Miller Lite	60.00	27.00
2 Rusty Wallace Miller Lite Japan	60.00	27.00
3 Dale Earnhardt Goodwrench Brickyard Special	60.00	27.00
3 Dale Earnhardt Wheaties	150.00	70.00
3 Dale Earnhardt Wheaties Mail-In	60.00	27.00
3 Dale Earnhardt Wheaties Snap-On	200.00	90.00
3 Dale Earnhardt Wheaties Sports Image	80.00	36.00
4 Sterling Marlin Kodak Mac Tools	60.00	27.00
6 Mark Martin Valvoline	60.00	27.00
6 Mark Martin Valvoline Mac Tools	75.00	34.00
8 Hut Stricklin Circuit City	40.00	18.00
10 Phil Parsons Channellock	40.00	18.00
11 Brett Bodine Close Call	40.00	18.00

CAR / DRIVER / SPONSOR	MINT	NRMT
12 Kenny Wallace Gray Bar	45.00	20.00
14 Steve Park Burger King	120.00	55.00

CAR / DRIVER / SPONSOR	MINT	NRMT
16 Ted Musgrave Primestar	35.00	16.00
18 Bobby Labonte Interstate Batteries	60.00	27.00
18 Bobby Labonte Interstate Batteries Hall of Fame	80.00	36.00
18 Bobby Labonte Interstate Batteries Mac Tools	75.00	34.00
22 Ward Burton MBNA	45.00	20.00
23 Jimmy Spencer Camel	90.00	40.00
24 Jeff Gordon DuPont	60.00	27.00
24 Jeff Gordon DuPont Brickyard Special	60.00	27.00
24 Jeff Gordon DuPont Mac Tools	75.00	34.00
24 Jeff Gordon DuPont Premier Promo	175.00	80.00
24 Jeff Gordon DuPont Premier Sports Image	100.00	45.00
24 Jeff Gordon Lost World Sports Image	75.00	34.00
27 Kenny Irwin Action	70.00	32.00
27 Kenny Irwin Tonka	55.00	25.00
29 Jeff Green Tom & Jerry	55.00	25.00
30 Jonny Benson Pennzoil	35.00	16.00
31 Mike Skinner Lowe's	55.00	25.00
37 Mike Green Timber Wolf	45.00	20.00

CAR / DRIVER / SPONSOR	MINT	NRMT
42 Joe Nemechek Bell South	35.00	16.00

CAR / DRIVER / SPONSOR	MINT	NRMT
46 Wally Dallenbach First Union	30.00	13.50
75 Rick Mast Remington Camo	35.00	16.00

CAR / DRIVER / SPONSOR	MINT	NRMT
75 Rick Mast Remington	30.00	13.50
88 Dale Jarrett Quality Care	60.00	27.00
88 Dale Jarrett Quality Care Brickyard Special	70.00	32.00
88 Dale Jarrett Quality Care Mac Tools	65.00	29.00
94 Bill Elliott Mac Tonight	60.00	27.00
99 Jeff Burton Exide	50.00	22.00
00 Buckshot Jones Aqua Fresh	55.00	25.00

1998 Action Racing Collectables 1:24

These 1:24 scale replicas were produced by Action Racing Collectibles. Most pieces were packaged in a blue box and have the Action Racing Collectibles logo or the Racing Collectibles Inc. logo on the box.

CAR / DRIVER / SPONSOR	MINT	NRMT
1 Dale Earnhardt Jr. Coke	70.00	32.00
1 Darrell Waltrip Pennzoil	90.00	40.00
1 Jeff Gordon Baby Ruth	80.00	36.00

CAR / DRIVER / SPONSOR	MINT	NRMT
1 Steve Park Pennzoil	120.00	55.00
1 Steve Park Pennzoil Indy	70.00	32.00
K2 D.Earnhardt/Dayvault's		
K2 Dale Earnhardt Dayvault's	90.00	40.00

2 Rusty Wallace Miller Lite TCB	55.00	25.00
2 Rusty Wallace Adventures of Rusty	60.00	27.00
2 Rusty Wallace Miller Lite	55.00	25.00
2 Rusty Wallace Miller Lite Elvis	55.00	25.00
3 Dale Earnhardt Goodwrench Plus	70.00	32.00

3 Dale Earnhardt Goodwrench Plus Bass Pro	90.00	40.00
3 Dale Earnhardt Goodwrench Plus Daytona	70.00	32.00

3 Dale Earnhardt Coke	65.00	29.00

CAR / DRIVER / SPONSOR	MINT	NRMT
3 Dale Earnhardt Jr. AC Delco	225.00	100.00
4 Bobby Hamilton Kodak	40.00	18.00
5 Terry Labonte Blasted Fruit Loops	90.00	40.00
5 Terry Labonte Kellogg's	70.00	32.00
5 Terry Labonte Kellogg's Corny	75.00	34.00

5 Terry Labonte Kellogg's Ironman	90.00	40.00

8 Dale Earnhardt 10,000 RPM '78 Dodge	70.00	32.00

8 Hut Stricklin Circuit City	35.00	16.00
9 Jerry Nadeau Power Puff	200.00	90.00
9 Jerry Nadeau Zombie Island	60.00	27.00
9 Lake Speed Birthday Cake	55.00	25.00
9 Lake Speed Huckleberry Hound	55.00	25.00

CAR / DRIVER / SPONSOR	MINT	NRMT
10 Ricky Rudd Tide Give Kids the World	70.00	32.00
10 Ricky Rudd Tide	60.00	27.00
12 Jeremy Mayfield Mobil 1	65.00	29.00
12 Jimmy Spencer Zippo	175.00	80.00
14 Patty Moise Rhodes	60.00	27.00
18 Bobby Labonte Interstate Batteries	65.00	29.00

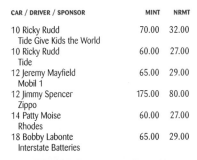

18 Bobby Labonte Interstate Batteries Hot Rod	70.00	32.00

18 Bobby Labonte Interstate Batteries Small Soldiers	65.00	29.00
21 Michael Waltrip Citgo	35.00	16.00

21 Michael Waltrip Citgo Woody	60.00	27.00

22 Ward Burton MBNA	55.00	25.00

CAR / DRIVER / SPONSOR	MINT	NRMT
23 Jimmy Spencer No Bull	100.00	45.00
24 Jeff Gordon DuPont	70.00	32.00
24 Jeff Gordon DuPont Brickyard Winner	80.00	36.00

24 Jeff Gordon DuPont Chromalusion	110.00	50.00
24 Jeff Gordon DuPont Chromalusion Mac Tools	120.00	55.00
24 Jeff Gordon DuPont Mac Tools	100.00	45.00

24 Jeff Gordon DuPont No Bull	80.00	36.00

28 Kenny Irwin Havoline	50.00	22.00

28 Kenny Irwin Havoline Joker	60.00	27.00

CAR / DRIVER / SPONSOR	MINT	NRMT
30 Derrike Cope Gumout	35.00	16.00
31 Dale Earnhardt Jr. Sikkens	150.00	70.00

31 Dale Earnhardt Jr. Wrangler	200.00	90.00
31 Mike Skinner Lowe's	50.00	22.00
31 Mike Skinner Lowe's Special Olympics	60.00	27.00

32 Dale Jarrett White Rain	60.00	27.00
33 Tim Fedewa Kleenex	65.00	29.00
33 Ken Schrader Skoal	65.00	29.00
34 Mike McLaughlin Goulds	90.00	40.00
35 Todd Bodine Tabasco	65.00	29.00

35 Todd Bodine Tabasco Red	65.00	29.00
36 Ernie Irvan M&M's	120.00	55.00

CAR / DRIVER / SPONSOR	MINT	NRMT
36 Ernie Irvan Skittles	60.00	27.00
36 Ernie Irvan Wildberry Skittles	70.00	32.00

40 Sterling Marlin Coors Light	70.00	32.00
41 Steve Grissom Kodiak	70.00	32.00

42 Joe Nemechek BellSouth	50.00	22.00

42 Marty Robbins 1974 Dodge	50.00	22.00

44 Tony Stewart Shell	80.00	36.00

CAR / DRIVER / SPONSOR	MINT	NRMT
44 Tony Stewart Shell Small Soldiers	80.00	36.00
50 Ricky Craven Budweiser	70.00	32.00
50 No Driver Association Bud Louie	90.00	40.00
72 Mike Dillon Detroit Gasket	50.00	22.00
81 Kenny Wallace Square D	45.00	20.00
81 Kenny Wallace Square D Lightning	60.00	27.00

88 Dale Jarrett Quality Care	70.00	32.00

88 Dale Jarrett Quality Care Batman	70.00	32.00

90 Dick Trickle Heilig-Meyers	65.00	29.00

96 David Green Caterpillar	50.00	22.00
98 Greg Sacks Thorn Apple Valley	50.00	22.00
98 Rich Bickle Thorn Apple Valley Go Grill Crazy	55.00	25.00

CAR / DRIVER / SPONSOR	MINT	NRMT
300 Darrell Waltrip Flock Special	80.00	36.00
00 Buckshot Jones Alka Seltzer	70.00	32.00

1999 Action Racing Collectables 1:24

ALCOHOL/TOBACCO CARS ON PIT WALL BASE

1 Jeff Gordon Carolina Ford	80.00	36.00

1 Steve Park Pennzoil	70.00	32.00
2 Rusty Wallace Miller Lite	70.00	32.00
2 Rusty Wallace Miller Texas	70.00	32.00

2 Rusty Wallace Harley-Davidson	70.00	32.00

2 Rusty Wallace Miller Lite Last Lap	75.00	34.00

3 Dale Earnhardt Goodwrench	75.00	34.00

CAR / DRIVER / SPONSOR	MINT	NRMT

3 Dale Earnhardt Goodwrench 25th Anniversary	75.00	34.00

3 Dale Earnhardt GM Goodwrench Sign	75.00	34.00

3 Dale Earnhardt Wrangler	100.00	45.00

3 Dale Earnhardt GM Goodwrench Last Lap	80.00	36.00

3 Dale Earnhardt Jr. AC Delco	90.00	40.00

CAR / DRIVER / SPONSOR	MINT	NRMT
3 Dale Earnhardt Jr. AC Delco Last Lap	100.00	45.00
3 Dale Earnhardt Jr. Superman	120.00	55.00
4 Bobby Hamilton Kodak Advantix	70.00	32.00

4 Jeff Purvis Lance Snacks	70.00	32.00
5 Terry Labonte Kellogg's	70.00	32.00
5 Terry Labonte K-Sentials	75.00	34.00
5 Terry Labonte Rice Krispies	75.00	34.00

5 Terry Labonte NASCAR Racers	80.00	36.00

8 Dale Earnhardt Jr. Budweiser	125.00	55.00

8 Dale Earnhardt Jr. Bud Track Cars	120.00	55.00

9 Jerry Nadeau Dexter's laboratory	70.00	32.00

9 Jerry Nadeau Jetsons	70.00	32.00
10 Ricky Rudd Tide	60.00	27.00

10 Ricky Rudd Tide Kids Car	70.00	32.00

11 Dale Jarrett Rayovac	70.00	32.00
11 Dale Jarrett Green Bay	75.00	34.00
12 Jeremy Mayfield Mobil 1	70.00	32.00

12 Jeremy Mayfield Mobil 1 Kentucky Derby	80.00	36.00

15 Ken Schrader Oakwood Homes	60.00	27.00
16 Ron Hornaday NAPA	100.00	45.00
17 Matt Kenseth DeWalt	150.00	70.00

18 Bobby Labonte Interstate Batteries	70.00	32.00

18 Bobby Labonte NASCAR Racers	75.00	34.00

18 Bobby Labonte MBNA	75.00	34.00
19 Mike Skinner Yellow Freight	100.00	45.00
20 Tony Stewart Home Depot	200.00	90.00
20 Tony Stewart Home Depot BW	200.00	90.00

Car / Driver / Sponsor	Mint	NRMT
20 Tony Stewart Habitat for Humanity	80.00	36.00

Car / Driver / Sponsor	Mint	NRMT
21 Elliott Sadler Citgo	60.00	27.00
22 Ward Burton Caterpillar	70.00	32.00
22 Ward Burton Caterpillar Mac Tools	80.00	36.00
23 Jimmy Spencer No Bull	70.00	32.00
23 Jimmy Spencer Winston Lights	80.00	36.00

Car / Driver / Sponsor	Mint	NRMT
24 Jeff Gordon Dupont	70.00	32.00

Car / Driver / Sponsor	Mint	NRMT
24 Jeff Gordon Superman	90.00	40.00
24 Jeff Gordon NASCAR Racers	75.00	34.00

Car / Driver / Sponsor	Mint	NRMT
24 Jeff Gordon Pepsi	70.00	32.00
24 Jeff Gordon Pepsi Star Wars	80.00	36.00
25 Wally Dallenbach Budweiser	70.00	32.00

Car / Driver / Sponsor	Mint	NRMT
27 Casey Atwood Castrol	100.00	45.00
27 Casey Atwood Castrol Last Lap	75.00	34.00
28 Kenny Irwin Havoline	60.00	27.00

Car / Driver / Sponsor	Mint	NRMT
30 Dale Earnhardt Army '76 Malibu	80.00	36.00
30 Darrike Cope Jimmy Dean	60.00	27.00

Car / Driver / Sponsor	Mint	NRMT
31 Dale Earnhardt Jr. Gargoyles 1997 Monte Carlo	100.00	45.00

Car / Driver / Sponsor	Mint	NRMT
31 Mike Skinner Lowe's	60.00	27.00

Car / Driver / Sponsor	Mint	NRMT
31 Dale Earnhardt Jr. Sikkens 1997 Monte Carlo White	100.00	45.00

Car / Driver / Sponsor	Mint	NRMT
32 Jeff Green Kleenex 75th	60.00	27.00

Car / Driver / Sponsor	Mint	NRMT
33 Ken Schrader Skoal	80.00	36.00
36 Ernie Irvan M&M's	60.00	27.00
36 Ernie Irvan Pedigree	70.00	32.00
36 Ernie Irvan Crispy M&M's	100.00	45.00
36 Ernie Irvan M&M's Countdown	90.00	40.00

CAR / DRIVER / SPONSOR	MINT	NRMT
36 Ernie Irvan M&M's Millennium	70.00	32.00
36 Tim Fedewa Stanley	60.00	27.00

37 Kevin Grubb Timber Wolf	70.00	32.00

40 Sterling Marlin Coors	70.00	32.00
40 Sterling Marlin John Wayne	80.00	36.00
40 Sterling Marlin Brooks & Dunn	70.00	32.00

40 Kerry Earnhardt Channellock	60.00	27.00
40 Coca-Cola 600 '99	60.00	27.00
44 Justin Labonte Slim Jim	70.00	32.00

45 Rich Bickle 10-10-345	70.00	32.00
50 Mark Green Dr Pepper	60.00	27.00

CAR / DRIVER / SPONSOR	MINT	NRMT

55 Kenny Wallace Square D	60.00	27.00

55 Kenny Wallace NASCAR Racers	70.00	32.00

59 Mike Dillion Kingsford	60.00	27.00
66 Darrell Waltrip Big K	70.00	32.00

66 Darrell Waltrip Bik K Victory Tour 2000	70.00	32.00
71 David Marcis RealTree	70.00	32.00

77 Dale Earnhardt Hy-Gain '76	80.00	36.00

CAR / DRIVER / SPONSOR	MINT	NRMT
88 Dale Jarrett Quality Care	60.00	27.00
88 Dale Jarrett Quality Care White	70.00	32.00
88 Dale Jarrett Quality Care Last Lap	75.00	34.00

99 Kevin LePage Red Man	70.00	32.00
00 Buckshot Jones Crown Fiber	60.00	27.00

0 Larry Pearson Cheez-it	60.00	27.00

2000 Action Racing Collectables 1:24

These 1:24 scale replicas were produced by Action Racing Collectibles. Most pieces were packaged in a blue box and have the Action Racing Collectibles logo or the Racing Collectibles Inc. logo on the box.

1 Randy LaJoie Bob Evans	60.00	27.00
3 Dale Earnhardt Goodwrench	90.00	40.00

3 Dale Earnhardt GW Taz	90.00	40.00
3 Ron Hornaday NAPA	70.00	32.00
4 Mark Martin Jim Magill '83 Monte Carlo	80.00	36.00

CAR / DRIVER / SPONSOR	MINT	NRMT
6 Mark Martin Jim Magill '83 Monte Carlo	80.00	36.00
8 Dale Earnhardt Jr. Budweiser	100.00	45.00
18 Bobby Labonte Interstate Batteries	80.00	36.00

	MINT	NRMT
20 Tony Stewart Home Depot	90.00	40.00
24 Jeff Gordon DuPont	80.00	36.00
31 Mike Skinner Lowe's	70.00	32.00
55 Kenny Wallace Square D	60.00	27.00

	MINT	NRMT
1 Mark Martin Activision '83 Monte Carlo	80.00	36.00

1993-95 Action Racing Collectables Banks 1:24

These cars were produced by Action Racing Collectibles. Each car has a slot in the back window for a coin bank. Most banks have blacked in windows. This is the easiest way to tell banks apart from a regular car.

	MINT	NRMT
2 Mark Martin Miller 1984 ASA	50.00	22.00
2 Rusty Wallace Ford Motorsports	175.00	80.00
2 Rusty Wallace Miller Geniune Draft	125.00	55.00
3 Dale Earnhardt Goodwrench 1994 Lumina	200.00	90.00
3 Dale Earnhardt Goodwrench 1995 Monte Carlo with headlights	150.00	70.00

CAR / DRIVER / SPONSOR	MINT	NRMT
3 Dale Earnhardt Goodwrench 1995 Monte Carlo without headlights	175.00	80.00
3 Dale Earnhardt Goodwrench 1995 Monte Carlo Sports Image	50.00	22.00
3 Dale Earnhardt Goodwrench Silver Car Black Wheels	350.00	160.00
3 Dale Earnhardt Goodwrench Silver Car Red Wheels	350.00	160.00
3 Dale Earnhardt Wrangler 1984 Monte Carlo	300.00	135.00
5 Terry Labonte Kellogg's	400.00	180.00
6 Mark Martin Folgers	200.00	90.00
6 Mark Martin Valvoline 1995	50.00	22.00
7 Alan Kulwicki Hooters AK Racing	100.00	45.00
8 Kenny Wallace Red Dog Beer	50.00	22.00
11 Bill Elliott Budweiser	90.00	40.00
11 Darrell Waltrip Budweiser 1986 Monte Carlo	90.00	40.00
12 Neil Bonnett Budweiser 1986 Monte Carlo	100.00	45.00
16 Ted Musgrave Family Channel	200.00	90.00
21 Buddy Baker Valvoline	60.00	27.00
21 Neil Bonnett Hodgdon	45.00	20.00
21 David Pearson Chattanooga Chew	60.00	27.00
22 Bobby Allison Miller Beer Acrylic Case	50.00	22.00
24 Jeff Gordon DuPont 1995 Champion	50.00	22.00
24 Jeff Gordon DuPont 1995 Monte Carlo	175.00	80.00
25 Tim Richmond Folgers Monte Carlo Fastback	50.00	22.00
25 Ken Schrader Budweiser	50.00	22.00
27 Rusty Wallace Kodiak	125.00	55.00
28 Ernie Irvan Havoline Employee Special	175.00	80.00
28 Ernie Irvan Havoline Retail Special	35.00	16.00
28 Dale Jarrett Havoline	60.00	27.00
35 Alan Kulwicki Quincy's Steakhouse	90.00	40.00
51 Neil Bonnett Country Time	110.00	50.00
75 Buddy Baker Valvoline	60.00	27.00
88 Darrell Waltrip Gatorade Oldsmobile	100.00	45.00
94 Bill Elliott McDonald's	50.00	22.00
94 Bill Elliott McDonald's Thunderbat	120.00	55.00
95 David Green Busch Beer	50.00	22.00

1996 Action Racing Collectables Banks 1:24

These cars were produced by Action Racing Collectibles. Each car has a slot in the back window for a coin bank. Most banks have blacked in windows. This is the easiest way to tell banks apart from a regular car.

CAR / DRIVER / SPONSOR	MINT	NRMT
2 Mark Martin Miller 1985 ASA	60.00	27.00
2 Rusty Wallace Miller Genuine Draft 1996	70.00	32.00
3 Richard Childress CRC Chemical	50.00	22.00
3 Dale Earnhardt Olympic	80.00	36.00
5 Terry Labonte Kellogg's Silver Car	150.00	70.00
5 Terry Labonte Kellogg's Japan	80.00	36.00
6 Mark Martin Valvoline 1996	60.00	27.00
7 Geoff Bodine QVC	50.00	22.00
10 Ricky Rudd Tide 1996	60.00	27.00
11 Brett Bodine Lowe's	40.00	18.00
21 Michael Waltrip Citgo Star Trek	50.00	22.00
24 Jeff Gordon DuPont 1996 Monte Carlo with Quaker State decal	60.00	27.00
29 Steve Grissom Cartoon Network	50.00	22.00
29 Steve Grissom WCW	50.00	22.00
29 No Driver Association Scooby-Doo	50.00	22.00
42 Robby Gordon Tonka	50.00	22.00
42 Kyle Petty Coors Light Black Paint Scheme	60.00	27.00
43 Bobby Hamilton STP Silver 25th Anniversary	300.00	135.00
43 Bobby Hamilton STP Silver car	100.00	45.00
43 Bobby Hamilton STP 5 car set	300.00	135.00
88 Ernie Irvan Havoline	60.00	27.00

1997 Action Racing Collectables Banks 1:24

These cars were produced by Action Racing Collectibles. Each car has a slot in the back window for a coin bank. Most banks have blacked in windows. This is the easiest way to tell banks apart from a regular car.

	MINT	NRMT
1 Hermie Sadler Dewalt	60.00	27.00
2 Rusty Wallace Miller Lite Texas Motor Speedway	65.00	29.00

	MINT	NRMT
3 Dale Earnhardt AC Delco	60.00	27.00
3 Dale Earnhardt Goodwrench	70.00	32.00
3 Dale Earnhardt Goodwrench Plus	60.00	27.00

CAR / DRIVER / SPONSOR	MINT	NRMT
3 Dale Earnhardt Lowes Food	75.00	34.00
3 Dale Earnhardt Wheaties Snap-On	150.00	70.00
3 Dale Earnhardt Wrangler 1984 Monte Carlo Daytona	100.00	45.00
3 Steve Park AC Delco	90.00	40.00
3 Ricky Rudd Piedmont	55.00	25.00
4 Sterling Marlin Kodak	50.00	22.00
9 Jeff Burton Track Gear	45.00	20.00
10 Ricky Rudd Tide	50.00	22.00
17 Darrell Waltrip Parts America 7 Car Bank set	300.00	135.00
17 Darrell Waltrip Parts America	50.00	22.00
22 Ward Burton MBNA	40.00	18.00
22 Ward Burton MBNA Gold	45.00	20.00
24 Jeff Gordon DuPont Million Dollar Date	75.00	34.00
24 Jeff Gordon DuPont Million Dollar Date Mac Tools	80.00	36.00
24 Jeff Gordon DuPont Chroma Premier	150.00	70.00
24 Jeff Gordon Lost World	80.00	36.00

CAR / DRIVER / SPONSOR	MINT	NRMT
25 Ricky Craven Budweiser	65.00	29.00
26 Rich Bickle KFC	50.00	22.00
27 Kenny Irwin G.I. Joe	50.00	22.00
27 Rusty Wallace Miller Genuine Draft 1990 Grand Prix	100.00	45.00
29 Elliott Sadler Phillips 66	60.00	27.00
32 Dale Jarrett White Rain	50.00	22.00
33 Ken Schrader Skoal	55.00	25.00
36 Todd Bodine Stanley Tools	45.00	20.00
36 Derrike Cope Skittles	45.00	20.00
37 Jeremy Mayfield Kmart	45.00	20.00
40 Robby Gordon Coors Light	55.00	25.00
41 Steve Grissom Kodiak	55.00	25.00
60 Mark Martin Winn Dixie	60.00	27.00
71 Dave Marcis Realtree	55.00	25.00
71 Dave Marcis Realtree Making of Champions	55.00	25.00

CAR / DRIVER / SPONSOR	MINT	NRMT
81 Kenny Wallace Square D	45.00	20.00
94 Bill Elliott McDonald's	80.00	36.00
96 David Green Caterpillar	45.00	20.00

1998 Action Racing Collectables Banks 1:24

These cars were produced by Action Racing Collectables. Each car has a slot in the back window for a coin bank. Most banks have blacked in windows. This is the easiest way to tell banks apart from a regular car.

CAR / DRIVER / SPONSOR	MINT	NRMT
1 Dale Earnhardt Jr. Coke	75.00	34.00
1 Darrell Waltrip Pennzoil	80.00	36.00
1 Jeff Gordon Baby Ruth '92 TB	80.00	36.00
1 Steve Park Pennzoil	100.00	45.00
K2 Dale Earnhardt Dayvault's	80.00	36.00
2 Rusty Wallace Miller Lite	60.00	27.00
2 Rusty Wallace Miller Lite Elvis	60.00	27.00
3 Dale Earnhardt Goodwrench Plus w/Coke	75.00	34.00
3 Dale Earnhardt Goodwrench Plus w/o Coke	125.00	55.00
3 Dale Earnhardt Goodwrench Plus Bass Pro	90.00	40.00
3 Dale Earnhardt Goodwrench Plus Daytona	60.00	27.00
3 Dale Earnhardt Coke	90.00	40.00
3 Dale Earnhardt Jr. AC Delco	200.00	90.00
3 Dale Earnhardt Jr. AC Delco Snap-On	200.00	90.00

CAR / DRIVER / SPONSOR	MINT	NRMT
4 Bobby Hamilton Kodak	70.00	32.00
5 Terry Labonte Kellogg's	75.00	34.00
5 Terry Labonte Blasted Fruit Loops	70.00	32.00
5 Terry Labonte Kellogg's Corny	70.00	32.00
5 Terry Labonte Kellogg's Ironman	80.00	36.00

CAR / DRIVER / SPONSOR	MINT	NRMT
8 Dale Earnhardt 10,000 RPM 1975 Dodge	60.00	27.00
8 Hut Stricklin Circuit City	40.00	18.00
9 Lake Speed Birthday Cake	50.00	22.00
9 Lake Speed Huckleberry Hound	70.00	32.00
10 Ricky Rudd Tide	60.00	27.00
12 Jeremy Mayfield Mobil 1	60.00	27.00
12 Jimmy Spencer Zippo	225.00	100.00
14 Patty Moise Rhodes	60.00	27.00
18 Bobby Labonte Interstate Batteries Hot Rod	70.00	32.00
18 Bobby Labonte Interstate Batteries Small Soldiers	70.00	32.00
23 Jimmy Spencer No Bull	100.00	45.00
24 Jeff Gordon DuPont	70.00	32.00
24 Jeff Gordon DuPont Chromalusion	100.00	45.00
24 Jeff Gordon DuPont No Bull	90.00	40.00
28 Kenny Irwin Havoline Joker	60.00	27.00

CAR / DRIVER / SPONSOR	MINT	NRMT
31 Dale Earnhardt Jr. Sikkens	200.00	90.00
31 Dale Earnhardt Jr. Wrangler	225.00	100.00
31 Mike Skinner Lowe's	60.00	27.00
31 Mike Skinner Lowe's Special Olympics	60.00	27.00
33 Tim Fedewa Kleenex	55.00	25.00
34 Mike McLaughlin Goulds	80.00	36.00
35 Todd Bodine Tabasco	75.00	34.00
35 Todd Bodine Tabasco Red	70.00	32.00

CAR / DRIVER / SPONSOR	MINT	NRMT
36 Ernie Irvan M&M's Mac Tools	90.00	40.00
41 Steve Grissom Kodiak	75.00	34.00
42 Joe Nemechek BellSouth	60.00	27.00
44 Tony Stewart Shell	70.00	32.00
44 Tony Stewart Shell Small Soldiers	70.00	32.00
50 Ricky Craven Budweiser	150.00	70.00
50 Ricky Craven Budweiser Mac Tools	150.00	70.00
50 No Driver Association Bud Louie	100.00	45.00
88 Dale Jarrett Quality Care	70.00	32.00
88 Dale Jarrett Quality Care Batman	70.00	32.00
300 Darrell Waltrip Tim Flock Special	90.00	40.00

1999 Action Racing Collectables Banks 1:24

ALL BANKS HAVE BLACK WINDOWS

	MINT	NRMT
1 Jeff Gordon Carolina Ford	80.00	36.00

	MINT	NRMT
1 Steve Park Pennzoil	70.00	32.00
2 Rusty Wallace Miller Lite	70.00	32.00
2 Rusty Wallace Harley-Davidson	70.00	32.00
2 Rusty Wallace Miller Lite Last Lap	75.00	34.00
3 Dale Earnhardt Goodwrench	70.00	32.00
3 Dale Earnhardt Goodwrench 25th Anniversary	70.00	32.00
3 Dale Earnhardt Wrangler	80.00	36.00
3 Dale Earnhardt GM Goodwrench Last Lap	100.00	45.00
3 Dale Earnhardt Jr. AC Delco	100.00	45.00
3 Dale Earnhardt Jr. Superman	120.00	55.00
3 Dale Earnhardt Jr. AC Delco Last Lap	120.00	55.00
5 Terry Labonte Kellogg's	70.00	32.00
8 Dale Earnhardt Jr. Budweiser	80.00	36.00
9 Jerry Nadeau Dexter's laboratory	65.00	29.00
18 Bobby Labonte Interstate Batteries	65.00	29.00
20 Tony Stewart Home Depot	300.00	135.00
23 Jimmy Spencer No Bull	70.00	32.00
23 Jimmy Spencer Winston Lights	70.00	32.00

CAR / DRIVER / SPONSOR	MINT	NRMT
24 Jeff Gordon DuPont	70.00	32.00
24 Jeff Gordon Star Wars	150.00	70.00
24 Jeff Gordon Pepsi	70.00	32.00
25 Wally Dallenbach Budwiser	65.00	29.00
27 Casey Atwood Last Lap	100.00	45.00
28 Kenny Irwin Havoline	65.00	29.00
30 Dale Earnhardt Army '76 Malibu	70.00	32.00
31 Dale Earnhardt Jr. Sikkens 1997 Monte Carlo White	100.00	45.00

	MINT	NRMT
31 Dale Earnhardt Jr. Gargoyles '97 MC	100.00	45.00
36 Ernie Irvan Crunchy M&M's	80.00	36.00
36 Tim Fedewa Stanley	65.00	29.00
40 Sterling Marlin Coors Brooks & Dunn	60.00	27.00
71 Dave Marcis ReelTree	70.00	32.00
77 Dale Earnhardt Hy-Gain '76 Malibu	70.00	32.00

	MINT	NRMT
88 Dale Jarrett Quality Care	60.00	27.00
88 Dale Jarrett QC White	70.00	32.00
88 Dale Jarrett Quality Care Last Lap	70.00	32.00

2000 Action Racing Collectables Banks 1:24

These cars are black window and low numbered.

	MINT	NRMT
3 Dale Earnhardt Goodwrench	100.00	45.00
3 Dale Earnhardt GM Goodwrench Taz No Bull	100.00	45.00
20 Tony Stewart Home Depot	100.00	45.00

1998-99 Action Racing Collectables 1:32

These 1:32 scale cars debuted in 1998. These cars were sold through GM and Ford dealerships as well as through various TV outlets.

	MINT	NRMT
3 Dale Earnhardt Goodwrench Plus Bass Pro	50.00	22.00
3 Dale Earnhardt Goodwrench Plus Daytona	50.00	22.00
3 Dale Earnhardt Jr. AC Delco	75.00	34.00
24 Jeff Gordon DuPont	50.00	22.00
28 Kenny Irwin Havoline Joker	50.00	22.00
88 Dale Jarrett Quality Care Batman	50.00	22.00

1993-95 Action Racing Collectables 1:64

These 1:64 scale cars feature the top cars in NASCAR racing. Since 1995, most of the cars are now produced with the Platinum Series label. Some of the Platinum Series cars comes with a SkyBox card. In most cases, the SkyBox card was specifically made for those Platinum Series pieces and was not distributed in any other method. Action now produces their own cards for inclusion with the die-cast pieces.

	MINT	NRMT
2 Ricky Craven DuPont Platinum Series	12.00	5.50
2 Dale Earnhardt Wrangler 1981 Pontiac Platinum Series	35.00	16.00

	MINT	NRMT
2 Mark Martin Miller 1985 ASA	18.00	8.00
2 Rusty Wallace Ford Motorsports Platinum Series	9.00	4.00
2 Rusty Wallace Miller Geniune Draft Platinum Series Acrylic display case	18.00	8.00
2 Rusty Wallace Pontiac Excitement AC Racing Promo	10.00	4.50
2 Rusty Wallace Pontiac Excitement Delco Remy Promo	10.00	4.50
Feb-43 Dale Earnhardt Richard Petty 7 and 7 Special	30.00	13.50
3 Richard Childress Black Gold Platinum Series	10.00	4.50
3 Dale Earnhardt Goodwrench AC Racing Promo	14.00	6.25
3 Dale Earnhardt Wrangler 1984 Monte Carlo Platinum Series	40.00	18.00
3 Dale Earnhardt Goodwrench 1988 Monte Carlo Platinum Series	40.00	18.00

CAR / DRIVER / SPONSOR	MINT	NRMT
3 Dale Earnhardt Goodwrench 1994 Lumina Platinum Series	25.00	11.00
3 Dale Earnhardt Goodwrench 1995 Monte Carlo Brickyard Special	25.00	11.00
3 Dale Earnhardt Goodwrench 1995 Monte Carlo Platinum Series	20.00	9.00
3 Dale Earnhardt Goodwrench Silver Car Blister without card package	50.00	22.00
3 Dale Earnhardt Goodwrench Silver Car Platinum Series	40.00	18.00
3 Dale Earnhardt Goodwrench Silver Car Race World Promo	25.00	11.00
3 Jeff Green Goodwrench Platinum Series	10.00	4.50
24-Mar Dale Earnhardt Jeff Gordon Dual package Brickyard Special	35.00	16.00
24-Mar Dale Earnhardt Jeff Gordon Dual package Kellogg's Promo	35.00	16.00
4 Ernie Irvan Kodak AC Racing Promo	9.00	4.00
4 Ernie Irvan Kodak Delco Remy Promo	8.00	3.60
4 Sterling Marlin Kodak 1994 Lumina Platinum Series	10.00	4.50
4 Sterling Marlin Kodak 1995 Monte Carlo Platinum Series	14.00	6.25
5 Terry Labonte Kellogg's Platinum Series	18.00	8.00
24-May Terry Labonte Jeff Gordon Dual package Kellogg's Promo	25.00	11.00
6 Tommy Houston Roses	8.00	3.60
6 Mark Martin Folgers Platinum Series	50.00	22.00
6 Mark Martin Valvoline Brickyard Special Blister package	12.00	5.50
6 Mark Martin Valvoline Brickyard Special Platinum Series	12.00	5.50
6 Mark Martin Valvoline Platinum Series	10.00	4.50
6 Mark Martin Valvoline Valvoline Team Promo	8.00	3.60

7 Geoff Bodine Exide 1995 Platinum Series	8.00	3.60

CAR / DRIVER / SPONSOR	MINT	NRMT
7 Alan Kulwicki Army	40.00	18.00
7 Alan Kulwicki Hooter's 1992 Ford Thunderbird	35.00	16.00
7 Alan Kulwicki Hooter's AK Racing	25.00	11.00
7 Alan Kulwicki Zerex Camaro ASA Platinum Series	20.00	9.00
7 Alan Kulwicki Zerex	25.00	11.00
8 Dale Earnhardt 1985 Camaro ASA Platinum Series	20.00	9.00
10 Ricky Rudd Tide Blister package	10.00	4.50

11 Bill Elliott Budweiser 1994 Platinum Series	20.00	9.00
11 Darrell Waltrip Budweiser 1985 Monte Carlo 1994 Platinum Series	35.00	16.00

11 Darrell Waltrip Mountain Dew 1982 Buick 1995 Platinum Series	15.00	6.75
11 Darrell Waltrip Pepsi Camaro ASA Platinum Series	10.00	4.50
11 Brett Bodine Lowe's	8.00	3.60
12 Neil Bonnett Budweiser 1985 Monte Carlo Platinum Series	20.00	9.00
15 Lake Speed Quality Car Platinum Series	8.00	3.60
16 Wally Dallenbach Jr. Roush Racing Valvoline Team Promo	30.00	13.50
16 Ted Musgrave Family Channel Platinum Series	8.00	3.60
17 Darrell Waltrip Superflo Camaro Platinum Series	12.00	5.50
17 Darrell Waltrip Tide Camaro Platinum Series	20.00	9.00
17 Darrell Waltrip Western Auto AC Racing Promo	9.00	4.00

CAR / DRIVER / SPONSOR	MINT	NRMT
17 Darrell Waltrip Western Auto Delco Remy Promo	8.00	3.60

17 Darrell Waltrip Western Auto 1995 Monte Carlo Platinum Series	10.00	4.50
18 Bobby Labonte Interstate Batteries	15.00	6.75

21 Neil Bonnett Hodgdon 1982 Thunderbird Platinum Series	12.00	5.50

22 Bobby Allison Miller Beer 1983 Buick Platinum Series in acrylic case	20.00	9.00

23 Jimmy Spencer Smokin' Joe's Platinum Series in acrylic case	35.00	16.00

CAR / DRIVER / SPONSOR	MINT	NRMT
24 Jeff Gordon DuPont AC Racing Promo	50.00	22.00
24 Jeff Gordon DuPont 1994 Lumina Platinum Series	40.00	18.00
24 Jeff Gordon DuPont 1995 Champion	20.00	9.00

24 Jeff Gordon DuPont 1995 Monte Carlo Platinum Series	25.00	11.00
24 Jeff Gordon DuPont Valvoline Team Promo	25.00	11.00
25 Tim Richmond Folgers Monte Carlo Fastback	14.00	6.25
25 Ken Schrader Budweiser Platinum Series	12.00	5.50
25 Ken Schrader GMAC AC Racing Promo	9.00	4.00
25 Ken Schrader GMAC Valvoline Team Promo	8.00	3.60
26 Sammy Swindell Bull Hannah Promo	8.00	3.60
27 Tim Richmond Old Milwaukee Beer Platinum Series	12.00	5.50
28 Ernie Irvan Havoline Platinum Series	12.00	5.50
28 Dale Jarrett Havoline Platinum Series	10.00	4.50
35 Shawna Robinson Polaroid	12.00	5.50
36 Todd Bodine Stanley Platinum Series	10.00	4.50

40 Kenny Wallace Dirt Devil AC Racing Promo	9.00	4.00

CAR / DRIVER / SPONSOR	MINT	NRMT
41 Joe Nemechek Meineke Platinum Series	8.00	3.60
41 Phil Parsons AC Racing	9.00	4.00

42 Kyle Petty Coors Light Platinum Series in Acrylic case	18.00	8.00
42 Kyle Petty Mello Yello AC Racing Promo	9.00	4.00
42 Kyle Petty Mello Yello Platinum Series	8.00	3.60
46 Al Unser Jr. Valvoline Valvoline Team Promo	10.00	4.50
51 Neil Bonnett Country Time Platinum Series	20.00	9.00
52 Ken Schrader AC Delco Platinum Series	10.00	4.50

88 Darrell Waltrip Gatorade 1980 Olds Platinum Sieries	10.00	4.50
93 Lumina Prototype	8.00	3.60
93 Pontiac Prototype	8.00	3.60
93 Thunderbird Prototype	8.00	3.60
94 Bill Elliott McDonald's 1995 Platinum Series	10.00	4.50
94 Casey Elliott Racing Collectibles Inc.	10.00	4.50
94 Bill Elliott Thunderbat Platinum Series	30.00	13.50
95 David Green Busch Platinum Series	10.00	4.50
98 Derrike Cope Fingerhut Platinum Series	8.00	3.60

1996 Action Racing Collectables 1:64

Most of these 1:64 scale cards were issued as part of the Platinum Series. Cars with alcohol and/or tobacco sponsorship are packaged in acrylic cases.

2 Rusty Wallace Miller Splash Paint Acrylic	15.00	6.75
2 Rusty Wallace Miller Genuine Draft Silver	15.00	6.75
3 Dale Earnhardt Goodwrench	15.00	6.75

3 Dale Earnhardt AC-Delco	12.00	5.50
3 Dale Earnhardt Goodwrench Blister with card package	12.00	5.50

3 Dale Earnhardt Olympic Hood Open Car	20.00	9.00
3 Dale Earnhardt Olympic Car Blister with card package	15.00	6.75
3 Dale Earnhardt Olympic Hood Open in Green Box	30.00	13.50
3 Dale Earnhardt 16-car set	250.00	110.00

CAR / DRIVER / SPONSOR	MINT	NRMT

| 5 Terry Labonte Kellogg's Iron Man | 30.00 | 13.50 |

5 Terry Labonte Kellogg's Japan	15.00	6.75
6 Mark Martin Valvoline	10.00	4.50
7 Geoff Bodine Exide	8.00	3.60
10 Ricky Rudd Tide	8.00	3.60
14 Jeff Green Racing For Kids	10.00	4.50
21 Michael Waltrip Citgo	10.00	4.50
21 Michael Waltrip Citgo Star Trek	12.00	5.50

| 22 Bobby Allison Miller 1985 MC | 12.00 | 5.50 |

CAR / DRIVER / SPONSOR	MINT	NRMT
22 Ward Burton MBNA	10.00	4.50
24 Jeff Gordon DuPont Monte Carlo	12.00	5.50
24 Jeff Gordon DuPont Monte Carlo Blister package	10.00	4.50
28 Davey Allison Vinyl Tech 1987	12.00	5.50
28 Ernie Irvan Havoline	10.00	4.50

29 Steve Grissom Cartoon Network	10.00	4.50
29 Steve Grissom WCW	10.00	4.50
29 No Driver Association Scooby-Doo	10.00	4.50
30 Johnny Benson Pennzoil	10.00	4.50

42 Kyle Petty Coors Light	12.00	5.50
42 Kyle Petty Coors Light Black Paint Scheme	12.00	5.50
43 Bobby Hamilton STP Silver 25th Anniversary	20.00	9.00
57 Jason Keller Halloween Havoc	10.00	4.50
88 Ernie Irvan Havoline	12.00	5.50
88 Dale Jarrett Quality Care	10.00	4.50

CAR / DRIVER / SPONSOR	MINT	NRMT
94 Bill Elliott McDonald's	10.00	4.50
96 David Green Caterpillar	8.00	3.60

1997 Action Racing Collectables 1:64

Most of these 1:64 scale cards were issued as part of the Platinum Series. Cars with alcohol and/or tobacco sponsorship are packaged in acrylic cases.

| 2 Rusty Wallace Miller Lite | 12.00 | 5.50 |

| 2 Rusty Wallace Miller Lite Japan | 18.00 | 8.00 |
| 2 Rusty Wallace Miller Lite Texas Motor Speedway | 15.00 | 6.75 |

| 3 Dale Earnhardt AC Delco | 12.00 | 5.50 |
| 3 Dale Earnhardt AC Delco Black Window Blister Pack | 10.00 | 4.50 |

	MINT	NRMT
3 Dale Earnhardt Goodwrench	12.00	5.50
3 Dale Earnhardt Goodwrench Brickyard Special	10.00	4.50
3 Dale Earnhardt Goodwrench Plus Box	15.00	6.75
3 Dale Earnhardt Wheaties	30.00	13.50
3 Dale Earnhardt Wheaties Black Window Blister Pack	15.00	6.75
3 Dale Earnhardt Wheaties Hood Open Sports Image	50.00	22.00
3 Dale Earnhardt Wheaties Mail-In	12.00	5.50

	MINT	NRMT
3 Steve Park AC Delco	18.00	8.00

	MINT	NRMT
10 Ricky Rudd Tide	10.00	4.50

	MINT	NRMT
3 Dale Earnhardt Goodwrench Plus	12.00	5.50

	MINT	NRMT
3 Ricky Rudd Piedmont	10.00	4.50
4 Sterling Marlin Kodak	10.00	4.50

	MINT	NRMT
11 Brett Bodine Close Call	8.00	3.60
12 Kenny Wallace Gray Bar	8.00	3.60

	MINT	NRMT
6 Mark Martin Valvoline	10.00	4.50
9 Jeff Burton Track Gear	8.00	3.60

	MINT	NRMT
14 Steve Park Burger King	20.00	9.00
17 Darrell Waltrip Parts America 7 Car set	60.00	27.00

CAR / DRIVER / SPONSOR	MINT	NRMT
18 Bobby Labonte Interstate Batteries	10.00	4.50
18 Bobby Labonte Interstate Batteries Hall of Fame	15.00	6.75
22 Ward Burton MBNA	10.00	4.50

22 Ward Burton MBNA Gold	10.00	4.50
23 Jimmy Spencer Camel	25.00	11.00
24 Jeff Gordon DuPont Bickyard Special	10.00	4.50
24 Jeff Gordon DuPont Million Dollar Date	12.00	5.50
24 Jeff Gordon DuPont Million Dollar Date Black Window	15.00	6.75

24 Jeff Gordon DuPont	12.00	5.50

24 Jeff Gordon DuPont Chroma Premier	25.00	11.00

24 Jeff Gordon Lost World	18.00	8.00
24 Jeff Gordon Lost World Black Window Blister Pack	15.00	6.75

24 Jeff Gordon Lost World Hood Open Sports Image	20.00	9.00

25 Ricky Craven Budweiser	10.00	4.50

26 Rich Bickle KFC	10.00	4.50

27 Kenny Irwin G.I. Joe	10.00	4.50

	MINT	NRMT
27 Kenny Irwin Tonka	10.00	4.50
27 Rusty Wallace Miller Genuine Draft 1990 Grand Prix	25.00	11.00
29 Jeff Green Tom & Jerry	15.00	6.75
29 Elliott Sadler Phillips 66	10.00	4.50

	MINT	NRMT
31 Mike Skinner Lowe's	10.00	4.50
31 Mike Skinner Lowe's Blister Pack	10.00	4.50

	MINT	NRMT
31 Mike Skinner Lowe's Japan	12.00	5.50

	MINT	NRMT
36 Todd Bodine Stanley Tools	10.00	4.50
36 Derrike Cope Skittles	8.00	3.60
37 Mark Green Timber Wolf	12.00	5.50

	MINT	NRMT
37 Jeremy Mayfield Kmart	10.00	4.50
40 Robby Gordon Coors Light	15.00	6.75
41 Steve Grissom Kodiak	15.00	6.75
46 Wally Dallenbach First Union	8.00	3.60
60 Mark Martin Winn Dixie	12.00	5.50
71 Dave Marcis Realtree	20.00	9.00
75 Rick Mast Remington	10.00	4.50
75 Rick Mast Remington Camo	10.00	4.50

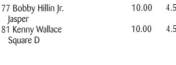

	MINT	NRMT
77 Bobby Hillin Jr. Jasper	10.00	4.50
81 Kenny Wallace Square D	10.00	4.50

	MINT	NRMT
88 Dale Jarrett Quality Care	10.00	4.50
88 Dale Jarrett Quality Care Brickyard Special	10.00	4.50

	MINT	NRMT
94 Bill Elliott McDonald's	12.00	5.50

	MINT	NRMT
94 Bill Elliott Mac Tonight	10.00	4.50
96 David Green Caterpillar	10.00	4.50
99 Jeff Burton Exide	10.00	4.50
00 Buckshot Jones Aqua Fresh	10.00	4.50

1998 Action Racing Collectables 1:64

Most of these 1:64 scale cards were issued as part of the Platinum Series. Cars with alcohol and/or tobacco sponsorship are packaged in acrylic cases.

	MINT	NRMT
1 Dale Earnhardt Jr. Coke	15.00	6.75

| 1 Steve Park Pennzoil | 15.00 | 6.75 |

| 1 Steve Park Pennzoil Reverse Paint | 15.00 | 6.75 |
| 1 Darrell Waltrip Pennzoil | 15.00 | 6.75 |

| K2 Dale Earnhardt Dayvault's | 15.00 | 6.75 |

| K2 Dale Earnhardt Dayvault's All Pink | 18.00 | 8.00 |

| 2 Rusty Wallace Miller Lite | 18.00 | 8.00 |
| 2 Rusty Wallace Adventures of Rusty | 18.00 | 8.00 |

| 2 Rusty Wallace Miller Lite Elvis | 18.00 | 8.00 |

| 2 Rusty Wallace Miller Lite TCB | 18.00 | 8.00 |
| 12-Feb Rusty Wallace Jeremy Mayfield on Pit Wall Base | 15.00 | 6.75 |

| 3 Dale Earnhardt Coke | 15.00 | 6.75 |

3 Dale Earnhardt Goodwrench Plus	12.00	5.50
3 Dale Earnhardt Goodwrench Plus Blister Pack	10.00	4.50
3 Dale Earnhardt Goodwrench Plus Daytona	10.00	4.50

| 3 Dale Earnhardt Goodwrench Plus Bass Pro | 20.00 | 9.00 |

3 Dale Earnhardt Jr.   25.00   11.00
   AC Delco

5 Terry Labonte   12.00   5.50
   Kellogg's

8 Dale Earnhardt   12.00   5.50
   10,000 RPM 1978 Dodge
8 Hut Stricklin   8.00   3.60
   Circuit City

3 Dale Earnhardt Jr.   20.00   9.00
   AC Delco Blister Pack

5 Terry Labonte   15.00   6.75
   Blasted Fruit Loops
5 Terry Labonte   15.00   6.75
   Kellogg's Corny

9 Jerry Nadeau   30.00   13.50
   Power Puff

4 Bobby Hamilton   10.00   4.50
   Kodak

5 Terry Labonte   12.00   5.50
   Kellogg's Ironman

9 Jerry Nadeau   12.00   5.50
   Zombie Island

9 Lake Speed   12.00   5.50
    Birthday Cake

9 Lake Speed   12.00   5.50
    Huckleberry Hound

10 Ricky Rudd   10.00   4.50
    Tide

10 Ricky Rudd	10.00	4.50
Give Kids the World		
14 Patty Moise	15.00	6.75
Rhodes Xena		
18 Bobby Labonte	10.00	4.50
Interstate Batteries		
18 Bobby Labonte	15.00	6.75
Interstate Batteries Hot Rod		
18 Bobby Labonte	15.00	6.75
Interstate Batteries Small Soldiers		

22 Ward Burton   10.00   4.50
    MBNA

23 Jimmy Spencer   15.00   6.75
    No Bull

24 Jeff Gordon   12.00   5.50
    DuPont

24 Jeff Gordon   12.00   5.50
    DuPont Brickyard Winner

24 Jeff Gordon   40.00   18.00
    DuPont Chromalusion

	MINT	NRMT
24 Jeff Gordon DuPont No Bull	12.00	5.50
31 Dale Earnhardt Jr. Sikkens	25.00	11.00
31 Mike Skinner Lowe's Special Olympic	10.00	4.50
32 Dale Jarrett White Rain	8.00	3.60

	MINT	NRMT
28 Kenny Irwin Havoline	8.00	3.60
28 Kenny Irwin Havoline Joker	15.00	6.75
31 Dale Earnhardt Wrangler	30.00	13.50
35 Todd Bodine Tabasco Orange	12.00	5.50

	MINT	NRMT
30 Derrike Cope Gumout	8.00	3.60
31 Mike Skinner Lowe's	10.00	4.50
35 Todd Bodine Tabasco Red	12.00	5.50
36 Ernie Irvan M&M's	18.00	8.00

| 36 Ernie Irvan Skittles | 12.00 | 5.50 |
| 36 Ernie Irvan Wildberry Skittles | 15.00 | 6.75 |

| 50 Ricky Craven Budweiser | 10.00 | 4.50 |

| 75 Rick Mast Remington | 8.00 | 3.60 |

| 40 Sterling Marlin Coors Light | 15.00 | 6.75 |

| 50 NDA Bud Louie | 12.00 | 5.50 |

| 81 Kenny Wallace Square D | 8.00 | 3.60 |
| 81 Kenny Wallace Square D Lightning | 10.00 | 4.50 |

41 Steve Grissom Kodiak	15.00	6.75
42 Joe Nemechek BellSouth	8.00	3.60
44 Tony Stewart Shell	15.00	6.75
44 Tony Stewart Shell Small Soldiers	15.00	6.75

| 72 Mike Dillon Detroit Gasket | 12.00 | 5.50 |

88 Dale Jarrett Quality Care	12.00	5.50
88 Dale Jarrett Quality Care Batman	15.00	6.75
90 Dick Trickle Heilig-Meyers	10.00	4.50

	MINT	NRMT
2 Rusty Wallace Miller Lite	15.00	6.75
2 Rusty Wallace True to Texas	12.00	5.50
2 Rusty Wallace Harley-Davidson	15.00	6.75
2 Rusty Wallace Miller Lite Last Lap	15.00	6.75

1999 Action Racing Collectables 1:64

These 1:64 scale cards were issued as part of the Platinum Series. The Alcohol/Tobacco cars were released on a pit wall base.

ALCOHOL AND TOBACCO CARS ON A BASE

OTHERS IN PLATINUM SERIES BLISTERS

	MINT	NRMT
3 Dale Earnhardt Goodwrench	12.00	5.50
3 Dale Earnhardt Goodwrench 25th Anniversary	15.00	6.75

	MINT	NRMT
1 Jeff Gordon Carolina Ford	15.00	6.75

96 David Green Caterpillar	8.00	3.60

1 Jeff Gordon Baby Ruth 1992 Thunderbird	12.00	5.50

300 Darrell Waltrip Flock Speical	12.00	5.50

	MINT	NRMT
3 Dale Earnhart Wrangler	20.00	9.00
3 Dale Earnhardt GM Goodwrench Sign	12.00	5.50
3 Dale Earnhardt GM Goodwrench Last Lap	15.00	6.75
3 Dale Earnhardt Jr. AC Delco Superman	16.00	7.25
3 Dale Earnhardt Jr. AC Delco Last Lap	16.00	7.25

00 Buckshot Jones Alka Seltzer	12.00	5.50

1 Steve Park Pennzoil	12.00	5.50

CAR / DRIVER / SPONSOR	MINT	NRMT
3 Dale Earnhardt Jr. AC Delco	15.00	6.75
3 Dale Earnhardt Jr. AC Delco Black Window Blister Pack	15.00	6.75
4 Bobby Hamilton Advantix	10.00	4.50

CAR / DRIVER / SPONSOR	MINT	NRMT
9 Jerry Nadeau Dexter's laboratory	12.00	5.50
9 Jerry Nadeau Jetsons	12.00	5.50
11 Dale Jarrett Rayovac	10.00	4.50
11 Dale Jarrett Green Bay	12.00	5.50
12 Jeremy Mayfield Mobil 1	10.00	4.50
12 Jeremy Mayfield Kentucky Derby	12.00	5.50

CAR / DRIVER / SPONSOR	MINT	NRMT
20 Tony Stewart Home Depot	40.00	18.00
20 Tony Stewart Habitat for Humanity	25.00	11.00

CAR / DRIVER / SPONSOR	MINT	NRMT
5 Terry Labonte Kellogg's	12.00	5.50
5 Terry Labonte K-Sentials	15.00	6.75
5 Terry Labonte Rice Krispies	15.00	6.75
5 Terry Labonte NASCAR Racers	15.00	6.75

CAR / DRIVER / SPONSOR	MINT	NRMT
15 Ken Schrader Oakwood Homes	10.00	4.50
17 Matt Kenseth DeWalt	15.00	6.75
18 Bobby Labonte Interstate Batteries	12.00	5.50
18 Bobby Labonte NASCAR Racers	15.00	6.75
18 Bobby Labonte MBNA	10.00	4.50

CAR / DRIVER / SPONSOR	MINT	NRMT
22 Ward Burton Caterpillar	10.00	4.50
23 Jimmy Spencer Winston	18.00	8.00

CAR / DRIVER / SPONSOR	MINT	NRMT
8 Dale Earnhardt Jr. Budweiser	15.00	6.75
8 Dale Earnhardt Bud Track Cars	15.00	6.75

CAR / DRIVER / SPONSOR	MINT	NRMT
24 Jeff Gordon DuPont	12.00	5.50
24 Jeff Gordon DuPont Superman	25.00	11.00
24 Jeff Gordon NASCAR Racers	15.00	6.75
24 Jeff Gordon Pepsi	12.00	5.50

CAR / DRIVER / SPONSOR	MINT	NRMT
24 Jeff Gordon Star Wars	15.00	6.75
27 Casey Atwood Castrol	30.00	13.50
27 Casey Atwood Castrol Last Lap	20.00	9.00
28 Kenny Irwin Texaco	10.00	4.50
28/88 Kenny Irwin Dale Jarrett Batman & Joker	30.00	13.50
30 Dale Earnhardt Army '76 Malibu	12.00	5.50

31 Dale Earnhardt Jr. Gargoyles	18.00	8.00

31 Dale Earnhardt Jr. Sikkens White	18.00	8.00
31 Mike Skinner Lowe's	10.00	4.50

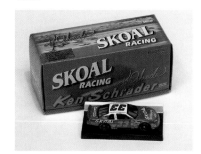

33 Ken Schrader Skoal	12.00	5.50

CAR / DRIVER / SPONSOR	MINT	NRMT
36 Ernie Irvan M&M's	12.00	5.50
40 Sterling Marlin Coors	12.00	5.50
40 Sterling Marlin Coors John Wayne	15.00	6.75
40 Sterling Marlin Coors Brooks & Dunn	12.00	5.50
40 Coca-Cola 600 '99	8.00	3.60

55 Kenny Wallace Square D	10.00	4.50
55 Kenny Wallace NASCAR Racers	10.00	4.50
66 Darrell Waltrip Big K 2000	10.00	4.50
71 Dave Marcus Real Tree	18.00	8.00

88 Dale Jarrett Quality Care	10.00	4.50

CAR / DRIVER / SPONSOR	MINT	NRMT
88 Dale Jarrett Quality Care White	12.00	5.50
88 Dale Jarrett Quality Care & Quality Care White 2 Car Tin	25.00	11.00
88 Dale Jarrett Quality Care Last Lap	15.00	6.75
00 Buckshot Jones Crown Fiber	12.00	5.50

2000 Action Racing Collectables 1:64

These 1:64 scale cards were issued as part of the Platinum Series. The Alcohol/Tobacco cars were released on a pit wall base.

1 Randy Lajoie Bob Evans	10.00	4.50
3 Dale Earnhardt Taz No Bull	15.00	6.75
3 Dale Earnhardt Goodwrench	12.00	5.50
8 Dale Earnhardt Jr. Budweiser	15.00	6.75
20 Tony Stewart Home Depot	12.00	5.50
24 Jeff Gordon DuPont	12.00	5.50
24 Jeff Gordon DuPont Millennium	15.00	6.75
31 Mike Skinner Lowe's	10.00	4.50
55 Kenny Wallace Square D	10.00	4.50

1995-96 Action Racing Collectables SuperTrucks 1:64

These pieces are 1:64 scale replicas of the SuperTrucks that race in the NASCAR SuperTruck Series.

3 Mike Skinner Goodwrench	12.00	5.50
3 Mike Skinner Goodwrench 1996	10.00	4.50
6 Rick Carelli Total Petroleum	8.00	3.60
7 Geoff Bodine Exide	8.00	3.60
16 Ron Hornaday Action	10.00	4.50
16 Ron Hornaday NAPA	10.00	4.50
16 Ron Hornaday Papa John's Pizza	16.00	7.25
24 Scott Lagasse DuPont	12.00	5.50

| 24 Jack Sprague | 10.00 | 4.50 |
| Quaker State | | |

28 Ernie Irvan	10.00	4.50
NAPA		
52 Ken Schrader	8.00	3.60
AC Delco		
71 Kenji Momota	8.00	3.60
Action Racing Collectables		
84 Joe Ruttman	8.00	3.60
Mac Tools		
98 Butch Miller	8.00	3.60
Raybestos		

1993-95 Action/RCCA 1:24

These 1:24 scale pieces were distributed through Action's Racing Collectibles Club of America. The pieces are 1:24 replicas of the cars that have raced in NASCAR.

1 Rick Mast	70.00	32.00
Skoal		
2 Rusty Wallace	90.00	40.00
Ford Motorsports		
2 Rusty Wallace	90.00	40.00
Miller Genuine Draft		
1995 Thunderbird		
Feb-43 Dale Earnhardt	200.00	90.00
Richard Petty		
7 and 7 Special		

3 Dale Earnhardt	300.00	135.00
Wrangler 1984 Monte Carlo Blue Sides		
3 Dale Earnhardt	300.00	135.00
Wrangler 1984 Monte Carlo Blue & Yellow		
3 Dale Earnhardt	500.00	220.00
Wrangler 1987 Monte Carlo		

3 Dale Earnhardt	600.00	275.00
Goodwrench 1988 Monte Carlo		
Fast Back		
3 Dale Earnhardt	250.00	110.00
Goodwrench 1994 Lumina		
3 Dale Earnhardt	225.00	100.00
Goodwrench 1995 Monte Carlo		
3 Dale Earnhardt	1000.00	450.00
Goodwrench Silver Car		
Black Wheels		
3 Dale Earnhardt	800.00	350.00
Goodwrench Silver Car		
Red Wheels		
6 Mark Martin	350.00	160.00
Folgers		
9 Ted Musgrave	45.00	20.00
Action Racing Collectables		
10 Ricky Rudd	65.00	29.00
Tide		
11 Brett Bodine	40.00	18.00
Lowe's		
18 Dale Jarrett	125.00	55.00
Interstate Batteries		
23 Jimmy Spencer	350.00	160.00
Smokin' Joe's		
24 Jeff Gordon	250.00	110.00
DuPont 1995 Monte Carlo		
25 Tim Richmond	50.00	22.00
Folgers Monte Carlo Fastback		
25 Ken Schrader	60.00	27.00
Budweiser		
26 Hut Stricklin	40.00	18.00
Quaker State		
28 Dale Jarrett	50.00	22.00
Havoline		
30 Michael Waltrip	100.00	45.00
Pennzoil		
42 Kyle Petty	200.00	90.00
Coors Light Pumpkin Special		
51 Neil Bonnett	200.00	90.00
Country Time		
94 Bill Elliott	50.00	22.00
McDonald's 1995		
94 Bill Elliott	175.00	80.00
McDonald's Thunderbat		
95 David Green	50.00	22.00
Busch Beer		

1996 Action/RCCA 1:24

These 1:24 scale pieces were distributed through Action's Racing Collectibles Club of America. The pieces are 1:24 replicas of the cars that have raced in NASCAR.

2 Rusty Wallace	90.00	40.00
Miller Genuine Draft		
3 Richard Childress	60.00	27.00
CRC Chemical		
5 Terry Labonte	175.00	80.00
Kellogg's Silver car		
5 Terry Labonte	80.00	36.00
Kellogg's Japan		
6 Mark Martin	80.00	36.00
Valvoline Thunderbird		

15 Dale Earnhardt	110.00	50.00
Wrangler 1982 Thunderbird		
17 Darrell Waltrip	60.00	27.00
Parts America		
17 Darrell Waltrip	100.00	45.00
Tide		
21 Neil Bonnett	60.00	27.00
Hodgdon		
21 Michael Waltrip	60.00	27.00
Citgo Star Trek		
22 Bobby Allison	60.00	27.00
Miller Beer		
24 Jeff Gordon	70.00	32.00
DuPont Monte Carlo		
27 Rusty Wallace	150.00	70.00
Kodiak		
29 Steve Grissom	60.00	27.00
Cartoon Network		
29 Steve Grissom	60.00	27.00
WCW		
33 Robert Pressley	60.00	27.00
Skoal		
42 Robby Gordon	60.00	27.00
Tonka		
42 Kyle Petty	65.00	29.00
Coors Light Black Paint Scheme		
43 Bobby Hamilton	100.00	45.00
STP Silver car with Black Windows		
43 Bobby Hamilton	250.00	110.00
STP 5 car set with Black Windows		

1997 Action/RCCA 1:24

These 1:24 scale pieces were distributed through Action's Racing Collectibles Club of America. The pieces are 1:24 replicas of the cars that have raced in NASCAR.

2 Rusty Wallace	100.00	45.00
Miller Lite Texas Motor Speedway		
3 Dale Earnhardt	80.00	36.00
AC Delco		
3 Dale Earnhardt	250.00	110.00
Goodwrench		
3 Dale Earnhardt	80.00	36.00
Goodwrench Plus		
3 Dale Earnhardt	110.00	50.00
Lowes Food		

CAR / DRIVER / SPONSOR	MINT	NRMT
3 Dale Earnhardt Wrangler 1984 Monte Carlo Daytona	200.00	90.00
3 Steve Park AC Delco	175.00	80.00
3 Ricky Rudd Piedmont	65.00	29.00
4 Sterling Marlin Kodak	60.00	27.00
9 Jeff Burton Track Gear	75.00	34.00
17 Darrell Waltrip Parts America 7 Car set	300.00	135.00
17 Darrell Waltrip Parts America Chrome	150.00	70.00
22 Ward Burton MBNA	50.00	22.00
22 Ward Burton MBNA Gold	50.00	22.00
24 Jeff Gordon DuPont Million Dollar Date	75.00	34.00
24 Jeff Gordon DuPont ChromaPremier	175.00	80.00
24 Jeff Gordon Lost World	100.00	45.00
25 Ricky Craven Budweiser	70.00	32.00
26 Rich Bickle KFC	50.00	22.00
27 Kenny Irwin Action	70.00	32.00
27 Kenny Irwin G.I. Joe	65.00	29.00
27 Rusty Wallace Miller Genuine Draft 1990 Grand Prix	125.00	55.00
29 Elliott Sadler Phillips 66	60.00	27.00
31 Mike Skinner Lowe's Japan	60.00	27.00
32 Dale Jarrett White Rain	60.00	27.00
33 Ken Schrader Skoal	90.00	40.00
36 Todd Bodine Stanley Tools	50.00	22.00
36 Derrike Cope Skittles	50.00	22.00
37 Jeremy Mayfield Kmart	80.00	36.00
40 Robby Gordon Coors Light	65.00	29.00
41 Steve Grissom Kodiak	60.00	27.00
60 Mark Martin Winn Dixie	80.00	36.00
71 Dave Marcis Realtree	70.00	32.00
71 Dave Marcis Realtree Making of Champions	60.00	27.00
81 Kenny Wallace Square D	50.00	22.00
94 Bill Elliott McDonald's	70.00	32.00
96 David Green Caterpillar	50.00	22.00
97 Chad Little John Deere	60.00	27.00
97 Chad Little John Deere 160th Anniversary	65.00	29.00

1993-95 Action/RCCA Banks 1:24

These cars were produced by Action and distributed through the club (RCCA). Each car has a slot in the back window for a coin bank. Most banks have blacked in windows.

CAR / DRIVER / SPONSOR	MINT	NRMT
1 Winston Show Car	60.00	27.00
2 Dale Earnhardt Wrangler 1981 Pontiac	175.00	80.00
3 Richard Childress Black Gold	50.00	22.00
3 Dale Earnhardt Goodwrench 1994 Lumina	175.00	80.00

CAR / DRIVER / SPONSOR	MINT	NRMT
3 Dale Earnhardt Wrangler 1981 Pontiac	150.00	70.00

CAR / DRIVER / SPONSOR	MINT	NRMT
3 Dale Earnhardt Wrangler 1985 Monte Carlo	250.00	110.00
3 Dale Earnhardt Wrangler 1987 Monte Carlo	300.00	135.00
3 Jeff Green Goodwrench	50.00	22.00
4 Sterling Marlin Kodak	40.00	18.00
6 Mark Martin Valvoline 1995	50.00	22.00
6 Mark Martin Valvoline Brickyard Special	70.00	32.00
7 Alan Kulwicki Hooters	150.00	70.00
7 Alan Kulwicki Zerex	150.00	70.00
11 Darrell Waltrip Budweiser 1986 Monte Carlo	75.00	34.00
11 Darrell Waltrip Mountain Dew	75.00	34.00
12 Neil Bonnett Budweiser 1986 Monte Carlo	75.00	34.00
15 Dale Earnhardt Wrangler 1982 Thunder Bird	150.00	70.00
16 Ted Musgrave Primestar	60.00	27.00
25 Ken Schrader Budweiser	60.00	27.00
28 Ernie Irvan Havoline	45.00	20.00
42 Kyle Petty Coors Light '95	55.00	25.00
88 Darrell Waltrip Gatorade Monte Carlo	100.00	45.00

1996 Action/RCCA Banks 1:24

These cars were produced by Action and distributed through the club (RCCA). Each car has a slot in the back window for a coin bank. All banks have blacked in windows.

CAR / DRIVER / SPONSOR	MINT	NRMT
2 Rusty Wallace Miller Genuine Draft	70.00	32.00
2 Rusty Wallace Miller Genuine Draft Silver Anniversary Car	60.00	27.00
3 Dale Earnhardt AC-Delco	80.00	36.00
3 Dale Earnhardt Goodwrench	70.00	32.00
7 Geoff Bodine Exide	50.00	22.00
11 Darrell Waltrip Budweiser 1984 Monte Carlo	60.00	27.00
12 Neil Bonnett Budweiser 1984 Monte Carlo	75.00	34.00
14 Jeff Green Racing For Kids	60.00	27.00
17 Darrell Waltrip Western Auto	50.00	22.00
18 Bobby Labonte Interstate Batteries	50.00	22.00
21 Michael Waltrip Citgo	50.00	22.00
28 Ernie Irvan Havoline	50.00	22.00
30 Johnny Benson Pennzoil	60.00	27.00
31 Mike Skinner Lowe's	80.00	36.00
31 Mike Skinner Snap-On	125.00	55.00
42 Kyle Petty Coors Light	65.00	29.00
57 Jason Keller Halloween Havoc	50.00	22.00
88 Ernie Irvan Havoline	60.00	27.00
88 Dale Jarrett Quality Care	60.00	27.00
94 Bill Elliott McDonald's	60.00	27.00

1997 Action/RCCA Banks 1:24

These cars were produced by Action and distributed through the club (RCCA). Each car has a slot in the back window for a coin bank. All banks have blacked in windows.

CAR / DRIVER / SPONSOR	MINT	NRMT
2 Rusty Wallace Miller Lite	70.00	32.00
2 Rusty Wallace Miller Lite Japan	65.00	29.00
3 Dale Earnhardt Goodwrench Plus	60.00	27.00
3 Dale Earnhardt Wheaties	120.00	55.00
6 Mark Martin Valvoline	60.00	27.00
10 Phil Parsons Channellock	50.00	22.00
11 Brett Bodine Close Call	60.00	27.00
12 Kenny Wallace Gray Bar	60.00	27.00
14 Steve Park Burger King	100.00	45.00
18 Bobby Labonte Interstate Batteries	50.00	22.00
18 Bobby Labonte Interstate Batteries Hall of Fame	50.00	22.00
23 Jimmy Spencer Camel	175.00	80.00
24 Jeff Gordon DuPont	150.00	70.00
27 Kenny Irwin Nerf	50.00	22.00
27 Kenny Irwin Tonka	50.00	22.00

CAR / DRIVER / SPONSOR	MINT	NRMT
37 Mark Green Timber Wolf	50.00	22.00
42 Joe Nemechek BellSouth	45.00	20.00
46 Wally Dallenbach First Union	45.00	20.00
75 Rick Mast Remington	45.00	20.00
75 Rick Mast Remington Camo	45.00	20.00
88 Dale Jarrett Quality Care	60.00	27.00
94 Bill Elliott Mac Tonight	80.00	36.00
97 Chad Little John Deere	45.00	20.00
97 Chad Little John Deere 160th Anniversary	55.00	25.00
99 Jeff Burton Exide	70.00	32.00
00 Buckshot Jones Aqua Fresh	60.00	27.00

1998 Action/RCCA Banks 1:24

These cars were produced by Action and distributed through the club (RCCA). Each car has a slot in the back window for a coin bank. All banks have clear windows.

CAR / DRIVER / SPONSOR	MINT	NRMT
1 Jeff Gordon Baby Ruth	125.00	55.00
1 Dale Earnhardt Jr. Coke	150.00	70.00
1 Steve Park Pennzoil	150.00	70.00
1 Darrell Waltrip Pennzoil	100.00	45.00
K2 Dale Earnhardt Dayvault's	80.00	36.00
2 Rusty Wallace Adventures of Rusty	60.00	27.00
2 Rusty Wallace Miller Lite	55.00	25.00
2 Rusty Wallace Miller Lite Elvis	45.00	20.00
2 Rusty Wallace Miller Lite TCB	40.00	18.00
3 Dale Earnhardt Coke	70.00	32.00
3 Dale Earnhardt Goodwrench Plus	80.00	36.00
3 Dale Earnhardt Goodwrench Plus Bass Pro	150.00	70.00
3 Dale Earnhardt Goodwrench Plus Daytona	75.00	34.00
3 Dale Earnhardt Jr. AC Delco	300.00	135.00
4 Bobby Hamilton Kodak	70.00	32.00
5 Terry Labonte Blasted Fruit Loops	80.00	36.00
5 Terry Labonte Kellogg's	90.00	40.00
5 Terry Labonte Kellogg's Corny	120.00	55.00
5 Terry Labonte Kellogg's Ironman	100.00	45.00
8 Dale Earnhardt 10,000 RPM 1978 Dodge	75.00	34.00
8 Hut Stricklin Circuit City	60.00	27.00
9 Jerry Nadeau Zombie Island	90.00	40.00
9 Lake Speed Birthday Cake	60.00	27.00

CAR / DRIVER / SPONSOR	MINT	NRMT
9 Lake Speed Huckleberry Hound	80.00	36.00
10 Ricky Rudd Tide	70.00	32.00
12 Jeremy Mayfield Mobil 1	50.00	22.00
12 Jimmy Spencer Zippo	225.00	100.00
14 Patty Moise Rhodes Xena	50.00	22.00
18 Bobby Labonte Interstate Batteries	75.00	34.00
18 Bobby Labonte Interstate Batteries Small Soldiers	80.00	36.00
23 Jimmy Spencer No Bull	150.00	70.00
24 Jeff Gordon DuPont	80.00	36.00
24 Jeff Gordon DuPont Chromalusion	150.00	70.00
28 Kenny Irwin Havoline	80.00	36.00
28 Kenny Irwin Havoline Joker	90.00	40.00
31 Dale Earnhardt Jr. Sikkens	250.00	110.00
31 Dale Earnhardt Jr. Wrangler	250.00	110.00
31 Mike Skinner Lowe's	60.00	27.00
31 Mike Skinner Lowe's Special Olympic	60.00	27.00
32 Dale Jarrett White Rain	65.00	29.00
33 Tim Fedewa Kleenex	70.00	32.00
34 Mike McLaughlin Goulds	100.00	45.00
35 Todd Bodine Tabasco	80.00	36.00
36 Ernie Irvan M&M's	125.00	55.00
36 Ernie Irvan Skittles	70.00	32.00
36 Ernie Irvan Wildberry Skittles	100.00	45.00
41 Steve Grissom Kodiak	75.00	34.00
42 Joe Nemechek BellSouth	60.00	27.00
44 Tony Stewart Shell	80.00	36.00
44 Tony Stewart Shell Small Soldiers	80.00	36.00
50 Ricky Craven Budweiser	100.00	45.00
50 No Driver Association Bud Louie	80.00	36.00
81 Kenny Wallace Square D	70.00	32.00
81 Kenny Wallace Square D Lightning	75.00	34.00
88 Dale Jarrett Quality Care	75.00	34.00
88 Dale Jarrett Quality Care No Bull	75.00	34.00
88 Dale Jarrett Quality Care Batman	80.00	36.00
90 Dick Trickle Heilig-Meyers	65.00	29.00
96 David Green Caterpillar	45.00	20.00
98 Greg Sacks Thorn Apple Valley	45.00	20.00
300 Darrell Waltrip Flock Special	100.00	45.00

1999 Action/RCCA Banks 1:24

These car were available only through the club, and were very limited. All banks have clear windows.

CAR / DRIVER / SPONSOR	MINT	NRMT
1 Steve Park Pennzoil	110.00	50.00
1 Jeff Gordon Carolina Ford	125.00	55.00
2 Rusty Wallace Miller Lite	120.00	55.00
2 Rusty Wallace Miller Lite Harley-Davidson	120.00	55.00
2 Rusty Wallace True to Texas	120.00	55.00
3 Dale Earnhardt Goodwrench	120.00	55.00
3 Dale Earnhardt Goodwrench 25th Anniversary	120.00	55.00
3 Dale Earnhardt GM Goodwrench Sign	120.00	55.00
3 Dale Earnhardt Wrangler	110.00	50.00
3 Dale Earnhardt Jr. AC Delco	110.00	50.00
3 Dale Earnhardt Jr. AC Delco Superman	150.00	70.00
4 Bobby Hamilton Advantix	100.00	45.00
5 Terry Labonte K-Sentials	110.00	50.00
5 Terry Labonte Rice Krispy	110.00	50.00
8 Dale Earnhardt Jr. Budwesier	120.00	55.00
8 Dale Earnhardt Jr. Budweiser Tracks	120.00	55.00
9 Jerry Nadeau Dextor's Lab	110.00	50.00
9 Jerry Nadeau Jetsons	110.00	50.00
10 Ricky Rudd Tide	100.00	45.00
10 Ricky Rudd Tide Peroxide	100.00	45.00
12 Jeremy Mayfield Kentucky Derby	100.00	45.00
12 Jeremy Mayfield Mobil 1	100.00	45.00
15 Ken Schrader Oakwood Homes	100.00	45.00
17 Matt Kenseth DeWalt	110.00	50.00
18 Bobby Labonte Interstate Batteries	110.00	50.00
19 Mike Skinner Yellow Fright	110.00	50.00
20 Tony Stewart Home Depot	200.00	90.00
20 Tony Stewart Habitat for Humanity	175.00	80.00
21 Elliott Sadler Citgo	100.00	45.00
23 Jimmy Spencer Winston	110.00	50.00
23 Jimmy Spencer Winston Lights	110.00	50.00
24 Jeff Gordon DuPont	100.00	45.00
24 Jeff Gordon DuPont Superman	120.00	55.00
24 Jeff Gordon Pepsi	120.00	55.00
24 Jeff Gordon Star Wars	120.00	55.00
25 Wally Dallenbach Budweiser	100.00	45.00

CAR / DRIVER / SPONSOR	MINT	NRMT
27 Casey Atwood Castrol	125.00	55.00
28 Kenny Irwin Havoline	100.00	45.00
30 Derrike Cope Jimmy Dean	100.00	45.00
31 Dale Earnhardt Jr. Gargoyles	100.00	45.00
31 Dale Earnhardt Jr. Wrangler	120.00	55.00
31 Mike Skinner Lowe's	100.00	45.00
33 Ken Schrader Skoal Red	100.00	45.00
36 Ernie Irvan M&M's	100.00	45.00
36 Ernie Irvan Pedigree	100.00	45.00
36 Ernie Irvan Crispy M&M's	120.00	55.00
40 Sterling Marlin Coors	100.00	45.00
40 Sterling Marlin Coors John Wayne	100.00	45.00
40 Sterling Marlin Coors Brooks & Dunn	100.00	45.00
40 Kerry Earnhardt Channellock	100.00	45.00
40 NDA Coca-Cola	100.00	45.00
44 Justin Labonte Slim Jim	100.00	45.00
45 Rich Bickle 10-10-345	100.00	45.00
50 Mark Green Dr Pepper	100.00	45.00
55 Kenny Wallace Square D	100.00	45.00
66 Darrell Waltrip Big K	100.00	45.00
71 Dave Marcis Realtree	100.00	45.00
77 Robert Pressley Jasper	100.00	45.00
88 Dale Jarrett Quality Care	100.00	45.00
88 Dale Jarrett No Bull	100.00	45.00
00 Buckshot Jones Crown Fiber	100.00	45.00

2000 Action/RCCA Banks 1:24

These banks are available solely through the RCCA club and feature clear windows.

CAR / DRIVER / SPONSOR	MINT	NRMT
3 Dale Earnhardt Taz No Bull	120.00	55.00
20 Tony Stewart Home Depot	120.00	55.00

1997 Action/RCCA Elite 1:24

This series consists of upgraded versions of their standard production cars. It was started in 1997. The cars from this series contain serial number plates on the undercarriage at the end of the car.

CAR / DRIVER / SPONSOR	MINT	NRMT
2 Rusty Wallace Miller Lite Texas Motor Speedway	125.00	55.00
2 Rusty Wallace Miller Lite	150.00	70.00
3 Dale Earnhardt AC Delco	100.00	45.00

CAR / DRIVER / SPONSOR	MINT	NRMT
3 Dale Earnhardt Goodwrench	400.00	180.00
3 Dale Earnhardt Goodwrench Plus	250.00	110.00
3 Dale Earnhardt Wheaties Gold number plate	250.00	110.00
3 Dale Earnhardt Wheaties Pewter number plate	200.00	90.00
3 Steve Park AC Delco	200.00	90.00
4 Sterling Marlin Kodak	80.00	36.00
6 Mark Martin Valvoline	150.00	70.00
9 Jeff Burton Track Gear	80.00	36.00
10 Ricky Rudd Tide	80.00	36.00
14 Steve Park Burger King	250.00	110.00
17 Darrell Waltrip Parts America	120.00	55.00
17 Darrell Waltrip Parts America Chrome	175.00	80.00
18 Bobby Labonte Interstate Batteries	150.00	70.00
22 Ward Burton MBNA Gold	150.00	70.00
24 Jeff Gordon Dupont	250.00	110.00
24 Jeff Gordon Dupont Million Dollar Date	150.00	70.00
24 Jeff Gordon Dupont Premier	350.00	160.00
24 Jeff Gordon Lost World	250.00	110.00
25 Ricky Craven Budweiser	100.00	45.00
29 Jeff Green Tom & Jerry	100.00	45.00
29 Elliot Sadler Phillips 66	70.00	32.00
29 No Driver Associated Scooby-Doo	150.00	70.00
31 Mike Skinner Lowe's	175.00	80.00
31 Mike Skinner Lowe's Japan	100.00	45.00
32 Dale Jarrett White Rain	175.00	80.00
36 Derrike Cope Skittles	100.00	45.00
36 Todd Bodine Stanley	150.00	70.00
37 Mark Green Timber Wolf	150.00	70.00
37 Jeremy Mayfield Kmart	100.00	45.00
46 Wally Dallenbach First Union	60.00	27.00
60 Mark Martin Winn Dixie	100.00	45.00
88 Dale Jarrett Ford Credit	150.00	70.00
94 Bill Elliott McDonald's	175.00	80.00
94 Bill Elliott Mac Tonight	100.00	45.00
96 David Green Caterpillar	60.00	27.00
97 Chad Little John Deere	100.00	45.00
97 Chad Little John Deere 160th Anniversary.	150.00	70.00
99 Jeff Burton Exide	100.00	45.00
00 Buckshot Jones Aqua Fresh	120.00	55.00

1998 Action/RCCA Elite 1:24

This series was consists of upgraded versions of their standard production cars. The cars from this series contain serial number plates on the undercarriage at the end of the car.

CAR / DRIVER / SPONSOR	MINT	NRMT
1 Dale Earnhardt Jr. Coke	175.00	80.00
1 Jeff Gordon Baby Ruth	200.00	90.00
1 Steve Park Pennzoil	175.00	80.00
1 Steve Park Pennzoil Indy	150.00	70.00
1 Darrell Waltrip Pennzoil	175.00	80.00
K2 Dale Earnhardt Dayvault's	100.00	45.00
2 Rusty Wallace Adventures of Rusty	150.00	70.00
2 Rusty Wallace Miller Lite	150.00	70.00
2 Rusty Wallace Miller Lite Elvis	150.00	70.00
3 Dale Earnhardt Coke	150.00	70.00
3 Dale Earnhardt Goodwrench Plus	150.00	70.00
3 Dale Earnhardt Goodwrench Plus Bass Pro	150.00	70.00
3 Dale Earnhardt Goodwrench Plus Daytona	200.00	90.00
3 Dale Earnhardt Goodwrench Silver	175.00	80.00
3 Dale Earnhardt Jr. AC Delco	450.00	200.00
4 Bobby Hamilton Kodak	100.00	45.00
5 Terry Labonte Blasted Fruit Loops	175.00	80.00
5 Terry Labonte Kellogg's	150.00	70.00
5 Terry Labonte Kellogg's Corny	200.00	90.00
5 Terry Labonte Kellogg's Ironman	175.00	80.00
8 Dale Earnhardt 10,000 RPM 1978 Dodge	150.00	70.00
8 Hut Stricklin Circuit City	100.00	45.00
9 Jerry Nadeau Zombie Island	150.00	70.00
9 Lake Speed Birthday Cake	150.00	70.00
9 Lake Speed Hucklerberry Hound	175.00	80.00
10 Ricky Rudd Tide	150.00	70.00
12 Jeremy Mayfield Mobil 1	150.00	70.00
12 Jimmy Spencer Zippo	350.00	160.00
14 Patty Moise Rhodes	175.00	80.00
18 Bobby Labonte Interstate Batteries Small Soldiers	150.00	70.00
23 Jimmy Spencer No Bull	200.00	90.00
24 Jeff Gordon DuPont	200.00	90.00
24 Jeff Gordon DuPont Chromalusion	300.00	135.00
28 Kenny Irwin Havoline	125.00	55.00
28 Kenny Irwin Havoline Joker	125.00	55.00
31 Dale Earnhardt Jr. Sikkens	250.00	110.00

CAR / DRIVER / SPONSOR	MINT	NRMT
31 Mike Skinner Lowe's	150.00	70.00
31 Mike Skinner Lowe's Special Olympics	150.00	70.00
33 Tim Fedewa Kleenex	175.00	80.00
34 Mike McLaughlin Goulds	175.00	80.00
35 Todd Bodine Tabasco	150.00	70.00
36 Ernie Irvan M&M's	200.00	90.00
36 Ernie Irvan Skittles	150.00	70.00
36 Ernie Irvan Wildberry Skittles	175.00	80.00
41 Steve Grissom Kodiak	150.00	70.00
44 Tony Stewart Shell	225.00	100.00
44 Tony Stewart Shell Small Soldiers	150.00	70.00
50 Ricky Craven Budweiser	150.00	70.00
50 No Driver Association Bud Louie	175.00	80.00
81 Kenny Wallace Square D	125.00	55.00
81 Kenny Wallace Square D Lightning	150.00	70.00
88 Dale Jarrett Quality Care	150.00	70.00
88 Dale Jarrett Quality Care Batman	150.00	70.00
88 Dale Jarrett Quality Care No Bull	150.00	70.00
96 David Green Caterpillar	150.00	70.00
98 Greg Sacks Thorn Apple Valley	125.00	55.00
300 Darrell Waltrip Tim Flock Special	200.00	90.00

1999 Action/RCCA Elite 1:24

CAR / DRIVER / SPONSOR	MINT	NRMT
1 Jeff Gordon Carolina '91 TB	175.00	80.00
1 Steve Park Pennzoil	175.00	80.00
2 Rusty Wallace Miller Lite	175.00	80.00
2 Rusty Wallace Miller Lite Last Lap	175.00	80.00
2 Rusty Wallace Harley-Davidson	200.00	90.00
3 Dale Earnhardt Goodwrench	175.00	80.00
3 Dale Earnhardt Goodwrench 25th Anniversary	175.00	80.00
3 Dale Earnhardt Goodwrench Last Lap	175.00	80.00
3 Dale Earnhardt GM Goodwrench Sign	175.00	80.00
3 Dale Earnhardt Wrangler	200.00	90.00
3 Dale Earnhardt Jr. AC Delco	225.00	100.00
3 Dale Earnhardt Jr. AC Delco Last Lap	200.00	90.00
3 Dale Earnhardt Jr. AC Delco Superman	200.00	90.00
4 Bobby Hamilton Advantix	150.00	70.00
5 Terry Labonte Kellogg's	175.00	80.00
5 Terry Labonte K-Sentials	200.00	90.00
5 Terry Labonte Rice Krispies	200.00	90.00
8 Dale Earnhardt Jr. Budweiser	200.00	90.00
8 Dale Earnhardt Jr. Budweiser Track Cars	200.00	90.00
9 Jerry Nadeau Dextor's Lab	175.00	80.00
9 Jerry Nadeau Jetsons	175.00	80.00
10 Ricky Rudd Tide Kids Car	175.00	80.00
10 Ricky Rudd Tide	175.00	80.00
11 Dale Jarrett Green Bay Packers	175.00	80.00
12 Jeremy Mayfield Mobil 1	175.00	80.00
12 Jeremy Mayfield Kentucky Derby	175.00	80.00
17 Matt Kenseth DeWalt Ford	225.00	100.00
18 Bobby Labonte Interstate Batteries	200.00	90.00
19 Mike Skinner Yellow Fright	200.00	90.00
20 Tony Stewart Home Depot	500.00	220.00
20 Tony Stewart Habitat	250.00	110.00
22 Ward Burton Caterpiller	225.00	100.00
23 Jimmy Spencer No Bull	200.00	90.00
23 Jimmy Spencer Winston Lights Gold	175.00	80.00
24 Jeff Gordon DuPont	175.00	80.00
24 Jeff Gordon Superman	225.00	100.00
24 Jeff Gordon Pepsi	225.00	100.00
24 Jeff Gordon Pepsi Star Wars	175.00	80.00
25 Wally Dallenbach Budweiser	175.00	80.00
27 Casey Atwood Castrol	200.00	90.00
28 Kenny Irwin Havoline	175.00	80.00
30 Dale Earnhardt Army '76 Malibu	175.00	80.00
30 Derrike Cope Jimmy Dean	175.00	80.00
31 Dale Earnhardt Jr. Sikkens White	250.00	110.00
31 Mike Skinner Lowe's	175.00	80.00
31 Dale Earnhardt Jr. Wrangler	200.00	90.00
33 Ken Schrader Skoal	200.00	90.00
33 Ken Schrader Skoal Red	200.00	90.00
36 Ernie Irvan M&M's	200.00	90.00
36 Ernie Irvan Pedigree	200.00	90.00
40 Sterling Marlin Coors	175.00	80.00
40 Sterling Marlin Coors John Wayne	175.00	80.00
40 Sterling Marlin Coors Brook & Dunn	175.00	80.00
40 Kerry Earnhardt Channellock	175.00	80.00
40 NDA Coca-Cola	175.00	80.00
45 Rich Bickle 10-10-345	175.00	80.00
50 Mark Green Dr Pepper	175.00	80.00
55 Kenny Wallace Square D	175.00	80.00
66 Darrell Waltrip Big K	175.00	80.00
71 Dave Marcis Reeltree	175.00	80.00
77 Dale Earnhardt Hy-Gain '76 Malibu	175.00	80.00
77 Robet Pressley Jasper	175.00	80.00
88 Dale Jarrett Quality Care	175.00	80.00
88 Dale Jarrett QC White	175.00	80.00
2 Mark Martin J-Mar Trucking	200.00	90.00

2000 Action/RCCA Elite 1:24

These cars are available solely through the RCCA club and feature exacting detail.

CAR / DRIVER / SPONSOR	MINT	NRMT
3 Dale Earnhardt Taz No Bull	200.00	90.00
8 Dale Earnhardt Jr. 2000 Test Car	175.00	80.00
20 Tony Stewart Home Depot	175.00	80.00

1995-96 Action/RCCA SuperTrucks 1:24

The top SuperTruck driver's trucks are featured in these die-cast pieces. Most pieces were distributed either through the Action Dealer Network or Action's Racing Collectibles Club of America. Some were made available through both outlets. There are two versions of most trucks, a bank and a regular version. The banks have a slot in the truck bed for the coin.

CAR / DRIVER / SPONSOR	MINT	NRMT
3 Mike Skinner Goodwrench	40.00	18.00
3 Mike Skinner Goodwrench Bank	50.00	22.00
3 Mike Skinner Goodwrench 1996	40.00	18.00
3 Mike Skinner Goodwrench 1996 Bank	60.00	27.00
6 Rick Carelli Total Petroleum	45.00	20.00
6 Rick Carelli Total Petroleum Bank	45.00	20.00
7 Geoff Bodine Exide	45.00	20.00
7 Geoff Bodine Exide Bank	45.00	20.00
16 Ron Hornaday Action	40.00	18.00
16 Ron Hornaday Action Bank	40.00	18.00
16 Ron Hornaday NAPA	40.00	18.00
16 Ron Hornaday NAPA Bank	40.00	18.00
16 Ron Hornaday NAPA Gold	60.00	27.00
16 Ron Hornaday NAPA Gold B	60.00	27.00
16 Ron Hornaday Papa John's	45.00	20.00
16 Ron Hornaday Papa John's Bank	45.00	20.00
24 Scott Lagasse DuPont	45.00	20.00
24 Scott Lagasse DuPont Bank	45.00	20.00

CAR / DRIVER / SPONSOR	MINT	NRMT
24 Jack Sprague Quaker State	40.00	18.00
24 Jack Sprague Quaker State Bank	40.00	18.00
28 Ernie Irvan NAPA	45.00	20.00
28 Ernie Irvan NAPA Bank	50.00	22.00
52 Ken Schrader AC Delco	40.00	18.00
52 Ken Schrader AC Delco Bank	45.00	20.00
71 Kenji Momota Action Racing Collectables	40.00	18.00
71 Kenji Momota Action Racing Collectables Bank	45.00	20.00
80 Joe Ruttman JR's Garage	60.00	27.00
84 Joe Ruttman Mac Tools	40.00	18.00
84 Joe Ruttman Mac Tools Bank	45.00	20.00
98 Butch Miller Raybestos Bank	45.00	20.00

1998 Action/RCCA Gold 1:32

These 1:32 scale cars were distributed by Action through RCCA.

1 Steve Park Pennzoil	75.00	34.00
2 Rusty Wallace Miller Lite	75.00	34.00
3 Dale Earnhardt Goodwrench Plus Bass Pro	75.00	34.00
3 Dale Earnhardt Jr. AC Delco	90.00	40.00
5 Terry Labonte Kellogg's	75.00	34.00
12 Jeremy Mayfield Mobil 1	75.00	34.00
18 Bobby Labonte Interstate Batteries	75.00	34.00
23 Jimmy Spencer No Bull	75.00	34.00
24 Jeff Gordon DuPont	75.00	34.00
28 Kenny Irwin Havoline	75.00	34.00
36 Ernie Irvan M&M's	75.00	34.00
88 Dale Jarrett Quality Care	75.00	34.00

1991 Action/RCCA Oldsmobile Series 1:64

This series consists of 1991 Oldsmobile 1:64 scale replicas. Included is a 2-car set of Rob Moroso plus two single cars of the 1990 Winston Cup Rookie of the Year.

20/25 Rob Moroso Swisher Sweet 2 car set	25.00	11.00
22 Ed Berrier Greased Lightning	4.00	1.80
22 Rob Moroso Moroso Racing	4.00	1.80
22 Rob Moroso Prestone	4.00	1.80
33 Harry Gant Skoal with Mug	15.00	6.75
44 Bobby Labonte Penrose	30.00	13.50
44 Sterling Marlin Piedmont	8.00	3.60

CAR / DRIVER / SPONSOR	MINT	NRMT
73 Phil Barkdoll XR-1	4.00	1.80
88 Buddy Baker Red Baron	25.00	11.00
91 Clifford Allison Mac Tools	15.00	6.75
93 Christmas Car Promo	4.00	1.80

1991 Action/RCCA 1983-86 T-Bird Series 1:64

The 1:64 die cast cars that appear in this series are replicas of Thunderbirds that were driven between 1983-1986. The series has one of the few die cast of Kyle Petty's 7-Eleven. The series also has Dale Earnhardt in a Ford Thunderbird.

7 Kyle Petty 7-Eleven	18.00	8.00
9 Bill Elliott Melling	18.00	8.00
15 Dale Earnhardt Wrangler	60.00	27.00
15 Ricky Rudd Motorcraft	12.00	5.50
21 Buddy Baker Valvoline with V on deck lid	6.00	2.70
21 Buddy Baker Valvoline with Valvoline on deck lid	8.00	3.60
21 David Pearson Black Bumper	20.00	9.00
21 David Pearson Brown Bumper	25.00	11.00

1993-95 Action/RCCA 1:64

These were the 1:64 scale cars that were made by Action and distributed through the club (RCCA). The most popular versions seem to be the hood open cars. Many of the first cars distributed throught the club were made for Action by Revell.

1 Jeff Gordon Baby Ruth Revell	70.00	32.00
1 No Driver Association Winston Cup Car Platinum Series in acrylic case	20.00	9.00
2 Mark Martin Miller Acrylic	15.00	6.75
2 Rusty Wallace Miller Genuine Draft Club Only	18.00	8.00
2 Rusty Wallace Miller Genuine Draft 1995 Hood Open in acrylic case	15.00	6.75
2 Rusty Wallace Pontiac Excitement Revell	8.00	3.60

3 Richard Childress CRC Chemical 1980 Olds	12.00	5.50

CAR / DRIVER / SPONSOR	MINT	NRMT

3 Dale Earnhardt Wrangler 1981 Pontiac	30.00	13.50
3 Dale Earnhardt Wrangler 1985 Monte Carlo Notchback	40.00	18.00
3 Dale Earnhardt Wrangler 1987 Monte Carlo Fastback	40.00	18.00
3 Dale Earnhardt Goodwrench Club Only	30.00	13.50

3 Dale Earnhardt Goodwrench 1994 Lumina Hood Open	30.00	13.50
3 Dale Earnhardt Goodwrench 1994 Lumina	18.00	8.00
3 Dale Earnhardt Goodwrench 1995 Monte Carlo Hood Open	25.00	11.00
3 Dale Earnhardt Goodwrench Silver Car Hood Open	100.00	45.00
3 Dale Earnhardt Jr. Mom-n-Pop's	60.00	27.00

5 Terry Labonte Kellogg's 1994 Lumina HO	30.00	13.50

5 Ricky Rudd Tide Revell Promo	12.00	5.50
6 Mark Martin Folgers Promo	50.00	22.00
6 Mark Martin Stroh's Light 2 car combo	50.00	22.00
6 Mark Martin Valvoline Hood Open Brickyard Special	16.00	7.25

6 Mark Martin   15.00   6.75
   Valvoline 1995 Thunderbird
   Hood Open

6 Mark Martin   6.00   2.70
   Valvoline Revell

7 Alan Kulwicki   40.00   18.00
   Hooters Hood Open
7 Alan Kulwicki   40.00   18.00
   Zerex

8 Kerry Earnhardt   20.00   9.00
   Mom-n-Pop's 1994

9 Bill Elliott   10.00   4.50
   Melling Club Only
10 Derrike Cope   10.00   4.50
   Purolator Revell
10 Ricky Rudd   10.00   4.50
   Tide Hood Open
11 Brett Bodine   12.00   5.50
   Lowe's Hood Open
11 Bill Elliott   15.00   6.75
   Budweiser Hood Open

11 Darrell Waltrip   15.00   6.75
   Budweiser 1984 Monte Carlo
12 Neil Bonnett   15.00   6.75
   Budweiser 1984 Monte Carlo
12 Hut Stricklin   5.00   2.20
   Raybestos Revell
15 Dale Earnhardt   50.00   22.00
   Wrangler Revell

15 Ricky Rudd   5.00   2.20
   Motorcraft Revell

15 Lake Speed   15.00   6.75
   Quality Care 1994 Hood Open
16 Ted Musgrave   15.00   6.75
   Family Channel Hood Open
17 Darrell Waltrip   15.00   6.75
   Superflo Camaro
17 Darrell Waltrip   15.00   6.75
   Western Auto Revell Club Only

17 Darrell Waltrip   12.00   5.50
   Western Auto 1994 Lumina
   Hood Open
17 Darrell Waltrip   15.00   6.75
   Western Auto 1995 Monte Carlo
   Hood Open

18 Dale Jarrett   25.00   11.00
   Interstate Batteries 1994 Hood Open

18 Dale Jarrett   5.00   2.20
   Interstate Batteries Revell
21 David Pearson   15.00   6.75
   Chattanooga Chew
   1985 Monte Carlo

21 David Pearson   20.00   9.00
   Pearson Racing

21 Morgan Shepherd   12.00   5.50
   Cheerwine Morema

21 Morgan Shepherd   5.00   2.20
   Citgo REV

22 Sterling Marlin   5.00   2.20
   Maxwell House Revell
23 Jimmy Spencer   50.00   22.00
   Smokin' Joe's Hood Open

24 Jeff Gordon	50.00	22.00	28 Davey Allison	30.00	13.50	41 Joe Nemechek	5.00	2.20
DuPont 1993 Lumina HO			Havoline Club Only			Meineke		
24 Jeff Gordon	30.00	13.50	28 Dale Jarrett	15.00	6.75	42 Kyle Petty	15.00	6.75
DuPont 1994 Lumina Hood Open			Havoline Hood Open			Coors Light Hood Open		
24 Jeff Gordon	20.00	9.00	30 Michael Waltrip	12.00	5.50	42 Kyle Petty	60.00	27.00
DuPont 1995 Monte Carlo Hood Open			Pennzoil Hood Open			Coors Light Pumpkin Special Hood Open		
25 Ricky Craven	15.00	6.75						
1991 BGN Champion Promo								
25 Tim Richmond	20.00	9.00						
25 Ken Schrader	15.00	6.75						
Budweiser Hood Open								
25 Bill Venturini	5.00	2.20						
Rain X Revell								
26 Brett Bodine	5.00	2.20						
Quaker State Revell								

26 Steve Kinser	15.00	6.75	30 Michael Waltrip	5.00	2.20	42 Kyle Petty	12.00	5.50
Quaker State 1995 Hood Open			Pennzoil Revell			Mello Yello Hood Open		
27 Rusty Wallace	30.00	13.50	35 Alan Kulwicki	50.00	22.00	42 Kyle Petty	5.00	2.20
Kodiak 1989 Pontiac HO Acrylic			Qunicy's			Mello Yello Revell		

27 Tim Richmond	15.00	6.75	36 Kenny Wallace	5.00	2.20	43 Richard Petty	25.00	11.00
Old Milwaukee 1994 Hood Open			Cox Lumber Revell			STP 1991 Grand Prix Revell		
						44 Larry Caudill	5.00	2.20
						Army Revell		
						51 Neil Bonnett	50.00	22.00
						Country Time		
						63 Chuck Bown	12.00	5.50
						Nescafe Promo		

28 Cale Yarborough	25.00	11.00	36 Kenny Wallace	5.00	2.20
Hardee's			Dirt Devil Revell		
28 Davey Allison	25.00	11.00			
Mac Tools Promo					
28 Davey Allison	20.00	9.00			
Havoline Hood Open Black Gold paint scheme					
28 Davey Allison	20.00	9.00			
Havoline Hood Open Black Orange paint scheme					

			38 Kelley Earnhardt	15.00	6.75	66 Jimmy Hensley	5.00	2.20
			Mom-n-Pop's 1994			TropArtic Revell		
						68 Bobby Hamilton	5.00	2.20
						Country Time Revell		
						87 Joe Nemechek	5.00	2.20
						Texas Pete Revell		

	MINT	NRMT
88 Ernie Irvan	10.00	4.50
Havoline HO		
88 Darrell Waltrip	15.00	6.75
Gatorade		
89 Jim Sauter	5.00	2.20
Evinrude Revell		
90 Bobby Hillin Jr.	12.00	5.50
Heilig-Meyers Promo		

	MINT	NRMT
90 Mike Wallace	10.00	4.50
Heilig-Meyers Revell Promo		
92 Circle Track Show Car Promo	12.00	5.50
93 Casey Elliott	12.00	5.50
Hood Open		
93 Mike Wallace	5.00	2.20
No Sponsor Revell		

	MINT	NRMT
94 Bill Elliott	15.00	6.75
McDonald's Hood Open		
94 Bill Elliott	50.00	22.00
McDonald's Thunderbat Hood Open		

	MINT	NRMT
95 David Green	15.00	6.75
Busch Beer Hood Open		

	MINT	NRMT
98 Derrike Cope	12.00	5.50
Fingerhut 1994 Hood Open		

	MINT	NRMT
99 Ricky Craven	5.00	2.20
DuPont Revell		

1996 Action/RCCA 1:64

These were the 1:64 scale cars that were made by Action and distributed through the club (RCCA). All cars have open hoods. These cars are packaged in boxes in contrast to their ARC counterparts.

	MINT	NRMT
2 Rusty Wallace	15.00	6.75
Miller Genuine Draft		
2 Rusty Wallace	20.00	9.00
Miller Genuine Draft Silver car in Acrylic Case		

	MINT	NRMT
3 Dale Earnhardt	25.00	11.00
AC Delco		

	MINT	NRMT
3 Dale Earnhardt	30.00	13.50
Goodwrench		
4 Sterling Marlin	15.00	6.75
Kodak		
5 Terry Labonte	30.00	13.50
Kellogg's Ironman		

	MINT	NRMT
5 Terry Labonte	20.00	9.00
Kellogg's Japan		
6 Mark Martin	15.00	6.75
Valvoline		
7 Geoff Bodine	12.00	5.50
Exide		

	MINT	NRMT
14 Jeff Green	12.00	5.50
Racing For Kids		

	MINT	NRMT
15 Dale Earnhardt	30.00	13.50
Wrangler 1982 Thunderbird		

	MINT	NRMT
17 Darrell Waltrip	15.00	6.75
Tide 1988 Monte Carlo		

	MINT	NRMT
18 Bobby Labonte	15.00	6.75
Interstate Batteries		

	MINT	NRMT
21 Michael Waltrip	15.00	6.75
Citgo Star Trek		

	MINT	NRMT
24 Jeff Gordon	20.00	9.00
DuPont		
25 Tim Richmond	15.00	6.75
Folgers 1986 Monte Carlo		

CAR / DRIVER / SPONSOR	MINT	NRMT

| 27 Rusty Wallace | 25.00 | 11.00 |
| Kodiak 1989 Grand Prix Acrylic | | |

28 Ernie Irvan	15.00	6.75
Havoline		
29 Steve Grissom	15.00	6.75
Cartoon Network		

29 No Driver Association	15.00	6.75
Scooby-Doo		
30 Johnny Benson	15.00	6.75
Pennzoil		
42 Kyle Petty	18.00	8.00
Coors Light		

| 42 Kyle Petty | 20.00 | 9.00 |
| Coors Light Black Paint Scheme In Acrylic Case | | |

| 43 Bobby Hamilton | 18.00 | 8.00 |
| STP Silver car | | |

CAR / DRIVER / SPONSOR	MINT	NRMT
43 Bobby Hamilton	80.00	36.00
STP 5 car set		
57 Jason Keller	15.00	6.75
Halloween Havoc		

88 Dale Jarrett	15.00	6.75
Quality Care		
94 Bill Elliott	15.00	6.75
McDonald's		

1997 Action/RCCA 1:64

These were the 1:64 scale cars that were made by Action and distributed through the club (RCCA). All cars have open hoods. These cars are packaged in boxes in contrast to their ARC counterparts.

2 Rusty Wallace	15.00	6.75
Miller Lite		
2 Rusty Wallace	18.00	8.00
Miller Lite Japan		
2 Rusty Wallace	18.00	8.00
Miller Lite Texas Motor Speedway		
3 Dale Earnhardt	25.00	11.00
AC Delco		
3 Dale Earnhardt	25.00	11.00
Goodwrench		
3 Dale Earnhardt	25.00	11.00
Goodwrench Plus		

3 Dale Earnhardt	50.00	22.00
Wheaties		
3 Steve Park	30.00	13.50
AC Delco		
4 Sterling Marlin	12.00	5.50
Kodak		
6 Mark Martin	15.00	6.75
Valvoline		
9 Jeff Burton	15.00	6.75
Track Gear		
10 Ricky Rudd	12.00	5.50
Tide		
11 Brett Bodine	12.00	5.50
Close Call		

CAR / DRIVER / SPONSOR	MINT	NRMT
12 Kenny Wallace	12.00	5.50
Gray Bar		
14 Steve Park	30.00	13.50
Burger King		
17 Darrell Waltrip	80.00	36.00
Parts America 7 Car set		
17 Darrell Waltrip	25.00	11.00
Parts America Chrome		

18 Bobby Labonte	15.00	6.75
Interstate Batteries		
18 Bobby Labonte	15.00	6.75
Interstate Batteries Hall of Fame		

22 Ward Burton	12.00	5.50
MBNA		
22 Ward Burton	12.00	5.50
MBNA Gold		

23 Jimmy Spencer	40.00	18.00
Camel		
24 Jeff Gordon	30.00	13.50
DuPont		

| 24 Jeff Gordon | 25.00 | 11.00 |
| DuPont Million Dollar Date | | |

24 Jeff Gordon
  DuPont ChromaPremier — 50.00 — 22.00

24 Jeff Gordon Lost World	30.00	13.50
24 Jeff Gordon Lost World w/card set	50.00	22.00
25 Ricky Craven Budweiser	18.00	8.00
26 Rich Bickle KFC	12.00	5.50
27 Kenny Irwin G.I. Joe	15.00	6.75
27 Kenny Irwin Tonka	18.00	8.00
29 Jeff Green Tom & Jerry	12.00	5.50
29 Elliott Sadler Phillips 66	12.00	5.50

31 Mike Skinner Lowe's	12.00	5.50
31 Mike Skinner Lowe's Japan	12.00	5.50
32 Dale Jarrett White Rain	15.00	6.75
36 Derrike Cope Skittles	12.00	5.50
37 Mark Green Timber Wolf	12.00	5.50
37 Jeremy Mayfield Kmart	15.00	6.75
41 Steve Grissom Kodiak	15.00	6.75
46 Wally Dallenbach First Union	12.00	5.50
60 Mark Martin Winn Dixie	15.00	6.75

71 Dave Marcis
  Realtree — 12.00 — 5.50

75 Rick Mast
  Remington — 12.00 — 5.50

| 75 Rick Mast Remington Camo | 12.00 | 5.50 |
| 77 Bobby Hillin Jr. Jasper | 12.00 | 5.50 |

81 Kenny Wallace Square D	12.00	5.50
88 Dale Jarrett Quality Care	15.00	6.75
94 Bill Elliott McDonald's	15.00	6.75
94 Bill Elliott Mac Tonight	15.00	6.75
96 David Green Caterpillar	12.00	5.50
97 Chad Little John Deere	12.00	5.50

| 97 Chad Little John Deere 160th Anniversary | 12.00 | 5.50 |
| 00 Buckshot Jones Aqua Fresh | 15.00 | 6.75 |

1998 Action/RCCA 1:64

These were the 1:64 scale cars that were made by Action and distributed through the club (RCCA). All cars have open hoods. These cars are packaged in boxes in contrast to their ARC counterparts.

1 Dale Earnhardt Jr.
  Coke — 30.00 — 13.50

| 1 Jeff Gordon Baby Ruth | 35.00 | 16.00 |
| 1 Steve Park Pennzoil | 30.00 | 13.50 |

| 1 Darrell Waltrip Pennzoil | 18.00 | 8.00 |
| K2 Dale Earnhardt Dayvault's | 18.00 | 8.00 |

2 Rusty Wallace
  Adventures of Rusty — 20.00 — 9.00

Car / Driver / Sponsor	MINT	NRMT
2 Rusty Wallace Miller Lite	20.00	9.00
2 Rusty Wallace Miller Lite Elvis	20.00	9.00
2 Rusty Wallace Miller Lite TCB	20.00	9.00

3 Dale Earnhardt Coke	30.00	13.50

3 Dale Earnhardt Goodwrench Plus	25.00	11.00
3 Dale Earnhardt Goodwrench Plus Bass Pro	35.00	16.00

3 Dale Earnhardt Jr. AC Delco	40.00	18.00

4 Bobby Hamilton Kodak	15.00	6.75
5 Terry Labonte Blasted Fruit Loops	20.00	9.00

5 Terry Labonte Kellogg's	18.00	8.00

5 Terry Labonte Kellogg's Corny	18.00	8.00

5 Terry Labonte Kellogg's Ironman	18.00	8.00

8 Dale Earnhardt RPM 1978 Dodge	15.00	6.75
8 Hut Stricklin Circuit City	15.00	6.75
9 Lake Speed Birthday Cake	15.00	6.75
9 Lake Speed Huckleberry Hound	15.00	6.75
10 Ricky Rudd Tide	15.00	6.75
12 Jeremy Mayfield Mobil 1	20.00	9.00
18 Bobby Labonte Interstate Batteries	15.00	6.75
18 Bobby Labonte Interstate Batteries Hot Rod	20.00	9.00
18 Bobby Labonte Interstate Batteries Small Soldiers	15.00	6.75

24 Jeff Gordon DuPont	20.00	9.00

24 Jeff Gordon DuPont Chromalusion	45.00	20.00

24 Jeff Gordon DuPont No Bull	25.00	11.00

28 Kenny Irwin Havoline	18.00	8.00
28 Kenny Irwin Havoline Joker	18.00	8.00

31 Dale Earnhardt Jr. Sikkens	45.00	20.00

CAR / DRIVER / SPONSOR	MINT	NRMT
31 Mike Skinner Lowe's	15.00	6.75
31 Mike Skinner Lowe's Special Olympics	15.00	6.75
32 Dale Jarrett White Rain	15.00	6.75
35 Todd Bodine Tabasco Orange	15.00	6.75

35 Todd Bodine Tabasco Red	15.00	6.75
36 Ernie Irvan Skittles	15.00	6.75
41 Steve Grissom Kodiak	20.00	9.00
44 Tony Stewart Shell	25.00	11.00
44 Tony Stewart Shell Small Soldiers	18.00	8.00
50 Ricky Craven Budweiser	20.00	9.00

81 Kenny Wallace Square D Lighting	15.00	6.75
88 Dale Jarrett Quality Care	18.00	8.00
88 Dale Jarrett Quality Care Batman	18.00	8.00

90 Dick Trickle Heilig-Meyers	15.00	6.75

CAR / DRIVER / SPONSOR	MINT	NRMT
98 Greg Sacks Thorn Apple Valley	15.00	6.75

300 Darrell Waltrip Tim Flock Special	18.00	8.00

1999 Action/RCCA 1:64

These car were available only through the club, and were very limited. All car have opening hoods.

1 Jeff Gordon Carolina Ford	20.00	9.00
1 Steve Park Pennzoil	18.00	8.00

3 Dale Earnhardt Goodwrench	20.00	9.00

3 Dale Earnhardt Goodwrench 25th Anniversary	20.00	9.00
3 Dale Earnhardt GM Goodwrench Sign	25.00	11.00
3 Dale Earnhardt Wrangler	25.00	11.00

CAR / DRIVER / SPONSOR	MINT	NRMT
3 Dale Earnhardt Jr. AC Delco	25.00	11.00
4 Bobby Hamilton Advantix	18.00	8.00
5 Terry Labonte K-Sentials	18.00	8.00
8 Dale Earnhardt Jr. Budweiser	20.00	9.00
8 Dale Earnhardt Jr. Budweiser Tracks	20.00	9.00

12 Jeremy Mayfield Kentucky Derby	20.00	9.00
18 Bobby Labonte Interstate Batteries	18.00	8.00

20 Tony Stewart Home Depot	60.00	27.00
20 Tony Stewart Habitat for Humanity	35.00	16.00

23 Jimmy Spencer Winston	20.00	9.00
23 Jimmy Spencer Winston Lights	20.00	9.00
24 Jeff Gordon DuPont	20.00	9.00
24 Jeff Gordon Superman	30.00	13.50

24 Jeff Gordon Pepsi	20.00	9.00
24 Jeff Gordon Star Wars	30.00	13.50

CAR / DRIVER / SPONSOR	MINT	NRMT

CAR / DRIVER / SPONSOR	MINT	NRMT
25 Wally Dallenbach Budweiser	18.00	8.00
27 Casey Atwood Castrol	35.00	16.00
28 Kenny Irwin Havoline	18.00	8.00
30 Dale Earnhardt Army '76 Malibu	25.00	11.00

	MINT	NRMT
31 Dale Earnhardt Jr. Gargoyles 1997 Monte Carlo	25.00	11.00

	MINT	NRMT
31 Dale Earnhardt Jr. Sikkens White 1997 Mote Carlo	25.00	11.00
31 Dale Earnhardt Jr. Wrangler	25.00	11.00

	MINT	NRMT
31 Mike Skinner Lowe's	18.00	8.00
33 Ken Schrader Skoal	25.00	11.00
36 Ernie Irvan M&M's	18.00	8.00
40 Kerry Earnhardt Channellock	18.00	8.00
71 Dave Marcis Realtree	18.00	8.00
77 Dale Earnhardt Hy-Gain '76 Malibu	25.00	11.00
88 Dale Jarrett QC White	25.00	11.00
00 Buckshot Jones Crown Fiber	18.00	8.00

2000 Action/RCCA 1:64

These cars are available solely through the club.

CAR / DRIVER / SPONSOR	MINT	NRMT
8 Dale Earnhardt Jr. Budweiser	20.00	9.00
20 Tony Stewart Home Depot	20.00	9.00

1993-98 Ertl 1:18

Some of the newer pieces are often sold in 2-car sets and 3-car sets. Many of the 1:18 scale cars are commonly refered to as American Muscle. This is due to the fact that the packaging many of the cars came in said American Muscle on the box. Ertl no longer produces a line of 1:18 scale cars to be distributed by themselves but does contract work for those companies that would like to add 1:18 scales to their product lines.

	MINT	NRMT
1 Davey Allison Lancaster	60.00	27.00
1 Jeff Gordon Baby Ruth	120.00	55.00
1 Rick Mast Hooter's	60.00	27.00
Jan-33 Rick Mast Skoal 2 car set	140.00	65.00
2 Rusty Wallace Miller Genuine Draft	160.00	70.00
2 Rusty Wallace Miller Silver car	75.00	34.00
3 Dale Earnhardt Goodwrench '93 Lumina	60.00	27.00
3 Dale Earnhardt Goodwrench '95 Monte Carlo	75.00	34.00
3 Dale Earnhardt Goodwrench 7-Time	75.00	34.00
3 Dale Earnhardt Goodwrench Silver Car	150.00	70.00
Mar-43 Dale Earnhardt Richard Petty 7-time Champions	110.00	50.00
3 Jeff Green Goodwrench Buck Fever	45.00	20.00
3 Mike Skinner Goodwrench	45.00	20.00
4 Ernie Irvan Kodak	45.00	20.00
4 Sterling Marlin Kodak '95 Monte Carlo	60.00	27.00
4 Sterling Marlin Kodak 1997 Monte Carlo	45.00	20.00
4-Apr Sterling Marlin Jeff Purvis Kodak Funsaver	150.00	70.00
4 Dennis Sensiba Lane Automotive	50.00	22.00
5 Terry Labonte Honey Crunch distributed by GMP	175.00	80.00
5 Terry Labonte Kellogg's	45.00	20.00
5 Terry Labonte Kellogg's Silver car	70.00	32.00
6 Mark Martin Valvoline	45.00	20.00
6 Mark Martin Valvoline 1996	45.00	20.00
6 Mark Martin Valvoline 1997	60.00	27.00
7 Geoff Bodine Exide GMP	65.00	29.00
7 Geoff Bodine QVC	45.00	20.00
7/33/54 Harry Gant Manheim 3 Car set	200.00	90.00
7 Alan Kulwicki Army Buck Fever	100.00	45.00

	MINT	NRMT
7 Alan Kulwicki Hooters Buck Fever	125.00	55.00
7 Alan Kulwicki Zerex Buck Fever	110.00	50.00
7 Gary St.Amant Wynn's ASA	65.00	29.00
8 Jeff Burton Raybestos	35.00	16.00
8 Bobby Dotter Lubteck ASA	60.00	27.00
8 Kenny Wallace Red Dog	60.00	27.00
8 Kenny Wallace Red Dog Bank	75.00	34.00
9 Lake Speed SPAM	60.00	27.00
10 Derrike Cope Purolator	90.00	40.00
10 Ricky Rudd Tide GMP	65.00	29.00
11 Brett Bodine Lowe's	75.00	34.00
11 Bill Elliott Budweiser	40.00	18.00
12 Jimmy Spencer Meineke White Rose Collectibles Bank	200.00	90.00
14 John Andretti Kanawha	40.00	18.00
15 Geoff Bodine Motorcraft	125.00	55.00
16 Chad Chaffin 31W Insulation	50.00	22.00
16 Ted Musgrave Primestar	45.00	20.00
17 Bill Sedgwick Die Hard Super Truck	50.00	22.00
17 Darrell Waltrip Parts America	45.00	20.00
17 Darrell Waltrip Western Auto	50.00	22.00
18 Dale Jarrett Interstate Batteries	40.00	18.00
20 Bobby Hamilton Fina Lube Bank	125.00	55.00
21 Doug George Ortho Super Truck	45.00	20.00
21 Bobby Bowsher Quality Farm	70.00	32.00
21 Morgan Shepherd Cheerwine	70.00	32.00
21 Michael Waltrip Citgo	70.00	32.00
23 Davey Allison Miller American Bank	60.00	27.00
23 Davey Allison Miller High Life Bank	60.00	27.00
23 Chad Little John Deere	150.00	70.00
23 Chad Little John Deere Autographed	600.00	275.00
23 Jimmy Spencer Smokin' Joe's	150.00	70.00
24 Jeff Gordon DuPont '94 Lumina	75.00	34.00
24 Jeff Gordon DuPont '95 Buck Fever	75.00	34.00
24 Jeff Gordon DuPont '95 GMP	75.00	34.00
24 Jeff Gordon DuPont White Rose Collectibles Bank	600.00	275.00
24 Jeff Gordon DuPont White Rose Collectibles Bank No serial number on bottom	140.00	65.00
24 Jack Sprague Quaker State Super Truck	50.00	22.00
25 Ken Schrader Budweiser	40.00	18.00

CAR / DRIVER / SPONSOR	MINT	NRMT
25 Ricky Craven	100.00	45.00
Bud Pre. Series		
26 Steve Kinser	110.00	50.00
Quaker State Hood Open		
27 Tim Richmond	50.00	22.00
Old Milwaukee		
27 Rusty Wallace	75.00	34.00
Kodiak		
27 Rusty Wallace	75.00	34.00
Miller Genuine Draft		
28 Davey Allison	50.00	22.00
Havoline		
28 Davey Allison	70.00	32.00
Havoline Black and Gold Paint Scheme		
28 Davey Allison	70.00	32.00
Havoline Black and White Paint Scheme		
28 Dale Jarrett	50.00	22.00
Havoline		
28 Ernie Irvan	70.00	32.00
Havoline		
30 Johnny Benson Jr.	50.00	22.00
Pennzoil		
30 Michael Waltrip	35.00	16.00
Pennzoil		
32 Dale Jarrett	65.00	29.00
Mac Tools		
33 Harry Gant	175.00	80.00
Skoal 2 car set		
33 Brad Loney	60.00	27.00
Winnebago		
33 Brad Loney	60.00	27.00
Winnebago 1996		
33 Robert Pressley	75.00	34.00
Skoal		
36 Derrike Cope	50.00	22.00
Skittles		
37 Jeremy Mayfield	60.00	27.00
Kmart distributed by GMP		
37 Jeremy Mayfield	90.00	40.00
Kmart Pre. Series		
41 Ricky Craven	70.00	32.00
Kodiak GMP		
42 Andy Hillenburg	75.00	34.00
Budget Gourmet Promo Bank		
42 Kyle Petty	65.00	29.00
Coors Light GMP		
42 Kyle Petty	75.00	34.00
Coors Light WRC		
42 Kyle Petty	40.00	18.00
Mello Yello		
43 John Andretti	70.00	32.00
STP		
43 Rodney Combs Jr.	85.00	38.00
French's		
43 Rodney Combs Jr.	80.00	36.00
Hulk Hogan		
43 Bobby Hamilton	250.00	110.00
STP 5-car set		
43 Bobby Hamilton	60.00	27.00
STP Silver		
43 Richard Petty	45.00	20.00
STP		
43 Richard Petty	65.00	29.00
STP 7-Time Champion		
43 Robert Pressley	85.00	38.00
French's		
44 David Green	75.00	34.00
Slim Jim		
52 Butch Miller	50.00	22.00
Liberty Ford		
52 Ken Schrader	60.00	27.00
AC Delco GMP Bank		
52 Ken Schrader	50.00	22.00
AC Delco Super Truck		
52 Ken Schrader	50.00	22.00
AC Delco 1995		

CAR / DRIVER / SPONSOR	MINT	NRMT
59 Andy Belmont	60.00	27.00
Dr. Die Cast		
59 Chad Chaffin	45.00	20.00
Dr. Die Cast		
59 Robert Pressley	325.00	145.00
Alliance		
59 Dennis Setzer	60.00	27.00
Alliance '95 2500 produced		
59 Dennis Setzer	75.00	34.00
Alliance 5000 produced		
59 Dennis Setzer	225.00	100.00
Alliance 2 car set		
60 Mark Martin	70.00	32.00
Winn Dixie GMP		
71 Dave Marcis	70.00	32.00
Olive Garden		
75 Todd Bodine	70.00	32.00
Factory Stores		
84 Benny Senneker	90.00	40.00
Lane Automotive		
87 Joe Nemechek	65.00	29.00
Burger King GMP		
87 Joe Nemechek	200.00	90.00
Dentyne White Rose Collectibles Bank		
88 Dale Jarrett	45.00	20.00
Quality Care		
90 Ernie Irvan	60.00	27.00
Bulls Eye		
90 Mike Wallace	50.00	22.00
Heilig-Meyers		
94 Ron Barfield	65.00	29.00
New Holland		
94 Bill Elliott	45.00	20.00
McDonald's		
94 Bill Elliott	45.00	20.00
McDonald's 1996		
94 Bill Elliott	60.00	27.00
McDonald's 1997		
94 Bill Elliott	90.00	40.00
MT Prestige Series		
94 Bill Elliott	45.00	20.00
McDonald's Thunderbat		
95 David Green	200.00	90.00
Busch 2 car set		
95 David Green	80.00	36.00
Caterpillar Bank		
95 Tim Richmond	45.00	20.00
Old Milwaukee		
96 David Green	60.00	27.00
Caterpillar GMP		
96 David Green	90.00	40.00
Cater. Pres. Series		
97 Chad Little	140.00	65.00
John Deere Autographed Box		
98 Jeremy Mayfield	45.00	20.00
Fingerhut		
99 Dick Trickle	50.00	22.00
Articat		

1992 Funstuf Pit Row 1:43

These 1:43 scale cars were distributed through retail outlets. The series features a Jeff Gordon Baby Ruth BGN car.

	MINT	NRMT
1 Jeff Gordon	30.00	13.50
Baby Ruth		
6 Mark Martin	5.00	2.20
Valvoline		
11 Bill Elliott	5.00	2.20
Amoco		
12 Hut Stricklin	5.00	2.20
Raybestos		
16 Wally Dallenbach Jr.	6.00	2.70
Roush Racing		

CAR / DRIVER / SPONSOR	MINT	NRMT
18 Dale Jarrett	5.00	2.20
Interstate Batteries		
21 Morgan Shepherd	5.00	2.20
Citgo		
22 Sterling Marlin	5.00	2.20
Maxwell House		
33 Harry Gant	5.00	2.20
Leo Jackson Motors		
41 Greg Sacks	6.00	2.70
Kellogg's		
49 Stanley Smith	5.00	2.20
Ameritron Batteries		
66 Jimmy Hensley	5.00	2.20
TropArtic		
66 Chad Little	5.00	2.20
TropArtic		
75 Joe Ruttman	5.00	2.20
Dinner Bell		
83 Jeff McClure	6.00	2.70
Collector's World		
98 Jimmy Spencer	5.00	2.20
Moly Black Gold		

1992 Funstuf Pit Row 1:64

This series of 1:64 cars was produced by Pit Row and distributed through retail outlets. The series features a Jeff Gordon Baby Ruth BGN car. Also in the series includes a variation of the #94 Terry Labonte car. Another variation in the series is some of the cars that come with a Winston Decal and without a Winston Decal.

	MINT	NRMT
1 Jeff Gordon	20.00	9.00
Baby Ruth		
11 Bill Elliott	3.00	1.35
Amoco on the Deck Lid		
11 Bill Elliott	3.00	1.35
Amoco on the Hood		
11 No Driver Association	3.00	1.35
Baby Ruth		
12 Ken Schulz	5.00	2.20
Piggly Wiggly		
15 Morgan Shepherd	3.00	1.35
Motorcraft		
15 Morgan Shepherd	7.00	3.10
Motorcraft with Winston Decal on Fender		
15 No Driver Association	3.00	1.35
Motorcraft		
18 Dale Jarrett	3.00	1.35
Interstate Batteries		
18 No Driver Association	3.00	1.35
Interstate Batteries		
20 Michael Waltrip	5.00	2.20
Orkin		
21 Dale Jarrett	3.00	1.35
Citgo		
21 Dale Jarrett	7.00	3.10
Citgo with Winston Decal on Fender		
21 Morgan Shepherd	3.00	1.35
Citgo		
23 Eddie Bierschwale	5.00	2.20
AutoFinders		
27 Ward Burton	5.00	2.20
Gaultney		
27 Jeff McClure	5.00	2.20
Race For Life		
41 Greg Sacks	5.00	2.20
Kellogg's		
43 Richard Petty	3.00	1.35
STP		
43 Richard Petty	7.00	3.10
STP with Winston Decal on Fender		
49 Stanley Smith	7.00	3.10
Ameritron Batteries		

CAR / DRIVER / SPONSOR	MINT	NRMT
66 Jimmy Hensley TropArtic	3.00	1.35
66 Chad Little TropArtic	3.00	1.35
66 Lake Speed TropArtic	3.00	1.35
75 No Driver Association Dinner Bell	3.00	1.35
75 Joe Ruttman Dinner Bell	3.00	1.35
83 Jeff McClure Collector's World	5.00	2.20
94 Terry Labonte Sunoco	3.00	1.35
94 Terry Labonte Sunoco with Busch decal	5.00	2.20

1999 Hot Wheels Crew's Choice 1:24

These 1:24 scale cars feature bodies that are detachable from the chassis.

	MINT	NRMT
10 Ricky Rudd Tide	30.00	13.50
22 Ward Burton Caterpillar	30.00	13.50
36 Ernie Irvan M&M's	30.00	13.50
40 Sterling Marlin Coors	30.00	13.50
94 Bill Elliott McDonald's	30.00	13.50
99 Jeff Burton Exide	30.00	13.50

1999 Hot Wheels Pro Racing 1:24

These 1:24 scale cars were available through retail outlets.

	MINT	NRMT
5 Terry Labonte Kellogg's	40.00	18.00
6 Mark Martin Hot Wheels	40.00	18.00
10 Ricky Rudd Tide	20.00	9.00
12 Jeremy Mayfield Mobil 1	20.00	9.00
14 Sterling Marlin Tennessee	45.00	20.00
26 Johnny Benson Cheerios	20.00	9.00
36 Ernie Irvan M&M's	40.00	18.00
42 Joe Nemechek BellSouth	20.00	9.00
43 Richard Petty STP '81 Buick	40.00	18.00
44 Kyle Petty Hot Wheels	40.00	18.00
58 Ricky Craven Tubine Solutions	40.00	18.00
94 Bill Elliott Drive Thru	20.00	9.00
97 Chad Little John Deere	20.00	9.00

1999 Hot Wheels Trading Paint 1:24

These 1:24 scale cars feature race wear and tear.

	MINT	NRMT
22 Ward Burton Caterpillar	20.00	9.00

	MINT	NRMT
43 John Andretti STP	20.00	9.00
44 Kyle Petty Hot Wheels	20.00	9.00
66 Darrell Waltrip Big K	20.00	9.00
94 Bill Elliott McDonald's	20.00	9.00

2000 Hot Wheels Crew's Choice 1:24

These cars feature bodies that are removable from the chassis.

	MINT	NRMT
14 Mike Bliss Conseco	40.00	18.00
32 Scott Pruit Tide	40.00	18.00
44 Kyle Petty Hot Wheels	40.00	18.00

2000 Hot Wheels Deluxe 1:24

These cars are available through retail outlets.

	MINT	NRMT
44 Kyle Petty Hot Wheels	30.00	13.50

1998 Hot Wheels Pro Racing 1:43

These 1:43 scale cars were produced by Hot Wheels and marks their introduction in the NASCAR market. These cars were distributed through hobby, retail and trackside outlets.

	MINT	NRMT
5 Terry Labonte Kellogg's	15.00	6.75
6 Mark Martin Valvoline	15.00	6.75
10 Ricky Rudd Tide	15.00	6.75
12 Jeremy Mayfield Mobil 1	15.00	6.75

	MINT	NRMT
35 Todd Bodine Tabasco	15.00	6.75
36 Ernie Irvan Skittles	15.00	6.75
43 John Andretti STP	15.00	6.75
44 Kyle Petty Hot Wheels	15.00	6.75

1999 Hot Wheels Crew's Choice 1:43

These 1:43 scale cars feature bodies that are detachable from the chassis.

CAR / DRIVER / SPONSOR	MINT	NRMT
36 Ernie Irvan M&M's	25.00	11.00
44 Kyle Petty Hot Wheels	25.00	11.00
94 Bill Elliott McDonald's	25.00	11.00

1999 Hot Wheels Pro Racing 1:43

These 1:43 scale cars were available through retail outlets.

	MINT	NRMT
5 Terry Labonte Kellogg's	15.00	6.75
6 Mark Martin Vavoline	15.00	6.75
10 Ricky Rudd Tide	15.00	6.75
12 Jeremy Mayfield Mobil 1	15.00	6.75
22 Ward Burton Caterpillar	15.00	6.75
26 Johnny Benson Cheerios	15.00	6.75
36 Ernie Irvan M&M's	15.00	6.75
43 John Andretti STP	15.00	6.75
94 Bill Elliott McDonald's	15.00	6.75
97 Chad Little John Deere	15.00	6.75

1999 Hot Wheels Track Edition 1:43

The track edition set comes with a 1:64 scale car.

	MINT	NRMT
12 Jeremy Mayfield Mobil 1	15.00	6.75
16 Kevin Lepage Primestar	15.00	6.75
36 Ernie Irvan M&M's	15.00	6.75
94 Bill Elliott Drive Thru	15.00	6.75
97 Chad Little John Deere	15.00	6.75

1997 Hot Wheels Collector Edition 1:64

	MINT	NRMT
4 Sterling Marlin Kodak	6.00	2.70

5 Terry Labonte   6.00   2.70
   Kellogg's

10 Ricky Rudd   6.00   2.70
   Tide

30 Johnny Benson   6.00   2.70
   Pennzoil

6 Mark Martin   6.00   2.70
   Valvoline

16 Ted Musgrave   6.00   2.70
   Primestar

43 Bobby Hamilton   6.00   2.70
   STP

7 Geoff Bodine   6.00   2.70
   QVC

21 Michael Waltrip   6.00   2.70
   Citgo

28 Ernie Irvan   6.00   2.70
   Havoline

44 Kyle Petty   6.00   2.70
   Hot Wheels

8 Hut Stricklin   6.00   2.70
   Circuit City

94 Bill Elliott   6.00   2.70
   McDonald's

| 91 Mike Wallace | 6.00 | 2.70 |
| Spam | | |

98 John Andretti — 6.00 — 2.70
RCA

99 Jeff Burton — 6.00 — 2.70
Exide

1997 Hot Wheels Collector Edition Short Track 1:64

| 4 Sterling Marlin | 6.00 | 2.70 |
| Kodak | | |

5 Terry Labonte — 6.00 — 2.70
Kellogg's

5 Terry Labonte	6.00	2.70
Kellogg's Tony		
6 Mark Martin	6.00	2.70
Valvoline		
7 Geoff Bodine	6.00	2.70
QVC		
8 Hut Stricklin	6.00	2.70
Circuit City		
10 Ricky Rudd	6.00	2.70
Spring Fresh		
10 Ricky Rudd	6.00	2.70
Tide		
16 Ted Musgrave	6.00	2.70
Primestar		
21 Michael Waltrip	6.00	2.70
Citgo		

21 Michael Waltrip	6.00	2.70
Citgo Red top		
28 Ernie Irvan	6.00	2.70
Havoline		
30 Johnny Benson	6.00	2.70
Pennzoil		
37 Jeremy Mayfield	6.00	2.70
K-Mart		
43 Bobby Hamilton	6.00	2.70
STP		

| 44 Kyle Petty | 6.00 | 2.70 |
| Hot Wheels | | |

94 Bill Elliott	6.00	2.70
MacTonight		
94 Bill Elliott	6.00	2.70
McDonald's		
96 David Green	6.00	2.70
Caterpillar		
99 Jeff Burton	6.00	2.70
Exide		

1997 Hot Wheels Collector Edition Speedway Edition 1:64

This series of 1:64 cars marks Hot Wheels second mass-market venture into NASCAR. These cars are the upgraded versions of those cars available in the Pro Racing series.

4 Sterling Marlin	6.00	2.70
Kodak		
5 Terry Labonte	6.00	2.70
Kellogg's		
6 Mark Martin	6.00	2.70
Valvoline		
7 Geoff Bodine	6.00	2.70
QVC		
8 Hut Stricklin	6.00	2.70
Circuit City		
10 Ricky Rudd	6.00	2.70
Tide		
16 Ted Musgrave	6.00	2.70
Primestar		
21 Michael Waltrip	6.00	2.70
Citgo		
28 Ernie Irvan	6.00	2.70
Havoline		
30 Johnny Benson	6.00	2.70
Penzoil		
37 Jeremy Mayfield	6.00	2.70
Kmart		
43 Bobby Hamilton	6.00	2.70
STP		

Car / Driver / Sponsor	MINT	NRMT
44 Kyle Petty Hot Wheels	6.00	2.70

Car / Driver / Sponsor	MINT	NRMT
91 Mike Wallace Spam	6.00	2.70
94 Bill Elliott McDonald's	6.00	2.70

Car / Driver / Sponsor	MINT	NRMT
96 David Green Caterpillar	6.00	2.70
98 John Andretti RCA	6.00	2.70
99 Jeff Burton Exide	6.00	2.70

1997 Hot Wheels Collector Edition Track Edition 1:64

Car / Driver / Sponsor	MINT	NRMT
4 Sterling Marlin Kodak	10.00	4.50

Car / Driver / Sponsor	MINT	NRMT
28 Ernie Irvan Havoline	10.00	4.50
28 Ernie Irvan Hot Wheels Super Truck	40.00	18.00

Car / Driver / Sponsor	MINT	NRMT
43 Bobby Hamilton STP	10.00	4.50
43 Bobby Hamilton STP With yellow nose	40.00	18.00

KYLE PETTY

Car / Driver / Sponsor	MINT	NRMT
44 Kyle Petty Hot Wheels Blue Box	25.00	11.00
44 Kyle Petty Hot Wheels White Box	250.00	110.00

1997 Hot Wheels Pro Racing 1:64

This series of 1:64 cars marks Hot Wheels first mass-market venture into NASCAR. These cars are packaged with cardboard backing shaped like a number one.

Car / Driver / Sponsor	MINT	NRMT
4 Sterling Marlin Kodak	4.00	1.80
5 Terry Labonte Kellogg's	4.00	1.80
6 Mark Martin Valvoline	4.00	1.80
7 Geoff Bodine QVC	4.00	1.80
10 Ricky Rudd Tide	4.00	1.80
16 Ted Musgrave Primestar	4.00	1.80
21 Michael Waltrip Citgo	4.00	1.80
28 Ernie Irvan Havoline	4.00	1.80
30 Johnny Benson Penzoil	4.00	1.80
37 Jeremy Mayfield Kmart	4.00	1.80
43 Bobby Hamilton STP	4.00	1.80
44 Kyle Petty Hot Wheels	4.00	1.80
91 Mike Wallace Spam	4.00	1.80
94 Bill Elliott McDonald's	4.00	1.80
96 David Green Caterpillar	4.00	1.80
98 John Andretti RCA	4.00	1.80
99 Jeff Burton Exide	4.00	1.80

1998 Hot Wheels Collector Edition Pit Crew 1:64

These 1:64 scale cars were produced by Hot Wheels and marks their introduction in the NASCAR market. They are packaged in blister packs with their corresponding pit wagon. The gold cars from this series are valued the same as the standard cars. These cars were distributed through hobby, retail and trackside outlets.

Car / Driver / Sponsor	MINT	NRMT
5 Terry Labonte Kellogg's	8.00	3.60
6 Mark Martin Valvoline	8.00	3.60

Car / Driver / Sponsor	MINT	NRMT
10 Ricky Rudd Tide	8.00	3.60
12 Jeremy Mayfield Mobil 1	8.00	3.60
13 Jerry Nadeau FirstPlus	8.00	3.60

33 Tim Fedewa — 8.00 — 3.60
  Kleenex
36 Matt Hutter — 8.00 — 3.60
  Stanley
43 Bobby Hamilton — 8.00 — 3.60
  STP

44 Kyle Petty — 8.00 — 3.60
  Hot Wheels
74 Randy LaJoie — 8.00 — 3.60
  Fina
94 Bill Elliott — 8.00 — 3.60
  McDonald's
97 Chad Little — 8.00 — 3.60
  John Deere

1998 Hot Wheels Collector Edition Preview Edition 1:64

These cars are basically a sneek peek at the 1998 season.

4 Bobby Hamilton — 8.00 — 3.60
  Kodak

5 Terry Labonte — 8.00 — 3.60
  Kellogg's
6 Mark Martin — 10.00 — 4.50
  Syntec

6 Mark Martin — 8.00 — 3.60
  Valvoline
6 Mark Martin — 10.00 — 4.50
  Eagle One

8 Hut Stricklin — 8.00 — 3.60
  Circuit City

10 Ricky Rudd — 8.00 — 3.60
  Tide

12 Jeremy Mayfield — 8.00 — 3.60
  Mobil 1

13 Jerry Nadeau — 8.00 — 3.60
  FirstPlus

16 Ted Musgrave — 8.00 — 3.60
  Primestar
21 Michael Waltrip — 8.00 — 3.60
  Citgo

26 Johnny Benson — 8.00 — 3.60
  Cheerios

						44 Kyle Petty Blues Brothers 2000	10.00	4.50
						44 Kyle Petty Players Inc.	8.00	3.60
						50 Ricky Craven Hendrick	8.00	3.60
						89 Dennis Setzer McRib	12.00	5.50

| 30 Derrike Cope
Gumout | 8.00 | 3.60 |
| 35 Todd Bodine
Tabasco Green | 10.00 | 4.50 |

| 40 Sterling Marlin
Sabco | 8.00 | 3.60 |
| 42 Joe Nemechek
BellSouth | 8.00 | 3.60 |

| 90 Dick Trickle
Helig-Meyers | 10.00 | 4.50 |

| 35 Todd Bodine
Tabasco | 8.00 | 3.60 |

| 42 Joe Nemechek
BellSouth Black | 8.00 | 3.60 |

| 94 Bill Elliott
McDonalds | 8.00 | 3.60 |

| 35 Todd Bodine
Tabasco Red | 8.00 | 3.60 |

| 43 John Andretti
STP | 8.00 | 3.60 |
| 43 John Andretti
STP Players | 8.00 | 3.60 |

| 96 David Green
Caterpiller | 8.00 | 3.60 |

| 36 Ernie Irvan
Skittles | 8.00 | 3.60 |

| 44 Kyle Petty
Hot Wheels | 8.00 | 3.60 |

97 Chad Little
John Deere — 8.00 3.60

99 Jeff Burton
Exide — 8.00 3.60

1998 Hot Wheels Collector Edition Test Track 1:64

These 1:64 scale cars were produced by Hot Wheels and marks their introduction in the NASCAR market. They are packaged in blister packs and have primer coating as most test cars do. These cars were distributed through hobby and retail.

4 Bobby Hamilton
Kodak — 5.00 2.20

5 Terry Labonte
Kellogg's — 5.00 2.20

6 Mark Martin
Valvoline — 5.00 2.20

10 Ricky Rudd
Tide — 5.00 2.20

21 Michael Waltrip
Citgo — 5.00 2.20

28 Ernie Irvan
Havoline — 5.00 2.20

43 John Andretti
STP — 5.00 2.20

44 Kyle Petty
Hot Wheels — 5.00 2.20

99 Jeff Burton
Exide — 5.00 2.20

1998 Hot Wheels Collector Edition Track Edition 1:64

These 1:64 scale cars were produced by Hot Wheels and marks their introduction in the NASCAR market. They are packaged in black boxes. These cars were distributed through hobby and trackside outlets.

4 Bobby Hamilton
Kodak — 20.00 9.00

5 Terry Labonte
Kellogg's — 20.00 9.00

	MINT	NRMT
42 Joe Nemechek BellSouth	20.00	9.00

	MINT	NRMT
6 Mark Martin Valvoline	20.00	9.00
21 Michael Waltrip Citgo	20.00	9.00
43 John Andretti STP	20.00	9.00
43 John Andretti Players Inc.	20.00	9.00

	MINT	NRMT
6 Mark Martin Eagle One	30.00	13.50
6 Mark Martin Synpower	20.00	9.00
8 Hut Stricklin Circuit City	20.00	9.00
26 Johnny Benson Cheerios	20.00	9.00
30 Derrike Cope Gumout	20.00	9.00
35 Todd Bodine Tabasco	20.00	9.00
44 Kyle Petty Hot Wheels	20.00	9.00
44 Kyle Petty Blues Brothers 2000	25.00	11.00

	MINT	NRMT
10 Ricky Rudd Tide	20.00	9.00
35 Todd Bodine Tabasco Red	20.00	9.00
35 Todd Bodine Tabasco Green	25.00	11.00
44 Kyle Petty Players Inc.	25.00	11.00

	MINT	NRMT
12 Jeremy Mayfield Mobil 1	20.00	9.00
13 Jerry Nadeau First Plus	20.00	9.00
36 Ernie Irvan Skittles	20.00	9.00
40 Sterling Marlin Sabco	20.00	9.00
42 Joe Nemechek BellSouth Black	25.00	11.00
50 Ricky Craven Hendrick	20.00	9.00
50 No Driver Association Boy Scouts	20.00	9.00

89 Dennis Setzer   30.00   13.50
   McRib

90 Dick Trickle   20.00   9.00
   Heilig-Meyers
94 Bill Elliott   20.00   9.00
   McDonald's

96 David Green   20.00   9.00
   Caterpiller

97 Chad Little   20.00   9.00
   John Deere
99 Jeff Burton   20.00   9.00
   Exide

1998 Hot Wheels Collector Edition Trading Paint 1:64

These 1:64 scale cars show the ware and tear a NASCAR is subjected to during a 500 mile race including road grime, paint scrapes, and wheel rub marks.

6 Mark Martin	20.00	9.00
Valvoline		
12 Jeremy Mayfield	12.00	5.50
Mobil 1		
13 Jerry Nadeau	15.00	6.75
FirstPlus		
16 Ted Musgrave	8.00	3.60
Primestar		
21 Michael Waltrip	8.00	3.60
Citgo		
35 Todd Bodine	20.00	9.00
Tabasco		
40 Sterling Marlin	8.00	3.60
Sabco		
42 Joe Nemechek	10.00	4.50
BellSouth		
43 John Andretti	20.00	9.00
STP		
44 Kyle Petty	15.00	6.75
Hot Wheels		
46 Wally Dallenbach	8.00	3.60
First Union		
96 David Green	5.00	2.20
Caterpillar		
99 Jeff Burton	15.00	6.75
Exide		

1999 Hot Wheels Collector Edition 1:64

These black box cars were available at the track or through hobby dealers.

4 Bobby Hamilton	4.00	1.80
Kodak		
5 Terry Labonte	4.00	1.80
Kellogg's		
6 Mark Martin	4.00	1.80
Valvoline		

7 Geoffery Bodine	8.00	3.60
Philips		
7 Geoff Bodine	8.00	3.60
Klaussner		
9 Jerry Nadeau	4.00	1.80
Jetsons		
10 Ricky Rudd	4.00	1.80
Tide		
11 Brett Bodine	4.00	1.80
Paychex		
12 Jeremy Mayfield	4.00	1.80
Mobil 1		
16 Kevin LePage	4.00	1.80
Primestar		
22 Ward Burton	4.00	1.80
Caterpillar		
25 Wally Dallenbach	4.00	1.80
Dallenbach		
26 Johnny Benson	4.00	1.80
Betty Crocker		
28 Davey Allison	8.00	3.60
Havoline		
36 Ernie Irvan	4.00	1.80
M&M's		
40 Sterling Marlin	4.00	1.80
Sabco		
42 Joe Nemechek	4.00	1.80
BellSouth		
43 Richard Petty	8.00	3.60
STP '64		
43 Richard Petty	8.00	3.60
STP '67		
43 Richard Petty	8.00	3.60
STP '72		
43 John Andreti	4.00	1.80
STP		
44 Kyle Petty	4.00	1.80
Hot Wheels		

66 Darrell Waltrip   4.00   1.80
   Big-K

CAR / DRIVER / SPONSOR	MINT	NRMT
94 Bill Elliott Drive Thru	4.00	1.80
97 Chad Little John Deere	4.00	1.80
99 Jeff Burton Exide	4.00	1.80

1999 Hot Wheels Collector Edition Pit Crew 1:64

These 1:64 scale cars came with a replica tool box.

CAR / DRIVER / SPONSOR	MINT	NRMT
4 Bobby Hamilton Advantix	4.00	1.80
5 Terry Labonte Kellogg's	4.00	1.80
6 Mark Martin Valvoline	4.00	1.80
9 Jerry Nadeau Dextor's Lab	8.00	3.60
10 Ricky Rudd Tide	4.00	1.80
12 Jeremy Mayfield Mobil 1	4.00	1.80
17 Matt Kenseth DeWalt	10.00	4.50
43 John Andretti STP	4.00	1.80
44 Kyle Petty Hot Wheels	4.00	1.80
58 Ricky Cravin Turbine	20.00	9.00
66 Darrell Waltip Big K	4.00	1.80
94 Bill Elliott McDonalds	4.00	1.80
97 Chad Little John Deere	4.00	1.80
99 Jeff Burton Exide	4.00	1.80

1999 Hot Wheels Collector Edition Pit Crew Gold 1:64

These 1:64 scale cars came with a replica tool box, both tool box and car were detailed in gold colored paint.

CAR / DRIVER / SPONSOR	MINT	NRMT
5 Terry Labonte Kellogg's	8.00	3.60
6 Mark Martin Valvoline	8.00	3.60
10 Ricky Rudd Tide	8.00	3.60
12 Jeremy Mayfield Moble 1	8.00	3.60
43 John Andretti STP	8.00	3.60

CAR / DRIVER / SPONSOR	MINT	NRMT
44 Kyle Petty Hot Wheels	8.00	3.60
94 Bill Elliott Drive Thru	8.00	3.60
97 Chad Little John Deere	8.00	3.60
99 Jeff Burton Exide	8.00	3.60

1999 Hot Wheels Collector Edition Pit Cruisers 1:64

These 1:64 scale cars were off the Mainline Hot wheels line and were limited to 15,000 each.

CAR / DRIVER / SPONSOR	MINT	NRMT
6 Mark Martin Valvoilne	12.00	5.50
10 Rudd Rudd Tide	12.00	5.50
43 John Andretti STP	12.00	5.50
44 Kyle Petty Hot Wheels	12.00	5.50

1999 Hot Wheels Collector Edition Track Edition 1:64

These 1:64 scale black box cars were available at the track or through a hobby dealer.

CAR / DRIVER / SPONSOR	MINT	NRMT
4 Bobby Hamilton Kodak	15.00	6.75
5 Terry Labonte Kellogg's	20.00	9.00
6 Mark Martin Valvoline	20.00	9.00

CAR / DRIVER / SPONSOR	MINT	NRMT
7 Michael Waltrip Klaussner/Philips	20.00	9.00
10 Ricky Rudd Tide	20.00	9.00
11 Brett Bodine Paychex	20.00	9.00
12 Jeremy Mayfield Mobil 1	20.00	9.00
14 Sterling Marlin Tennessee	25.00	11.00
21 Elliott Sadler Citgo	20.00	9.00
22 Ward Burton Caterpillar	20.00	9.00
25 Wally Dallenbach Dallenbach	20.00	9.00
26 Johnny Benson Cheerios	20.00	9.00
28 D.Allison/Havoline	20.00	9.00
36 Ernie Irvan M&M's	20.00	9.00
40 Sterling Marlin Sabco	20.00	9.00
42 Joe Nemechek BellSouth	20.00	9.00
43 Richard Petty STP '64	20.00	9.00
43 Richard Petty STP '67	20.00	9.00

CAR / DRIVER / SPONSOR	MINT	NRMT
43 Richard Petty STP '72	20.00	9.00
43 John Andretti STP	20.00	9.00
44 Kyle Petty Hot Wheels	20.00	9.00
66 Darrell Waltrip Big K	20.00	9.00
94 Bill Elliott Drive Thru	20.00	9.00
97 Chad Little John Deere	20.00	9.00

1999 Hot Wheels Collector Edition Test Track 1:64

This is the first in a series of Treasure Hunt Cars limited to 15,000

CAR / DRIVER / SPONSOR	MINT	NRMT
10 Ricky Rudd Tide	20.00	9.00
12 Jeremy Mayfield Mobil 1	20.00	9.00

CAR / DRIVER / SPONSOR	MINT	NRMT
44 Kyle Petty Hot Wheels	20.00	9.00

CAR / DRIVER / SPONSOR	MINT	NRMT
99 Jeff Burton Exide	20.00	9.00

1999 Hot Wheels Collector Edition Trading Paint 1:64

This is second in a series of Treasure Hunt Cars limited to 15,000.

Car / Driver / Sponsor	MINT	NRMT
5 Terry Labonte Kellogg's	20.00	9.00

Car / Driver / Sponsor	MINT	NRMT
6 Mark Martin Valvoline	20.00	9.00
44 Kyle Petty Hot Wheels	20.00	9.00

Car / Driver / Sponsor	MINT	NRMT
97 Chad Little John Deere	15.00	6.75

2000 Hot Wheels Crew's Choice 1:64

These cars feature bodies that are removable from the chassis.

Car / Driver / Sponsor	MINT	NRMT
33 Joe Nemechek Oakwood Homes	15.00	6.75
43 John Andretti STP	20.00	9.00
43 J.Andretti/Cheerios		
44 Kyle Petty Hot Wheels	20.00	9.00
66 Darrell Waltrip Route 66	15.00	6.75

2000 Hot Wheels Deluxe 1:64

These cars are available through retail outlets.

Car / Driver / Sponsor	MINT	NRMT
4 Bobby Hamilton Kodak	5.00	2.20
5 Terry Labonte Kellogg's	5.00	2.20

Car / Driver / Sponsor	MINT	NRMT
33 Joe Nemechek Oakwood Homes	4.00	1.80
43 John Andretti STP	5.00	2.20
44 Kyle Petty Hot Wheels	7.00	3.10
55 Kenny Wallace Aerosmith	10.00	4.50

2000 Hot Wheels Deluxe Scorchin Scooter 1:64

These are from the Hot Wheels mainline release, and are limited.

Car / Driver / Sponsor	MINT	NRMT
4 Bobby Hamilton Kodak	12.00	5.50
5 Terry Labonte Kellogg's	12.00	5.50
6 Mark Martin Valvoline	12.00	5.50
12 Jeremy Mayfield Mobil 1	12.00	5.50
22 Ward Burton Caterpillar	12.00	5.50
43 John Andretti STP	12.00	5.50
44 Kyle Petty Hot Wheels	12.00	5.50
45 Adam Petty Sprint	12.00	5.50
55 Kenny Wallace Square D	12.00	5.50
60 Geoffery Bodine Power Team	12.00	5.50
94 Bill Elliott McDonald's	12.00	5.50
97 Chad Little John Deere	12.00	5.50
98 Rick Mast Woodie	15.00	6.75
99 Jeff Burton Exide	12.00	5.50

2000 Hot Wheels Select 1:64

This is the first year of the Select series in 1:64 scale. It was sold in a blister pack featuring a display stand which resembles a track wall complete with fence and tire marks.

Car / Driver / Sponsor	MINT	NRMT
4 Bobby Hamilton Kodak	8.00	3.60
22 Ward Burton Caterpillar	10.00	4.50
43 John Andretti STP	12.00	5.50
44 Kyle Petty Hot Wheels	12.00	5.50
55 Kenny Wallace Square D	8.00	3.60
60 Geoffery Bodine Power Team	10.00	4.50

1998 Johnny Lighting Stock Car Legends 1:64

These cars take a look back at some of the most successful drivers that turned a lap.

Car / Driver / Sponsor	MINT	NRMT
5 Neil Bonnett Jim Stacy '77 Dodge	12.00	5.50

Car / Driver / Sponsor	MINT	NRMT
6 Buddy Baker Dodge 1969 Dodge Daytona	12.00	5.50

Car / Driver / Sponsor	MINT	NRMT
6 Pete Hamilton American Brakeblok 1971 Plymouth GTX	12.00	5.50

Car / Driver / Sponsor	MINT	NRMT
11 Mario Andretti Bunnell Motor 1967 Ford Fairlane	12.00	5.50

21 Buddy Baker   12.00   5.50
Vavoline 1984 Thunderbird

11 Cale Yarborough   15.00   6.75
First American City Travelers Checks
1978 Oldsmobile 442

27 Benny Parsons   12.00   5.50
Melling 1980 Monty Carlo

40 Pete Hamilton   12.00   5.50
7-up 1970 Plymouth
42 Marty Robbins 1973 Dodge Charger 15.00 6.75

11 Darrell Waltrip   12.00   5.50
Pepsi 1983 Monte Carlo

28 Cale Yarborough   12.00   5.50
Hardee's 1984 Monte Carlo

50 Geoff Bodine   12.00   5.50
Spectrum 1982 Grand Prix
51 A.J. Foyt   15.00   6.75
Valvoline 1979 Olds

17 David Pearson   12.00   5.50
East Tenn. Motor 1969 Ford Troino
17 David Pearson 1967 Ford Fairlane 12.00 5.50

32 Richard Brooks   12.00   5.50
Bestline 1970

71 Bobby Isaac   12.00   5.50
K&K Insurance 1970 Dodge Daytona

21 Donnie Allison   12.00   5.50
Purolator 1971 Mercury Cylone

88 Darrell Waltrip   12.00   5.50
Gatorade 1979 Monte Carlo

88 Rusty Wallace 12.00 5.50
Gatorade 1984 Grand Prix

98 Leeroy Yarborough 12.00 5.50
1969 Ford Torino

99 Fred Lorenzen 12.00 5.50
STP 1971 Plymouth

1990-92 Matchbox White Rose Super Stars 1:64

The was the first series of NASCAR replica cars distributed by White Rose. The cars were produced by Matchbox. They come in either a blister package, a box or a polybag.

CAR / DRIVER / SPONSOR	MINT	NRMT
1 Jeff Gordon	20.00	9.00
Baby Ruth Orange Lettering '92 BX		
1 Jeff Gordon	12.00	5.50
Baby Ruth Red Lettering '92 BX		
2 Rusty Wallace	5.00	2.20
Penske '92 BL		
3 Dale Earnhardt	50.00	22.00
GM '90 BX		
3 Dale Earnhardt	30.00	13.50
GM Parts '91 BX		

CAR / DRIVER / SPONSOR	MINT	NRMT
3 Dale Earnhardt	12.00	5.50
Goodwrench '92 BL		
3 Dale Earnhardt	10.00	4.50
Mom-n-Pop's '92 polly bag		
4 Ernie Irvan	5.00	2.20
Kodak '92 BL		
7 Harry Gant	8.00	3.60
Mac Tools '92 BX		
7 Jimmy Hensley	8.00	3.60
White Rose Collectibles '92 BX		
7 Alan Kulwicki	25.00	11.00
Hooters '92 BL		
7 Alan Kulwicki	16.00	7.25
Hooters Naturally Fresh '92 BL		
8 Jeff Burton	4.00	1.80
TIC Financial '92 BX		
8 Dick Trickle	4.00	1.80
Snicker's '92 BL		
9 No Driver Association	4.00	1.80
Melling '92 BL		
10 Derrike Cope	4.00	1.80
Purolator '92 BL		
10 Ernie Irvan	20.00	9.00
Mac Tools '91 BX		
11 Bill Elliott	4.00	1.80
Amoco '92 BL		
12 Hut Stricklin	4.00	1.80
Raybestos '92 BL		
15 No Driver Association	4.00	1.80
Motorcraft '92 BL		
15 Morgan Shepherd	4.00	1.80
Motorcraft '92 BL		
18 Dale Jarrett	4.00	1.80
Interstate Batteries '92 BL		
22 Sterling Marlin	4.00	1.80
Maxwell House '92 BL		
26 Brett Bodine	4.00	1.80
Quaker State '92 BL		
28 Davey Allison	15.00	6.75
Havoline '92 BL		
28 Davey Allison	15.00	6.75
Havoline Mac Tools '92 BL		
29 No Driver Association	5.00	2.20
Matchbox Racing		
White Rose Collectibles '92 BX		
29 Phil Parsons	20.00	9.00
Parsons Racing '92 BX		
30 Michael Waltrip	4.00	1.80
Pennzoil '92 BL		
41 James Smith	5.00	2.20
White House Apple Juice '92 BL		
42 Kyle Petty	4.00	1.80
Mello Yello '92 BL		
43 Richard Petty	4.00	1.80
STP '92 BL		
44 Bobby Labonte	8.00	3.60
Penrose '92 BX		
44 Bobby Labonte	8.00	3.60
Slim Jim '92 BX		
48 James Hylton	4.00	1.80
Valtrol '92 BL		
49 Ed Feree	4.00	1.80
Fergaed Racing '92 BX		
55 Ted Musgrave	4.00	1.80
Jasper Engines		
66 Chad Little	4.00	1.80
Phillips 66 red car '92 BL		
66 No Driver Association	4.00	1.80
Phillips 66 black car '92 BL		
68 Bobby Hamilton	4.00	1.80
Country Time '92 BL		
87 Joe Nemechek	4.00	1.80
Texas Pete '92 BX		
89 Jim Sauter	4.00	1.80
Evinrude '92 BL		
92 No Driver Association	35.00	16.00
White Rose Collectibles '92 BL		
92 Hut Stricklin	4.00	1.80
Stanley Tools '92 BX		

1993 Matchbox White Rose Super Stars 1:64

This series features six Jimmy Hensley cars honoring many of the sponsors of the number 7 car. Each piece either comes in a blister package or a box. The year is on the end of each of the box packages.

CAR / DRIVER / SPONSOR	MINT	NRMT
1 Rodney Combs Jr.	18.00	8.00
Luxaire BL		
1 Rodney Combs Jr.	16.00	7.25
Goody's BX		
6 Mark Martin	5.00	2.20
Valvoline BX		
7 Jimmy Hensley	9.00	4.00
Bobsled BX		
7 Jimmy Hensley	9.00	4.00
Bojangles BL		
7 Jimmy Hensley	9.00	4.00
Cellular One BX		
7 Jimmy Hensley	9.00	4.00
Family Channel BX		
7 Jimmy Hensley	9.00	4.00
Hanes BX		
7 Jimmy Hensley	9.00	4.00
Matchbox BX		
8 Jeff Burton	4.00	1.80
TIC Financal BX		
8 Jeff Burton	4.00	1.80
Baby Ruth BX		
8 Sterling Marlin	4.00	1.80
Raybestos BL		
8 Bobby Dotter	4.00	1.80
Dewalt BX		
9 Mike Wallace	4.00	1.80
FDP Brakes BX		
12 Jimmy Spencer	4.00	1.80
Meineke BL		
14 Terry Labonte	4.00	1.80
MW Windows BX		
21 Morgan Shepherd	4.00	1.80
Citgo BL		
22 Bobby Labonte	4.00	1.80
Maxwell House BL		
24 Jeff Gordon	10.00	4.50
DuPont BL		
25 Hermie Sadler	4.00	1.80
VA is for Lovers BX		
28 Davey Allison	18.00	8.00
Havoline BL		
29 Phil Parsons	4.00	1.80
Matchbox BL		
31 Bobby Hillin Jr.	4.00	1.80
Team Ireland BL		
32 Jimmy Horton	4.00	1.80
Active Racing BL		
32 Dale Jarrett	4.00	1.80
Pic-N-Pay BX		
40 Kenny Wallace	4.00	1.80
Dirt Devil BL		
41 Phil Parsons	4.00	1.80
Manheim BL		
48 Sterling Marlin	4.00	1.80
Cappio BX		
69 Jeff Sparker	12.00	5.50
WFE Challenge BL		
71 Dave Marcis	4.00	1.80
Enick's Catering BL		
83 Lake Speed	4.00	1.80
Purex		
87 Joe Nemechek	4.00	1.80
Dentyne		
93 No Driver Association	35.00	16.00
White Rose Collectibles BL		
93 No Driver Association	8.00	3.60
American Zoom poly bag		
94 Terry Labonte	4.00	1.80
Sunoco BL		

CAR / DRIVER / SPONSOR	MINT	NRMT
98 Derrike Cope Bojangles BL	4.00	1.80
98 Jimmy Spencer Moly Black Gold BL	4.00	1.80
99 Ricky Craven DuPont BX	4.00	1.80

1994 Matchbox White Rose Super Stars 1:64

This is considered the second Super Stars Series distributed by White Rose Collectibles. There were speical cars issued that featured Future Cup Stars and drivers who won Super Star Awards. The boxes for the Future Cup Stars' cars is different from the regular Series 2 boxes. The Super Star Awards cars come in a jewelry type box and the car is gold.

CAR / DRIVER / SPONSOR	MINT	NRMT
2 Ricky Craven DuPont BX	4.00	1.80
2 Rusty Wallace Ford Motorsports BX	5.00	2.20
3 Dale Earnhardt Gold Lumina Super Star Awards	30.00	13.50
4 Sterling Marlin Kodak BX	4.00	1.80
4 Sterling Marlin Kodak FunSaver BX	4.00	1.80
5 Terry Labonte Kellogg's BX	4.00	1.80
6 Mark Martin Valvoline BX	4.00	1.80
7 Geoff Bodine Exide BX	8.00	3.60
7 Harry Gant Manheim BX	4.00	1.80
8 Jeff Burton Raybestos BX	4.00	1.80
12 Derrike Cope Straight Arrow BX	4.00	1.80
15 Lake Speed Quality Care BX	4.00	1.80
16 Ted Musgrave Family Channel BX	4.00	1.80
17 Darrell Waltrip Western Auto BX	4.00	1.80
19 Loy Allen Jr. Hooters BX	4.00	1.80
23 Hut Stricklin Smokin' Joe's BX	20.00	9.00
24 Jeff Gordon DuPont BX	8.00	3.60
26 Brett Bodine Quaker State BX	4.00	1.80
29 Phil Parsons Baltimore CFL BL	20.00	9.00
29 Phil Parsons Matchbox White Rose Collectibles BX	4.00	1.80
30 Michael Waltrip Pennzoil BX	4.00	1.80
32 Dale Jarrett Pic-N-Pay BX	4.00	1.80
33 Harry Gant Gold Lumina Super Star Awards	22.00	10.00
34 Mike McLaughlin Fiddle Faddle BL	4.00	1.80
37 Loy Allen Jr. Naturally Fresh Future Cup Stars '94 BX	8.00	3.60
40 Bobby Hamilton Kendall BX	4.00	1.80
41 Joe Nemechek Meineke BX	4.00	1.80
43 Rodney Combs Jr. Black Flag BX	8.00	3.60

CAR / DRIVER / SPONSOR	MINT	NRMT
43 Rodney Combs Jr. French's Black Flag BL	25.00	11.00
43 Rodney Combs Jr. French's BX	8.00	3.60
46 Shawna Robinson Polaroid BL	15.00	6.75
52 Ken Schrader AC Delco BX	4.00	1.80
55 Jimmy Hensley Petron Plus BL	15.00	6.75
60 Mark Martin Winn Dixie BX	10.00	4.50
66 Mike Wallace Duron Paint Future Cup Stars '94 BX	8.00	3.60
75 Todd Bodine Factory Stores of America BX	4.00	1.80
87 Joe Nemechek Cintas Future Cup Stars '94 BX	8.00	3.60
92 Larry Pearson Stanley Tools BX	4.00	1.80
94 No Driver Association Matchbox White Rose Collectibles BL	25.00	11.00
94 No Driver Association Series 2 preview BX	8.00	3.60
98 Derrike Cope Fingerhut BX	4.00	1.80
!0 Jeff Burton TIC Financial Future Cup Stars '94 BX	9.00	4.00

1995 Matchbox White Rose Super Stars 1:64

This is the continuation of the second Super Stars Series. The boxes the cars come each of the year on the end of them. The Super Star Awards cars again come in a special box and are gold.

CAR / DRIVER / SPONSOR	MINT	NRMT
1 Hermie Sadler DeWalt	5.00	2.20
2 Ricky Craven DuPont	5.00	2.20
3 Dale Earnhardt Gold 7-Time Champion Super Star Awards	30.00	13.50
3 Dale Earnhardt Goodwrench	8.00	3.60
5 Terry Labonte Kellogg's	5.00	2.20
6 Mark Martin Valvoline	5.00	2.20
7 Geoff Bodine Exide	5.00	2.20
8 Jeff Burton Raybestos	5.00	2.20
8 Jeff Burton Raybestos Super Star Awards	18.00	8.00
8 Bobby Dotter Hyde Tools	5.00	2.20
11 Brett Bodine Lowe's	5.00	2.20
12 Derrike Cope Straight Arrow	5.00	2.20
18 Bobby Labonte Interstate Batteries	5.00	2.20
24 Jeff Gordon DuPont	8.00	3.60
24 York Cobra Promo	10.00	4.50
25 Ken Schrader Budweiser in Acrylic Case	16.00	7.25
26 Steve Kinser Quaker State	5.00	2.20
28 Dale Jarrett Havoline	5.00	2.20

CAR / DRIVER / SPONSOR	MINT	NRMT
40 Patty Moise Dial Purex	5.00	2.20
42 Kyle Petty Coors Light in Acrylic Case	15.00	6.75
57 Jason Keller Budget Gourmet	5.00	2.20
71 Kevin Lepage Vermont Teddy Bear	5.00	2.20
72 Tracy Leslie Detroit Gasket	5.00	2.20
74 Johnny Benson Jr. Lipton Tea	5.00	2.20
87 Joe Nemechek Bell South	15.00	6.75
87 Joe Nemechek Burger King	5.00	2.20
90 Mike Wallace Heilig-Meyers	5.00	2.20
94 Bill Elliott Gold Thunderbird Super Star Awards	18.00	8.00
94 Bill Elliott McDonald's	5.00	2.20
94 Bill Elliott McDonald's Thunderbat	16.00	7.25
95 John Tanner Caterpillar	5.00	2.20
99 Phil Parsons Luxaire	5.00	2.20

1995 Matchbox White Rose SuperTrucks 1:64

This is the first series of SuperTrucks that White Rose Collectibles distributed.

CAR / DRIVER / SPONSOR	MINT	NRMT
1 Mike Chase Sears Diehard	5.00	2.20
3 Mike Skinner Goodwrench	5.00	2.20
6 Rick Carelli Total	5.00	2.20
24 Scott Lagasse DuPont	5.00	2.20

1996 Matchbox White Rose Super Stars 1:64

This series of 1:64 replicas features four Super Star Awards cars. The cars are gold in color and feature winners of the SuperTruck series, the Winston Cup Rookie of the Year and the Busch Grand National winner.

CAR / DRIVER / SPONSOR	MINT	NRMT
4 Sterling Marlin Kodak	5.00	2.20
5 Terry Labonte Kellogg's	6.00	2.70
6 Mark Martin Valvoline	5.00	2.20
9 Lake Speed SPAM	5.00	2.20
10 Ricky Rudd Tide	5.00	2.20
12 Derrike Cope Badcock Promo	10.00	4.50
15 Wally Dallenbach Hayes Promo	10.00	4.50
16 Ted Musgrave Family Channel	5.00	2.20
21 Michael Waltrip Citgo	5.00	2.20
22 Ward Burton MBNA	5.00	2.20
24 Jeff Gordon DuPont SSA	25.00	11.00
24 Jeff Gordon DuPont	8.00	3.60

CAR / DRIVER / SPONSOR	MINT	NRMT
34 Mike McLaughlin Royal Oak	5.00	2.20
37 John Andretti K-Mart	5.00	2.20
40 Tim Fedewa Kleenex	5.00	2.20
41 Ricky Craven Gold Monte Carlo Super Star Awards	18.00	8.00
41 Ricky Craven Kodiak	5.00	2.20
43 Rodney Combs Lance's	5.00	2.20
74 Johnny Benson Jr. Gold Super Star Awards	18.00	8.00
87 Joe Nemechek Bell South Promo	10.00	4.50
87 Joe Nemechek Burger King	5.00	2.20
88 Dale Jarrett Quality Care	5.00	2.20
94 Ron Barfield New Holland	5.00	2.20
94 Bill Elliott McDonald's	5.00	2.20
95 David Green Caterpiller	5.00	2.20
99 Jeff Burton Exide	5.00	2.20

1996 Matchbox White Rose SuperTrucks 1:64

This is the second series of SuperTrucks that White Rose distributed.

CAR / DRIVER / SPONSOR	MINT	NRMT
0 Rick Eckert Rayvest Promo	8.00	3.60
2 Mike Bliss ASE	5.00	2.20
3 Mike Skinner Gold Super Star Awards	18.00	8.00
10 Phil Parsons Channellock	5.00	2.20
21 Tobey Butler Ortho	5.00	2.20
24 Jack Sprague Quaker State	5.00	2.20

1997 Matchbox White Rose Super Stars 1:64

This series of 1:64 replicas features two Super Star Awards cars and three other cars packaged in glass bottles. The most unique car from this series is that of Rick Mast which is packaged in a glass replica of a shotgun shell.

CAR / DRIVER / SPONSOR	MINT	NRMT
2 Rusty Wallace Miller Lite packaged in a bottle	75.00	34.00
5 Terry Labonte Kellogg's	6.00	2.70
5 Terry Labonte Kellogg's SSA Gold	25.00	11.00
25 Ricky Craven Budweiser packaged in a bottle	60.00	27.00
36 Derrike Cope Skittles	5.00	2.20
40 Robby Gordon Coors Light packaged in a bottle	60.00	27.00
74 Randy Lajoie Fina	5.00	2.20
74 Randy Lajoie Fina SSA Gold	20.00	9.00

CAR / DRIVER / SPONSOR	MINT	NRMT
75 Rick Mast Remington packaged in a shotgun shell	50.00	22.00
88 Kevin Lepage Hype	5.00	2.20
94 Bill Elliott McDonald's	5.00	2.20
95 David Green Caterpillar	5.00	2.20

1996 Press Pass 1:24

Card manufactuer Press Pass ventured into die-cast with these two pieces. Each piece is a boxed set containing a 1:24 bank produced by Action, a 1:64 hood opened car produced by Action, and one Burning Rubber card produced by Press Pass. Each of the pieces were done in a quantity of 1,996.

CAR / DRIVER / SPONSOR	MINT	NRMT
2 Rusty Wallace Miller Silver car	170.00	75.00
5 Terry Labonte Kellogg's Silver car	170.00	75.00

1992-97 Raceway Replicas 1:24

This manufacturer of high end 1:24 scale die cast replicas has produced this series of four cars. The cars are sold directly to the public usually through ads in racing publications.

CAR / DRIVER / SPONSOR	MINT	NRMT
4 Sterling Marlin Kodak 1996	130.00	57.50
6 Mark Martin Valvoline 1994	130.00	57.50
11 Bill Elliott Budweiser 1992	130.00	57.50
27 Hut Stricklin McDonald's 1993	130.00	57.50
28 Davey Allison Havoline 1993	130.00	57.50
96 David Green Caterpillar 1997	130.00	57.50

1995-96 Racing Champions 1:18

This series of 1:18 scale cars were the first entries into the 1:18 scale size by manufacturer Racing Champions. The cars were sold through retail outlets and through hobby shops.

CAR / DRIVER / SPONSOR	MINT	NRMT
2 Ricky Craven DuPont	30.00	13.50
2 Rusty Wallace MGD	30.00	13.50
4 Sterling Marlin Kodak	30.00	13.50
5 Terry Labonte Bayer	30.00	13.50
9 Joe Bessey Delco Remy	30.00	13.50
15 Wally Dallenbach Hayes Modems	40.00	18.00
16 Ted Musgrave Primestar	30.00	13.50
17 Darrell Waltrip Western Auto	30.00	13.50
18 Bobby Labonte Interstate Batteries	30.00	13.50
22 Ward Burton MBNA	30.00	13.50
24 Jeff Gordon DuPont	40.00	18.00

CAR / DRIVER / SPONSOR	MINT	NRMT
24 Jeff Gordon DuPont Signature Series	40.00	18.00
25 Ken Schrader Budweiser	30.00	13.50
25 Ken Schrader Budweiser Hood Open	50.00	22.00
25 Ken Schrader Budweiser Hood Open Chrome	400.00	180.00
29 Steve Grissom Cartoon Network	30.00	13.50
30 Johnny Benson Pennzoil	30.00	13.50
31 Mike Skinner Realtree Hood Open	90.00	40.00
34 Mike McLaughlin Royal Oak	30.00	13.50
43 Bobby Hamilton STP Silver car	35.00	16.00
43 Bobby Hamilton STP 5 car set	180.00	80.00
47 Jeff Fuller Sunoco	30.00	13.50
51 Chuck Bown Lucks	30.00	13.50
52 Ken Schrader AC Delco	30.00	13.50
57 Jim Bown Matco	40.00	18.00
57 Jason Keller Halloween Havoc	30.00	13.50
57 Jason Keller Slim Jim	30.00	13.50
74 Johnny Benson Lipton Tea	30.00	13.50
87 Joe Nemechek Burger King	30.00	13.50
88 Dale Jarrett Quality Care	30.00	13.50
94 Bill Elliott McDonald's Monopoly	30.00	13.50
97 Chad Little Sterling Cowboy	30.00	13.50

1996 Racing Champions SuperTrucks 1:18

This is a 1:18 scale series of SuperTrucks. The Mike Skinner piece is available both in a hood open version and the regular hood sealed version.

CAR / DRIVER / SPONSOR	MINT	NRMT
2 Mike Bliss ASE	30.00	13.50
3 Mike Skinner Goodwrench	40.00	18.00
3 Mike Skinner Goodwrench Hood Open	45.00	20.00
6 Rick Carelli Total	30.00	13.50
7 Geoff Bodine QVC	30.00	13.50
9 Joe Bessey New Hampshire Speedway	30.00	13.50
14 Butch Gilliland Stroppe	30.00	13.50
17 Bill Sedgwick Die Hard	30.00	13.50
17 Darrell Waltrip Western Auto	40.00	18.00
20 Walker Evans Dana	30.00	13.50
21 Doug George Ortho	30.00	13.50
24 Jack Sprague Quaker State	30.00	13.50
29 Bob Keselowski Winnebago	30.00	13.50
30 Jimmy Hensley Mopar	30.00	13.50

CAR / DRIVER / SPONSOR	MINT	NRMT
35 Bill Venturini Rain X	30.00	13.50
43 Rich Bickle Cummins	30.00	13.50
52 Ken Schrader AC Delco	40.00	18.00
75 Bobby Gill Spears	30.00	13.50
83 Steve Portenga Coffee Critic	30.00	13.50
98 Butch Miller Raybestos	30.00	13.50

1997 Racing Champions 1:18

This series of cars is highlighted by the Premier Gold cars. These cars were distributed through hobby outlets. There are 166 of each of the gold cars.

CAR / DRIVER / SPONSOR	MINT	NRMT
2 Rusty Wallace Miller Lite Gold	400.00	180.00
2 Rusty Wallace Miller Lite Hobby	60.00	27.00
6 Mark Martin Valvoline Gold	400.00	180.00
6 Mark Martin Valvoline Hobby	60.00	27.00
10 Ricky Rudd Tide Gold	350.00	160.00
10 Ricky Rudd Tide Hobby	50.00	22.00
17 Darrell Waltrip Parts America Chrome	60.00	27.00
18 Bobby Labonte Interstate Batteries Gold	350.00	160.00
18 Bobby Labonte Interstate Batteries Hobby	50.00	22.00
36 Derrike Cope Skittles Gold	350.00	160.00
36 Derrike Cope Skittles Hobby	50.00	22.00
75 Rick Mast Remington Gold	350.00	160.00
75 Rick Mast Remington Hobby	50.00	22.00
94 Bill Elliott McDonald's Gold	400.00	180.00
94 Bill Elliott McDonald's Hobby	60.00	27.00
96 David Green Caterpillar Promo	40.00	18.00

1997 Racing Champions SuperTrucks 1:18

This is the series edition of 1:18 SuperTrucks released by Racing Champions.

CAR / DRIVER / SPONSOR	MINT	NRMT
2 Mike Bliss Team ASE	30.00	13.50
15 Mike Cope Penrose	30.00	13.50
18 Mike Dokken Dana	30.00	13.50
24 Jack Sprague Quaker State	30.00	13.50
44 Boris Said Federated Auto	30.00	13.50
66 Bryan Refner Carlin	30.00	13.50
75 Dan Press Spears	30.00	13.50
80 Joe Ruttman LCI	30.00	13.50
87 Joe Nemechek BellSouth	30.00	13.50
7 Tammy Jo Kirk Loveable	30.00	13.50

1998 Racing Champions Gold Hood Open 1:18

This is a special series produced by Racing Champions to celebrate NASCAR's 50th anniversary. Each car is a limited edition of 1,998. Each car is also plated in gold chrome and contains a serial number on its chassis.

CAR / DRIVER / SPONSOR	MINT	NRMT
4 Bobby Hamilton Kodak	60.00	27.00
5 Terry Labonte Kellogg's	100.00	45.00
30 Derrike Cope Gumout	60.00	27.00
33 Ken Schrader Petree	60.00	27.00
35 Todd Bodine Tabasco	60.00	27.00
36 Ernie Irvan Skittles	80.00	36.00

1991-92 Racing Champions 1:24

This series of 1:24 cars features some of the most expensive and toughest to find die cast pieces. The pieces were packaged in a black box and were distributed through retail outlets and hobby shops. The Kenny Wallace Dirt Devil car and the Cox Lumber car are the two toughest to come by.

CAR / DRIVER / SPONSOR	MINT	NRMT
1 Jeff Gordon Baby Ruth	1000.00	450.00
1 Rick Mast Majik Market	40.00	18.00
2 Rusty Wallace AC Delco	40.00	18.00
2 Rusty Wallace Pontiac Excitement	40.00	18.00
3 Dale Earnhardt Goodwrench with Fender Stickers	30.00	13.50
3 Dale Earnhardt Goodwrench with Tampo Decals	45.00	20.00
4 Ernie Irvan Kodak	20.00	9.00
5 Ricky Rudd Tide	20.00	9.00
6 Mark Martin Valvoline	30.00	13.50
7 Harry Gant Morema	50.00	22.00
7 No Driver Association Easy Off	50.00	22.00
7 No Driver Association French's	60.00	27.00
7 No Driver Association Gulf Lite	60.00	27.00
7 Jimmy Hensley Bojangles	50.00	22.00
7 Tommy Kendall Family Channel	50.00	22.00
7 Alan Kulwicki Hooters	150.00	70.00
9 Joe Bessey AC Delco	600.00	275.00
9 Bill Elliott Melling	80.00	36.00
10 Derrike Cope Purolator	20.00	9.00
11 Bill Elliott Amoco	22.00	10.00
15 Geoff Bodine Motorcraft	20.00	9.00
15 Morgan Shepherd Motorcraft	20.00	9.00

CAR / DRIVER / SPONSOR	MINT	NRMT
16 Wally Dallenbach Jr. Roush Racing	60.00	27.00
17 Darrell Waltrip Western Auto with Fender Stickers	20.00	9.00
17 Darrell Waltrip Western Auto with Tampo Decals	25.00	11.00
18 Dale Jarrett Interstate Batteries	30.00	13.50
18 Gregory Trammell Melling	20.00	9.00
21 Dale Jarrett Citgo	80.00	36.00
21 Morgan Shepherd Citgo	20.00	9.00
22 Sterling Marlin Maxwell House	20.00	9.00
25 Ken Schrader No Sponsor with Large K on roof	30.00	13.50
25 Ken Schrader No Sponsor	20.00	9.00
25 Bill Venturini Rain X	500.00	220.00
28 Davey Allison Havoline	80.00	36.00
30 Michael Waltrip Pennzoil	20.00	9.00
33 Harry Gant No Sponsor Oldsmobile	40.00	18.00
33 Harry Gant No Sponsor Chevrolet	30.00	13.50
36 Kenny Wallace Cox Lumber	300.00	135.00
36 Kenny Wallace Dirt Devil	400.00	180.00
42 Bobby Hillin Jr. Mello Yello	40.00	18.00
42 Kyle Petty Mello Yello	30.00	13.50
43 Richard Petty STP with Blue Wheels	25.00	11.00
49 Stanley Smith Ameritron Batteries	400.00	180.00
51 No Driver Association Racing Champions	160.00	70.00
55 Ted Musgrave Jasper	1000.00	450.00
59 Andy Belmont FDP Brakes	500.00	220.00
60 Mark Martin Winn Dixie with Red Numbers	175.00	80.00
60 Mark Martin Winn Dixie with White Numbers	100.00	45.00
63 Chuck Bown Nescafe	800.00	350.00
66 Jimmy Hensley TropArtic	22.00	10.00
66 Chad Little TropArtic	22.00	10.00
66 No Driver Association TropArtic Red Car	25.00	11.00
66 Cale Yarborough TropArtic	20.00	9.00
68 Bobby Hamilton Country Time	30.00	13.50
70 J.D. McDuffie Son's Auto	20.00	9.00
71 Dave Marcis Big Apple Market	20.00	9.00
75 Butch Miller Food Country	400.00	180.00
83 Lake Speed Purex	175.00	80.00
87 Joe Nemechek Texas Pete	400.00	180.00
94 Terry Labonte Sunoco	40.00	18.00
94 Terry Labonte Sunoco Arrow on decal points at tire	60.00	27.00

1993 Racing Champions 1:24

These 1:24 scale cars come in a Red box and feature some of the top names in racing.

CAR / DRIVER / SPONSOR	MINT	NRMT
2 Davey Allison True Value IROC car	100.00	45.00
2 Rusty Wallace Pontiac Excitement	25.00	11.00
3 Dale Earnhardt Goodwrench Goodyear in White	30.00	13.50
3 Dale Earnhardt Goodwrench Goodyear in Yellow	30.00	13.50
3 Dale Earnhardt Goodwrench Mom-n-Pop's	30.00	13.50
4 Ernie Irvan Kodak Gold Film	20.00	9.00
4 Ernie Irvan Kodak Gold Film Plus	20.00	9.00
5 Ricky Rudd Tide Exxon	20.00	9.00
5 Ricky Rudd Tide Valvoline	20.00	9.00
6 Mark Martin Valvoline	30.00	13.50
7 Alan Kulwicki Hooters	75.00	34.00
8 Sterling Marlin Raybestos	20.00	9.00
8 Sterling Marlin Raybestos Douglas Batteries	22.00	10.00
10 Bill Elliott True Value IROC car	22.00	10.00
11 Bill Elliott Amoco	20.00	9.00
12 Jimmy Spencer Meineke	20.00	9.00
14 Terry Labonte Kellogg's	100.00	45.00
15 Geoff Bodine Motorcraft	20.00	9.00
17 Darrell Waltrip Western Auto	20.00	9.00
18 Dale Jarrett Interstate Batteries	20.00	9.00
21 Morgan Shepherd Citgo Red Pillar Post	20.00	9.00
21 Morgan Shepherd Citgo Tri-color Pillar Post	20.00	9.00
22 Bobby Labonte Maxwell House	80.00	36.00
24 Jeff Gordon DuPont	90.00	40.00
25 Ken Schrader No Sponsor	40.00	18.00
26 Brett Bodine Quaker State	20.00	9.00
27 Hut Stricklin McDonald's	20.00	9.00
28 Davey Allison Havoline Black and Gold paint scheme	80.00	36.00
28 Davey Allison Havoline Black and White paint scheme	100.00	45.00
30 Michael Waltrip Pennzoil	35.00	16.00
42 Kyle Petty Mello Yello	30.00	13.50
44 Rick Wilson STP	20.00	9.00
49 Stanley Smith Ameritron Batteries	125.00	55.00
59 Andy Belmont FDP Brakes	100.00	45.00
60 Mark Martin Winn Dixie	22.00	10.00
75 No Driver Association Auto Value	25.00	11.00
75 No Driver Association Factory Stores	20.00	9.00
87 Joe Nemechek Dentyne	20.00	9.00
98 Derrike Cope Bojangles	25.00	11.00

1994 Racing Champions 1:24

These 1:24 scale cars were mostly available in red boxes but some could be found in black boxes. The cars were distributed through both hobby and retail outlets.

CAR / DRIVER / SPONSOR	MINT	NRMT
0 Dick McCabe Fisher Snow Plows	20.00	9.00
1 Rick Mast Percision Products	16.00	7.25
2 Ricky Craven DuPont	30.00	13.50
2 Rusty Wallace Ford Motorsports Black Ford Oval	20.00	9.00
2 Rusty Wallace Ford Motorsports Blue Ford Oval	20.00	9.00
3 Dale Earnhardt Goodwrench	40.00	18.00
4 Sterling Marlin Kodak	16.00	7.25
5 Terry Labonte Kellogg's	25.00	11.00
6 Mark Martin Valvoline Reese's	40.00	18.00
7 Geoff Bodine Exide	16.00	7.25
7 Harry Gant Manheim	25.00	11.00
7 Alan Kulwicki Zerex	60.00	27.00
8 Jeff Burton Raybestos with Goodyear tires	20.00	9.00
8 Jeff Burton Raybestos with Hoosier tires	20.00	9.00
8 Kenny Wallace TIC Financial	20.00	9.00
12 Clifford Allison Sports Image	50.00	22.00
14 John Andretti Kanawha	25.00	11.00
14 Terry Labonte MW Windows	100.00	45.00
15 Lake Speed Quality Care	16.00	7.25
16 Chad Chaffin Dr. Die Cast	18.00	8.00
16 Ted Musgrave Family Channel	18.00	8.00
17 Darrell Waltrip Western Auto	16.00	7.25
18 Dale Jarrett Interstate Batteries	18.00	8.00
19 Loy Allen Hooters	16.00	7.25
20 Bobby Hillin Jr. Fina	20.00	9.00
20 Randy LaJoie Fina	22.00	10.00
21 Morgan Shepherd Citgo	16.00	7.25
22 Bobby Labonte Maxwell House	50.00	22.00
23 Chad Little Bayer	16.00	7.25
23 Hut Stricklin Smokin' Joe's	100.00	45.00
24 Jeff Gordon Coca-Cola Winner	60.00	27.00
24 Jeff Gordon DuPont Brickyard Special Purple Box	60.00	27.00
24 Jeff Gordon DuPont	40.00	18.00
24 Jeff Gordon DuPont Snickers	40.00	18.00
25 Ken Schrader GMAC	40.00	18.00
26 Brett Bodine Quaker State	16.00	7.25
27 Jimmy Spencer McDonald's	80.00	36.00
28 Ernie Irvan Havoline	22.00	10.00
30 Michael Waltrip Pennzoil	16.00	7.25
31 Steve Grissom Channellock	20.00	9.00
31 Tom Peck Channellock	16.00	7.25
33 Harry Gant No Sponsor	18.00	8.00
33 Harry Gant Leo Jackson Motorsports	18.00	8.00
33 Harry Gant Manheim Auctions	35.00	16.00
33 Bobby Labonte Dentyne	100.00	45.00
34 Mike McLaughlin Fiddle Faddle	20.00	9.00
35 Shawna Robinson Polaroid Captiva	20.00	9.00
38 Elton Sawyer Ford Credit	16.00	7.25
40 Bobby Hamilton Kendall	16.00	7.25
42 Kyle Petty Mello Yello	20.00	9.00
44 David Green Slim Jim	20.00	9.00
44 Bobby Hillin Jr. Buss Fuses	16.00	7.25
46 Shawna Robinson Polaroid	20.00	9.00
52 Ken Schrader AC Delco	20.00	9.00
54 Robert Pressley Manheim	20.00	9.00
59 Andy Belmont Metal Arrester	20.00	9.00
59 Dennis Setzer Alliance	30.00	13.50
60 Mark Martin Winn Dixie	25.00	11.00
63 Jim Bown Lysol	16.00	7.25
70 J.D. McDuffie Son's Auto	16.00	7.25
75 Todd Bodine Factory Stores of America	16.00	7.25
79 Dave Rezendes Lipton Tea	20.00	9.00
83 Sherry Blakley Ramses	40.00	18.00
92 Larry Pearson Stanley Tools	16.00	7.25
94 No Driver Association Auto Value	25.00	11.00
94 No Driver Association Brickyard 400 Purple Box	30.00	13.50
97 Joe Bessey Johnson	16.00	7.25
98 Derrike Cope Fingerhut	18.00	8.00

1995 Racing Champions Previews 1:24

This is the first time Racing Champions did a preview series for its 1:24 scale series. The cars were a preview of some of the cars that raced in the 1995 season.

CAR / DRIVER / SPONSOR	MINT	NRMT
2 Rusty Wallace Ford Motorsports	18.00	8.00
6 Mark Martin Valvoline	18.00	8.00
7 Geoff Bodine Exide with Goodyear tires	18.00	8.00
7 Geoff Bodine Exide with Hoosier tires	18.00	8.00
10 Ricky Rudd Tide	18.00	8.00
57 Jason Keller Budget Gourmet	18.00	8.00
63 Curtis Markham Lysol	18.00	8.00
94 Bill Elliott McDonald's	18.00	8.00
98 Jeremy Mayfield Fingerhut	40.00	18.00

1995 Racing Champions 1:24

This series of 1:24 cars features both Winston Cup cars and Busch Grand National cars. Featured in the series is Bill Elliott's Thunderbat car. The car was a promotion done inconjunction with the movie Batman Forever.

CAR / DRIVER / SPONSOR	MINT	NRMT
2 Ricky Craven DuPont	20.00	9.00
2 Rusty Wallace Ford Motorsports	20.00	9.00
4 Sterling Marlin Kodak	18.00	8.00
4 Jeff Purvis Kodak Fun Saver	18.00	8.00

CAR / DRIVER / SPONSOR	MINT	NRMT
5 Terry Labonte Kellogg's	20.00	9.00
6 Tommy Houston Red Devil	18.00	8.00
6 Mark Martin Valvoline	18.00	8.00
7 Geoff Bodine Exide	18.00	8.00
7 Stevie Reeves Clabber Girl	18.00	8.00
8 Jeff Burton Raybestos	25.00	11.00
8 Kenny Wallace Red Dog	25.00	11.00
8 Bobby Dotter Hyde Tools	20.00	9.00
10 Ricky Rudd Tide	18.00	8.00
12 Derrike Cope Mane N' Tail	18.00	8.00

CAR / DRIVER / SPONSOR	MINT	NRMT
15 Dick Trickle Quality Care	18.00	8.00
16 Ted Musgrave Family Channel	18.00	8.00
17 Darrell Waltrip Western Auto	18.00	8.00
18 Bobby Labonte Interstate Batteries	20.00	9.00
21 Morgan Shepherd Citgo	18.00	8.00
23 Chad Little Bayer	20.00	9.00
24 Jeff Gordon DuPont	30.00	13.50
24 Jeff Gordon DuPont Signature Series	40.00	18.00
24 Jeff Gordon DuPont Signature Series Hood Open	60.00	27.00
25 Johnny Rumley Big Johnson	20.00	9.00
25 Ken Schrader Budweiser	20.00	9.00
26 Steve Kinser Quaker State	24.00	11.00
27 Loy Allen Hooters	18.00	8.00
28 Dale Jarrett Havoline	18.00	8.00
29 Steve Grissom Meineke	18.00	8.00
34 Mike McLaughlin French's	18.00	8.00
37 John Andretti K-Mart	20.00	9.00
38 Elton Sawyer Red Carpet Lease	18.00	8.00
40 Patty Moise Dial Purex	20.00	9.00
41 Ricky Craven Larry Hedrick	18.00	8.00
44 David Green Slim Jim	18.00	8.00
44 Jeff Purvis Jackaroo	18.00	8.00
51 Jim Bown Luck's	20.00	9.00
60 Mark Martin Winn Dixie	20.00	9.00
71 Kevin Lepage Vermont Teddy Bear	18.00	8.00
71 Dave Marcis Olive Garden	25.00	11.00
75 Todd Bodine Factory Stores of America	18.00	8.00
81 Kenny Wallace TIC Financial	18.00	8.00
87 Joe Nemechek Burger King	18.00	8.00
88 Ernie Irvan Havoline	25.00	11.00
90 Mike Wallace Heilig-Meyers	18.00	8.00
94 Bill Elliott McDonald's	20.00	9.00

CAR / DRIVER / SPONSOR	MINT	NRMT
94 Bill Elliott McDonald's Thunderbat	35.00	16.00

1995 Racing Champions SuperTrucks 1:24

This 1:24 scale series is representitive of the many different trucks that raced in the inaugural SuperTruck series. There are many different variation with with sponsors or paint schemes throughout the series.

CAR / DRIVER / SPONSOR	MINT	NRMT
1 P.J. Jones Sears Diehard Chevrolet	20.00	9.00
1 P.J. Jones Vessells Ford	25.00	11.00
2 David Ashley Southern California Ford	18.00	8.00
3 Mike Skinner Goodwrench	20.00	9.00
6 Mike Bliss Ultra Wheels	18.00	8.00
6 Butch Gilliland Ultra Wheels	18.00	8.00
6 Rick Carelli Total Petroleum	18.00	8.00
7 Geoff Bodine Exide	18.00	8.00
7 Geoff Bodine Exide Salsa	18.00	8.00
7 Dave Rezendes Exide	18.00	8.00
8 Mike Bliss Ultra Wheels	18.00	8.00
10 Stan Fox Made for You	18.00	8.00
12 Randy MacCachren Venable	18.00	8.00
18 Johnny Benson Hella Lights	18.00	8.00
21 Tobey Butler Ortho with Green Nose piece	18.00	8.00
21 Tobey Butler Ortho with Yellow Nose piece	18.00	8.00
23 T.J. Clark ASE with Blue scheme	18.00	8.00
23 T.J. Clark ASE with White scheme	18.00	8.00
24 Jeff Gordon DuPont Signature Series	25.00	11.00
24 Scott Lagasse DuPont	20.00	9.00
24 Scott Lagasse DuPont Bank	22.00	10.00
37 Bob Strait Target Expediting	18.00	8.00
38 Sammy Swindell Channellock	18.00	8.00
51 Kerry Teague Rosenblum Racing	18.00	8.00
52 Ken Schrader AC Delco	18.00	8.00
54 Steve McEachern McEachern Racing	18.00	8.00
61 Todd Bodine Roush Racing	18.00	8.00
75 Bill Sedgwick Spears Motorsports	18.00	8.00
83 Steve Portenga Coffee Critic	18.00	8.00
95 No Driver Association Brickyard 400 Special	20.00	9.00
95 No Driver Association Brickyard 400 Special Bank	25.00	11.00
98 Butch Miller Raybestos	18.00	8.00

1996 Racing Champions Previews 1:24

This series of 1:24 die cast replicas featured a preview at some of the new paint jobs to run in

the 1996 season. The Terry Labonte Bayer car is one of the first for this new car.

CAR / DRIVER / SPONSOR	MINT	NRMT
2 Ricky Craven DuPont	18.00	8.00
4 Sterling Marlin Kodak	18.00	8.00
5 Terry Labonte Kellogg's	18.00	8.00
5 Terry Labonte Bayer	18.00	8.00
6 Mark Martin Valvoline	18.00	8.00
7 Stevie Reeves Clabber Girl	18.00	8.00
9 Joe Bessey Delco Remy	18.00	8.00
9 Lake Speed SPAM	18.00	8.00
10 Ricky Rudd Tide	18.00	8.00
11 Brett Bodine Lowe's	18.00	8.00
12 Derrike Cope Mane N' Tail	18.00	8.00
14 Patty Moise Dial Purex	18.00	8.00
16 Ted Musgrave Family Channel	18.00	8.00
17 Darrell Waltrip Western Auto	18.00	8.00
18 Bobby Labonte Interstate Batteries	18.00	8.00
22 Ward Burton MBNA	18.00	8.00
24 Jeff Gordon DuPont	20.00	9.00
30 Johnny Benson Pennzoil	18.00	8.00
40 Tim Fedewa Kleenex	18.00	8.00
41 Ricky Craven Kodiak	18.00	8.00
47 Jeff Fuller Sunoco	18.00	8.00
51 Chuck Bown Lucks	18.00	8.00
52 Ken Schrader AC Delco	18.00	8.00
57 Jason Keller Slim Jim	18.00	8.00
74 Johnny Benson Lipton Tea	18.00	8.00
87 Joe Nemechek Burger King	18.00	8.00
90 Mike Wallace Heilig-Meyers	18.00	8.00
94 Bill Elliott McDonald's	18.00	8.00

1996 Racing Champions 1:24

The 1:24 scale cars that appear in this series are replicas of many of the cars that ran in the 1996 season. The Rusty Wallace Miller Genuine Draft car is one of the few times that Racing Champions has offered a collectible die cast with a beer logo.

CAR / DRIVER / SPONSOR	MINT	NRMT
1 Rick Mast Hooter's	30.00	13.50
1 Rick Mast Hooter's Hood Open	30.00	13.50
2 Ricky Craven DuPont	18.00	8.00
2 Ricky Craven DuPont Hood Open	25.00	11.00
2 Rusty Wallace Miller Genuine Draft	30.00	13.50

CAR / DRIVER / SPONSOR	MINT	NRMT
2 Rusty Wallace Miller Genuine Draft Hood Open	40.00	18.00
2 Rusty Wallace Penske Racing	25.00	11.00
3 Mike Skinner Goodwrench	25.00	11.00
4 Sterling Marlin Kodak Back to Back Special	25.00	11.00

CAR / DRIVER / SPONSOR	MINT	NRMT
5 Terry Labonte Bayer Hood Open	25.00	11.00
5 Terry Labonte Kellogg's	20.00	9.00
5 Terry Labonte Kellogg's Hood Open	35.00	16.00
5 Terry Labonte Kellogg's Silver car	40.00	18.00

CAR / DRIVER / SPONSOR	MINT	NRMT
5 Terry Labonte Kellogg's Silver Hood Open	40.00	18.00
6 Tommy Houston Suburban Propane	18.00	8.00
6 Mark Martin Valvoline	18.00	8.00
6 Mark Martin Valvoline Hood Open	35.00	16.00
7 Geoff Bodine QVC	18.00	8.00
8 Hut Stricklin Circuit City	18.00	8.00
9 Joe Bessey Delco Remy	18.00	8.00
9 Joe Bessey Delco Remy Hood Open	25.00	11.00
9 Lake Speed SPAM	20.00	9.00
10 Ricky Rudd Tide	18.00	8.00
11 Brett Bodine Lowe's	18.00	8.00
11 Brett Bodine Lowe's Hood Open	25.00	11.00
11 Brett Bodine Lowe's 50th Anniversary Paint Scheme	40.00	18.00
11 Brett Bodine Lowe's 50th Anniversary Paint Scheme Hood Open	25.00	11.00

CAR / DRIVER / SPONSOR	MINT	NRMT
14 Patty Moise Purex	20.00	9.00
15 Wally Dallenbach Hayes Modems	50.00	22.00
15 Wally Dallenbach Hayes Modems Hood Open	35.00	16.00
16 Ted Musgrave Primestar	18.00	8.00
17 Darrell Waltrip Parts America	18.00	8.00
18 Bobby Labonte Interstate Bat.	25.00	11.00
19 Loy Allen Healthsource	25.00	11.00
21 Michael Waltrip Citgo	18.00	8.00
21 Michael Waltrip Citgo Hood Open	30.00	13.50
22 Ward Burton MBNA	18.00	8.00
23 Chad Little John Deere	30.00	13.50
23 Chad Little John Deere Hood Open	40.00	18.00
23 Chad Little John Deere in a John Deere Box	40.00	18.00
24 Jeff Gordon DuPont	40.00	18.00
24 Jeff Gordon DuPont 1995 Champion	35.00	16.00
24 Jeff Gordon DuPont 1995 Champion Hood Open	40.00	18.00
25 Ken Schrader Budweiser	40.00	18.00
25 Ken Schrader Budweiser Chrome	300.00	135.00
25 Ken Schrader Hendrick Motorsports	18.00	8.00
28 Ernie Irvan Havoline	18.00	8.00
28 Ernie Irvan Havoline Hood Open	30.00	13.50
29 Steve Grissom Cartoon Network	20.00	9.00
29 Steve Grissom Cartoon Network Hood Open	25.00	11.00
29 Steve Grissom WCW	20.00	9.00
29 Steve Grissom WCW Hood Open	25.00	11.00
29 No Driver Association Scooby-Doo in Scooby Box	24.00	11.00
29 No Driver Association WCW Sting	18.00	8.00
30 Johnny Benson Pennzoil	18.00	8.00
30 Johnny Benson Pennzoil Hood Open	50.00	22.00
31 Mike Skinner Realtree	100.00	45.00
31 Mike Skinner Realtree Hood Open	70.00	32.00
34 Mike McLaughlin Royal Oak	18.00	8.00
37 John Andretti K-Mart	18.00	8.00
38 Dennis Setzer Lipton	18.00	8.00
40 Tim Fedewa Kleenex	18.00	8.00
40 Jim Sauter First Union	20.00	9.00
41 Ricky Craven Hedrick Racing	18.00	8.00
41 Ricky Craven Kodiak in Acrylic case	50.00	22.00
41 Ricky Craven Manheim	18.00	8.00
43 Bobby Hamilton STP 5 car set	100.00	45.00

CAR / DRIVER / SPONSOR	MINT	NRMT
43 Bobby Hamilton STP 5 car trailer set	150.00	70.00
43 Bobby Hamilton STP Silver car	25.00	11.00
44 Bobby Labonte Shell	30.00	13.50
47 Jeff Fuller Sunoco Hood Open	25.00	11.00
51 Jim Bown Lucks Hood Open	25.00	11.00
52 Ken Schrader AC Delco	18.00	8.00
52 Ken Schrader AC Delco Hood Open	25.00	11.00
57 Jason Keller Halloween Havoc	18.00	8.00
57 Jason Keller Slim Jim Hood Open	30.00	13.50
60 Mark Martin Winn Dixie	20.00	9.00
60 Mark Martin Winn Dixie Hood Open	35.00	16.00
63 Curtis Markham Lysol	18.00	8.00
74 Johnny Benson Lipton Tea 1995 BGN Champion	20.00	9.00
74 Johnny Benson Lipton Tea 1995 BGN Champion Hood Open	30.00	13.50
75 Morgan Shepherd Remington	30.00	13.50
75 Morgan Shepherd Remington Hood Open	35.00	16.00
77 Bobby Hillin Jr. Jasper Engines	18.00	8.00
81 Kenny Wallace Square D	18.00	8.00
87 Joe Nemechek Burger King	60.00	27.00
88 Dale Jarrett Quality Care	18.00	8.00

	MINT	NRMT
88 Dale Jarrett Quality Care Hood Open	30.00	13.50
90 Mike Wallace Duron	18.00	8.00
94 Ron Barfield New Holland	18.00	8.00
94 Bill Elliott McDonald's	18.00	8.00
94 Bill Elliott McDonald's Hood Open	30.00	13.50
94 Bill Elliott McDonald's Monopoly	20.00	9.00
94 Bill Elliott McDonald's Monopoly Hood Open	30.00	13.50
96 David Green Busch Chrome	250.00	110.00
96 David Green Busch Hobby	35.00	16.00
97 Chad Little Sterling Cowboy	18.00	8.00
99 Glenn Allen Luxaire	18.00	8.00
99 Jeff Burton Exide	18.00	8.00

1996 Racing Champions SuperTrucks 1:24

Racing Champions continued there line of 1:24 SuperTrucks in 1996. This series features many of the circuit's first-time drivers.

CAR / DRIVER / SPONSOR	MINT	NRMT
2 Mike Bliss ASE	18.00	8.00
2 Mike Bliss Super Wheels	18.00	8.00
6 Rick Carelli Chesrown	18.00	8.00
7 Geoff Bodine QVC	18.00	8.00
14 Butch Gilliland Stropps	18.00	8.00
17 Bill Sedgwick Die Hard	18.00	8.00
19 Lance Norlock Maclanerg-Duncan	18.00	8.00
20 Walker Evans Dana	18.00	8.00
21 Doug George Ortho	18.00	8.00
24 Jack Sprague Quaker State	18.00	8.00
29 Bob Keselowski Winnebago	18.00	8.00
30 Jimmy Hensley Mopar	18.00	8.00
34 Bob Brevak Concor	18.00	8.00
43 Rich Bickle Cummins	18.00	8.00
44 Bryan Refner 1-800-Collect	18.00	8.00
52 Ken Schrader AC Delco	18.00	8.00
57 Robbie Pyle Aisyn	18.00	8.00
75 Bobby Gill Spears	18.00	8.00
78 Mike Chase Petron Plus	18.00	8.00
83 Steve Portenga Coffee Critic	18.00	8.00
98 Butch Miller Raybestos	18.00	8.00

1997 Racing Champions Previews 1:24

This series of 1:24 die cast replicas featured a preview at some of the new paint jobs to run in the 1997 season. The Rick Mast Remington car and the Robert Pressley Scooby Doo car features two of the numerous driver changes for the 97 Winston Cup season.

	MINT	NRMT
4 Sterling Marlin Kodak	16.00	7.25
5 Terry Labonte Kellogg's	16.00	7.25
6 Mark Martin Valvoline	16.00	7.25
10 Ricky Rudd Tide	16.00	7.25
18 Bobby Labonte Interstate Batteries	16.00	7.25
21 Michael Waltrip Citgo	16.00	7.25
24 Jeff Gordon DuPont	20.00	9.00
28 Ernie Irvan Havoline	16.00	7.25
29 Robert Pressley Scooby-Doo	16.00	7.25

CAR / DRIVER / SPONSOR	MINT	NRMT
30 Johnny Benson Pennzoil	16.00	7.25
75 Rick Mast Remington	16.00	7.25
94 Bill Elliott McDonald's	16.00	7.25

1997 Racing Champions 1:24

The 1:24 scale cars that appear in this series are replicas of many of the cars that ran in the 1996 season. The series is higlighted by the Terry Labonte Kellogg's car commenerating his 1996 Winston Cup Championship. This car is available in two variations: standard and hood open. The Lake Speed University of Nebraska car is believed to be in short supply becuase of the dissolved team sponsorship. It is also believed to be available in a red tampo and black tampo.

	MINT	NRMT
1 Hermie Sadler DeWalt	16.00	7.25
1 Morgan Shepherd Crusin' America	16.00	7.25
1 Morgan Shepherd R&L Carriers	20.00	9.00
2 Ricky Craven Raybestos	16.00	7.25
2 Rusty Wallace Miller Lite distributed by Matco	60.00	27.00
2 Rusty Wallace Penske	16.00	7.25
4 Sterling Marlin Kodak	16.00	7.25
5 Terry Labonte Bayer	20.00	9.00
5 Terry Labonte Kellogg's	18.00	8.00
5 Terry Labonte Kellogg's 1996 Champion	25.00	11.00

	MINT	NRMT
5 Terry Labonte Kellogg's 1996 Champion Hood Open	40.00	18.00
5 Terry Labonte Tony the Tiger	25.00	11.00
6 Tommy Houston Suburban Propane	16.00	7.25
6 Mark Martin Valvoline	16.00	7.25
7 Geoff Bodine QVC	16.00	7.25
7 Geoff Bodine QVC Gold Rush	25.00	11.00
8 Hut Stricklin Circuit City	16.00	7.25
9 Lake Speed University of Nebraska	80.00	36.00
9 Joe Bessey Power Team	16.00	7.25
9 Jeff Burton Track Gear	16.00	7.25
10 Phil Parsons Channellock	16.00	7.25
10 Ricky Rudd Tide	16.00	7.25

CAR / DRIVER / SPONSOR	MINT	NRMT
11 Jimmy Foster Speedvision	18.00	8.00
11 Brett Bodine Close Call	16.00	7.25
16 Ted Musgrave Primestar	16.00	7.25
17 Darrell Waltrip Parts America	18.00	8.00
17 Darrell Waltrip Parts America Chrome	25.00	11.00
17 Darrell Waltrip Parts America Chrome Promo	25.00	11.00
18 Bobby Labonte Interstate Batt.	16.00	7.25
19 Gary Bradberry CSR	16.00	7.25
21 Michael Waltrip Citgo	16.00	7.25
24 Jeff Gordon DuPont	25.00	11.00
25 Ricky Craven Bud Lizard 3-car set	75.00	34.00
25 Ricky Craven Bud Lizard	30.00	13.50
25 Ricky Craven Hendrick	16.00	7.25
28 Ernie Irvan Havoline	16.00	7.25
28 Ernie Irvan Havoline 10th Anniversary	25.00	11.00
29 Robert Pressley Cartoon Network	16.00	7.25
29 Jeff Green Tom and Jerry	16.00	7.25
29 Elliott Sadler Phillips 66	25.00	11.00
30 Johnny Benson Pennzoil	16.00	7.25
32 Dale Jarrett Gillette	16.00	7.25
32 Dale Jarrett White Rain	16.00	7.25
33 Ken Schrader Petree Racing	16.00	7.25
34 Mike McLaughlin Royal Oak	16.00	7.25
36 Todd Bodine Stanley Tools	16.00	7.25
36 Derrike Cope Skittles	16.00	7.25
37 Jeremy Mayfield K-Mart	16.00	7.25
38 Elton Sawyer Barbasol	16.00	7.25
40 Robby Gordon Sabco Racing	16.00	7.25
41 Steve Grissom Hedrick	16.00	7.25
42 Joe Nemechek Bell South	16.00	7.25
46 Wally Dallenbach First Union	16.00	7.25
47 Jeff Fuller Sunoco	16.00	7.25
49 Kyle Petty nWo	30.00	13.50
57 Jason Keller Slim Jim	16.00	7.25
60 Mark Martin Winn-Dixie Promo	35.00	16.00
72 Mike Dillon Detroit Gasket	16.00	7.25
74 Randy LaJoie Fina	16.00	7.25
74 Randy LaJoie Fina 1996 Busch Champion	30.00	13.50
75 Rick Mast Remington	16.00	7.25
75 Rick Mast Remington Camo	16.00	7.25

CAR / DRIVER / SPONSOR	MINT	NRMT
75 Rick Mast Remington Stren	16.00	7.25
87 Joe Nemechek Bell South	16.00	7.25
88 Kevin Lepage Hype	16.00	7.25
90 Dick Trickle Heilig-Meyers	16.00	7.25
91 Mike Wallace Spam	16.00	7.25
94 Bill Elliott McDonald's	16.00	7.25
94 Ron Barfield New Holland	16.00	7.25

CAR / DRIVER / SPONSOR	MINT	NRMT
94 Bill Elliott Mac Tonight	18.00	8.00
94 Bill Elliott Mac Tonight 3-car set	80.00	36.00
96 David Green Caterpillar	16.00	7.25
96 David Green Caterpillar Promo	20.00	9.00
97 Chad Little John Deere Promo	30.00	13.50
97 No Driver Association Brickyard 500	20.00	9.00
97 Chad Little John Deere	16.00	7.25
99 Jeff Burton Exide	16.00	7.25
99 Glenn Allen Luxaire	16.00	7.25
00 Buckshot Jones Aqua-Fresh	20.00	9.00

1997 Racing Champions Stock Rods 1:24

These 1:24 scale cars are replicas of vintage stock rods with NASCAR paint schemes. Cars are listed by issue number instead of car number.

CAR / DRIVER / SPONSOR	MINT	NRMT
1 Darrell Waltrip Parts America	20.00	9.00
2 Sterling Marlin Kodak	20.00	9.00
3 Steve Grissom Hedrick	20.00	9.00
4 Ken Schrader Petree	20.00	9.00
5 Dennis Setzer Lance	20.00	9.00
6 Ricky Craven Hendrick	20.00	9.00
7 Ricky Rudd Tide	20.00	9.00
8 Rusty Wallace Penske	20.00	9.00
9 Rick Mast Remington	20.00	9.00
10 Terry Labonte Spooky Loops	40.00	18.00
11 Bill Elliott MacTonight	25.00	11.00
12 Bobby Hamilton Kodak	20.00	9.00
13 Terry Labonte Spooky Loops	25.00	11.00
14 Terry Labonte Kellogg's	25.00	11.00

1997 Racing Champions SuperTrucks 1:24

Racing Champions continued their line of 1:24 SuperTrucks in 1997. This series features many of the circuit's first-time drivers and Winston Cup regulars.

CAR / DRIVER / SPONSOR	MINT	NRMT
1 Michael Waltrip MW Windows	16.00	7.25

CAR / DRIVER / SPONSOR	MINT	NRMT
2 Mike Bliss Team ASE	16.00	7.25
4 Bill Elliott Team ASE	16.00	7.25
6 Rick Carelli ReMax	16.00	7.25
7 Tammy Kirk Loveable	16.00	7.25
15 Mike Colabacci VISA	16.00	7.25
15 Mike Cope Penrose	16.00	7.25
18 Johnny Benson Pennzoil	16.00	7.25
18 Mark Dokken Dana	16.00	7.25
19 Tony Raines Pennzoil	16.00	7.25
24 Jack Sprague Quaker State	16.00	7.25
29 Bob Keselowski Mopar	16.00	7.25
35 Dave Rezendes Ortho	16.00	7.25
49 Rodney Combs Lance	16.00	7.25
52 Tobey Butler Purolator	16.00	7.25
66 Bryan Refner Carlin	16.00	7.25
75 Dan Press Spears	16.00	7.25
80 Joe Ruttman LCI	16.00	7.25
86 Stacy Compton Valvoline	16.00	7.25
87 Joe Nemechek Bell South	16.00	7.25
92 Mark Kinser Rotary	16.00	7.25
98 Kenny Irwin Raybestos	25.00	11.00
99 Chuck Bown Exide	16.00	7.25
99 Jeff Burton Exide	16.00	7.25
99 Mark Martin Exide	16.00	7.25

1998 Racing Champions 1:24

The 1:24 scale cars that appear in this series are replicas of many of the cars that ran in the 1998 season. The Mark Martin Kosei car is one of the cars that highlights this series.

CAR / DRIVER / SPONSOR	MINT	NRMT
4 Bobby Hamilton Kodak	16.00	7.25
5 Terry Labonte Blasted Fruit Loops	20.00	9.00
5 Terry Labonte Kellogg's	20.00	9.00
5 Terry Labonte Kellogg's Corny	20.00	9.00
6 Joe Bessey Power Team	16.00	7.25

CAR / DRIVER / SPONSOR	MINT	NRMT
6 Mark Martin Eagle One	20.00	9.00
6 Mark Martin Kosei	175.00	80.00
6 Mark Martin Synpower	30.00	13.50
6 Mark Martin Valvoline	18.00	8.00
7 Geoff Bodine Phillips	25.00	11.00
8 Hut Stricklin Circuit City	16.00	7.25
9 Jeff Burton Track Gear	16.00	7.25
9 Lake Speed Birthday Cake	18.00	8.00
9 Lake Speed Huckleberry Hound	20.00	9.00

CAR / DRIVER / SPONSOR	MINT	NRMT
10 Ricky Rudd Give Kids The World	16.00	7.25
10 Ricky Rudd Tide	16.00	7.25
11 Brett Bodine Paychex	16.00	7.25
13 Jerry Nadeau First Plus	25.00	11.00
16 Ted Musgrave Primestar	16.00	7.25
17 Matt Kenseth Lycos	40.00	18.00
17 Darrell Waltrip Builders' Square	30.00	13.50
20 Blaise Alexander Rescue Engine	16.00	7.25
21 Michael Waltrip Citgo	16.00	7.25
23 Jimmy Spencer No Bull	125.00	55.00
26 Johnny Benson Betty Crocker	30.00	13.50
26 Johnny Benson Cheerios	20.00	9.00

CAR / DRIVER / SPONSOR	MINT	NRMT
28 Kenny Irwin Havoline	35.00	16.00
29 Hermie Sadler Dewalt	16.00	7.25
30 Derrike Cope Gumout	16.00	7.25
30 Mike Cope Slim Jim	16.00	7.25
33 Ken Schrader Petree	16.00	7.25
35 Todd Bodine Tabasco	20.00	9.00
36 Ernie Irvan M&M's	25.00	11.00
36 Ernie Irvan Skittles	16.00	7.25
36 Ernie Irvan Wildberry Skittles	16.00	7.25
40 Sterling Marlin Sabco	16.00	7.25
41 Steve Grissom Hedrick	16.00	7.25
42 Joe Nemechek BellSouth	16.00	7.25
46 Wally Dallenbach First Union	16.00	7.25
50 Ricky Craven Hendrick	16.00	7.25
50 NDA Dr. Pepper	16.00	7.25
59 Robert Pressley Kingsford	16.00	7.25
66 Elliott Sadler Phillips 66	16.00	7.25
72 Mike Dillon Detroit Gasket	16.00	7.25
75 Rick Mast Remington	16.00	7.25
78 Gary Bradberry Pilot	16.00	7.25
87 Joe Nemechek Bell South	25.00	11.00
88 Kevin Schwantz Ryder	16.00	7.25
90 Dick Trickle Heilig-Meyers	16.00	7.25
94 Bill Elliott Happy Meal	16.00	7.25
94 Bill Elliott McDonald's	16.00	7.25
94 Bill Elliott Mac Tonight	16.00	7.25

CAR / DRIVER / SPONSOR	MINT	NRMT
94 Bill Elliott McDonald's NASCAR 50th Anniversary Gold	95.00	45.00
96 David Green Caterpiller	16.00	7.25
96 David Green Caterpillar P	25.00	11.00
98 Greg Sacks Thorn Apple Valley	16.00	7.25
99 Glenn Allen Luxaire	16.00	7.25
99 Jeff Burton Exide	16.00	7.25
300 Darrell Waltrip Tim Flock Special	16.00	7.25

CAR / DRIVER / SPONSOR	MINT	NRMT
00 Buckshot Jones Aquafresh	16.00	7.25
00 Buckshot Jones Bayer	16.00	7.25

1998 Racing Champions Gold 1:24

This is a special series produced by Racing Champions to celebrate NASCAR's 50th anniversary. It parallels the regular 1998 1:24 scale series. Each car is a limited edition of 2,500. Each car is also plated in gold chrome and contains a serial number on its chassis.

CAR / DRIVER / SPONSOR	MINT	NRMT
2 Ron Barfield New Holland	30.00	13.50
4 Bobby Hamilton Kodak	30.00	13.50
5 Terry Labonte Blasted Fruit Loops	75.00	34.00
5 Terry Labonte Kellogg's	75.00	34.00
5 Terry Labonte Kellogg's Corny	75.00	34.00
6 Joe Bessey Power Team	25.00	11.00
6 Mark Martin Eagle One	75.00	34.00
6 Mark Martin Syntec	75.00	34.00
6 Mark Martin Valvoline	75.00	34.00
8 Hut Stricklin Circuit City	25.00	11.00
9 Jeff Burton Track Gear	30.00	13.50
9 Jerry Nadeau Zombie Island	30.00	13.50
9 Lake Speed Huckleberry Hound	30.00	13.50
9 Lake Speed Birthday Cake	30.00	13.50
10 Phil Parsons Duralube	25.00	11.00
10 Ricky Rudd Tide	30.00	13.50
11 Brett Bodine Paychex	30.00	13.50
13 Jerry Nadeau First Plus	50.00	22.00
14 Patty Moise Rhodes	25.00	11.00
16 Ted Musgrave Primestar	30.00	13.50
17 Matt Kenseth Lycos	50.00	22.00
17 Darrell Waltrip Builders' Square	40.00	18.00
19 Tony Raines Yellow	25.00	11.00
20 Blaise Alexander Rescue Engine	25.00	11.00
21 Michael Waltrip Citgo	30.00	13.50
23 Lance Hooper WCW	25.00	11.00
23 Jimmy Spencer No Bull	150.00	70.00
26 Johnny Benson Cheerios	40.00	18.00
28 Kenny Irwin Havoline Mac Tools	125.00	55.00
29 Hermie Sadler Dewalt	25.00	11.00
30 Derrike Cope Gumout	25.00	11.00
30 Mike Cope Slim Jim	25.00	11.00

CAR / DRIVER / SPONSOR	MINT	NRMT
33 Ken Schrader Petree	30.00	13.50
34 Mike McLaughlin Goulds	25.00	11.00
35 Todd Bodine Tabasco	30.00	13.50
36 Matt Hutter Stanley	25.00	11.00
36 Ernie Irvan M&M's	50.00	22.00
36 Ernie Irvan Skittles	25.00	11.00
36 Ernie Irvan Wildberry Skittles	40.00	18.00
40 Rick Fuller Channellock	25.00	11.00
40 Kevin Lepage Channellock	25.00	11.00
40 Sterling Marlin Sabco	30.00	13.50
41 Steve Grissom Hedrick	30.00	13.50
42 Joe Nemechek BellSouth	30.00	13.50
46 Wally Dallenbach First Union	30.00	13.50
47 Andy Santerie Monroe	30.00	13.50
50 Ricky Craven Hendrick	40.00	18.00
50 No Driver Association 50th Anniversary	40.00	18.00
59 Robert Pressley Kingsford	25.00	11.00
60 Mark Martin Winn Dixie	75.00	34.00
64 Dick Trickle Schneider	30.00	13.50
66 Eliott Sadler Phillips 66	30.00	13.50
72 Mike Dillon Detroit Gasket	25.00	11.00
75 Rick Mast Remington	25.00	11.00
77 Robert Pressley Jasper	25.00	11.00
78 Gary Bradberry Pilot	25.00	11.00
87 Joe Nemechek BellSouth	25.00	11.00
88 Kevin Schwantz Ryder	25.00	11.00
90 Dick Trickle Helig-Meyers	25.00	11.00
94 Bill Elliott Happy Meal	80.00	36.00
94 Bill Elliott McDonald's	80.00	36.00
96 David Green Caterpiller	25.00	11.00
97 Chad Little John Deere P	100.00	45.00
98 Greg Sacks Thorn Apple Valley	25.00	11.00
99 Glen Allen Luxaire	25.00	11.00
99 Jeff Burton Exide	30.00	13.50
300 Darrell Waltrip Flock Special	40.00	18.00
400 No Driver Association Brickyard 400	30.00	13.50
00 Buckshot Jones Alka Seltzer	30.00	13.50
00 Buckshot Jones Bayer	30.00	13.50
00 Buckshot Jones Aquafresh	30.00	13.50

1998 Racing Champions Gold Hood Open 1:24

This is a special series produced by Racing Champions to celebrate NASCAR's 50th anniversary. It parallels the regular 1998 1:24 scale series. Each car is a limited edition of 1,998. Each car is also plated in gold chrome and contains a serial number on its chassis.

CAR / DRIVER / SPONSOR	MINT	NRMT
4 Bobby Hamilton Kodak	40.00	18.00
5 Terry Labonte Blasted Fruit Loops	75.00	34.00
5 Terry Labonte Kellogg's	75.00	34.00
5 Terry Labonte Kellogg's Corny	75.00	34.00
6 Joe Bessey Power Team	30.00	13.50
6 Mark Martin Syntec	75.00	34.00
6 Mark Martin Valvoline	75.00	34.00
8 Hut Stricklin Circuit City	30.00	13.50
9 Lake Speed Huckleberry Hound	40.00	18.00
10 Ricky Rudd Tide	40.00	18.00
11 Brett Bodine Paychex	30.00	13.50
16 Ted Musgrave Primestar	30.00	13.50
17 Darrell Waltrip Builders' Square	50.00	22.00
19 Tony Raines Yellow	30.00	13.50
21 Michael Waltrip Goodwill Games	30.00	13.50
30 Derrike Cope Gumout	30.00	13.50
33 Ken Schrader Petree	40.00	18.00
35 Todd Bodine Tabasco	40.00	18.00
36 Ernie Irvan Skittles	40.00	18.00
36 Ernie Irvan Wildberry Skittles	50.00	22.00
40 Sterling Marlin Sabco	40.00	18.00
50 Ricky Craven Hendrick	40.00	18.00
77 Robert Pressley Jasper	30.00	13.50
78 Gary Bradberry Pilot	30.00	13.50
90 Dick Trickle Heilig-Meyers	30.00	13.50
94 Bill Elliott Happy Meal	75.00	34.00
94 Bill Elliott McDonald's	75.00	34.00
98 Greg Sacks Thorn Apple Valley	30.00	13.50
99 Jeff Burton Exide	40.00	18.00
400 No Driver Association Brickyard 400	40.00	18.00

1998 Racing Champions Reflections of Gold 1:24

This is a special series produced by Racing Champions to celebrate NASCAR's 50th anniversary. It parallels the regular 1998 1:24 scale series. Each car is a limited edition of 4,998. Each car is also plated in gold chrome and contains a serial number on its chassis.

CAR / DRIVER / SPONSOR	MINT	NRMT
4 Bobby Hamilton Kodak	25.00	11.00
5 Terry Labonte Kellogg's	50.00	22.00
6 Joe Bessey Power Team	25.00	11.00
6 Mark Martin Valvoline	75.00	34.00
8 Hut Stricklin Circuit City	25.00	11.00
9 Lake Speed Huckleberry Hound	25.00	11.00
10 Phil Parsons Duralube	25.00	11.00
10 Ricky Rudd Tide	30.00	13.50
11 Brett Bodine Paychex	25.00	11.00
13 Jerry Nadeau First Plus	50.00	22.00
16 Ted Musgrave Primestar	25.00	11.00
20 Blaisè Alexander Rescue Engine	25.00	11.00
21 Michael Waltrip Citgo	25.00	11.00
23 Lance Hooper WCW	25.00	11.00
26 Johnny Benson Cheerios	30.00	13.50
29 Hermie Sadler Dewalt	25.00	11.00
30 Derrike Cope Gumout	25.00	11.00
33 Tim Fedewa Kleenex	25.00	11.00
33 Ken Schrader Petree	30.00	13.50
34 Mike McLaughlin Goulds	25.00	11.00
35 Todd Bodine Tabasco	30.00	13.50
36 Ernie Irvan Skittles	45.00	20.00
40 Sterling Marlin Sabco	30.00	13.50
41 Steve Grissom Hedrick	25.00	11.00
42 Joe Nemechek Bell South	25.00	11.00
46 Wally Dallenbach First Union	25.00	11.00
47 Andy Santerie Monroe	25.00	11.00
59 Robert Pressley Kingsford	25.00	11.00
60 Mark Martin Winn Dixie	50.00	22.00
63 Tracy Leslie Lysol	25.00	11.00
64 Dick Trickle Scheinder	25.00	11.00
72 Mike Dillon Detroit Gasket	25.00	11.00
74 Randy Lajoie Fina	25.00	11.00
75 Rick Mast Remington	25.00	11.00
90 Dick Trickle Heilig-Meyers	30.00	13.50
94 Bill Elliott McDonald's	50.00	22.00
99 Jeff Burton Exide	45.00	20.00
00 Buckshot Jones Aqua Fresh	25.00	11.00

CAR / DRIVER / SPONSOR	MINT	NRMT

1998 Racing Champions Signature Series 1:24

This is a special series produced by Racing Champions to celebrate NASCAR's 50th anniversary. It parallels the regular 1998 1:24 scale series. Each car is a packaged in a decorative box with the driver's facsimile autograph on the front.

CAR / DRIVER / SPONSOR	MINT	NRMT
5 Terry Labonte Kellogg's	20.00	9.00
6 Mark Martin Valvoline	20.00	9.00
9 Jeff Burton Track Gear	20.00	9.00
9 Lake Speed Huckleberry Hound	20.00	9.00
10 Phil Parsons Duralube	20.00	9.00
10 Ricky Rudd Tide	20.00	9.00
11 Brett Bodine Paychex	20.00	9.00
13 Jerry Nadeau First Plus	20.00	9.00
16 Ted Musgrave Primestar	20.00	9.00
26 Johnny Benson Cheerios	20.00	9.00
30 Derrike Cope Gumout	20.00	9.00
33 Ken Schrader Petree	20.00	9.00
35 Todd Bodine Tabasco	20.00	9.00
36 Ernie Irvan Skittles	20.00	9.00
50 Ricky Craven Hendrick	20.00	9.00
75 Rick Mast Remington	20.00	9.00

CAR / DRIVER / SPONSOR	MINT	NRMT
94 Bill Elliott McDonald's	20.00	9.00
98 Greg Sacks Thorn Apple Valley	20.00	9.00

1998 Racing Champions Stock Rods 1:24

These 1:24 scale cars are replicas of vintage stock rods with NASCAR paint schemes. Cars are listed by issue number instead of car number.

CAR / DRIVER / SPONSOR	MINT	NRMT
15 Jeff Green Cartoon Network	15.00	6.75
16 Kevin Schwantz Ryder	15.00	6.75
17 Glen Allen Luxaire	15.00	6.75
18 Jeff Burton Exide	15.00	6.75
19 Michael Waltrip Citgo	15.00	6.75
20 Robert Pressley Kingsford	15.00	6.75

CAR / DRIVER / SPONSOR	MINT	NRMT
21 Kevin Schwantz Ryder	15.00	6.75
22 Ken Schrader Petree	15.00	6.75
23 Dick Trickle Heilig-Meyers	15.00	6.75
24 Joe Bessey Power Team	15.00	6.75
25 Glen Allen Luxaire	15.00	6.75
26 Jerry Nadeau First Plus	15.00	6.75
27 Hut Stricklin Circuit City	15.00	6.75
28 Terry Labonte Kellogg's	20.00	9.00
29 Wally Dallenbach First Union	15.00	6.75
30 Joe Nemechek BellSouth	15.00	6.75
31 Robert Pressley Kingsford	15.00	6.75
32 Hut Stricklin Circuit City	15.00	6.75
33 Elliot Sadler Phillips 66	15.00	6.75
34 Hermie Sadler Dewalt	15.00	6.75
35 Steve Grissom Hedrick Gold	20.00	9.00
36 Lake Speed Huckleberry Hound	15.00	6.75
37 Bill Elliott McDonald's Gold	40.00	18.00
38 Michael Waltrip Citgo	15.00	6.75
39 Jeff Burton Track Gear	15.00	6.75
40 Mark Martin Valvoline	20.00	9.00
41 Bill Elliott McDonald's	20.00	9.00
42 Jeff Burton Exide Gold	25.00	11.00
43 Jerry Nadeau First Plus Gold	20.00	9.00
44 Jeff Burton Exide	15.00	6.75
45 Rick Fuller Channellock	15.00	6.75
46 Ted Musgrave Primestar	15.00	6.75
47 Ricky Craven Hendrick	15.00	6.75
48 Terry Labonte Kellogg's Gold	40.00	18.00
49 Hut Stricklin Circuit City Gold	20.00	9.00
50 NDA NASCAR 50th Anniversary	15.00	6.75
51 Wally Dallenbach First Union	15.00	6.75
52 Terry Labonte Kellogg's Corny	20.00	9.00
53 Elliot Sadler Phillips 66	15.00	6.75
54 Bill Elliott McDonald's Gold	40.00	18.00
55 Steve Grissom Hedrick Gold	20.00	9.00
56 Terry Labonte Kellogg's	20.00	9.00
57 Bobby Hamilton Kodak	15.00	6.75
58 Bill Elliott McDonald's Gold	40.00	18.00
59 Mark Martin Valvoline	20.00	9.00
60 Hut Stricklin Circuit City Gold	20.00	9.00

CAR / DRIVER / SPONSOR	MINT	NRMT
61 Ricky Rudd Tide	15.00	6.75
62 Johnny Benson Cheerios	15.00	6.75
63 Ricky Craven Hendrick Gold	25.00	11.00
64 Michael Waltrip Citgo	15.00	6.75
65 Hermie Sadler Dewalt	15.00	6.75
66 Ken Schrader Petree	15.00	6.75
67 Bill Elliott McDonald's Gold	40.00	18.00
68 Joe Nemechek Bell South Gold	20.00	9.00
69 Bill Elliott McDonald's	20.00	9.00
70 Steve Grissom Hedrick	15.00	6.75
71 Mark Martin Valvoline	20.00	9.00
72 Ken Schrader Petree	15.00	6.75
73 Michael Waltrip Citgo Gold	20.00	9.00

1998 Racing Champions Stock Rods Reflections of Gold 1:24

These 1:24 scale cars are replicas of vintage stock rods with NASCAR paint schemes and gold plating. Cars are listed by issue number instead of car number.

CARS ARE LISTED BY ISSUE NUMBER

CAR / DRIVER / SPONSOR	MINT	NRMT
1 Bill Elliott McDonald's	50.00	22.00
2 Todd Bodine Tabasco	25.00	11.00
3 Terry Labonte Kellogg's	50.00	22.00
4 Bobby Hamilton Kodak	25.00	11.00
5 Mark Martin Valvoline	50.00	22.00
6 Jeff Burton Exide	35.00	16.00
7 Ernie Irvan Skittles	35.00	16.00
8 Ted Musgrave Primestar	25.00	11.00
9 Terry Labonte Kellogg's	50.00	22.00
10 Ken Schrader Petree	25.00	11.00
11 Dick Trickle Scheinder	25.00	11.00
12 Michael Waltrip Citgo	25.00	11.00

1998 Racing Champions Authentics 1:24

These 1:24 scale cars marks the first in a series by Racing Champions. These cars were distributed through hobby and trackside outlets. Each car is packaged in a special black snap case.

CAR / DRIVER / SPONSOR	MINT	NRMT
6 Mark Martin Eagle One	80.00	36.00
6 Mark Martin Synpower	80.00	36.00
6 Mark Martin Valvoline	70.00	32.00
16 Kevin Lepage Primestar	70.00	32.00

CAR / DRIVER / SPONSOR	MINT	NRMT
26 Johnny Benson Betty Crocker	70.00	32.00
26 Johnny Benson Cheerios	70.00	32.00
26 Johnny Benson Trix	70.00	32.00
97 Chad Little John Deere	70.00	32.00
99 Jeff Burton Exide	80.00	36.00
99 Jeff Burton Bruce Lee	80.00	36.00

1998 Racing Champions SuperTrucks 1:24

Racing Champions continued there line of 1:24 SuperTrucks in 1998. This series features many of the circuit's first-time drivers and Winston Cup regulars.

CAR / DRIVER / SPONSOR	MINT	NRMT
2 Mike Bliss Team ASE	16.00	7.25
6 Rick Carelli Remax	16.00	7.25
18 No Driver Association Dana	16.00	7.25
29 Bob Keselowski Mopar	16.00	7.25
31 Tony Roper Concor Tools	16.00	7.25
35 Ron Barfield Ortho	16.00	7.25
44 Boris Said Federated	16.00	7.25
52 Mike Wallace Pure One	16.00	7.25
66 Bryan Refner Carlin	16.00	7.25
84 Wayne Anderson Porter Cable	16.00	7.25
86 Stacy Compton RC Cola	16.00	7.25
87 Joe Nemechek BellSouth	16.00	7.25
90 Lance Norick National Hockey League	16.00	7.25
94 Bill Elliott Team ASE	16.00	7.25

1998 Racing Champions SuperTrucks Gold 1:24

This is a special series produced by Racing Champions to celebrate NASCAR's 50th anniversary. It parallels the regular 1998 1:24 scale series. Each truck is a limited edition of 2,500. Each truck is also plated in gold chrome and contains a serial number on its chassis.

CAR / DRIVER / SPONSOR	MINT	NRMT
2 Mike Bliss Team ASE	25.00	11.00
6 Rick Carelli Remax	25.00	11.00
29 Bob Keselowski Mopar	25.00	11.00
66 Bryan Refner Carlin	25.00	11.00
86 Stacy Compton RC Cola	25.00	11.00

1999 Racing Champions 1:24

The 1:24 scale cars that appear in this series are replicas of many of the cars that ran in the 1999 season.

CAR / DRIVER / SPONSOR	MINT	NRMT
4 Bobby Hamilton Kodak	16.00	7.25
4 Bobby Hamilton Kodak Advantix	16.00	7.25
5 Terry Labonte Kellogg's	16.00	7.25
6 Mark Martin Valvoline	16.00	7.25
6 Mark Martin Zerex	35.00	16.00
7 Michael Waltip Philips	16.00	7.25
9 Jerry Nadeau Dexter	16.00	7.25
9 Jerry Nadeau WCW nWo	16.00	7.25
9 Jerry Nadeau Goldberg	20.00	9.00
10 Ricky Rudd Tide	16.00	7.25
10 Ricky Rudd Tide Peroxide	18.00	8.00
11 Brett Bodine Paychex	16.00	7.25
12 Jeremy Mayfield Mobil 1	16.00	7.25
12 Jimmy Spencer Zippo	30.00	13.50
14 Rick Crawford Circle Bar Super Truck	16.00	7.25
16 Kevin Lepage Primestar	16.00	7.25
17 Matt Kenseth DeWalt	30.00	13.50
21 Elliott Sadler Citgo	16.00	7.25
23 Jimmy Spencer TCE Lights	16.00	7.25
24 Jack Sprague GMAC Super Truck	16.00	7.25
25 Wally Dallenbach Hendrick	16.00	7.25
26 Johnny Benson Cheerios	16.00	7.25
30 Derrike Cope Bryan Foods	16.00	7.25
32 Jeff Green Kleenex	16.00	7.25
33 Ken Schrader Petree	16.00	7.25
34 Mike McLaughiln Goulds Pumps	16.00	7.25

CAR / DRIVER / SPONSOR	MINT	NRMT
36 Ernie Irvan M&M's	25.00	11.00
36 Ernie Irvan Crispy M&M's	25.00	11.00
38 Glen Allen Barbasol	16.00	7.25
40 Sterling Marlin John Wayne	30.00	13.50
40 Sterling Marlin Brooks&Dunn	18.00	8.00
42 Joe Nemechek BellSouth	16.00	7.25
43 John Andretti STP	16.00	7.25

CAR / DRIVER / SPONSOR	MINT	NRMT
44 Justin Labonte Slim Jim	16.00	7.25
45 Adam Petty Spree	35.00	16.00
50 Mark Green Dr.Pepper	18.00	8.00
55 Kenny Wallace Square D	16.00	7.25
59 Mike Dillion Kingsford	16.00	7.25
60 Mark Martin Winn Dixie	35.00	16.00
66 Darrell Waltrip Big K	16.00	7.25
75 Ted Musgrave Remington	16.00	7.25
77 Robert Pressley Jasper	16.00	7.25
86 Stacy Compton RC Cola ST	16.00	7.25
94 Bill Elliott Drive Thru	16.00	7.25
97 Chad Little John Deere	18.00	8.00
99 Jeff Burton Exide	16.00	7.25
99 Jeff Burton Exide Bruce Lee	18.00	8.00
0 Larry Pearson Cheez-It	16.00	7.25

1999 Racing Champions Chrome Chase 1:24

This car featured chrome paint, special packaging and a low production run.

CAR / DRIVER / SPONSOR	MINT	NRMT
5 Terry Labonte Kellogg's	80.00	36.00
6 Mark Martin Zerex	80.00	36.00
6 Mark Martin Valvoline	80.00	36.00
12 Jeremy Mayfield Mobil 1	40.00	18.00
21 Elliott Sadler Citgo	40.00	18.00
23 Jimmy Spencer TCE	60.00	27.00
36 Ernie Irvan M&M's	80.00	36.00

1999 Racing Champions Chrome Signature Series 1:24

This car featured chrome paint, special packaging, low production run and a simulated driver signature on the base of the car.

CAR / DRIVER / SPONSOR	MINT	NRMT
4 Bobby Hamilton Kodak	40.00	18.00
5 Terry Labonte Kellogg's	60.00	27.00
6 Mark Martin Valvoline	60.00	27.00
9 Jerry Nadeau Dexter's laboratory	60.00	27.00
12 Jeremy Mayfield Mobil 1	40.00	18.00
16 Kevin LePage Primestar	40.00	18.00
25 Wally Dallenbach Hendrick	40.00	18.00
36 Ernie Irvan M&M's	60.00	27.00
77 Robert Pressley Jasper	40.00	18.00

Car / Driver / Sponsor	MINT	NRMT
94 Bill Elliott Drive Thru	60.00	27.00

1999 Racing Champions Gold 1:24

This is a special series produced by Racing Champions to celebrate their 10th anniversary. It parallels the regular 1999 1:24 scale series. Each car is a limited edition of 4,999. Each car is also plated in gold chrome and contains a serial number on its chassis.

Car / Driver / Sponsor	MINT	NRMT
4 Bobby Hamilton Kodak	25.00	11.00
5 Terry Labonte Kellogg's	40.00	18.00
6 Mark Martin Valvoline	40.00	18.00
9 Jerry Nadeau Dexter	25.00	11.00
10 Ricky Rudd Tide	25.00	11.00
11 Brett Bodine Paychex	25.00	11.00
15 Ken Schrader Oakwood Homes	25.00	11.00
25 Wally Dallenbach Hendrick	25.00	11.00
26 Johnny Benson Cheerios	25.00	11.00
33 Ken Schrader Petree	25.00	11.00
36 Ernie Irvan M&M's	30.00	13.50
55 Kenny Wallace Square D	25.00	11.00
60 Mark Martin Winn Dixie	40.00	18.00
66 Darrell Waltrip Big K	30.00	13.50
77 Robert Pressley Jasper	25.00	11.00
94 Bill Elliott McDonald's	40.00	18.00
99 Jeff Burton Exide Bruce Lee	30.00	13.50
99 Jeff Burton Exide	30.00	13.50

1999 Racing Champions Platinum 1:24

This is a special series produced by Racing Champions to celebrate their 10th anniversary. It parallels the regular 1999 1:24 scale series. Each car is a limited edition of 4,999. Each car is also plated in platinum chrome and contains a serial number on its chassis.

Car / Driver / Sponsor	MINT	NRMT
4 Bobby Hamilton Kodak	40.00	18.00
5 Terry Labonte Kellog's	75.00	34.00

Car / Driver / Sponsor	MINT	NRMT
6 Mark Martin Valvoine	75.00	34.00
9 Jerry Nadeau Dexter's laboratory	40.00	18.00
9 Jeff Burton Track Gear	40.00	18.00
10 Ricky Rudd Tide	40.00	18.00
11 Brett Bodine Paychex	40.00	18.00
16 Kevin LePage Primestar	40.00	18.00
25 Wally Dallenbach Hendrick	40.00	18.00
26 Johnny Benson Cheerios	40.00	18.00
33 Ken Schrader Petree	40.00	18.00
36 Ernie Irvan M&M's	40.00	18.00
42 Joe Nemechek BellSouth	40.00	18.00
55 Kenny Wallace Square D	40.00	18.00
77 Robert Pressley Jasper	40.00	18.00
94 Bill Elliott Drive Thru	75.00	34.00
97 Chad Little John Deere	40.00	18.00
99 Jeff Burton Exide	40.00	18.00

1999 Racing Champions Signature Series 1:24

This is a special series produced by Racing Champions to celebrate their 10th anniversary. It parallels the regular 1999 1:24 scale series. Each car is a packaged in a decorative box with the driver's facsimile autograph on the front.

Car / Driver / Sponsor	MINT	NRMT
4 Bobby Hamilton Kodak	20.00	9.00
5 Terry Labonte Kellogg's	20.00	9.00
6 Mark Martin Valvoline	20.00	9.00
6 Joe Bessey Power Team	20.00	9.00
9 Jerry Nadeau Dexter's laboratory	20.00	9.00
10 Ricky Rudd Tide	20.00	9.00
11 Brett Bodine Paychex	20.00	9.00
12 Jeremy Mayfield Mobil 1	20.00	9.00
16 Kevin LePage Primestar	20.00	9.00
25 Wally Dallenbach Hendrick	20.00	9.00
26 Johnny Benson Cheerios	20.00	9.00
32 Jeff Green Kleenex	20.00	9.00
34 Mike McLaughlin Goulds Pump	20.00	9.00
36 Ernie Irvan M&M's	20.00	9.00
40 Sterling Marlin John Wayne	20.00	9.00
77 Robert Pressley Jasper	20.00	9.00
94 Bill Elliott Drive Thru	20.00	9.00
99 Jeff Burton Exide	20.00	9.00

1999 Racing Champions Stock Rods 1:24

These 1:24 scale cars are replicas of vintage stock rods with NASCAR paint schemes. Cars are listed by issue number instead of car number.

Car / Driver / Sponsor	MINT	NRMT
74 Jeff Burton Exide	15.00	6.75
75 Kevin Lepage Primestar	15.00	6.75
76 Terry Labonte Kellogg's Iron Man	20.00	9.00
77 Bobby Hamilton Kodak	15.00	6.75
78 Terry Labonte Blasted Fruit Loops	20.00	9.00
79 Rick Mast Remington	15.00	6.75
80 Kevin Lepage Primestar Gold	20.00	9.00
81 Bobby Hamilton Kodak Gold	20.00	9.00
82 Bobby Hamilton Kodak	15.00	6.75
83 Terry Labonte Kellogg's Iron Man	20.00	9.00
84 Mark Martin Valvoline	20.00	9.00
85 Jeff Burton Exide	15.00	6.75
86 Bobby Hamilton Kodak	15.00	6.75
87 Brett Bodine Paychex	15.00	6.75
88 Wally Dallenbach Hendrick	15.00	6.75
89 Wally Dallenbach Hendrick Gold	20.00	9.00
90 Ernie Irvan M&M's	20.00	9.00
91 Ernie Irvan M&M's Gold	30.00	13.50
92 Bobby Hamilton Kodak Gold	20.00	9.00
93 Brett Bodine Paychex Gold	20.00	9.00
94 Bill Elliott Drive Thru Gold	40.00	18.00
95 Bill Elliott Drive Thru	20.00	9.00
96 Jerry Nadeau Dexter's Lab	15.00	6.75
97 Sterling Marlin John Wayne	20.00	9.00
99 Robert Pressley Jasper	15.00	6.75
100 Robert Pressley Jasper Gold	20.00	9.00
101 Ken Schrader Andy Petree Racing	15.00	6.75
102 Serling Marlin John Wayne	20.00	9.00
103 Jeff Burton Bruce Lee	20.00	9.00
104 Terry Labonte Kellogg's	20.00	9.00
105 Ricky Rudd Tide	20.00	9.00
106 Derrike Cope Bryan Foods	15.00	6.75
107 Ken Schrader APR Blue	15.00	6.75
108 Jimmy Spencer TCE	15.00	6.75

1999 Racing Champions
Trackside 1:24

These 1:24 cars were only available at the track.

Car / Driver / Sponsor	MINT	NRMT
9 Jerry Nadeau Dexter's Lab	60.00	27.00
23 Jimmy Spencer Winston	60.00	27.00
45 Adam Petty Spree	80.00	36.00

1999 Racing Champions
Under the Lights 1:24

These 1:24 scale cars feature special anodized paint to give that under the lights appearance.

Car / Driver / Sponsor	MINT	NRMT
4 Bobby Hamilton Kodak	15.00	6.75
6 Mark Martin Valvoline	20.00	9.00
12 Jeremy Mayfield Mobil 1	15.00	6.75
94 Bill Elliott Drive Thru	20.00	9.00
99 Jeff Burton Exide	20.00	9.00

1999 Racing Champions 24K
Gold 1:24

This is a special series produced by Racing Champions to celebrate their 10th anniversary. It parallels the regular 1998 1:24 scale series. Each car is a limited edition of 4,999. Each car is also plated in gold chrome and contains a serial number on its chassis.

Car / Driver / Sponsor	MINT	NRMT
4 Bobby Hamilton Kodak	40.00	18.00
5 Terry Labonte Kellog's	75.00	34.00
6 Joe Bessey Power Team	40.00	18.00
6 Mark Martin Valvoine	75.00	34.00
9 Jerry Nadeau Dexter's Lab	50.00	22.00
9 Jeff Burton Track Gear	40.00	18.00
10 Ricky Rudd Tide	40.00	18.00
11 Brett Bodine Paychex	40.00	18.00
16 Kevin LePage Primestar	40.00	18.00
26 Johnny Benson Cheerios	40.00	18.00
42 Joe Nemechek BellSouth	40.00	18.00
77 Robert Pressley Jasper	40.00	18.00
97 Chad Little John Deere	40.00	18.00
99 Jeff Burton Exide	40.00	18.00

2000 Racing Champions Time
Trial 2000 1:24

New for 2000, Racing Champions introduces a series that focuses on the testing and development of NASCAR stock cars rather than the final race-ready car - Time Trial stock car replicas. Sporting just a coat of gray primer and the team number.

Car / Driver / Sponsor	MINT	NRMT
6 Mark Martin Valvoline	20.00	9.00
97 Chad Little John Deere	20.00	9.00
99 Jeff Burton Exide	20.00	9.00

1992-94 Racing Champions
Banks 1:24

These 1:24 scale cars feature banks in each car. There is usually a slot in the back window to slip your money into. The cars, as with most die cast banks, have blacked in windows.

Car / Driver / Sponsor	MINT	NRMT
0 Dick McCabe Fisher Snow Plows	30.00	13.50
1 Rick Mast Precision Products	22.00	10.00
2 Ward Burton Hardee's	22.00	10.00
2 Ricky Craven DuPont	25.00	11.00
2 Rusty Wallace Ford Motorsports	35.00	16.00
2 Rusty Wallace Pontiac Excitement	250.00	110.00
3 Dale Earnhardt Goodwrench BGN car	40.00	18.00
3 Dale Earnhardt Goodwrench with numbered box	45.00	20.00
3 Dale Earnhardt Goodwrench with unnumbered box	40.00	18.00
3 Dale Earnhardt Goodwrench wtih Snap On	40.00	18.00
3 Dale Earnhardt Mom-n-Pop's	45.00	20.00
4 Ernie Irvan Kodak	32.00	14.50
4 Sterling Marlin Kodak	25.00	11.00
4 Sterling Marlin Kodak Fun Saver	25.00	11.00
5 Terry Labonte Kellogg's	35.00	16.00
5 Ricky Rudd Tide	22.00	10.00
6 Mark Martin Valvoline	30.00	13.50
6 Mark Martin Valvoline Reese's	25.00	11.00
7 Geoff Bodine Exide	25.00	11.00
7 Harry Gant Black Flag	45.00	20.00
7 Harry Gant Easy Off	45.00	20.00
7 Harry Gant French's	45.00	20.00
7 Harry Gant Gulf Lite	45.00	20.00
7 Harry Gant Manheim	45.00	20.00
7 Harry Gant Morema	45.00	20.00
7 Harry Gant Woolite	45.00	20.00
7 Jimmy Hensley Bojangles	25.00	11.00
7 Tommy Kendall Family Channel	30.00	13.50
7 Alan Kulwicki Army	65.00	29.00
7 Alan Kulwicki Hooters	250.00	110.00
7 Alan Kulwicki Zerex	90.00	40.00
8 Sterling Marlin Raybestos	22.00	10.00

Car / Driver / Sponsor	MINT	NRMT
8 Kenny Wallace TIC Financial	32.00	14.50
10 Ricky Rudd Tide	32.00	14.50
10 Jimmy Spencer Kleenex	100.00	45.00
11 Bill Elliott Amoco	40.00	18.00
11 Bill Elliott Budweiser	50.00	22.00
11 Bill Elliott Budweiser Hardy Boys car	40.00	18.00
12 Clifford Allison Sports Image	40.00	18.00
12 Jimmy Spencer Meineke	65.00	29.00
14 John Andretti Kanawha	30.00	13.50
14 Terry Labonte MW Windows	100.00	45.00
15 Geoff Bodine Motorcraft	22.00	10.00
15 Lake Speed Quality Care	22.00	10.00
16 Chad Chaffin Dr. Die Cast	25.00	11.00
16 Ted Musgrave Family Channel	25.00	11.00
17 Darrell Waltrip Tide Orange paint scheme	50.00	22.00
17 Darrell Waltrip Tide Primer gray car	40.00	18.00
17 Darrell Waltrip Western Auto	150.00	70.00
18 Dale Jarrett Interstate Batteries	30.00	13.50
20 Randy LaJoie Fina	32.00	14.50
20 Joe Ruttman Fina	35.00	16.00
20 Joe Ruttman Fina 520 made	40.00	18.00
21 Morgan Shepherd Cheerwine	30.00	13.50
21 Morgan Shepherd Citgo	22.00	10.00
22 Bobby Labonte Maxwell House	22.00	10.00
23 Chad Little Bayer	22.00	10.00
24 Jeff Gordon DuPont	55.00	25.00
24 Jeff Gordon DuPont Brickyard Special	100.00	45.00
24 Jeff Gordon DuPont Coca-Cola 600 Winner	175.00	80.00
24 Jeff Gordon DuPont Snickers	40.00	18.00
25 Hermie Sadler Virginia is for Lovers	22.00	10.00
26 Brett Bodine Quaker State	22.00	10.00
27 Hut Stricklin McDonald's	30.00	13.50
28 Davey Allison Havoline	80.00	36.00
28 Davey Allison Havoline with Black and Gold paint scheme	125.00	55.00
28 Davey Allison Havoline with Black and White paint scheme	50.00	22.00
28 Davey Allison Mac Tools	125.00	55.00
28 Ernie Irvan Havoline	40.00	18.00
28 Ernie Irvan Mac Tools	40.00	18.00
30 Michael Waltrip Pennzoil	22.00	10.00

CAR / DRIVER / SPONSOR	MINT	NRMT
31 Steve Grissom Channellock	22.00	10.00
31 Tom Peck Channellock	22.00	10.00
33 Harry Gant Farewell Tour	32.00	14.50
33 Harry Gant Leo Jackson	25.00	11.00
33 Harry Gant Manheim Auctions	75.00	34.00
33 Harry Gant Manheim Auctions Autographed	125.00	55.00
33 Bobby Labonte Dentyne	60.00	27.00
34 Mike McLaughlin Fiddle Faddle	22.00	10.00
35 Shawna Robinson Polaroid Captiva	30.00	13.50
38 Elton Sawyer Ford Credit	25.00	11.00
41 Ernie Irvan Mac Tools	40.00	18.00
42 Kyle Petty Mello Yello	30.00	13.50
43 Rodney Combs French's	22.00	10.00
43 Wally Dallenbach Jr. STP	22.00	10.00
43 Richard Petty STP	50.00	22.00
44 David Green Slim Jim	32.00	14.50
44 Bobby Hillin Jr. Buss Fuses	25.00	11.00
44 Rick Wilson STP	25.00	11.00
46 Shawna Robinson Polaroid	30.00	13.50
51 No Driver Association Racing Champions	100.00	45.00
52 Ken Schrader AC Delco	25.00	11.00
52 Ken Schrader Morema	35.00	16.00
54 Robert Pressley Manheim Auctions	35.00	16.00
55 Ted Musgrave US Air	50.00	22.00
59 Andy Belmont Metal Arrester	32.00	14.50
59 Robert Pressley Alliance	70.00	32.00
59 Dennis Setzer Alliance	45.00	20.00
60 Mark Martin Winn Dixie of 5000	75.00	34.00
60 Mark Martin Winn Dixie of 10,000	35.00	16.00
63 Jim Bown Lysol	22.00	10.00
70 J.D. McDuffie Son's Auto	25.00	11.00
71 Dave Marcis Earnhardt Chevrolet	45.00	20.00
75 Todd Bodine Factory Stores	22.00	10.00
77 Greg Sacks US Air	32.00	14.50
83 Sherry Blakely Ramses	30.00	13.50
87 Joe Nemechek Dentyne	25.00	11.00
92 Larry Pearson Stanley Tools	22.00	10.00
93 No Driver Associations Racing Champions	175.00	80.00
94 No Driver Association Brickyard 400 Special	32.00	14.50
97 Joe Bessey Auto Palace	30.00	13.50

CAR / DRIVER / SPONSOR	MINT	NRMT
97 Joe Bessey Johnson AC Delco	30.00	13.50
98 Derrike Cope Bojangles Black car	35.00	16.00
98 Derrike Cope Bojangles Yellow car	35.00	16.00
98 Jody Ridley Ford Motorsports	40.00	18.00

1995 Racing Champions Banks 1:24

This series of 1:24 cars offers the collector the option to use them as bank. Each car has a slot in the rear window or in some cases the deck lid.

CAR / DRIVER / SPONSOR	MINT	NRMT
2 Rusty Wallace Ford Motorsports	25.00	11.00
4 Sterling Marlin Kodak	25.00	11.00
5 Terry Labonte Kellogg's	25.00	11.00
6 Mark Martin Valvoline	25.00	11.00
7 Geoff Bodine Exide	25.00	11.00
8 Jeff Burton Raybestos	25.00	11.00

CAR / DRIVER / SPONSOR	MINT	NRMT
8 Kenny Wallace Red Dog Hood Open	35.00	16.00
12 Derrike Cope Straight Arrow	25.00	11.00
16 Ted Musgrave Family Channel	25.00	11.00
24 Jeff Gordon DuPont	30.00	13.50
24 Jeff Gordon DuPont Signature Series Hood Open	40.00	18.00
24 Jeff Gordon DuPont Signature Series HO 1995 Champion	40.00	18.00
25 Ken Schrader Budweiser	25.00	11.00
25 Ken Schrader Budweiser Hood Open	32.00	14.50
27 Loy Allen Hooters	25.00	11.00
28 Dale Jarrett Havoline Hood Open	35.00	16.00
32 Dale Jarrett Mac Tools	32.00	14.50
37 John Andretti K-Mart Hood Open	35.00	16.00
44 David Green Slim Jim	25.00	11.00
59 Dennis Setzer Alliance	32.00	14.50
60 Mark Martin Winn Dixie	35.00	16.00
74 Johnny Benson Lipton Tea Hood Open	40.00	18.00
88 Ernie Irvan Texaco Hood Open	40.00	18.00
94 Bill Elliott McDonald's	32.00	14.50
94 Bill Elliott McDonald's Thunderbat	40.00	18.00

1996 Racing Champions Banks 1:24

This series of 1:24 cars offers the collector the option to use them as bank. Each car has a slot in the rear window or in some cases the deck lid. These banks have blacked in windows.

CAR / DRIVER / SPONSOR	MINT	NRMT
6 Mark Martin Valvoline	25.00	11.00
23 Chad Little John Deere	40.00	18.00
29 Steve Grissom Cartoon Network	30.00	13.50
32 Dale Jarrett Band-Aid	35.00	16.00
47 Jeff Fuller Sunoco	25.00	11.00
51 Chuck Bown Lucks	25.00	11.00
94 Bill Elliott McDonald's	25.00	11.00
94 Bill Elliott McDonald's Monopoly	30.00	13.50

1996 Racing Champions Chrome Banks 1:24

These chrome banks were produced in quantites of 166 for each bank. This series is also highlighted two different beer diecast programs: The Ken Schrader Budweiser banks and the David Green Busch banks

CAR / DRIVER / SPONSOR	MINT	NRMT
2 Rusty Wallace Penske Chrome	400.00	180.00
4 Sterling Marlin Kodak	350.00	160.00
5 Terry Labonte Kellogg's Silver Hood Open	800.00	350.00
6 Mark Martin Valvoline Chrome	400.00	180.00
10 Ricky Rudd Tide Chrome	350.00	160.00
17 Darrell Waltrip Parts America Chrome	350.00	160.00
18 Bobby Labonte Interstate Batteries Chrome	350.00	160.00
24 Jeff Gordon DuPont	1100.00	500.00
25 Ken Schrader Budweiser	400.00	180.00
29 Steve Grissom Cartoon Network Chrome	350.00	160.00
29 No Driver Association Scooby-Doo Chrome	350.00	160.00
37 John Andretti Kmart	300.00	135.00
88 Dale Jarrett Quality Care	400.00	180.00
94 Bill Elliott McDonald's	400.00	180.00
96 David Green Busch Chrome	250.00	110.00

1996 Racing Champions Hobby Banks 1:24

These 1:24 scale banks were distributed with the chrome banks through hobby outlets.

CAR / DRIVER / SPONSOR	MINT	NRMT
2 Rusty Wallace Penske Hobby	40.00	18.00
4 Sterling Marlin Kodak Hobby	40.00	18.00
5 Terry Labonte Kellogg's Hobby	40.00	18.00

CAR / DRIVER / SPONSOR	MINT	NRMT
6 Mark Martin Valvoline Hobby	40.00	18.00
10 Ricky Rudd Tide Hobby	40.00	18.00
11 Brett Bodine Lowe's 50th Anniversary Hobby	40.00	18.00
17 Darrell Waltrip Parts America Hobby	40.00	18.00
18 Bobby Labonte Interstate Batteries Hobby	40.00	18.00
24 Jeff Gordon DuPont Hobby	40.00	18.00
25 Ken Schrader Bud Olympic	50.00	22.00
29 Steve Grissom Cartoon Hobby	40.00	18.00
29 No Driver Association Scooby-Doo Hobby	40.00	18.00
37 John Andretti K-Mart Hobby	40.00	18.00
88 Dale Jarrett Quality Care Hobby	40.00	18.00
94 Bill Elliott McDonald's Hobby	40.00	18.00
96 David Green Busch Hobby	40.00	18.00

1996 Racing Champions Hood Open Banks 1:24

These 1:24 scale banks have open hood and were distributed through hobby and retail outlets.

	MINT	NRMT
2 Rusty Wallace Miller Genuine Draft Hood Open	35.00	16.00
5 Terry Labonte Kellogg's Silver Hood Open	35.00	16.00
21 Michael Waltrip Citgo Hood Open	35.00	16.00
23 Chad Little John Deere Hood Open	50.00	22.00
25 Ken Schrader Budweiser Hood Open	35.00	16.00
60 Mark Martin Winn Dixie Hood Open	40.00	18.00
75 Morgan Shepherd Remington Hood Open	35.00	16.00
88 Dale Jarrett Quality Care Hood Open	35.00	16.00
94 Bill Elliott McDonald's Monopoly Hood Open	35.00	16.00

1997 Racing Champions Banks 1:24

This series of 1:24 cars offers the collector the option to use them as bank. Each car has a slot in the rear window or in some cases the deck lid. These banks have blacked in windows. he Mark Martin Winn Dixie bank was offered solely through Winn Dixie. There are 166 of each of the Terry Labonte Kellogg's Champions Chrome bank.

	MINT	NRMT
2 Rusty Wallace Miller Lite Matco	60.00	27.00
2 Rusty Wallace Miller Lite Matco Chrome	200.00	90.00
5 Terry Labonte Kellogg's 1996 Champion	45.00	20.00
5 Terry Labonte Kellogg's Champion Chrome	450.00	200.00
28 Ernie Irvan Havoline 10th Anniversary paint scheme	40.00	18.00
28 Ernie Irvan Havoline 10th Anniversary paint scheme Chrome	300.00	135.00

	MINT	NRMT
60 Mark Martin Winn Dixie	40.00	18.00
94 Bill Elliott Mac Tonight	50.00	22.00
96 David Green Caterpillar Promo	40.00	18.00

1997 Racing Champions Gold Banks 1:24

These were 166 of each of these 1:24 scale banks produced. There were distributed through hobby outlets.

	MINT	NRMT
2 Rusty Wallace Miller Lite Gold	350.00	160.00
6 Mark Martin Valvoline Gold	350.00	160.00
10 Ricky Rudd Tide Gold	300.00	135.00
18 Bobby Labonte Interstate Batteries Gold	300.00	135.00
36 Derrike Cope Skittles Gold	300.00	135.00
75 Rick Mast Remington Gold	300.00	135.00
94 Bill Elliott McDonald's Gold	350.00	160.00

1997 Racing Champions Hobby Banks 1:24

These 1:24 scale banks were distributed through hobby outlets.

	MINT	NRMT
2 Rusty Wallace Miller Lite Hobby	40.00	18.00
6 Mark Martin Valvoline Hobby	40.00	18.00
10 Ricky Rudd Tide Hobby	40.00	18.00
18 Bobby Labonte Interstate Batteries Hobby	40.00	18.00
36 Derrike Cope Skittles Hobby	40.00	18.00
75 Rick Mast Remington Hobby	40.00	18.00
94 Bill Elliott McDonald's Hobby	40.00	18.00

1997 Racing Champions Hood Open Banks 1:24

These 1:24 scale banks were distributed through retail outlets and have open hoods.

	MINT	NRMT
5 Terry Labonte Kellogg's Hood Open	35.00	16.00
6 Mark Martin Valvoline Hood Open	35.00	16.00
10 Ricky Rudd Tide Hood Open	35.00	16.00
28 Ernie Irvan Havoline Hood Open	35.00	16.00
29 Robert Pressley Scooby-Doo Hood Open	35.00	16.00

CAR / DRIVER / SPONSOR	MINT	NRMT
36 Derrike Cope Skittles Hood Open	35.00	16.00
75 Rick Mast Remington Hood Open	35.00	16.00
94 Bill Elliott McDonald's Hood Open	35.00	16.00
96 David Green Caterpillar Hood Open	35.00	16.00

	MINT	NRMT
97 Chad Little John Deere Hood Open	35.00	16.00

1998 Racing Champions Driver's Choice Banks 1:24

These 1:24 scale banks were distributed through trackside and hobby outlets.

	MINT	NRMT
5 Terry Labonte Kellogg's	50.00	22.00
6 Mark Martin Valvoline	50.00	22.00
10 Ricky Rudd Tide	45.00	20.00
94 Bill Elliott McDonald's	50.00	22.00

1998 Racing Champions Gold Banks 1:24

This is a special series produced by Racing Champions to celebrate NASCAR's 50th anniversary. It parallels the regular 1998 1:24 scale series. Each bank is a limited edition of 2,500. Each car is also plated in gold chrome and contains a serial number on its chassis.

	MINT	NRMT
6 Mark Martin Valvoline	100.00	45.00
9 Lake Speed Huckleberry Hound	60.00	27.00
10 Ricky Rudd Tide	60.00	27.00
11 Brett Bodine Paychex	60.00	27.00
26 Johnny Benson Cheerios	75.00	34.00
94 Bill Elliott McDonald's	100.00	45.00
99 Jeff Burton Exide	60.00	27.00

1998 Racing Champions Gold Hood Open Banks 1:24

This is a special series produced by Racing Champions to celebrate NASCAR's 50th anniversary. It parallels the regular 1998 1:24 scale series. Each car is a limited edition of 1,998. Each car is also plated in gold chrome and contains a serial number on its chassis.

	MINT	NRMT
5 Terry Labonte Blasted Fruit Loops	50.00	22.00
5 Terry Labonte Kellogg's Corny	50.00	22.00

CAR / DRIVER / SPONSOR	MINT	NRMT
6 Mark Martin Eagle One	50.00	22.00
6 Mark Martin Synpower	50.00	22.00
6 Mark Martin Valvoline	50.00	22.00
10 Ricky Rudd Tide	40.00	18.00
36 Ernie Irvan M&M's	40.00	18.00
36 Ernie Irvan Skittles	40.00	18.00
36 Ernie Irvan Wildberry Skittles	40.00	18.00
99 Jeff Burton Exide	40.00	18.00

1998 Racing Champions Authentics Banks 1:24

These 1:24 scale cars marks the first in a series by Racing Champions. These banks were distributed through hobby and trackside outlets. Each bank is packaged in a special black snap case.

CAR / DRIVER / SPONSOR	MINT	NRMT
6 Mark Martin Eagle One	80.00	36.00
6 Mark Martin Synpower	80.00	36.00
6 Mark Martin Valvoline	80.00	36.00
16 Kevin Lepage Primestar	80.00	36.00
26 Johnny Benson Betty Crocker	80.00	36.00
26 Johnny Benson Betty Crocker	80.00	36.00
26 Johnny Benson Cheerios	80.00	36.00
26 Johnny Benson Trix	80.00	36.00
97 Chad Little John Deere	80.00	36.00
99 Jeff Burton Exide	80.00	36.00

1991 Racing Champions 1:43

This was the first 1:43 scale size series from Racing Champions. Included in the sets are racing greats like Richard Petty, Mark Martin, Cale Yarborough, Bill Elliott and Rusty Wallace

CAR / DRIVER / SPONSOR	MINT	NRMT
2 Rusty Wallace Pontiac Excitement	12.00	5.50
4 Ernie Irvan Kodak	6.00	2.70
6 Mark Martin Valvoline	12.00	5.50
9 Bill Elliott Melling	12.00	5.50
11 Geoff Bodine No Sponsor	6.00	2.70
15 Morgan Shepherd Motorcraft	6.00	2.70
18 Gregory Trammell Melling	6.00	2.70
21 Dale Jarrett Citgo	12.00	5.50
22 Sterling Marlin Maxwell House	6.00	2.70
25 Ken Schrader No Sponsor	6.00	2.70
36 Kenny Wallace Cox Lumber	6.00	2.70
42 Kyle Petty Mello Yello	6.00	2.70

CAR / DRIVER / SPONSOR	MINT	NRMT
43 Richard Petty STP	6.00	2.70
66 Cale Yarborough TropArtic	6.00	2.70
70 J.D. McDuffie Son's Auto	10.00	4.50
72 Ken Bouchard ADAP	6.00	2.70
89 Jim Sauter Evinrude	6.00	2.70

1992 Racing Champions 1:43

This series of 1:43 scale cars was issued in black boxes. They were distributed through both hobby stores and retail outlets.

CAR / DRIVER / SPONSOR	MINT	NRMT
1 Jeff Gordon Baby Ruth	75.00	34.00
1 Rick Mast Majik Market	6.00	2.70
3 Dale Earnhardt Goodwrench	12.00	5.50
5 Ricky Rudd Tide	8.00	3.60
7 Alan Kulwicki Hooters	35.00	16.00
11 Bill Elliott Amoco	10.00	4.50
17 Darrell Waltrip Western Auto	8.00	3.60
17 Darrell Waltrip Western Auto Promo	8.00	3.60
18 Dale Jarrett Interstate Batteries	10.00	4.50
28 Davey Allison Havoline	20.00	9.00
30 Michael Waltrip Pennzoil	8.00	3.60
33 Harry Gant NS	30.00	13.50
66 Chad Little TropArtic	8.00	3.60
72 Ken Bouchard Auto Palace	6.00	2.70

1993 Racing Champions 1:43

This series of 1:43 cars features all the top names in racing. Racing Champions did a primer edition for each of the car makes that were running in NASCAR in 1993.

CAR / DRIVER / SPONSOR	MINT	NRMT
2 Rusty Wallace Pontiac Excitement	8.00	3.60
3 Dale Earnhardt Goodwrench	12.00	5.50
4 Ernie Irvan Kodak	6.00	2.70
5 Ricky Rudd Tide	6.00	2.70
6 Mark Martin Valvoline	8.00	3.60
7 Alan Kulwicki Hooters in Box	20.00	9.00
8 Sterling Marlin Raybestos	20.00	9.00
11 Bill Elliott Amoco	8.00	3.60
14 Terry Labonte Kellogg's	8.00	3.60
15 Geoff Bodine Motorcraft	6.00	2.70
17 Darrell Waltrip Western Auto	6.00	2.70
21 Morgan Shepherd Citgo	6.00	2.70

CAR / DRIVER / SPONSOR	MINT	NRMT
24 Jeff Gordon DuPont	12.00	5.50
25 Bill Venturini Rain X	12.00	5.50
26 Brett Bodine Quaker State	6.00	2.70
27 Hut Stricklin McDonald's	6.00	2.70
28 Davey Allison Havoline	12.00	5.50
33 Harry Gant No Sponsor	6.00	2.70
42 Kyle Petty Mello Yello	6.00	2.70
44 Rick Wilson STP	6.00	2.70
51 No Driver Association Chevrolet with Primer paint	12.00	5.50
51 No Driver Association Ford with Primer paint	12.00	5.50
51 No Driver Association Pontiac with Primer paint	12.00	5.50
59 Andy Belmont FDP Brakes	12.00	5.50
60 Mark Martin Winn Dixie	10.00	4.50

1993 Racing Champions Premier 1:43

This is the first year that Racing Champions did a Premier series for its 1:43 scale size.

CAR / DRIVER / SPONSOR	MINT	NRMT
2 Ward Burton Hardee's	18.00	8.00
3 Dale Earnhardt Goodwrench	40.00	18.00
5 Ricky Rudd Tide	16.00	7.25
6 Mark Martin Valvoline	18.00	8.00
7 Alan Kulwicki Hooters	75.00	34.00
8 Sterling Marlin Raybestos	16.00	7.25
11 Bill Elliott Amoco	18.00	8.00
11 Bill Elliott Budweiser	22.00	10.00
17 Darrell Waltrip Western Auto	16.00	7.25
24 Jeff Gordon DuPont	40.00	18.00
27 Hut Stricklin McDonald's	16.00	7.25
28 Davey Allison Havoline	35.00	16.00
28 Davey Allison Havoline with Black and White paint scheme	30.00	13.50
28 Ernie Irvan Havoline	30.00	13.50
33 Harry Gant No Sponsor	16.00	7.25
42 Kyle Petty Mello Yello	16.00	7.25
59 Robert Pressley Alliance	45.00	20.00
60 Mark Martin Winn Dixie	25.00	11.00
87 Joe Nemechek Dentyne	60.00	27.00
97 Joe Bessey AC Delco	20.00	9.00
98 Derrike Cope Bojangles by RCCC	75.00	34.00

1994 Racing Champions 1:43

This was the last year that Racing Champions did a full size 1:43 scale series. The most popular piece in the series is a special Jeff Gordon Coca-Cola 600 winner car.

CAR / DRIVER / SPONSOR	MINT	NRMT
1 Rick Mast Precision Products	5.00	2.20
4 Sterling Marlin Kodak	5.00	2.20
5 Terry Labonte Kellogg's	6.00	2.70
10 Ricky Rudd Tide	5.00	2.20
19 Loy Allen Hooter's	5.00	2.20
24 Jeff Gordon DuPont	10.00	4.50
24 Jeff Gordon DuPont Coca-Cola 600 Winner	25.00	11.00
26 Brett Bodine Quaker State	5.00	2.20
33 Harry Gant Farewell Tour	16.00	7.25
33 Harry Gant Leo Jackson	5.00	2.20
42 Kyle Petty Mello Yello	5.00	2.20
60 Mark Martin Winn Dixie	10.00	4.50

1994 Racing Champions Premier 1:43

This was the second year that Racing Champions did a 1:43 Premier series. Highlighting the series are two Alan Kulwicki cars (Zerex and Army).

CAR / DRIVER / SPONSOR	MINT	NRMT
1 Rick Mast Precision Products	16.00	7.25
2 Rusty Wallace Ford Motorsports	18.00	8.00
3 Dale Earnhardt Goodwrench	22.00	10.00
4 Sterling Marlin Kodak	16.00	7.25
5 Terry Labonte Kellogg's	20.00	9.00
6 Mark Martin Valvoline	18.00	8.00
7 Harry Gant Manheim	25.00	11.00
7 Jimmy Hensley Bojangles	20.00	9.00
7 Tommy Kendall Family Channel	20.00	9.00
7 Alan Kulwicki Army	25.00	11.00
7 Alan Kulwicki Zerex	25.00	11.00
12 Clifford Allison Sports Image	20.00	9.00
15 Lake Speed Quality Care	16.00	7.25
16 Ted Musgrave Family Channel	16.00	7.25
21 Morgan Shepherd Cheerwine	18.00	8.00
22 Bobby Labonte Maxwell House	18.00	8.00
24 Jeff Gordon DuPont Snickers	25.00	11.00
25 Ken Schrader GMAC	16.00	7.25
26 Brett Bodine Quaker State	16.00	7.25

CAR / DRIVER / SPONSOR	MINT	NRMT
28 Ernie Irvan Havoline	20.00	9.00
28 Ernie Irvan Mac Tools	25.00	11.00
30 Michael Waltrip Pennzoil	16.00	7.25
33 Harry Gant Farewell Tour	18.00	8.00
33 Harry Gant Leo Jackson Motorsports	16.00	7.25
59 Dennis Setzer Alliance	20.00	9.00
60 Mark Martin Winn Dixie	20.00	9.00
77 Greg Sacks US Air	20.00	9.00

1995 Racing Champions Premier 1:43

In 1995, Racing Champions only produce 1:43 size cars for special circumstances. The Jeff Gordon was a salute to the inaugural Brickyard Winner and the Mark Martin was done as a promo. The Martin piece was available through Winn Dixie stores.

CAR / DRIVER / SPONSOR	MINT	NRMT
24 Jeff Gordon Brickyard Win	70.00	32.00
60 Mark Martin Winn Dixie	20.00	9.00

1989 Racing Champions Flat Bottom 1:64

This was the first series of NASCAR die cast cars produced by Racing Champions. The series is commonly refered to as flat bottoms because the blister package the car came in was flat across the bottom. In all subsequent years there was a bubble across the bottom to help the package freely stand up.

CAR / DRIVER / SPONSOR	MINT	NRMT
3 Dale Earnhardt Goodwrench	150.00	70.00
9 Bill Elliott Motorcraft Melling Ford	100.00	45.00
16 Larry Pearson No Sponsor	70.00	32.00
28 Davey Allison Havoline	120.00	55.00
30 Michael Waltrip Country Time	70.00	32.00
94 Sterling Marlin Sunoco	75.00	34.00

1990 Racing Champions 1:64

This was the first full series of 1:64 scale cars produced by Racing Champions. Many of the cars came with rubber tires as opposed to plastic. Cars with rubber tires usually carry a $5.00 to $10.00 premium. The cars used many different body styles.

CAR / DRIVER / SPONSOR	MINT	NRMT
1 Terry Labonte Oldsmobile	60.00	27.00
3 Dale Earnhardt Goodwrench	150.00	70.00
3 Dale Earnhardt GM Performance Parts	90.00	40.00

CAR / DRIVER / SPONSOR	MINT	NRMT
9 Bill Elliott Orange and Blue Stripe No Melling on the car	100.00	45.00
9 Bill Elliott Orange and Blue Stripe with Melling on the car	60.00	27.00
9 Bill Elliott Red and Blue Stripe with Melling on the car	50.00	22.00
10 Derrike Cope Lumina	100.00	45.00
14 A.J. Foyt Buick	100.00	45.00
14 A.J. Foyt Lumina	100.00	45.00
14 A.J. Foyt Old Pontiac body style	50.00	22.00
14 A.J. Foyt Oldsmobile	40.00	18.00
14 A.J. Foyt Pontiac	35.00	16.00
15 Morgan Shepherd Red and White color scheme	40.00	18.00
15 Morgan Shepherd Red and Cream color scheme	30.00	13.50
16 Larry Pearson Buick with White Bumper	125.00	55.00
16 Larry Pearson Buick with Brown Bumper Name in script	35.00	16.00
16 Larry Pearson Buick with Brown Bumper Name in print	30.00	13.50
16 Larry Pearson Lumina with Brown Bumper	75.00	34.00
16 Larry Pearson Old Pontiac with Brown Bumper	75.00	34.00
16 Larry Pearson Oldsmobile with Brown Bumper	75.00	34.00
16 Larry Pearson Pontiac with Brown Bumper	25.00	11.00
20 Rob Moroso Red Stripe	30.00	13.50
21 Neil Bonnett Citgo	80.00	36.00
26 Kenny Bernstein Buick	40.00	18.00
26 Kenny Bernstein Lumina	50.00	22.00
26 Kenny Bernstein Old Pontiac body style	50.00	22.00
26 Kenny Bernstein Oldsmobile	40.00	18.00
27 Rusty Wallace Old Pontiac Miller Genuine Draft	80.00	36.00
27 Rusty Wallace Oldsmobile	100.00	45.00
27 Rusty Wallace Pontiac Miller Genuine Draft	80.00	36.00
27 Rusty Wallace Pontiac Miller	60.00	27.00
27 Rusty Wallace Pontiac with Silver Decals	80.00	36.00
28 Davey Allison Black and White paint scheme	100.00	45.00
28 Davey Allison Black and Gold paint scheme	50.00	22.00
30 Michael Waltrip Country Time	70.00	32.00
30 Michael Waltrip Maxwell House	40.00	18.00
33 Harry Gant Pontiac	40.00	18.00
42 Kyle Petty Buick with Blue and White paint	125.00	55.00
42 Kyle Petty Lumina with Blue and White paint	125.00	55.00

CAR / DRIVER / SPONSOR	MINT	NRMT
42 Kyle Petty	60.00	27.00
Old Pontiac with Blue and White paint		
42 Kyle Petty	100.00	45.00
Oldsmobile with Blue and White paint		
42 Kyle Petty	30.00	13.50
Sabco on the deck lid		
42 Kyle Petty	30.00	13.50
without Sabco on the deck lid		
Blue and Pink paint scheme		
43 Richard Petty	40.00	18.00
Pontiac		
94 Sterling Marlin	90.00	40.00
Buick		
94 Sterling Marlin	75.00	34.00
Lumina		
94 Sterling Marlin	90.00	40.00
Old Pontiac		
94 Sterling Marlin	40.00	18.00
Oldsmobile		

1991 Racing Champions 1:64

This series of 1:64 scale Racing Champion cars has many different package variations. There were three variations that most of the pieces came in. One has Dale Earnhardt on the back of the package (abbreviated EB in the listing). Another has Richard Petty on the back of the package (abbreviated PB). Finally a third variation comes with NASCAR Properties on the stand the car sits on. Again many different body styles were used.

CAR / DRIVER / SPONSOR	MINT	NRMT
1 Terry Labonte	20.00	9.00
Oldsmobile EB		
1 Terry Labonte	40.00	18.00
Oldsmobile NP		
1 Terry Labonte	20.00	9.00
Oldsmobile PB		
1 Rick Mast	6.00	2.70
Buick PB		
1 Rick Mast	5.00	2.20
Oldsmobile PB		
2 Rusty Wallace	15.00	6.75
Pontiac EB		
2 Rusty Wallace	10.00	4.50
Pontiac PB		
3 Dale Earnhardt	40.00	18.00
Lumina EB		
3 Dale Earnhardt	150.00	70.00
Lumina NP		
3 Dale Earnhardt	25.00	11.00
Lumina PB		
4 Ernie Irvan	5.00	2.20
Kodak PB		
5 Jay Fogelman	12.00	5.50
Lumina PB		
9 Bill Elliott	5.00	2.20
Ford PB		
9 Bill Elliott	25.00	11.00
Ford EB		
Car is 1/2 blue		
9 Bill Elliott	18.00	8.00
Ford EB		
Car is 3/4 blue		
9 Bill Elliott	30.00	13.50
Old Ford body style EB		
Orange and White paint scheme		
9 Bill Elliott	35.00	16.00
Old Ford body style NP		
Orange and White paint scheme		
10 Derrike Cope	6.00	2.70
Purolator EB		
with 2 rows of checkers		
10 Derrike Cope	25.00	11.00
Purolator EB		
with 3 rows of checkers		

CAR / DRIVER / SPONSOR	MINT	NRMT
10 Derrike Cope	5.00	2.20
Purolator PB		
with 2 rows of checkers		
10 Derrike Cope	15.00	6.75
Purolator PB		
with 3 rows of checkers		
11 Geoff Bodine	5.00	2.20
Ford EB		
11 Geoff Bodine	5.00	2.20
Ford PB		
12 Bobby Allison	5.00	2.20
Buick PB		
12 Hut Stricklin	5.00	2.20
Buick PB		
12 Hut Stricklin	5.00	2.20
Lumina PB		
14 A.J. Foyt	20.00	9.00
Buick PB		
14 A.J. Foyt	20.00	9.00
Oldsmobile EB		
14 A.J. Foyt	60.00	27.00
Oldsmobile NP		
14 A.J. Foyt	10.00	4.50
Oldsmobile PB		
15 Morgan Shepherd	10.00	4.50
Ford with Red paint scheme EB		
15 Morgan Shepherd	15.00	6.75
Ford EB		
with Red and White paint scheme		
15 Morgan Shepherd	5.00	2.20
Ford PB		
15 Morgan Shepherd	10.00	4.50
Old Ford EB		
15 Morgan Shepherd	60.00	27.00
Old Ford NP		
16 Larry Pearson	6.00	2.70
Buick EB		
16 Larry Pearson	60.00	27.00
Buick NP		
16 Larry Pearson	5.00	2.20
Buick PB		
16 Larry Pearson	25.00	11.00
Lumina PB		
18 Gregory Trammell	5.00	2.20
Ford Melling PB		
20 Rob Moroso	30.00	13.50
Oldsmobile EB		
20 Rob Moroso	50.00	22.00
Oldsmobile with STP decal NP		
21 Neil Bonnett	25.00	11.00
Oldsmobile Ford EB		
21 Neil Bonnett	90.00	40.00
Old Ford NP		
21 Dale Jarrett	20.00	9.00
Ford EB		
21 Dale Jarrett	8.00	3.60
Ford PB		
22 Sterling Marlin	5.00	2.20
Ford with Black wheels PB		
22 Sterling Marlin	30.00	13.50
Ford with Silver Wheels PB		
25 Ken Schrader	5.00	2.20
Lumina PB		
26 Kenny Bernstein	6.00	2.70
Buick EB		
26 Kenny Bernstein	60.00	27.00
Buick Quaker State NP		
26 Kenny Bernstein	5.00	2.20
Buick PB		
26 Kenny Bernstein	10.00	4.50
Oldsmobile PB		
26 Brett Bodine	5.00	2.20
Buick Quaker State PB		
26 Brett Bodine	5.00	2.20
Lumina PB		
27 Rusty Wallace	60.00	27.00
Pontiac Miller Genuine Draft EB		
27 Rusty Wallace	90.00	40.00
Pontiac Miller Genuine Draft NP		

CAR / DRIVER / SPONSOR	MINT	NRMT
27 Rusty Wallace	50.00	22.00
Pontiac no MGD EB		
27 Rusty Wallace	40.00	18.00
Pontiac Miller EB		
28 Davey Allison	50.00	22.00
Ford EB		
28 Davey Allison	35.00	16.00
Ford PB		
28 Davey Allison	40.00	18.00
Old Ford EB		
28 Davey Allison	90.00	40.00
Old Ford NP		
28 Davey Allison	30.00	13.50
Old Ford PB		
30 Michael Waltrip	25.00	11.00
Pontiac Country Time EB		
30 Michael Waltrip	12.00	5.50
Pontiac Pennzoil EB		
with STP decal		
30 Michael Waltrip	12.00	5.50
Pontiac Pennzoil EB		
without STP decal		
30 Michael Waltrip	60.00	27.00
Pontiac NP		
30 Michael Waltrip	5.00	2.20
Pontiac PB		
33 Harry Gant	20.00	9.00
Buick PB		
33 Harry Gant	15.00	6.75
Oldsmobile EB		
33 Harry Gant	12.00	5.50
Oldsmobile PB		
33 Harry Gant	15.00	6.75
Pontiac EB		
33 Harry Gant	60.00	27.00
Pontiac NP		
34 Todd Bodine	5.00	2.20
Lumina Welco		
36 Kenny Wallace	5.00	2.20
Pontiac Cox Lumber		
42 Kyle Petty	15.00	6.75
Pontiac Peak EB		
42 Kyle Petty	35.00	16.00
Pontiac Peak NB		
42 Kyle Petty	20.00	9.00
Pontiac Peak PB		
42 Kyle Petty	8.00	3.60
Pontiac Mello Yello PB		
43 Richard Petty	15.00	6.75
Pontiac EB		
43 Richard Petty	60.00	27.00
Pontiac NP		
43 Richard Petty	8.00	3.60
Pontiac PB		
52 Jimmy Means	5.00	2.20
Pontiac PB		
59 Robert Pressley	5.00	2.20
Alliance		
66 Cale Yarborough	8.00	3.60
Pontiac PB		
68 Bobby Hamilton	5.00	2.20
Oldsmobile PB		
68 Bobby Hamilton	20.00	9.00
Buick PB		
70 J.D. McDuffie	5.00	2.20
Son's Auto		
71 Dave Marcis	8.00	3.60
Lumina PB		
72 Ken Bouchard	20.00	9.00
Pontiac ADAP PB		
72 Tracy Leslie	5.00	2.20
Oldsmobile Detroit Gaskets PB		
89 Jim Sauter	5.00	2.20
Pontiac PB		
89 Jim Sauter	10.00	4.50
Pontiac Day Glow PB		
94 Terry Labonte	12.00	5.50
Buick PB		

CAR / DRIVER / SPONSOR	MINT	NRMT
94 Terry Labonte	8.00	3.60
Oldsmobile PB		
94 Sterling Marlin	10.00	4.50
Oldsmobile EB		
94 Sterling Marlin	25.00	11.00
Oldsmobile NP		
96 Tom Peck	35.00	16.00
Lumina PB		
96 Tom Peck	5.00	2.20
Oldsmobile PB		

1992 Racing Champions 1:64

Every piece in this series either has a Petty back or a copyright list on the back. This was Jeff Gordon's first appearance in a Racing Champions die cast series.

CAR / DRIVER / SPONSOR	MINT	NRMT
1 Jeff Gordon	100.00	45.00
Baby Ruth		
1 Rick Mast	3.00	1.35
Majik Market		
2 Rusty Wallace	12.00	5.50
Pontiac Excitement		
3 Dale Earnhardt	25.00	11.00
Goodwrench		
4 Ernie Irvan	8.00	3.60
Kodak		
5 Jay Fogelman	3.00	1.35
Inn Keeper		
5 Ricky Rudd	3.00	1.35
Tide		
6 Mark Martin	20.00	9.00
Valvoline		
7 Harry Gant	20.00	9.00
Mac Tools		
7 Alan Kulwicki	40.00	18.00
Hooter's		
8 Bobby Dotter	3.00	1.35
Team R		
9 Joe Bessey	12.00	5.50
AC Delco		
9 Bill Elliott	12.00	5.50
Melling		
9 Chad Little	10.00	4.50
Melling Performance		
10 Derrike Cope	5.00	2.20
Purolator Adam's Mark		
10 Derrike Cope	5.00	2.20
Purolator with name in Blue		
10 Derrike Cope	15.00	6.75
Purolator with name in White		
10 Sterling Marlin	8.00	3.60
Maxwell House		
11 Geoff Bodine	5.00	2.20
No Sponsor		
11 Bill Elliott	12.00	5.50
Amoco		
12 Bobby Allison	4.00	1.80
No Sponsor		
12 Hut Stricklin	3.00	1.35
Raybestos		
14 A.J. Foyt	15.00	6.75
No Sponsor		

CAR / DRIVER / SPONSOR	MINT	NRMT
15 Geoff Bodine	3.00	1.35
Motorcraft		
16 Wally Dallenbach Jr.	15.00	6.75
Roush Racing		
17 Darrell Waltrip	3.00	1.35
Western Auto		
18 Dale Jarrett	8.00	3.60
Interstate Batteries		
18 Gregory Trammell	3.00	1.35
Melling		
19 Chad Little	3.00	1.35
Tyson		
20 Mike Wallace	8.00	3.60
First Aide		
21 Dale Jarrett	5.00	2.20
Citgo		
21 Morgan Shepherd	3.00	1.35
Citgo		
22 Sterling Marlin	3.00	1.35
Maxwell House		
25 Ken Schrader	5.00	2.20
Hendrick Motorsports		
25 Bill Venturini	5.00	2.20
Amoco Rain X		
26 Brett Bodine	3.00	1.35
Quaker State		
28 Davey Allison	15.00	6.75
Havoline		
28 Bobby Hillin Jr.	15.00	6.75
Havoline		
30 Michael Waltrip	3.00	1.35
Pennzoil		
31 Bobby Hillin Jr.	5.00	2.20
Team Ireland		
33 Harry Gant	5.00	2.20
No Sponsor		
34 Todd Bodine	5.00	2.20
Welco Quick Stop		
36 Kenny Wallace	5.00	2.20
Cox Lumber		
36 Kenny Wallace	6.00	2.70
Dirt Devil		
42 Bobby Hillin Jr.	18.00	8.00
Mello Yello		
42 Kyle Petty	8.00	3.60
Mello Yello		
43 Richard Petty	12.00	5.50
STP with Black wheels		
43 Richard Petty	12.00	5.50
STP with Blue wheels		
44 Bill Caudill	5.00	2.20
Army		
49 Stanley Smith	10.00	4.50
Ameritron		
55 Ted Musgrave	10.00	4.50
Jasper Engines		
56 Jerry Glanville	6.00	2.70
Atlanta Falcons		
59 Andy Belmont	6.00	2.70
FDP Brakes		
60 Mark Martin	6.00	2.70
Winn Dixie		
63 Chuck Bown	5.00	2.20
Nescafe		
66 Jimmy Hensley	3.00	1.35
TropArtic		
66 Chad Little	3.00	1.35
TropArtic		
66 Cale Yarborough	6.00	2.70
TropArtic Ford		
66 Cale Yarborough	5.00	2.20
TropArtic Pontiac		
68 Bobby Hamilton	3.00	1.35
Country Time		
70 J.D. McDuffie	3.00	1.35
Son's Auto		
71 Dave Marcis	5.00	2.20
Big Apple Market		
72 Ken Bouchard	8.00	3.60
ADAP		

CAR / DRIVER / SPONSOR	MINT	NRMT
72 Tracy Leslie	3.00	1.35
Detroit Gasket		
75 Butch Miller	5.00	2.20
Food Country		
83 Lake Speed	6.00	2.70
Purex		
87 Joe Nemechek	5.00	2.20
Texas Pete		
89 Jim Sauter	3.00	1.35
Evinrude		
94 Terry Labonte	10.00	4.50
Sunoco with Blue bumper		
94 Terry Labonte	10.00	4.50
Suncoo with Yellow bumper		
96 Tom Peck	3.00	1.35
Thomas Brothers		

1992 Racing Champions Premier 1:64

This 5-piece series was the first time Racing Champions did a Premier Series. Each piece comes in a black shadow box and the number of quantity produced is on the front of the box.

CAR / DRIVER / SPONSOR	MINT	NRMT
3 Dale Earnhardt	30.00	13.50
Goodwrench		
11 Bill Elliott	15.00	6.75
Amoco		
17 Darrell Waltrip	14.00	6.25
Western Auto		
28 Davey Allison	30.00	13.50
Havoline		

CAR / DRIVER / SPONSOR	MINT	NRMT
43 Richard Petty	20.00	9.00
STP		

1993 Racing Champions 1:64

This series of 1:64 scale cars features the top names in racing. The cars came in a blister pack and were sold through both hobby and retail outlets.

CAR / DRIVER / SPONSOR	MINT	NRMT
0 Dick McCabe	4.00	1.80
Fisher Snow Plows		
2 Rusty Wallace	5.00	2.20
Pontiac Excitement		
3 Dale Earnhardt	15.00	6.75
Goodwrench		
3 Dale Earnhardt	12.00	5.50
Goodwrench Mom-n-Pop's		
4 Ernie Irvan	5.00	2.20
Kodak		

5 Ricky Rudd	4.00	1.80
Tide		
6 Mark Martin	10.00	4.50
Valvoline		
7 Alan Kulwicki	15.00	6.75
Hooters		
8 Sterling Marlin	4.00	1.80
Raybestos		
11 Bill Elliott	5.00	2.20
Amoco		
12 Jimmy Spencer	4.00	1.80
Meineke		

14 Terry Labonte	20.00	9.00
Kellogg's		
15 Geoff Bodine	4.00	1.80
Motorcraft		
17 Darrell Waltrip	4.00	1.80
Western Auto		
18 Dale Jarrett	5.00	2.20
Interstate Batteries		
21 Morgan Shepherd	4.00	1.80
Citgo		

22 Bobby Labonte	25.00	11.00
Maxwell House		
24 Jeff Gordon	30.00	13.50
DuPont		

25 Ken Schrader	10.00	4.50
Kodiak		
25 Bill Venturini	6.00	2.70
Rain X		
26 Brett Bodine	4.00	1.80
Quaker State		
27 Hut Stricklin	4.00	1.80
McDonald's		

28 Davey Allison	10.00	4.50
Havoline		
28 Davey Allison	12.00	5.50
Havoline		
with Black and White paint scheme		
28 Ernie Irvan	10.00	4.50
Havoline		
33 Harry Gant	4.00	1.80
No Sponsor Lumina		
33 Harry Gant	4.00	1.80
No Sponsor Oldsmobile		
42 Kyle Petty	4.00	1.80
Mello Yello		

44 Rick Wilson	4.00	1.80
STP		
59 Andy Belmont	8.00	3.60
FDP Brakes		
59 Robert Pressley	8.00	3.60
Alliance		
60 Mark Martin	8.00	3.60
Winn Dixie		
71 Dave Marcis	4.00	1.80
STG		
75 Butch Mock	4.00	1.80
Factory Stores of America		
87 Joe Nemechek	4.00	1.80
Dentyne		
98 Derrike Cope	4.00	1.80
Bojangles		

1993 Racing Champions Premier 1:64

This was the second year of the 1:64 scale Premier series. The series is highlighted by the Alan Kulwicki Hooters car and the three different Champion Forever Davey Allison pieces.

1 Rodney Combs	10.00	4.50
Jebco Clocks		
2 Ward Burton	14.00	6.25
Hardee's		
2 Rusty Wallace	7.00	3.10
Pontiac Excitement		
3 Dale Earnhardt	25.00	11.00
Goodwrench		
3 Dale Earnhardt	15.00	6.75
Dale Earnhardt Inc.		
4 Ernie Irvan	6.00	2.70
Kodak		
4 Jeff Purvis	15.00	6.75
Kodak		
5 Ricky Rudd	6.00	2.70
Tide		
6 Mark Martin	7.00	3.10
Valvoline		
6 Mark Martin	14.00	6.25
Valvoline		
Four in a Row Promo		
6 Mike Stefanik	10.00	4.50
Valvoline Auto Palace		
7 Jimmy Hensley	30.00	13.50
Alan Kulwicki Racing		

7 Alan Kulwicki	40.00	18.00
Hooter's		
7 Alan Kulwicki	25.00	11.00
Zerex		
8 Sterling Marlin	6.00	2.70
Raybestos		
11 Bill Elliott	20.00	9.00
Budweiser Promo		
12 Jimmy Spencer	6.00	2.70
Meineke		

14 Terry Labonte	20.00	9.00
Kellogg's		

CAR / DRIVER / SPONSOR	MINT	NRMT
15 Geoff Bodine Motorcraft	6.00	2.70
18 Dale Jarrett Interstate Batteries	8.00	3.60
21 Morgan Shepherd Citgo	6.00	2.70

CAR / DRIVER / SPONSOR	MINT	NRMT
24 Jeff Gordon DuPont	20.00	9.00
26 Brett Bodine Quaker State	6.00	2.70
27 Hut Stricklin McDonald's	6.00	2.70
27 Hut Stricklin Mr. Pibb	6.00	2.70
28 Davey Allison Havoline with Black paint scheme	20.00	9.00
28 Davey Allison Havoline with Champion Forever card and Black and Gold paint scheme	15.00	6.75
28 Davey Allison Havoline with Champion Forever card and Black and Orange paint scheme	20.00	9.00
28 Davey Allison Havoline with Champion Forever card and Black and White paint scheme	20.00	9.00
28 Ernie Irvan Havoline	20.00	9.00
31 Neil Bonnett Mom-n-Pop's	50.00	22.00
33 Harry Gant No Sponsor	6.00	2.70
41 Ernie Irvan Mac Tools	15.00	6.75
42 Kyle Petty Mello Yello	6.00	2.70
44 Jimmy Hensley STP	12.00	5.50
59 Robert Pressley Alliance	20.00	9.00
59 Dennis Setzer Alliance	15.00	6.75
60 Mark Martin Winn Dixie	20.00	9.00
87 Joe Nemechek Dentyne	6.00	2.70
97 Joe Bessey Auto Palace	6.00	2.70
98 Derrike Cope Bojangles with Black paint scheme	10.00	4.50
98 Derrike Cope Bojangles with Yellow paint scheme	10.00	4.50
2 Frank Kimmel Harley Davidson	15.00	6.75

1993 Racing Champions PVC Box 1:64

Almost each die cast in this series was done for a special occasion. Each piece comes a clear PVC box. The box has the drivers name, what the occasion is and the quantity produced in gold foil on top of it.

CAR / DRIVER / SPONSOR	MINT	NRMT
3 Dale Earnhardt Back in Black	15.00	6.75
3 Dale Earnhardt Darlington Win	15.00	6.75
3 Dale Earnhardt Busch Clash Win	15.00	6.75
3 Dale Earnhardt Twin 125 Win	15.00	6.75
4 Ernie Irvan Kodak Talladega Win	10.00	4.50
7 Harry Gant Morema	8.00	3.60
7 Jimmy Hensley Hanes	10.00	4.50
7 Jimmy Hensley Purolator	10.00	4.50
8 Sterling Marlin Raybestos	10.00	4.50
12 David Bonnett Plasti-Kote	8.00	3.60
18 Dale Jarrett Interstate Batteries	8.00	3.60
21 Morgan Shepherd Cheerwine	8.00	3.60
24 Jeff Gordon DuPont	30.00	13.50
24 Jeff Gordon DuPont Fan Club	30.00	13.50
24 Jeff Gordon DuPont Daytona	25.00	11.00
24 Jeff Gordon DuPont Twin 125 Win	25.00	11.00
27 Hut Stricklin McDonald's All-American	8.00	3.60
27 Hut Stricklin McDonald's Daytona	20.00	9.00
27 Hut Stricklin McDonald's 250 produced	50.00	22.00
27 Hut Stricklin McDonald's Taylorsville	8.00	3.60
28 Alan Kulwicki Hardee's	40.00	18.00
28 Davey Allison Havoline	20.00	9.00
28 Ernie Irvan Havoline	20.00	9.00
28 Ernie Irvan Havoline Charlotte	20.00	9.00
40 Kenny Wallace Dirt Devil	25.00	11.00
42 Kyle Petty Mello Yello	20.00	9.00
44 David Green Slim Jim	20.00	9.00
44 Rick Wilson STP	20.00	9.00
46 Al Unser Jr. Valvoline	25.00	11.00
51 No Driver Association Pontiac Racing Champions	40.00	18.00
51 No Driver Association Lumina Racing Champions	40.00	18.00
51 No Driver Association Thunderbird Racing Champions	40.00	18.00
51 No Driver Association Racing Champions Mascot	40.00	18.00
52 Ken Schrader Morema	10.00	4.50
56 Ernie Irvan Earnhardt Chevrolet	25.00	11.00
59 Robert Pressley Alliance Fan Club	20.00	9.00
59 Robert Pressley Alliance September 1993	35.00	16.00
59 Robert Pressley Alliance Pressley	20.00	9.00

CAR / DRIVER / SPONSOR	MINT	NRMT
60 Mark Martin Winn Dixie	15.00	6.75
68 Bobby Hamilton Country Time	75.00	34.00
89 Jeff McClure Bero Motors	8.00	3.60
93 No Driver Association Budweiser 500	15.00	6.75
93 No Driver Association Food City 500	15.00	6.75
93 No Driver Association Slick 50 300	15.00	6.75
93 No Driver Association Racing Champions Club Car	15.00	6.75

1994 Racing Champions 1:64

These 1:64 scale pieces were mainly packaged in a red blister pack and distributed through hobby shops and retail outlets. The highlight to the series is the Jeff Gordon Brickyard peice.

CAR / DRIVER / SPONSOR	MINT	NRMT
1 Rick Mast Precision Products	4.00	1.80
2 Ricky Craven DuPont	6.00	2.70
2 Rusty Wallace Ford Motorsports	8.00	3.60
2 Rusty Wallace Ford Motorsports with no Blue	8.00	3.60
4 Sterling Marlin Kodak	4.00	1.80
5 Terry Labonte Kellogg's	6.00	2.70
6 Mark Martin Valvoline	5.00	2.20
7 Geoff Bodine Exide	4.00	1.80
7 Harry Gant Manheim	8.00	3.60
8 Jeff Burton Raybestos	8.00	3.60
8 Kenny Wallace TIC Financial	4.00	1.80
10 Ricky Rudd Tide	4.00	1.80
12 Clifford Allison Sports Image	10.00	4.50
14 John Andretti Kanawaha	4.00	1.80
15 Lake Speed Quality Care	4.00	1.80
16 Ted Musgrave Family Channel	4.00	1.80
17 Darrell Waltrip Western Auto	4.00	1.80
18 Dale Jarrett Interstate Batteries	10.00	4.50
19 Loy Allen Hooters	8.00	3.60
20 Randy LaJoie Fina	4.00	1.80
21 Morgan Shepherd Citgo	4.00	1.80
22 Bobby Labonte Maxwell House	8.00	3.60
23 Hut Stricklin Smokin' Joe's in PVC box	10.00	4.50
24 Jeff Gordon DuPont	30.00	13.50

CAR / DRIVER / SPONSOR	MINT	NRMT
24 Jeff Gordon DuPont Brickyard special	20.00	9.00
25 Hermie Sadler Virginia is for Lovers	4.00	1.80
25 Ken Schrader GMAC	4.00	1.80
26 Brett Bodine Quaker State	4.00	1.80
27 Jimmy Spencer McDonald's	4.00	1.80
28 Ernie Irvan Havoline	5.00	2.20
30 Michael Waltrip Pennzoil	4.00	1.80
31 Tom Peck Channellock	6.00	2.70
33 Harry Gant No Sponsor	40.00	18.00
38 Elton Sawyer Ford Credit	4.00	1.80
40 Bobby Hamilton Kendall	4.00	1.80
42 Kyle Petty Mello Yello	4.00	1.80
44 Bobby Hillin Jr. Buss Fuses	4.00	1.80
46 Shawna Robinson Polaroid	4.00	1.80
52 Ken Schrader AC Delco	6.00	2.70
54 Robert Pressley Manheim	4.00	1.80
60 Mark Martin Winn Dixie	10.00	4.50
63 Jim Bown Lysol	4.00	1.80
75 Todd Bodine Factory Stores of America	4.00	1.80
83 Sherry Blakely Ramses	4.00	1.80
92 Larry Pearson Stanley Tools	4.00	1.80

CAR / DRIVER / SPONSOR	MINT	NRMT
94 No Driver Association Brickyard 400 special	6.00	2.70

CAR / DRIVER / SPONSOR	MINT	NRMT
97 Joe Bessey Johnson	4.00	1.80
98 Derrike Cope Fingerhut	4.00	1.80
0 Johnny Rumley Big Dog Coal	8.00	3.60

1994 Racing Champions Hobby 1:64

This series was distributed through hobby channels. Each piece came in a yellow box.

CAR / DRIVER / SPONSOR	MINT	NRMT
1 Rick Mast Precision Products	4.00	1.80
2 Ricky Craven DuPont	4.00	1.80
2 Rusty Wallace Ford Motorsports	5.00	2.20
4 Sterling Marlin Kodak	4.00	1.80
4 Sterling Marlin Kodak Funsaver	4.00	1.80
5 Terry Labonte Kellogg's	6.00	2.70
6 Mark Martin Valvoline	8.00	3.60
7 Geoff Bodine Exide	4.00	1.80
8 Jeff Burton Raybestos	4.00	1.80

CAR / DRIVER / SPONSOR	MINT	NRMT
14 Terry Labonte MW Windows	10.00	4.50
15 Lake Speed Quality Care	4.00	1.80
16 Ted Musgrave Family Channel	4.00	1.80
17 Darrell Waltrip Western Auto	6.00	2.70
18 Dale Jarrett Interstate Batteries	8.00	3.60
19 Loy Allen Hooter's	4.00	1.80
22 Brett Bodine Maxwell House	4.00	1.80
23 Chad Little Bayer	4.00	1.80
24 Jeff Gordon DuPont	15.00	6.75
25 Hermie Sadler Virginia is for Lovers	4.00	1.80
26 Brett Bodine Quaker State	4.00	1.80
27 Jimmy Spencer McDonald's	4.00	1.80
30 Michael Waltrip Pennzoil	4.00	1.80
31 Tom Peck Channellock	4.00	1.80

CAR / DRIVER / SPONSOR	MINT	NRMT
33 Harry Gant No Sponsor	4.00	1.80
34 Mike McLaughlin Fiddle Faddle	4.00	1.80
38 Elton Sawyer Ford Credit	4.00	1.80
40 Bobby Hamilton Kendall	4.00	1.80
42 Kyle Petty Mello Yello	4.00	1.80
46 Shawna Robinson Polaroid	4.00	1.80
63 Jim Bown Lysol	4.00	1.80
75 Todd Bodine Factory Stores of America	4.00	1.80
92 Larry Pearson Stanley Tools	4.00	1.80
94 No Driver Association Brickyard 400	6.00	2.70
98 Derrike Cope Fingerhut	4.00	1.80

1994 Racing Champions Premier 1:64

This series of 1:64 Premier series was issued by Racing Champions through retail outlets and hobby dealers. The pieces come in a black shadow box and have the quantity produced stamped in gold on the front of the box.

CAR / DRIVER / SPONSOR	MINT	NRMT
0 Dick McCabe Fisher Snow Plows	10.00	4.50
1 Davey Allison Lancaster	20.00	9.00
2 Ricky Craven DuPont	6.00	2.70
2 Rusty Wallace Miller Genuine Draft	10.00	4.50
2 Rusty Wallace Mac Tools	20.00	9.00

CAR / DRIVER / SPONSOR	MINT	NRMT
3 Dale Earnhardt Goodwrench	20.00	9.00
4 Sterling Marlin Kodak	6.00	2.70
4 Sterling Marlin Kodak Funsaver	10.00	4.50
5 Terry Labonte Kellogg's	20.00	9.00
6 Mark Martin Valvoline	6.00	2.70
6 Mark Martin Valvoline four in a row special	14.00	6.25
7 Geoff Bodine Exide	6.00	2.70
7 Harry Gant Manheim	15.00	6.75
7 Alan Kulwicki Army	30.00	13.50

CAR / DRIVER / SPONSOR	MINT	NRMT
8 Jeff Burton Raybestos	6.00	2.70
8 Kenny Wallace TIC Financial	10.00	4.50
12 Clifford Allison Sports Image	20.00	9.00
15 Lake Speed Quality Care	6.00	2.70
16 Chad Chaffin 31W Insulation	12.00	5.50
16 Ted Musgrave Family Channel	6.00	2.70
18 Dale Jarrett Interstate Batteries	10.00	4.50
19 Loy Allen Hooters	6.00	2.70
20 Randy LaJoie Fina	6.00	2.70
21 Johnny Benson Berger	15.00	6.75
24 Jeff Gordon DuPont	30.00	13.50
24 Jeff Gordon DuPont 1993 Rookie of the Year	16.00	7.25
25 Hermie Sadler Virgina is for Lovers	12.00	5.50
25 Ken Schrader Kodiak	6.00	2.70
26 Brett Bodine Quaker State	6.00	2.70
27 Jimmy Spencer McDonald's	6.00	2.70
28 Ernie Irvan Mac Tools in Yellow box	18.00	8.00
31 Steve Grissom Channellock	12.00	5.50

CAR / DRIVER / SPONSOR	MINT	NRMT
33 Bobby Labonte Dentyne	50.00	22.00
34 Mike McLaughlin Fiddle Faddle	6.00	2.70
35 Shawna Robinson Polaroid Captiva	15.00	6.75
40 Bobby Hamilton Kendall	6.00	2.70
43 Rodney Combs French's	15.00	6.75
43 Wally Dallenbach Jr. STP	15.00	6.75
46 Shawna Robinson Polaroid	10.00	4.50
54 Robert Pressley Alliance	12.00	5.50
59 Andy Belmont Metal Arrester	10.00	4.50
59 Dennis Setzer Alliance 2000 produced	25.00	11.00
59 Dennis Setzer Alliance	12.00	5.50
60 Mark Martin Winn Dixie	15.00	6.75
70 J.D. McDuffie Son's Auto	15.00	6.75
71 Dave Marcis Earnhardt Chevrolet	15.00	6.75

CAR / DRIVER / SPONSOR	MINT	NRMT
75 Todd Bodine Factory Stores of America	6.00	2.70
77 Greg Sacks US Air Jasper Engines	15.00	6.75
85 Jim Sauter Rheem AC	10.00	4.50
89 Jeff McClure FSU Seminoles	10.00	4.50
98 Jody Ridley Ford Motorsports	6.00	2.70

1994 Racing Champions Premier Brickyard 400 1:64

This series was issued in conjunction with the first Brickyard 400. The boxes are easily distinguishable due to their purple color. The Jeff Gordon pieces is the most popular due to his winning of the first Brickyard 400.

CAR / DRIVER / SPONSOR	MINT	NRMT
3 Dale Earnhardt Goodwrench	35.00	16.00
6 Mark Martin Valvoline	10.00	4.50
18 Dale Jarrett Interstate Batteries	10.00	4.50
21 Morgan Shepherd Citgo	7.00	3.10
24 Jeff Gordon DuPont	75.00	34.00
26 Brett Bodine Quaker State	7.00	3.10
27 Jimmy Spencer McDonald's	7.00	3.10
30 Michael Waltrip Pennzoil	7.00	3.10
42 Kyle Petty Mello Yello	7.00	3.10

1994 Racing Champions To the Maxx 1:64

This was the first series issued by Racing Champions that included a Maxx Premier Plus card.

CAR / DRIVER / SPONSOR	MINT	NRMT
2 Rusty Wallace Ford Motorsports	8.00	3.60
4 Sterling Marlin Kodak	7.00	3.10

CAR / DRIVER / SPONSOR	MINT	NRMT
5 Terry Labonte Kellogg's	8.00	3.60
6 Mark Martin Valvoline	8.00	3.60
16 Ted Musgrave Family Channel	7.00	3.10
24 Jeff Gordon DuPont	12.00	5.50

CAR / DRIVER / SPONSOR	MINT	NRMT
28 Ernie Irvan Havoline	8.00	3.60
42 Kyle Petty Mello Yello	7.00	3.10

1995 Racing Champions Previews 1:64

This series of 1:64 replica cars was a Preview to many of the cars that raced in the 1995 season. The Geoff Bodine car came with either Hoosier or Goodyear tires.

CAR / DRIVER / SPONSOR	MINT	NRMT
1 Rick Mast Precision Products	4.00	1.80
2 Ricky Craven DuPont	4.00	1.80
2 Rusty Wallace Ford Motorsports	5.00	2.20
4 Sterling Marlin Kodak	4.00	1.80
6 Mark Martin Valvoline	4.00	1.80
7 Geoff Bodine Exide with Goodyear tires	4.00	1.80
7 Geoff Bodine Exide with Hoosier tires	4.00	1.80
10 Ricky Rudd Tide	4.00	1.80
14 Terry Labonte MW Windows	5.00	2.20
16 Ted Musgrave Family Channel	4.00	1.80
21 Morgan Shepherd Citgo	4.00	1.80
23 Chad Little Bayer	4.00	1.80
24 Jeff Gordon DuPont	6.00	2.70
25 Kirk Shelmerdine Big Johnson	6.00	2.70
26 Steve Kinser Quaker State	4.00	1.80
28 Dale Jarrett Havoline	4.00	1.80
30 Michael Waltrip Pennzoil	4.00	1.80
38 Elton Sawyer Ford Credit	4.00	1.80
40 Bobby Hamilton Kendall	4.00	1.80
40 Patty Moise Dial Purex	4.00	1.80
52 Ken Schrader AC Delco	4.00	1.80
57 Jason Keller Budget Gourmet	4.00	1.80
63 Curtis Markham Lysol	4.00	1.80
75 Todd Bodine Factory Stores of America	4.00	1.80
92 Larry Pearson Stanley Tools	4.00	1.80
94 Bill Elliott McDonald's	4.00	1.80
98 Jeremy Mayfield Fingerhut	4.00	1.80

1995 Racing Champions 1:64

This is the regular issued of the 1:64 scale 1995 Racing Champions series. The Bobby Labonte car comes with and wthout roof flaps. This was one of the first cars to incorporate the new NASCAR safety feature into a die cast.

CAR / DRIVER / SPONSOR	MINT	NRMT
1 Rick Mast Precision	4.00	1.80

CAR / DRIVER / SPONSOR	MINT	NRMT
2 Ricky Craven DuPont	6.00	2.70
2 Rusty Wallace Ford Motorsports	5.00	2.20
4 Sterling Marlin Kodak	4.00	1.80
4 Jeff Purvis Kodak Funsaver	4.00	1.80
5 Terry Labonte Kellogg's	5.00	2.20
6 Tommy Houston Red Devil	4.00	1.80
6 Mark Martin Valvoline	5.00	2.20
7 Geoff Bodine Exide	4.00	1.80
7 Stevie Reeves Clabber Girl	4.00	1.80
8 Jeff Burton Raybestos with Blue numbers	4.00	1.80
8 Jeff Burton Raybestos	4.00	1.80
8 Kenny Wallace Red Dog	8.00	3.60
8 Bobby Dotter Hyde Tools	4.00	1.80
10 Ricky Rudd Tide	4.00	1.80
12 Derrike Cope Straight Arrow	4.00	1.80
14 Terry Labonte MW Windows	30.00	13.50
15 Jack Nadeau Buss Fuses	4.00	1.80
15 Dick Trickle Ford Quality	4.00	1.80
16 Stub Fadden NAPA	4.00	1.80
16 Ted Musgrave Family Channel	4.00	1.80
17 Darrell Waltrip Western Auto	4.00	1.80
18 Bobby Labonte Interstate Batteries with roof flaps	6.00	2.70

CAR / DRIVER / SPONSOR	MINT	NRMT
18 Bobby Labonte Interstate Batteries without roof flaps	4.00	1.80
21 Morgan Shepherd Citgo	4.00	1.80
22 Randy LaJoie MBNA	5.00	2.20
23 Chad Little Bayer	4.00	1.80
24 Jeff Gordon DuPont	25.00	11.00

CAR / DRIVER / SPONSOR	MINT	NRMT
24 Jeff Gordon DuPont Coca-Cola	25.00	11.00

CAR / DRIVER / SPONSOR	MINT	NRMT
24 Jeff Gordon DuPont Signature Series	25.00	11.00
24 Jeff Gordon DuPont Signature Series combo with SuperTruck	25.00	11.00
25 Johnny Rumley Big Johnson	4.00	1.80
25 Ken Schrader Hendrick	4.00	1.80
25 Kirk Shelmerdine Big Johnson	4.00	1.80
26 Steve Kinser Quaker State	4.00	1.80
27 Loy Allen Hooters	4.00	1.80

CAR / DRIVER / SPONSOR	MINT	NRMT
28 Dale Jarrett Havoline	5.00	2.20
29 Steve Grissom Meineke	4.00	1.80
30 Michael Waltrip Pennzoil	4.00	1.80
34 Mike McLaughlin French's	4.00	1.80
37 John Andretti K-Mart	4.00	1.80
40 Patty Moise Dial Purex	4.00	1.80
41 Ricky Craven Hedrick	4.00	1.80
44 David Green Slim Jim	4.00	1.80

CAR / DRIVER / SPONSOR	MINT	NRMT
44 Jeff Purvis Jackaroo	4.00	1.80
47 Jeff Fuller Sunoco	4.00	1.80
51 Jim Bown Luck's	4.00	1.80
52 Ken Schrader AC Delco	4.00	1.80
57 Jason Keller Budget Gourmet	4.00	1.80
60 Mark Martin Winn Dixie	5.00	2.20
71 Kevin Lepage Vermont Teddy Bear	8.00	3.60
71 Dave Marcis Olive Garden	8.00	3.60
75 Todd Bodine Factory Stores of America	4.00	1.80
81 Kenny Wallace TIC Financial	4.00	1.80
82 Derrike Cope FDP Brakes	4.00	1.80
87 Joe Nemechek Burger King	4.00	1.80
90 Mike Wallace Heilig-Meyers	4.00	1.80
92 Larry Pearson Stanley Tools	4.00	1.80
94 Bill Elliott McDonald's	8.00	3.60

CAR / DRIVER / SPONSOR	MINT	NRMT
94 Bill Elliott McDonald's Thunderbat	10.00	4.50
99 Phil Parsons Luxaire	4.00	1.80

1995 Racing Champions Matched Serial Numbers 1:64

This series features cards and die cast whose serial numbers match. The cars come in a black blister pack with a card. The card has a gold border and features the driver of the car.

CAR / DRIVER / SPONSOR	MINT	NRMT
2 Rusty Wallace Ford	7.00	3.10
5 Terry Labonte Kellogg's	7.00	3.10
6 Mark Martin Valvoline	7.00	3.10

CAR / DRIVER / SPONSOR	MINT	NRMT
7 Geoff Bodine	6.00	2.70
Exide		
18 Bobby Labonte	7.00	3.10
Interstate Batteries		
24 Jeff Gordon	25.00	11.00
DuPont		

1995 Racing Champions Premier 1:64

This is the 1995 series of the 1:64 Premier pieces. The cars are again packaged in a black shadow box and feature a gold foil number on the front of the box that states how many pieces were made. The cars were distributed through both hobby and retail.

CAR / DRIVER / SPONSOR	MINT	NRMT
2 Rusty Wallace	7.00	3.10
Ford Motorsports		
4 Sterling Marlin	6.00	2.70
Kodak		
6 Mark Martin	7.00	3.10
Valvoline		

CAR / DRIVER / SPONSOR	MINT	NRMT
8 Jeff Burton	10.00	4.50
Raybestos		
18 Bobby Labonte	6.00	2.70
Interstate Batteries		

CAR / DRIVER / SPONSOR	MINT	NRMT
24 Jeff Gordon	30.00	13.50
DuPont		
25 Ken Schrader	7.00	3.10
Budweiser		
26 Steve Kinser	6.00	2.70
Quaker State		
27 Loy Allen	6.00	2.70
Hooters		
28 Dale Jarrett	6.00	2.70
Havoline		
40 Bobby Hamilton	6.00	2.70
Kendall		
40 Patty Moise	6.00	2.70
Dial Purex		
59 Dennis Setzer	6.00	2.70
Alliance		
60 Mark Martin	10.00	4.50
Winn Dixie		
75 Todd Bodine	6.00	2.70
Factory Stores of America		
81 Kenny Wallace	6.00	2.70
TIC Financial		
94 Bill Elliott	20.00	9.00
McDonald's		

1995 Racing Champions To the Maxx 1:64

These pieces represent the second through fifth series of Racing Champions To the Maxx line. Each package includes a Maxx Premier Plus card that is only available with the die cast piece and was not inserted in any packs of the Premier Plus product.

CAR / DRIVER / SPONSOR	MINT	NRMT
2 Rusty Wallace	8.00	3.60
Ford Motorsports		
4 Sterling Marlin	7.00	3.10
Kodak		
4 Jeff Purvis	7.00	3.10
Kodak		
6 Tommy Houston	7.00	3.10
Dirt Devil		
6 Mark Martin	8.00	3.60
Valvoline		
7 Geoff Bodine	7.00	3.10
Exide		
7 Stevie Reeves	7.00	3.10
Clabber Girl		
8 Jeff Burton	7.00	3.10
Raybestos		
10 Ricky Rudd	7.00	3.10
Tide		
12 Derrike Cope	7.00	3.10
Mane N Tail		

CAR / DRIVER / SPONSOR	MINT	NRMT
14 Terry Labonte	7.00	3.10
MW Windows		
15 Dick Trickle	7.00	3.10
Quality Car		
17 Darrell Waltrip	7.00	3.10
Western Auto		
18 Bobby Labonte	8.00	3.60
Interstate Batteries		
21 Morgan Shepherd	7.00	3.10
Citgo		
22 Randy LaJoie	7.00	3.10
MBNA		
23 Chad Little	7.00	3.10
Bayer		

CAR / DRIVER / SPONSOR	MINT	NRMT
24 Jeff Gordon	10.00	4.50
DuPont		
26 Steve Kinser	7.00	3.10
Quaker State		
28 Dale Jarrett	8.00	3.60
Havoline		
29 Steve Grissom	7.00	3.10
Meineke		
34 Mike McLaughlin	7.00	3.10
French's		
38 Elton Sawyer	7.00	3.10
Ford Credit		
44 David Green	7.00	3.10
Slim Jim		
44 Jeff Purvis	7.00	3.10
Jackaroo		
52 Ken Schrader	7.00	3.10
AC Delco		
57 Jason Keller	7.00	3.10
Budget Gourmet		
75 Todd Bodine	7.00	3.10
Factory Stores of America		
81 Kenny Wallace	7.00	3.10
TIC Financial		
90 Mike Wallace	7.00	3.10
Heilig-Meyers		
92 Larry Pearson	7.00	3.10
Stanley Tools		
94 Bill Elliott	8.00	3.60
McDonald's		

1995 Racing Champions SuperTrucks 1:64

This series of 1:64 SuperTrucks is a good sample of many of the trucks that competed in the first SuperTruck series. There are numerous variations in the series.

CAR / DRIVER / SPONSOR	MINT	NRMT
1 P.J. Jones	6.00	2.70
Sears Diehard		
1 P.J. Jones	10.00	4.50
Vessells Ford		

	MINT	NRMT
1 Richmond Night Race Special	18.00	8.00
2 David Ashley	6.00	2.70
Southern California Ford		
3 Mike Skinner	6.00	2.70
Goodwrench		
6 Mike Bliss	6.00	2.70
Ultra Wheels		
6 Butch Gilliland	6.00	2.70
Ultra Wheels		
6 Rick Carelli	6.00	2.70
Total Petroleum		
7 Geoff Bodine	6.00	2.70
Exide		
7 Geoff Bodine	6.00	2.70
Exide Salsa		
7 Dave Rezendes	6.00	2.70
Exide		

	MINT	NRMT
8 Mike Bliss	6.00	2.70
Ultra Wheels		
8 C. Huartson	6.00	2.70
AC Delco		
10 Stan Fox	6.00	2.70
Made for You		
12 Randy MacCachren	6.00	2.70
Venable		
18 Johnny Benson	6.00	2.70
Hella Lights		

	MINT	NRMT
21 Tobey Butler	6.00	2.70
Ortho with Green Nose		
21 Tobey Butler	6.00	2.70
Ortho with Yellow Nose		
23 T.J. Clark	6.00	2.70
ASE with Blue paint scheme		
23 T.J. Clark	6.00	2.70
ASE with White paint scheme		
24 No Driver Association	6.00	2.70
DuPont Gordon Signature Series		

	MINT	NRMT
24 No Driver Association	8.00	3.60
DuPont with Gordon on the card		
37 Bob Strait	6.00	2.70
Target Expediting		
38 Sammy Swindell	6.00	2.70
Channellock		
with White Goodyear on tires		
38 Sammy Swindell	6.00	2.70
Channellock		
with Yellow Goodyear on tires		
51 Kerry Teague	6.00	2.70
Rosenblum Racing		
52 Ken Schrader	6.00	2.70
AC Delco		

	MINT	NRMT
54 Steve McEachern	6.00	2.70
McEachern Racing		
61 Todd Bodine	6.00	2.70
Roush Racing		
75 Bill Sedgwick	6.00	2.70
Spears Motorsports		
83 Steve Portenga	6.00	2.70
Coffee Critic		
95 No Driver Association	4.00	1.80
Brickyard 400 special		

	MINT	NRMT
98 Butch Miller	6.00	2.70
Raybestos		

1995 Racing Champions SuperTrucks Matched Serial Numbers 1:64

This series featues trucks and cards wtih matching serial numbers. The truck has a serial number stamp on the bottom of it. The card has a black serial number stamped on the front of it. The truck sits on a stand that also has a serial number that matches

	MINT	NRMT
1 Mike Chase	7.00	3.10
Sears Diehard		
3 Mike Skinner	7.00	3.10
Goodwrench		
6 Rick Carelli	7.00	3.10
Total Petroleum		
24 Scott Lagasse	7.00	3.10
DuPont		
75 Bill Sedgwick	7.00	3.10
Spears Motorsports		
98 Butch Miller	7.00	3.10
Raybestos		

1995 Racing Champions SuperTrucks To the Maxx 1:64

This is the first series of SuperTruck To the Maxx pieces. Each piece is packaged in a red blister pack and comes with a Crown Chrome accetate card.

	MINT	NRMT
1 P.J. Jones	7.00	3.10
Sears Diehard		
3 Mike Skinner	8.00	3.60
Goodwrench		
6 Rick Carelli	7.00	3.10
Total Petroleum		

	MINT	NRMT
7 Geoff Bodine	7.00	3.10
Exide		
21 Tobey Butler	7.00	3.10
Ortho		
24 Jeff Gordon	10.00	4.50
DuPont		
38 Sammy Swindell	7.00	3.10
Channellock		
98 Butch Miller	7.00	3.10
Raybestos		

1996 Racing Champions Previews 1:64

This series features some of the new paint schemes and driver changes for the 1996 season. The cars again come in a red blister with the word preview appearing below the year in the upper right hand corner.

	MINT	NRMT
2 Ricky Craven	4.00	1.80
DuPont		
4 Sterling Marlin	4.00	1.80
Kodak		
5 Terry Labonte	4.00	1.80
Kellogg's		
6 Mark Martin	4.00	1.80
Valvoline		
7 Stevie Reeves	4.00	1.80
Clabber Girl		

CAR / DRIVER / SPONSOR	MINT	NRMT
9 Joe Bessey Delco Remy	4.00	1.80
9 Lake Speed SPAM	4.00	1.80
10 Ricky Rudd Tide	4.00	1.80
11 Brett Bodine Lowe's	4.00	1.80

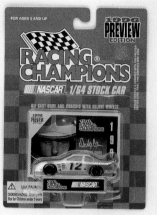

CAR / DRIVER / SPONSOR	MINT	NRMT
12 Derrike Cope Mane N' Tail	4.00	1.80
14 Patty Moise Dial Purex	4.00	1.80
16 Ted Musgrave Family Channel	4.00	1.80
17 Darrell Waltrip Western Auto	4.00	1.80
18 Bobby Labonte Interstate Batteries	4.00	1.80
22 Ward Burton MBNA	4.00	1.80
24 Jeff Gordon DuPont	16.00	7.25
30 Johnny Benson Pennzoil	4.00	1.80
40 Tim Fedewa Kleenex	4.00	1.80
41 Ricky Craven Kodiak	4.00	1.80
47 Jeff Fuller Sunoco	4.00	1.80
52 Ken Schrader AC Delco	4.00	1.80
57 Jason Keller Slim Jim	4.00	1.80
74 Johnny Benson Lipton Tea	4.00	1.80

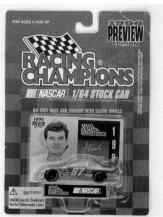

CAR / DRIVER / SPONSOR	MINT	NRMT
87 Joe Nemechek Burger King	4.00	1.80

CAR / DRIVER / SPONSOR	MINT	NRMT
90 Mike Wallace Heilig-Meyers	4.00	1.80
94 Bill Elliott McDonald's	4.00	1.80

1996 Racing Champions 1:64

This set features some unique pieces that Racing Champions had never issued before. Some piece came with a metal and plastic medallion in the blister package with the car. The Rusty Wallace was also available in both the Penske Racing and the MGD car.

CAR / DRIVER / SPONSOR	MINT	NRMT
1 Rick Mast Hooter's	20.00	9.00
2 Ricky Craven DuPont	4.00	1.80
2 Rusty Wallace Miller Genuine Draft	15.00	6.75
2 Rusty Wallace Penske Racing	4.00	1.80
4 Sterling Marlin Kodak	4.00	1.80
5 Terry Labonte Kellogg's	4.00	1.80

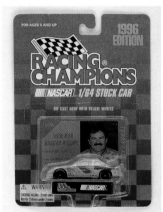

CAR / DRIVER / SPONSOR	MINT	NRMT
5 Terry Labonte Kellogg's with Iron Man card	18.00	8.00
5 Terry Labonte Kellogg's Silver car	8.00	3.60
6 Mark Martin Valvoline	4.00	1.80
6 Tommy Houston Suburban Propane	4.00	1.80
6 Mark Martin Valvoline Dura Blend	20.00	9.00

CAR / DRIVER / SPONSOR	MINT	NRMT
6 Mark Martin Roush Box Promo	12.00	5.50

CAR / DRIVER / SPONSOR	MINT	NRMT
7 Geoff Bodine QVC	4.00	1.80
8 Hut Stricklin Circuit City	4.00	1.80
10 Phil Parsons Channellock	4.00	1.80
10 Ricky Rudd Tide	4.00	1.80
11 Brett Bodine Lowe's	4.00	1.80
11 Brett Bodine Lowe's 50th Anniversary	18.00	8.00

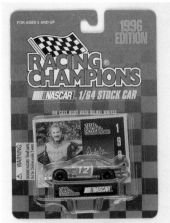

CAR / DRIVER / SPONSOR	MINT	NRMT
12 Derrike Cope Badcock	15.00	6.75
12 Michael Waltrip MW Windows	6.00	2.70
14 Patty Moise Dial Purex	4.00	1.80
16 Ted Musgrave Family Channel	4.00	1.80
17 Darrell Waltrip Parts America	4.00	1.80
18 Bobby Labonte Interstate Batteries	4.00	1.80
19 Loy Allen Healthsource	15.00	6.75
21 Michael Waltrip Citgo	4.00	1.80

CAR / DRIVER / SPONSOR	MINT	NRMT
22 Ward Burton MBNA	15.00	6.75
23 Chad Little John Deere	6.00	2.70
23 Chad Little John Deere Promo	12.00	5.50
24 Jeff Gordon DuPont	30.00	13.50

CAR / DRIVER / SPONSOR	MINT	NRMT
28 Ernie Irvan Havoline	4.00	1.80
29 Steve Grissom Cartoon Network	10.00	4.50
29 Steve Grissom WCW	12.00	5.50
29 No Driver Association Scooby-Doo	8.00	3.60
29 No Driver Association WCW Sting	12.00	5.50
30 Johnny Benson Pennzoil	4.00	1.80

CAR / DRIVER / SPONSOR	MINT	NRMT
31 Mike Skinner Realtree	30.00	13.50
32 Dale Jarrett Band-Aid Promo	6.00	2.70
34 Mike McLaughlin Royal Oak	12.00	5.50
37 John Andretti K-Mart	4.00	1.80
38 Dennis Setzer Lipton Tea	4.00	1.80
40 Tim Fedewa Kleenex	4.00	1.80
40 Jim Sauter First Union	6.00	2.70
41 Ricky Craven Hedrick Motorsports	4.00	1.80
41 Ricky Craven Manheim	4.00	1.80
43 Rodney Combs Lance	4.00	1.80
43 Bobby Hamilton 25th Anniversary 5 car set	100.00	45.00
43 Bobby Hamilton 5-car 25th Anniversary	30.00	13.50
43 Bobby Hamilton 5-car 25th Anniversary Hood Open	50.00	22.00
43 Bobby Hamilton STP Anniversary 1972 Red and Blue paint scheme	8.00	3.60
43 Bobby Hamilton STP Anniversary 1972 Blue paint scheme	8.00	3.60

43 Bobby Hamilton 8.00 3.60
STP Anniversary 1979 Red and Blue paint scheme

CAR / DRIVER / SPONSOR	MINT	NRMT
43 Bobby Hamilton STP Anniversary 1984 Blue and Red paint scheme	8.00	3.60
43 Bobby Hamilton STP Anniversary 1996 Silver car	15.00	6.75
43 Bobby Hamilton STP Anniversary 1996 Silver car in Red and Blue Box	18.00	8.00
44 Bobby Labonte Shell	10.00	4.50
47 Jeff Fuller Sunoco	8.00	3.60
51 Jim Bown Lucks	4.00	1.80
57 Jim Bown Matco Tools	10.00	4.50
57 Jason Keller Halloween Havoc	4.00	1.80
57 Jason Keller Slim Jim	4.00	1.80
58 Mike Cope Penrose	4.00	1.80
60 Mark Martin Winn Dixie Promo	8.00	3.60
61 Mike Olsen Little Trees	6.00	2.70
63 Curtis Markham Lysol	4.00	1.80
74 Randy LaJoie Fina	4.00	1.80

CAR / DRIVER / SPONSOR	MINT	NRMT
75 Morgan Shepherd Remington	8.00	3.60
81 Kenny Wallace TIC Financial	15.00	6.75
87 Joe Nemechek Bell South	12.00	5.50
87 Joe Nemechek Burger King	25.00	11.00

CAR / DRIVER / SPONSOR	MINT	NRMT
88 Dale Jarrett Quality Care	10.00	4.50
90 Mike Wallace Duron	4.00	1.80
92 David Pearson Stanley Tools	4.00	1.80
94 Ron Barfield New Holland	4.00	1.80
94 Bill Elliott McDonald's	4.00	1.80
94 Bill Elliott McDonald's Monopoly	4.00	1.80
94 Bill Elliott 10-Time Most Popular Driver Silver car	70.00	32.00
94 Harry Gant McDonald's	6.00	2.70
96 David Green Busch	10.00	4.50
96 Stevie Reeves Clabber Girl	4.00	1.80
97 Chad Little Sterling Cowboy	12.00	5.50
99 Glenn Allen Luxaire	4.00	1.80
99 Jeff Burton Exide	4.00	1.80

1996 Racing Champions Hobby 1:64

These pieces were released through Hobby outlets. The car came in a different box than the mainstream series.

	MINT	NRMT
4 Sterling Marlin Kodak	6.00	2.70
6 Mark Martin Valvoline	6.00	2.70

	MINT	NRMT
18 Bobby Labonte Interstate Batteries	6.00	2.70
24 Jeff Gordon DuPont	6.00	2.70
47 Jeff Fuller Sunoco	6.00	2.70
81 Kenny Wallace Square D	6.00	2.70

1996 Racing Champions Premier with Medallion 1:64

These pieces are the same as the standard Racing Champions 1:64 1996 pieces with the exception of the packaging. Each car is packaged with a medallion instead of a card.

	MINT	NRMT
1 Rick Mast Hooters	12.00	5.50
1 Hermie Sadler DeWalt	8.00	3.60
2 Ricky Craven DuPont	8.00	3.60
2 Ricky Craven DuPont Hood Open	10.00	4.50

2 Rusty Wallace
   Miller Genuine Draft Hood Open
   In Miller Package
	12.00	5.50

	MINT	NRMT
3 Mike Skinner Goodwrench	8.00	3.60
4 Sterling Marlin Kodak	8.00	3.60

	MINT	NRMT
5 Terry Labonte Bayer Hood Open	10.00	4.50

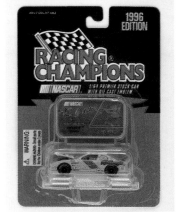

	MINT	NRMT
5 Terry Labonte Kellogg's Silver car Hood Open	10.00	4.50
6 Mark Martin Valvoline Dura Blend Hood Open	10.00	4.50
7 Geoff Bodine QVC	8.00	3.60

	MINT	NRMT
10 Ricky Rudd Tide Hood Open	10.00	4.50
11 Brett Bodine Lowe's	8.00	3.60
15 Wally Dallenbach Hayes Modems	20.00	9.00
16 Ted Musgrave Family Channel	8.00	3.60
18 Bobby Labonte Interstate Batteries	8.00	3.60

	MINT	NRMT
18 Bobby Labonte Interstate Batteries Hood Open	10.00	4.50

	MINT	NRMT
22 Ward Burton MBNA	8.00	3.60
23 Chad Little John Deere Hood Open	10.00	4.50

CAR / DRIVER / SPONSOR	MINT	NRMT
23 Chad Little	16.00	7.25
John Deere Hood Open Promo		
24 Jeff Gordon	12.00	5.50
DuPont		
24 Jeff Gordon	15.00	6.75
DuPont Hood Open		

24 Jeff Gordon	12.00	5.50
DuPont 1995 Champion		
25 Ken Schrader	12.00	5.50
Budweiser		
25 Ken Schrader	90.00	40.00
Budweiser Silver		
25 Ken Schrader	8.00	3.60
Hendrick		
28 Ernie Irvan	10.00	4.50
Havoline Hood Open		
29 Steve Grissom	10.00	4.50
Cartoon Network		
29 Steve Grissom	12.00	5.50
Cartoon Network Hood Open		
29 Steve Grissom	50.00	22.00
Cartoon Network 5-car set		
29 No Driver Association	8.00	3.60
Scooby-Doo		
29 No Driver Association	8.00	3.60
Shaggy		

30 Johnny Benson	8.00	3.60
Pennzoil		

CAR / DRIVER / SPONSOR	MINT	NRMT
31 Mike Skinner	35.00	16.00
Realtree		
34 Mike McLaughlin	8.00	3.60
Royal Oak		

37 John Andretti	8.00	3.60
K-Mart		
41 Ricky Craven	8.00	3.60
Hedrick		
43 Bobby Hamilton	12.00	5.50
STP Hood Open		
43 Bobby Hamilton	12.00	5.50
STP Silver Hood Open		
43 Bobby Hamilton	55.00	25.00
STP 5-car set		

44 Bobby Labonte	20.00	9.00
Shell		
52 Ken Schrader	8.00	3.60
AC Delco		

CAR / DRIVER / SPONSOR	MINT	NRMT
52 Ken Schrader	10.00	4.50
AC Delco Hood Open		
57 Chuck Bown	10.00	4.50
Matco		

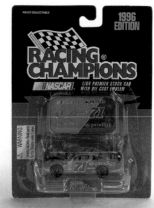

71 Dave Marcis	20.00	9.00
Prodigy		
74 Johnny Benson	8.00	3.60
Lipton Tea		
87 Joe Nemechek	18.00	8.00
Burger King		
88 Dale Jarrett	8.00	3.60
Quality Care		
92 Larry Pearson	8.00	3.60
Stanley Tools		
94 Bill Elliott	10.00	4.50
McDonald's Hood Open		
94 Bill Elliott	10.00	4.50
McDonald's Monopoly Hood Open		
96 David Green	10.00	4.50
Busch		
97 Chad Little	8.00	3.60
Sterling Cowboy		

1996 Racing Champions
Silver Chase 1:64

Each of these 1:64 scale Silver cars were done in a quantity of 1,996. These cars were randomly inserted in the cases that were shipped to retail outlets.

1 Rick Mast	50.00	22.00
Hooter's		
2 Rusty Wallace	80.00	36.00
Miller Genuine Draft		
4 Sterling Marlin	60.00	27.00
Kodak		
5 Terry Labonte	125.00	55.00
Kellogg's		
6 Mark Martin	80.00	36.00
Valvoline		
10 Ricky Rudd	50.00	22.00
Tide		
17 Darrell Waltrip	50.00	22.00
Parts America		
18 Bobby Labonte	80.00	36.00
Interstate Batteries		
24 Jeff Gordon	175.00	80.00
DuPont		
28 Ernie Irvan	75.00	34.00
Havoline		
88 Dale Jarrett	80.00	36.00
Quality Care		
94 Bill Elliott	80.00	36.00
McDonald's		

1996 Racing Champions SuperTrucks 1:64

Racing Champions continued their line of 1:24 SuperTrucks in 1996. This series features many of the circuit's first-time drivers.

		MINT	NRMT
2	Mike Bliss Team ASE	4.00	1.80
3	Mike Skinner Goodwrench	4.00	1.80
5	Darrell Waltrip Die Hard	4.00	1.80
6	Rick Carelli Chesrown	4.00	1.80
6	Rick Carelli Total	4.00	1.80
9	Joe Bessey New Hampshire Speedway	4.00	1.80
14	Butch Gilliland Stroppe	4.00	1.80
17	Bill Sedgwick Die Hard	4.00	1.80
17	Darrell Waltrip Western Auto	4.00	1.80
19	Lance Norick Macklanburg-Duncan	4.00	1.80
20	Walker Evans Dana	4.00	1.80
21	Doug George Ortho	4.00	1.80
24	Jack Sprague Quaker State	4.00	1.80
29	Bob Keselowski Winnebago	4.00	1.80
30	Jimmy Hensley Mopar	4.00	1.80
52	Ken Schrader AC Delco	4.00	1.80
57	Robbie Pyne Aisyn	4.00	1.80
75	Bobby Gill Spears	4.00	1.80
78	Mike Chase Petron Plus	4.00	1.80
80	Joe Ruttman J.R.Garage	4.00	1.80
83	Steve Portenga Coffee Critic	4.00	1.80
98	Butch Miller Raybestos	4.00	1.80

1997 Racing Champions Previews 1:64

This series of 1:64 die cast replicas featured a preview at some of the new paint jobs to run in the 1997 season. The Rick Mast Remington car and the Robert Pressley Scooby Doo car features two of the numerous driver changes for the 97 Winston Cup season.

		MINT	NRMT
4	Sterling Marlin Kodak	4.00	1.80
5	Terry Labonte Kellogg's	4.00	1.80
6	Mark Martin Valvoline	4.00	1.80
18	Bobby Labonte Interstate Batteries	4.00	1.80
21	Michael Waltrip Citgo	4.00	1.80
24	Jeff Gordon DuPont	4.00	1.80
28	Ernie Irvan Havoline	4.00	1.80

		MINT	NRMT
29	Robert Pressley Scooby-Doo	4.00	1.80
30	Johnny Benson Pennzoil	4.00	1.80
75	Rick Mast Remington	4.00	1.80
94	Bill Elliott McDonald's	4.00	1.80
99	Jeff Burton Exide	4.00	1.80

1997 Racing Champions Premier Preview with Medallion 1:64

This is the first time Racing Champions has issued a Premier Preview car. Each car comes with a medallion like the standard Premier cars.

		MINT	NRMT
4	Sterling Marlin Kodak	6.00	2.70
5	Terry Labonte Kellogg's	8.00	3.60
6	Mark Martin Valvoline	6.00	2.70

		MINT	NRMT
18	Bobby Labonte Interstate Batteries	6.00	2.70
24	Jeff Gordon DuPont	8.00	3.60
29	Robert Pressley Scooby-Doo	6.00	2.70
94	Bill Elliott McDonald's	6.00	2.70

1997 Racing Champions 1:64

The 1:64 scale cars that appear in this series are replicas of many of the cars that ran in the 1997 season. The series is highlighted by the Terry Labonte Kellogg's car commemorating his 1996 Winston Cup Championship. This car is available in two variations: standard and hood open.

		MINT	NRMT
1	Hermie Sadler DeWalt	4.00	1.80

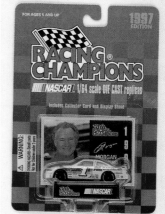

		MINT	NRMT
1	Morgan Shepherd R&L Carriers	4.00	1.80
2	Ricky Craven Raybestos	4.00	1.80
2	Rusty Wallace Miller Lite Matco	10.00	4.50
2	Rusty Wallace Penske Racing	4.00	1.80
4	Sterling Marlin Kodak	4.00	1.80
5	Terry Labonte Bayer	4.00	1.80
5	Terry Labonte Kellogg's 1996 Champion	8.00	3.60
5	Terry Labonte Kellogg's 2-car set	20.00	9.00

		MINT	NRMT
5	Terry Labonte Tony the Tiger	6.00	2.70
6	Joe Bessey Power Team	4.00	1.80
6	Mark Martin Valvoline	4.00	1.80
7	Geoff Bodine QVC	4.00	1.80

CAR / DRIVER / SPONSOR	MINT	NRMT
24 Jeff Gordon	8.00	3.60
DuPont		

CAR / DRIVER / SPONSOR	MINT	NRMT
7 Geoff Bodine	8.00	3.60
QVC Gold Rush		
8 Hut Stricklin	4.00	1.80
Circuit City		
9 Joe Bessey	4.00	1.80
Power Team		
9 Jeff Burton	4.00	1.80
Track Gear		
10 Phil Parsons	4.00	1.80
Channellock		
10 Ricky Rudd	4.00	1.80
Tide		
11 Brett Bodine	4.00	1.80
Close Call		
11 Jimmy Foster	4.00	1.80
Speedvision		
16 Ted Musgrave	4.00	1.80
Primestar		
17 Darrell Waltrip	8.00	3.60
Parts America Chrome		

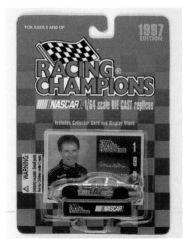

CAR / DRIVER / SPONSOR	MINT	NRMT
17 Darrell Waltrip	4.00	1.80
Parts America		
18 Bobby Labonte	4.00	1.80
Interstate Batteries		
19 Gary Bradberry	4.00	1.80
CSR		
21 Michael Waltrip	4.00	1.80
Citgo		

CAR / DRIVER / SPONSOR	MINT	NRMT
25 Ricky Craven	12.00	5.50
Bud Lizard		
25 Ricky Craven	4.00	1.80
Hendrick		
28 Ernie Irvan	4.00	1.80
Havoline		
28 Ernie Irvan	5.00	2.20
Havoline 10th Anniversary		
29 Robert Pressley	4.00	1.80
Cartoon Network		
29 Jeff Green	4.00	1.80
Tom and Jerry		
29 Elliott Sadler	4.00	1.80
Phillips 66		
30 Johnny Benson	4.00	1.80
Pennzoil		
32 Dale Jarrett	4.00	1.80
White Rain		
33 Ken Schrader	4.00	1.80
Petree Racing		
34 Mike McLaughlin	4.00	1.80
Royal Oak		
36 Todd Bodine	4.00	1.80
Stanley Tools		
36 Derrike Cope	4.00	1.80
Skittles		
37 Jeremy Mayfield	4.00	1.80
K-Mart		
38 Elton Sawyer	4.00	1.80
Barbasol		
40 Tim Fedewa	4.00	1.80
Kleenex		
40 Robby Gordon	4.00	1.80
Sabco Racing		

CAR / DRIVER / SPONSOR	MINT	NRMT
41 Steve Grissom	4.00	1.80
Hedrick		
42 Joe Nemechek	4.00	1.80
Bell South		
43 Rodney Combs	4.00	1.80
Lance		
43 Dennis Setzer	4.00	1.80
Lance		
46 Wally Dallenbach	4.00	1.80
First Union		
47 Jeff Fuller	4.00	1.80
Sunoco		
49 Kyle Petty	8.00	3.60
nWo		
57 Jason Keller	4.00	1.80
Slim Jim		
60 Mark Martin	8.00	3.60
Winn Dixie		
72 Mike Dillon	4.00	1.80
Detriot Gasket		
74 Randy LaJoie	4.00	1.80
Fina		
74 Randy Lajoie	8.00	3.60
Fina Promo		
75 Rick Mast	4.00	1.80
Remington		
75 Rick Mast	4.00	1.80
Remington Camo		
75 Rick Mast	4.00	1.80
Remington Stren		
88 Kevin LePage	4.00	1.80
Hype		
90 Dick Trickle	4.00	1.80
Heilig-Meyers		
91 Mike Wallace	4.00	1.80
Spam		
94 Ron Barfield	4.00	1.80
New Holland		
94 Bill Elliott	4.00	1.80
McDonald's		
94 Bill Elliott	4.00	1.80
Mac Tonight		
96 David Green	4.00	1.80
Caterpillar		
96 David Green	8.00	3.60
Caterpillar Promo		
97 No Driver Association	6.00	2.70
Brickyard 500		
97 No Driver Association	18.00	8.00
www.racingchamps.com		
97 Chad Little	4.00	1.80
John Deere		
97 Chad Little	8.00	3.60
John Deere Promo		
98 No Driver Association	6.00	2.70
EA Sports		
99 Glenn Allen	4.00	1.80
Luxaire		
99 Jeff Burton	4.00	1.80
Exide		
00 Buckshot Jones	6.00	2.70
Aqua-Fresh		

1997 Racing Champions Gold 1:64

These 1:64 scale cars were distributed through hobby outlets.

CAR / DRIVER / SPONSOR	MINT	NRMT
2 Rusty Wallace	100.00	45.00
Miller Lite		
6 Mark Martin	100.00	45.00
Valvoline		
10 Ricky Rudd	80.00	36.00
Tide		
18 Bobby Labonte	80.00	36.00
Interstate Batteries		
36 Derrike Cope	80.00	36.00
Skittles		

CAR / DRIVER / SPONSOR	MINT	NRMT
75 Rick Mast Remington	80.00	36.00
94 Bill Elliott McDonald's	100.00	45.00

1997 Racing Champions Hobby 1:64

These 1:64 scale cars were distributed through hobby outlets.

CAR / DRIVER / SPONSOR	MINT	NRMT
2 Rusty Wallace Miller Lite	8.00	3.60
6 Mark Martin Valvoline	8.00	3.60
10 Ricky Rudd Tide	8.00	3.60
18 Bobby Labonte Interstate Batteries	8.00	3.60
36 Derrike Cope Skittles	8.00	3.60
75 Rick Mast Remington	8.00	3.60
94 Bill Elliott McDonald's	8.00	3.60

1997 Racing Champions Pinnacle Series 1:64

This marks the second time Racing Champions have teamed up with a card manufacturer to product a line of diecast cars with trading cards. Each car is boxed in similar packaging as the standard cars, but Pinnacle cards are featured in place of Racing Champions generic cards.

CAR / DRIVER / SPONSOR	MINT	NRMT
4 Sterling Marlin Kodak	8.00	3.60
5 Terry Labonte Kellogg's	10.00	4.50
6 Mark Martin Valvoline	8.00	3.60
7 Geoff Bodine QVC	8.00	3.60
8 Hut Stricklin Circuit City	8.00	3.60
10 Ricky Rudd Tide	8.00	3.60
16 Ted Musgrave Primestar	8.00	3.60
18 Bobby Labonte Interstate Batteries	8.00	3.60
21 Michael Waltrip Citgo	8.00	3.60
28 Ernie Irvan Havoline	8.00	3.60
29 Robert Pressley Cartoon Network	8.00	3.60
30 Johnny Benson Pennzoil	8.00	3.60
36 Derrike Cope Skittles	8.00	3.60
37 Jeremy Mayfield K-Mart	8.00	3.60
75 Rick Mast Remington	8.00	3.60
87 Joe Nemechek BellSouth	8.00	3.60
94 Bill Elliott McDonald's	8.00	3.60
96 David Green Caterpillar	8.00	3.60
97 Chad Little John Deere	8.00	3.60
99 Jeff Burton Exide	8.00	3.60

1997 Racing Champions Premier with Medallion

These pieces are the same as the standard Racing Champions 1:64 1997 pieces with the exception of the packaging. Each car is packaged with a medallion instead of a card. The Lake Speed/University of Nebraska car highlights this series.

CAR / DRIVER / SPONSOR	MINT	NRMT
1 Morgan Shepherd Crusin' America	8.00	3.60
2 Rusty Wallace Penske	8.00	3.60
5 Terry Labonte Tony the Tiger	10.00	4.50
6 Mark Martin Valvoline	8.00	3.60
7 Geoff Bodine QVC	8.00	3.60
8 Hut Stricklin Circuit City	8.00	3.60

CAR / DRIVER / SPONSOR	MINT	NRMT
9 Lake Speed University of Nebraska	30.00	13.50
10 Ricky Rudd Tide	8.00	3.60
11 Brett Bodine Close Call	8.00	3.60
16 Ted Musgrave Primestar	8.00	3.60
17 Darrell Waltrip Parts America	8.00	3.60

CAR / DRIVER / SPONSOR	MINT	NRMT
17 Darrell Waltrip Parts America Chrome	10.00	4.50
18 Bobby Labonte Interstate Batteries	8.00	3.60

CAR / DRIVER / SPONSOR	MINT	NRMT
21 Michael Waltrip Citgo	8.00	3.60
28 Ernie Irvan Havoline	8.00	3.60
28 Ernie Irvan Havoline 10th Anniversary	10.00	4.50
29 Robert Pressley Scooby-Doo	8.00	3.60

CAR / DRIVER / SPONSOR	MINT	NRMT
29 No Driver Assocation Tom and Jerry	8.00	3.60
30 Johnny Benson Pennzoil	8.00	3.60
36 Derrike Cope Skittles	8.00	3.60
37 Jeremy Mayfield Kmart	8.00	3.60
75 Rick Mast Remington	8.00	3.60
75 Rick Mast Remington Camo	8.00	3.60
75 Rick Mast Remington Stren	8.00	3.60

CAR / DRIVER / SPONSOR	MINT	NRMT
94 Bill Elliott Mac Tonight	8.00	3.60
96 David Green Caterpillar	8.00	3.60
96 David Green Caterpillar Promo	12.00	5.50
97 Chad Little John Deere	8.00	3.60

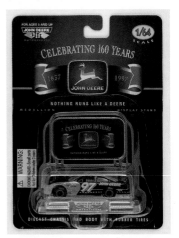

CAR / DRIVER / SPONSOR	MINT	NRMT
97 Chad Little	12.00	5.50
John Deere Promo		
99 Jeff Burton	8.00	3.60
Exide		

1997 Racing Champions Premier with Medallion Silver Chase 1:64

These 1:64 scale Silver Chase cars were limited in production to 997 of each car.

CAR / DRIVER / SPONSOR	MINT	NRMT
5 Terry Labonte	150.00	70.00
Kellogg's		
7 Geoff Bodine	75.00	34.00
QVC		
10 Ricky Rudd	75.00	34.00
Tide		
16 Ted Musgrave	75.00	34.00
Primestar		
18 Bobby Labonte	90.00	40.00
Interstate Batteries		
28 Ernie Irvan	90.00	40.00
Havoline		

1997 Racing Champions Silver Chase 1:64

Each of these 1:64 scale Silver cars were done in a quantity of 1,997. These cars were randomly inserted in the cases that were shipped to retail outlets.

CAR / DRIVER / SPONSOR	MINT	NRMT
5 Terry Labonte	125.00	55.00
Kellogg's 1996 Champion		
7 Geoff Bodine	50.00	22.00
QVC		
16 Ted Musgrave	50.00	22.00
Primestar		
21 Michael Waltrip	50.00	22.00
Citgo		
30 Johnny Benson	50.00	22.00
Pennzoil		
36 Derrike Cope	50.00	22.00
Skittles		
40 Robby Gordon	50.00	22.00
Sabco Racing		
42 Joe Nemechek	50.00	22.00
Bell South		
46 Wally Dallenbach	50.00	22.00
First Union		
75 Rick Mast	50.00	22.00
Remington		
96 David Green	50.00	22.00
Caterpillar		

CAR / DRIVER / SPONSOR	MINT	NRMT
97 Chad Little	50.00	22.00
John Deere		
99 Jeff Burton	60.00	27.00
Exide		

1997 Racing Champions Stock Rods 1:64

These 1:64 scale cars are replicas of vintage stock rods with NASCAR paint schemes. Cars are listed by issue number instead of car number.

CAR / DRIVER / SPONSOR	MINT	NRMT
1 Terry Labonte	15.00	6.75
Kellogg's		

CAR / DRIVER / SPONSOR	MINT	NRMT
2 Bill Elliott	12.00	5.50
McDonald's		
3 Mark Martin	12.00	5.50
Valvoline		
4 Robert Pressley	8.00	3.60
Scooby-Doo		
5 Ted Musgrave	8.00	3.60
Primestar		
6 Jeff Burton	8.00	3.60
Exide		
7 Bobby Labonte	8.00	3.60
Interstate Batteries		
8 Ricky Craven	8.00	3.60
Hendrick		
9 Darrell Waltrip	8.00	3.60
Parts America		
10 Rusty Wallace	100.00	45.00
Miller Lite		
11 Derrike Cope	6.00	2.70
Skittles		
12 Ricky Rudd	6.00	2.70
Tide		

CAR / DRIVER / SPONSOR	MINT	NRMT
13 Rick Mast	6.00	2.70
Remington		
14 Ricky Craven	6.00	2.70
Hendrick		
15 Jeff Green	6.00	2.70
Tom & Jerry		
16 Bill Elliott	8.00	3.60
Mac Tonight		
17 Mark Martin	8.00	3.60
Valvoline		
18 Rusty Wallace	8.00	3.60
Penske		
19 Ted Musgrave	6.00	2.70
Primestar		
20 Jeff Burton	6.00	2.70
Exide		
21 Darrell Waltrip	6.00	2.70
Parts America		
22 Ricky Rudd	6.00	2.70
Tide		
23 Rick Mast	6.00	2.70
Remington		
24 Steve Grissom	6.00	2.70
Hedrick		
25 Bill Elliott	8.00	3.60
Mac Tonight		
26 Glen Allen	6.00	2.70
Luxaire		
27 Dennis Setzer	6.00	2.70
Lance		
28 Bill Elliott	8.00	3.60
McDonald's		
29 Ricky Craven	6.00	2.70
Hendrick		
30 Sterling Marlin	6.00	2.70
Sabco		
31 Jeff Green	6.00	2.70
Cartoon Network		
32 Joe Nemechek	6.00	2.70
Bell South		
33 Ernie Irvan	6.00	2.70
Havoline		
34 Ricky Rudd	6.00	2.70
Tide		
35 Rusty Wallace	8.00	3.60
Penske		
36 Ernie Irvan	6.00	2.70
Havoline		
37 Mark Martin	8.00	3.60
Valvoline		
38 Terry Labonte	10.00	4.50
Spooky Loops		
39 Terry Labonte	10.00	4.50
Spooky Loops		
40 Derrike Cope	6.00	2.70
Skittles		
41 Steve Grissom	6.00	2.70
Hedrick		
42 Terry Labonte	50.00	22.00
Spooky Loops Chrome		
43 Terry Labonte	15.00	6.75
Spooky Loops		
44 Jeff Burton	6.00	2.70
Exide		
45 Bill Elliott	8.00	3.60
McDonald's		
46 Ted Musgrave	6.00	2.70
Primestar		
47 Mark Martin	8.00	3.60
Valvoline		
48 Ricky Rudd	6.00	2.70
Tide		
49 Glen Allen	6.00	2.70
Luxaire		
50 Terry Labonte	8.00	3.60
Spooky Loops		
51 Joe Bessey	6.00	2.70
Power Team		
52 Terry Labonte	8.00	3.60
Kellogg's		

CAR / DRIVER / SPONSOR	MINT	NRMT
53 Wally Dallenbach First Union	6.00	2.70
54 Ricky Craven Hendrick	6.00	2.70
55 Ricky Craven Hendrick	6.00	2.70

1997 Racing Champions SuperTrucks 1:64

Racing Champions continued their line of 1:64 SuperTrucks in 1997. This series features many of the circuit's first-time drivers and Winston Cup regulars.

CAR / DRIVER / SPONSOR	MINT	NRMT
1 Michael Waltrip MW Windows	4.00	1.80
2 Mike Bliss Team ASE	4.00	1.80
4 Bill Elliott Team ASE	4.00	1.80
6 Rick Carelli Remax	4.00	1.80
7 Tammy Kirk Loveable	4.00	1.80
13 Mike Colabucci Visa	4.00	1.80
15 Mike Cope Penrose	4.00	1.80
15 Mike Colabacci VISA	4.00	1.80
18 Johnny Benson Pennzoil	4.00	1.80
18 Mike Dokken Dana	4.00	1.80
19 Tony Raines Pennzoil	4.00	1.80
20 Butch Miller The Orleans	4.00	1.80
23 T.J. Clark CRG Motorsports	4.00	1.80

CAR / DRIVER / SPONSOR	MINT	NRMT
24 Jack Sprague Quaker State	4.00	1.80
29 Bob Keselowski Mopar	4.00	1.80
35 Dave Rezendes Ortho	4.00	1.80
44 Boris Said Federated Auto	4.00	1.80
49 Rodney Combs Lance	4.00	1.80
52 Tobey Butler Purolator	4.00	1.80
66 Bryan Refner Carlin	4.00	1.80
75 Dan Press Spears	4.00	1.80

CAR / DRIVER / SPONSOR	MINT	NRMT
80 Joe Ruttman LCI	4.00	1.80
86 Stacy Compton Valvoline	4.00	1.80
87 Joe Nemechek Bell South	4.00	1.80
92 Mark Kinser Rotary	4.00	1.80
94 Ron Barfield Super 8	4.00	1.80
99 Chuck Bown Exide	4.00	1.80
99 Jeff Burton Exide	4.00	1.80
99 Mark Martin Exide	4.00	1.80

1998 Racing Champions 1:64

The 1:64 scale cars that appear in this series are replicas of many of the cars that ran in the 1997 season, but also many replicas are of the cars slated to appear in the 1998 season. The cars in this series are packaged in special blister packs that display the NASCAR 50th anniversary logo.

CAR / DRIVER / SPONSOR	MINT	NRMT
4 Bobby Hamilton Kodak	4.00	1.80
4 Jeff Purvis Lance	4.00	1.80
5 Terry Labonte Kellogg's	5.00	2.20
5 Terry Labonte Kellogg's Corny	5.00	2.20
6 Joe Bessey Power Team	4.00	1.80
6 Mark Martin Eagle One	4.00	1.80

CAR / DRIVER / SPONSOR	MINT	NRMT
6 Mark Martin Kosei	30.00	13.50
6 Mark Martin Valvoline	4.00	1.80

CAR / DRIVER / SPONSOR	MINT	NRMT
8 Hut Stricklin Circuit City 4th of July	4.00	1.80
9 Lake Speed Birthday Cake	4.00	1.80
9 Jeff Burton Track Gear	4.00	1.80
10 Ricky Rudd Tide	4.00	1.80
11 Brett Bodine Paychex	4.00	1.80
12 Jeremy Mayfield Mobil One	4.00	1.80

CAR / DRIVER / SPONSOR	MINT	NRMT
13 Jerry Nadeau First Plus	4.00	1.80

CAR / DRIVER / SPONSOR	MINT	NRMT
16 Ted Musgrave Primestar	4.00	1.80

CAR / DRIVER / SPONSOR	MINT	NRMT
17 Matt Kenseth Lycos	12.00	5.50

CAR / DRIVER / SPONSOR	MINT	NRMT
17 Darrell Waltrip Speedblock	6.00	2.70

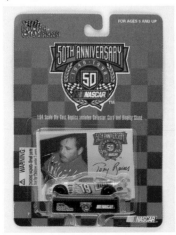

CAR / DRIVER / SPONSOR	MINT	NRMT
19 Tony Raines Yellow	4.00	1.80
20 Blaise Alexander Rescue Engine	4.00	1.80
21 Michael Waltrip Citgo	4.00	1.80
21 Michael Waltrip Goodwill Games	4.00	1.80

CAR / DRIVER / SPONSOR	MINT	NRMT
23 Lance Hooper WCW	4.00	1.80
23 Jimmy Spencer No Bull	30.00	13.50
23 Jimmy Spencer No Bull Gold	50.00	22.00
26 Johnny Benson Betty Crocker	50.00	22.00

CAR / DRIVER / SPONSOR	MINT	NRMT
26 Johnny Benson Lucky Charms	8.00	3.60
26 Johnny Benson Cheerios	4.00	1.80
29 Hermie Sadler Dewalt	4.00	1.80
30 Derrike Cope Gumout	4.00	1.80
30 Mike Cope Slim Jim	4.00	1.80
33 Tim Fedewa Kleenex	4.00	1.80
33 Ken Schrader Petree	4.00	1.80

CAR / DRIVER / SPONSOR	MINT	NRMT
35 Todd Bodine Tabasco Orange	4.00	1.80
36 Matt Hutter Stanley	4.00	1.80
36 Ernie Irvan Skittles	4.00	1.80
40 Kevin Lepage Chanellock	4.00	1.80
40 Sterling Marlin Coors Light	25.00	11.00
40 Sterling Marlin Coors Light Gold	40.00	18.00
40 Sterling Marlin Sabco	4.00	1.80

CAR / DRIVER / SPONSOR	MINT	NRMT
41 Steve Grissom Hedrick	4.00	1.80
42 Joe Nemechek BellSouth	4.00	1.80
46 Wally Dallenbach First Union	4.00	1.80
50 Ricky Craven Hendrick	4.00	1.80
59 Robert Pressley Kingsford	4.00	1.80
60 Mark Martin Winn Dixie	4.00	1.80
60 Mark Martin Winn Dixie Promo	8.00	3.60
64 Dick Trickle Scheinder	4.00	1.80
66 Elliot Sadler Phillips 66	4.00	1.80
74 Randy Lajoie Fina	4.00	1.80

CAR / DRIVER / SPONSOR	MINT	NRMT
75 Rick Mast Remington	4.00	1.80
78 Gary Bradberry Pilot	4.00	1.80
90 Dick Trickle Helig Meyers	4.00	1.80
94 Bill Elliott McDonald's	4.00	1.80
96 David Green Caterpiller	4.00	1.80
97 Chad Little John Deere Promo	8.00	3.60
99 Glen Allen Luxaire	4.00	1.80
99 Jeff Burton Exide	4.00	1.80

CAR / DRIVER / SPONSOR	MINT	NRMT
300 Darrell Waltrip Flock Special	6.00	2.70

CAR / DRIVER / SPONSOR	MINT	NRMT
00 Buckshot Jones / Aquafresh	4.00	1.80
00 Buckshot Jones / Aqua Fresh	4.00	1.80

1998 Racing Champions Chrome Chase 1:64

Each of these 1:64 scale Chrome cars were done in a quantity of 5,050 for Winston Cup cars and 1,000 for Busch cars. These cars were randomly inserted in the cases that were shipped to retail outlets.

CAR / DRIVER / SPONSOR	MINT	NRMT
5 Terry Labonte / Kellogg's	75.00	34.00
5 Terry Labonte / Kellogg's Corny	75.00	34.00
6 Mark Martin / Eagle One	75.00	34.00
6 Mark Martin / Valvoline	75.00	34.00
8 Hut Stricklin / Circuit City	40.00	18.00
9 Jeff Burton / Track Gear	50.00	22.00
10 Ricky Rudd / Tide	50.00	22.00
16 Ted Musgrave / Primestar	40.00	18.00
20 Blaise Alexander / Rescue Engine	40.00	18.00
23 Lance Hooper / WCW	40.00	18.00
26 Johnny Benson / Cheerios	50.00	22.00
33 Tim Fedewa / Kleenex	40.00	18.00
34 Mike McLaughlin / Goulds	40.00	18.00
35 Todd Bodine / Tabasco	40.00	18.00
36 Matt Hutter / Stanley	40.00	18.00
36 Ernie Irvan / Skittles	50.00	22.00
38 Elton Sawyer / Barbasol	40.00	18.00
40 Kevin Lepage / Channellock	40.00	18.00
60 Mark Martin / Winn Dixie	75.00	34.00
64 Dick Trickle / Schneider	40.00	18.00
74 Randy Lajoie / Fina	40.00	18.00
94 Bill Elliott / McDonald's	75.00	34.00
99 Jeff Burton / Exide	50.00	22.00
00 Buckshot Jones / Alka Seltzer	40.00	18.00

1998 Racing Champions Gold with Medallion 1:64

This is a special series produced by Racing Champions to celebrate NASCAR's 50th anniversary. It parallels the regular 1998 1:64 scale series. Each car is a limited edition of 5,000. Each car is also plated in gold chrome and contains a serial number on its chassis. This series is packaged with medallion sponsor emblems in blister packs.

CAR / DRIVER / SPONSOR	MINT	NRMT
2 Ron Barfield / New Holland	15.00	6.75
4 Bobby Hamilton / Kodak	20.00	9.00
4 Jeff Purvis / Lance	15.00	6.75
5 Terry Labonte / Blasted Fruit Loops	40.00	18.00
5 Terry Labonte / Kellogg's	40.00	18.00
5 Terry Labonte / Kellogg's Corny	40.00	18.00
6 Joe Bessey / Power Team	15.00	6.75
6 Mark Martin / Eagle One	40.00	18.00
6 Mark Martin / Syntec	40.00	18.00
6 Mark Martin / Valvoline	40.00	18.00
8 Hut Stricklin / Circuit City	15.00	6.75
9 Jeff Burton / Track Gear	20.00	9.00
9 Jerry Nadeau / Zombie Island	20.00	9.00
9 Lake Speed / Birthday Cake	20.00	9.00
9 Lake Speed / Huckleberry Hound	20.00	9.00
10 Phil Parsons / Duralube	15.00	6.75
10 Ricky Rudd / Tide	20.00	9.00
11 Brett Bodine / Paychex	20.00	9.00
13 Jerry Nadeu / First Plus	25.00	11.00

CAR / DRIVER / SPONSOR	MINT	NRMT
14 Patty Moise / Rhodes	15.00	6.75
16 Ted Musgrave / Primestar	15.00	6.75
17 Matt Kenseth / Lycos.com	50.00	22.00
19 Tony Raines / Yellow	15.00	6.75
20 Blaise Alexander / Rescue Engine	15.00	6.75
21 Michael Waltrip / Citgo	15.00	6.75
23 Lance Hooper / WCW	15.00	6.75
26 Johnny Benson / Cheerios	25.00	11.00
29 Hermie Sadler / Dewalt	15.00	6.75
30 Mike Cope / Slim Jim	15.00	6.75
30 Derrike Cope / Gumout	15.00	6.75
33 Ken Schrader / Petree	15.00	6.75
33 Tim Fedewa / Kleenex	15.00	6.75
34 Mike McLaughlin / Goulds	15.00	6.75
35 Todd Bodine / Tabasco	20.00	9.00
36 Matt Hutter / Stanley	15.00	6.75
36 Ernie Irvan / M&M's	30.00	13.50
36 Ernie Irvan / Skittles	20.00	9.00
36 Ernie Irvan / Wildberry Skittles	25.00	11.00
38 Elton Sawyer / Barbasol	15.00	6.75
40 Rick Fuller / Channellock	15.00	6.75
40 Kevin Lepage / Channellock	15.00	6.75
40 Sterling Marlin / Sabco	20.00	9.00
41 Steve Grissom / Hedrick	20.00	9.00
42 Joe Nemechek / BellSouth	15.00	6.75
46 Wally Dallenbach / First Union	15.00	6.75
50 Ricky Craven / Hendrick	25.00	11.00
50 NDA / Dr.Pepper	15.00	6.75
59 Robert Pressley / Kingsford	15.00	6.75
60 Mark Martin / Winn Dixie	40.00	18.00
63 Tracy Leslie / Lysol	15.00	6.75
64 Dick Trickle / Schneider	15.00	6.75
66 Elliot Sadler / Phillips 66	20.00	9.00
72 Mike Dillon / Detroit Gasket	15.00	6.75
74 Randy Lajoie / Fina	15.00	6.75
75 Rick Mast / Remington	15.00	6.75
78 Gary Bradberry / Pilot	15.00	6.75
87 Joe Nemechek / BellSouth	15.00	6.75
88 Kevin Schwantz / Ryder	15.00	6.75
90 Dick Trickle / Heilig-Meyers	20.00	9.00
94 Bill Elliott / Happy Meal	40.00	18.00

CAR / DRIVER / SPONSOR	MINT	NRMT
94 Bill Elliott McDonald's	40.00	18.00
96 David Green Caterpillar	15.00	6.75
97 Chad Little John Deere Promo	75.00	34.00

CAR / DRIVER / SPONSOR	MINT	NRMT
98 Greg Sacks Thorn Apple Valley	20.00	9.00
99 Glen Allen Luxaire	15.00	6.75
99 Jeff Burton Exide	20.00	9.00
300 Darrell Waltrip Flock Special	25.00	11.00
00 Buckshot Jones Alka Seltzer	20.00	9.00
00 Buckshot Jones Aqua Fresh	20.00	9.00

1998 Racing Champions Pinnacle Series 1:64

This marks the second year Racing Champions have teamed up with Pinnacle to produce a line of diecast car with trading cards. Each car is boxed in similar packaging as the standard cars, but Pinnacle cards are featured in place of Racing Champions generic cards.

CAR / DRIVER / SPONSOR	MINT	NRMT
4 Bobby Hamilton Kodak	6.00	2.70

CAR / DRIVER / SPONSOR	MINT	NRMT
5 Terry Labonte Kellogg's	6.00	2.70
6 Mark Martin Valvoline	6.00	2.70
8 Hut Stricklin Circuit City	6.00	2.70
9 Jeff Burton Track Gear	6.00	2.70
10 Ricky Rudd Tide	6.00	2.70
21 Michael Waltrip Citgo	6.00	2.70
33 Tim Fedewa Kleenex	6.00	2.70
33 Ken Schrader Petree Racing	6.00	2.70

CAR / DRIVER / SPONSOR	MINT	NRMT
35 Todd Bodine Tabasco	6.00	2.70
36 Ernie Irvan Skittles	6.00	2.70
40 Sterling Marlin Sabco Racing	6.00	2.70
42 Joe Nemechek Bell South	6.00	2.70
46 Wally Dallenbach First Union	6.00	2.70
50 Ricky Craven Hendrick	6.00	2.70
74 Randy Lajoie Fina	6.00	2.70
75 Rick Mast Remington	6.00	2.70
90 Dick Trickle Helig Meyers	6.00	2.70
94 Bill Elliott McDonald's	6.00	2.70
96 David Green Caterpiller	6.00	2.70

1998 Racing Champions Press Pass Series 1:64

This series is a continuation of the Pinnacle series that was stopped when Press Pass was purchased by Racing Champions. Each car is boxed in similar packaging as the standard cars, but Press Pass cards are featured in place of Racing Champions generic cards.

CAR / DRIVER / SPONSOR	MINT	NRMT
4 Bobby Hamilton Kodak	6.00	2.70

CAR / DRIVER / SPONSOR	MINT	NRMT
5 Terry Labonte Kellogg's	6.00	2.70
6 Mark Martin Eagle One	6.00	2.70
6 Mark Martin Valvoline	6.00	2.70
9 Jeff Burton Track Gear	6.00	2.70
10 Ricky Rudd Tide	6.00	2.70
11 Brett Bodine Paychex	6.00	2.70
13 Jerry Nadeau First Plus	6.00	2.70
16 Ted Musgrave Primestar	6.00	2.70

CAR / DRIVER / SPONSOR	MINT	NRMT
17 Darrell Waltrip Builders Square	6.00	2.70

CAR / DRIVER / SPONSOR	MINT	NRMT
21 Michael Waltrip Goodwill Games	6.00	2.70
26 Johnny Benson Cheerios	6.00	2.70
30 Derrike Cope Gumout	6.00	2.70
33 Tim Fedewa Kleenex	6.00	2.70
33 Ken Schrader Petree	6.00	2.70
35 Todd Bodine Tabasco	6.00	2.70
36 Ernie Irvan M&M's	6.00	2.70
40 Sterling Marlin Sabco	6.00	2.70
41 Steve Grissom Hedrick	6.00	2.70
42 Joe Nemechek Bell South	6.00	2.70
50 Ricky Craven Hendrick	6.00	2.70

CAR / DRIVER / SPONSOR	MINT	NRMT
59 Robert Pressley Kingsford	6.00	2.70
60 Mark Martin Winn Dixie	6.00	2.70
66 Elliott Sadler Phillips 66	6.00	2.70
75 Rick Mast Remington	6.00	2.70
90 Dick Trickle Heilig-Meyers	6.00	2.70
94 Bill Elliott McDonald's	6.00	2.70

CAR / DRIVER / SPONSOR	MINT	NRMT
94 Bill Elliott Happy Meal	6.00	2.70
96 David Green Caterpillar	6.00	2.70
97 Chad Little John Deere	6.00	2.70
98 Greg Sacks Thorn Apple Valley	6.00	2.70
99 Jeff Burton Exide	6.00	2.70
00 Buckshot Jones Aqua Fresh	6.00	2.70

1998 Racing Champions Reflections of Gold 1:64

This is a special series produced by Racing Champions to celebrate NASCAR's 50th anniversary. It parallels the regular 1998 1:64 scale series. Each car is a limited edition of 9,998. Each car is also plated in gold chrome and contains a serial number on its chassis.

CAR / DRIVER / SPONSOR	MINT	NRMT
4 Bobby Hamilton Kodak	15.00	6.75
4 Jeff Purvis Lance	15.00	6.75
5 Terry Labonte Kellogg's	30.00	13.50
6 Joe Bessey Power Team	15.00	6.75
6 Mark Martin Valvoline	30.00	13.50
8 Hut Stricklin Circuit City	15.00	6.75
9 Jeff Burton Track Gear	20.00	9.00
9 Lake Speed Huckleberry Hound	15.00	6.75
10 Phil Parsons Duralube	15.00	6.75

CAR / DRIVER / SPONSOR	MINT	NRMT
10 Ricky Rudd Tide	20.00	9.00
11 Brett Bodine Paychex	15.00	6.75
13 Jerry Nadeau First Plus	20.00	9.00
16 Ted Musgrave Primestar	15.00	6.75
20 Blaise Alexander Rescue	15.00	6.75
21 Michael Waltrip Citgo	15.00	6.75
26 Johnny Benson Cheerios	20.00	9.00
29 Hermie Sadler Dewalt	15.00	6.75
30 Derrike Cope Gumout	15.00	6.75
30 Mike Cope Slim Jim	15.00	6.75
33 Tim Fedewa Kleenex	15.00	6.75
33 Ken Schrader Petree	15.00	6.75
34 Mike McLaughlin Goulds	15.00	6.75
35 Todd Bodine Tabasco	20.00	9.00
36 Ernie Irvan Skittles	20.00	9.00
38 Elton Sawyer Barbasol	15.00	6.75
40 Sterling Marlin Sabco	15.00	6.75
41 Steve Grissom Hedrick	15.00	6.75
42 Joe Nemechek Bell South	15.00	6.75
46 Wally Dallenbach First Union	15.00	6.75
47 Andy Santerre Monroe	15.00	6.75
50 Ricky Craven Hendrick	15.00	6.75
59 Robert Pressley Kingsford	15.00	6.75
60 Mark Martin Winn Dixie	30.00	13.50
63 Tracy Leslie Lysol	15.00	6.75
75 Rick Mast Remington	15.00	6.75
77 Robert Pressley Jasper	15.00	6.75
90 Dick Trickle Heilig-Meyers	15.00	6.75
94 Bill Elliott McDonald's	30.00	13.50
98 Greg Sacks Thorn Apple Valley	20.00	9.00
99 Glen Allen Luxaire	15.00	6.75
99 Jeff Burton Exide	20.00	9.00
00 Buckshot Jones Aqua Fresh	15.00	6.75

1998 Racing Champions Signature Series 1:64

This is a special series produced by Racing Champions to celebrate NASCAR's 50th anniversary. It parallels the regular 1998 1:64 scale series. Each car is packaged in a decorative box with the driver's facsimile autograph on the front.

CAR / DRIVER / SPONSOR	MINT	NRMT
4 Bobby Hamilton Kodak	6.00	2.70

CAR / DRIVER / SPONSOR	MINT	NRMT
5 Terry Labonte Kellogg's	6.00	2.70
6 Mark Martin Valvoline	6.00	2.70
8 Hut Stricklin Circuit City	6.00	2.70
9 Jeff Burton Track Gear	6.00	2.70
9 Lake Speed Hucklerberry Hound	6.00	2.70

CAR / DRIVER / SPONSOR	MINT	NRMT
10 Ricky Rudd Tide	6.00	2.70
11 Brett Bodine Paychex	6.00	2.70
13 Jerry Nadeau First Plus	6.00	2.70
21 Michael Waltrip Citgo	6.00	2.70
26 Johnny Benson Cheerios	6.00	2.70
30 Mike Cope Slim Jim	6.00	2.70
33 Ken Schrader Petree	6.00	2.70
35 Todd Bodine Tabasco	6.00	2.70

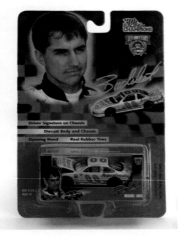

	MINT	NRMT
36 Ernie Irvan Skittles	6.00	2.70
38 Elton Sawyer Barbasol	6.00	2.70
40 Sterling Marlin Saboc	6.00	2.70
42 Joe Nemechek Bell South	6.00	2.70
46 Wally Dallenbach First Union	6.00	2.70
50 Ricky Craven Hendrick	6.00	2.70
59 Robert Pressley Kingsford	6.00	2.70
75 Rick Mast Remington	6.00	2.70

	MINT	NRMT
94 Bill Elliott Happy Meal	6.00	2.70

	MINT	NRMT
00 Buckshot Jones AquaFresh	6.00	2.70

	MINT	NRMT
94 Bill Elliott McDonald's	6.00	2.70
97 Chad Little John Deere	6.00	2.70

	MINT	NRMT
90 Dick Trickle Helig-Meyers	6.00	2.70

	MINT	NRMT
98 Greg Sacks Thorn Apple Valley	6.00	2.70
99 Jeff Burton Exide	6.00	2.70

1998 Racing Champions Stock Rods 1:64

These 1:64 scale cars are replicas of vintage stock rods with NASCAR paint schemes. Cars are listed by issue number instead of car number.

	MINT	NRMT
56 Terry Labonte Spooky Loops	8.00	3.60
57 Terry Labonte Kellogg's	8.00	3.60
58 Glen Allen Luxaire	6.00	2.70
59 Bobby Hamilton Kodak	6.00	2.70
60 Dick Trickle Heilig-Meyers	6.00	2.70
61 Robert Pressley Kingsford	6.00	2.70
62 Ted Musgrave Primestar	6.00	2.70
63 Hut Stricklin Circuit City	6.00	2.70
64 Kevin Schwantz Ryder	6.00	2.70
65 Michael Waltrip Citgo	6.00	2.70
66 Buckshot Jones Alka-Seltzer	6.00	2.70
67 Ken Schrader Petree	6.00	2.70
68 Bobby Hamilton Kodak	6.00	2.70
69 Hut Stricklin Circuit City	6.00	2.70
70 Terry Labonte Kellogg's	8.00	3.60
71 Rick Mast Remington	6.00	2.70
72 Joe Nemechek Bell South	6.00	2.70
73 Ricky Rudd Tide	6.00	2.70
74 Bill Elliott McDonald's	8.00	3.60
75 Ernie Irvan M&M's	6.00	2.70
76 Terry Labonte Kellogg's	8.00	3.60
77 Michael Waltrip Citgo	6.00	2.70
78 Ricky Rudd Tide Gold	8.00	3.60
79 Bill Elliott McDonald's Gold	20.00	9.00

CAR / DRIVER / SPONSOR	MINT	NRMT
80 Bobby Hamilton Kodak Gold	8.00	3.60
81 Hut Stricklin Circuit City Gold	8.00	3.60
82 Mark Martin Valvoline	8.00	3.60
83 Ted Musgrave Primestar	6.00	2.70
84 Jeff Burton Exide	6.00	2.70
85 Mark Martin Winn Dixie	8.00	3.60
86 Jeff Burton Exide Gold	12.00	5.50
87 Bill Elliott McDonald's Gold	20.00	9.00
88 Todd Bodine Tabasco	6.00	2.70
89 Lake Speed Huckleberry Hound	6.00	2.70
90 Jeff Burton Exide	6.00	2.70
91 Bill Elliott McDonald's	8.00	3.60
92 Mark Martin Winn Dixie	8.00	3.60
93 Mark Martin Valvoline	8.00	3.60
94 Lake Speed Cartoon Network	6.00	2.70
95 Terry Labonte Kellogg's Corny	8.00	3.60
96 Terry Labonte Kellogg's Corny Gold	20.00	9.00
97 Jeff Burton Exide Gold	15.00	6.75
98 Rick Mast Remington	6.00	2.70
99 Terry Labonte Kellogg's	8.00	3.60
100 Joe Nemechek Bell South	6.00	2.70
101 Robert Pressley Kingsford	6.00	2.70
102 Bill Elliott McDonald's	8.00	3.60
103 Mark Martin Winn Dixie	8.00	3.60
104 Jeff Burton Exide Gold	15.00	6.75
105 Bobby Hamilton Kodak Gold	8.00	3.60
106 Terry Labonte Kellogg's	8.00	3.60
107 Bill Elliott McDonald's	8.00	3.60
108 Mark Martin Valvoline	8.00	3.60
109 Jeff Burton Track Gear	6.00	2.70
110 Ted Musgrave Primestar	6.00	2.70
111 Lake Speed Huckleberry Hound	6.00	2.70
112 Terry Labonte Kellogg's Corny Gold	20.00	9.00
113 Ricky Rudd Tide Gold	8.00	3.60
114 Bobby Hamilton Kodak	6.00	2.70
115 Ken Schrader Petree	6.00	2.70
116 Dick Trickle Heilig-Meyers	6.00	2.70
117 Todd Bodine Tabasco	6.00	2.70
118 Terry Labonte Kellogg's	8.00	3.60
119 Terry Labonte Kellogg's	8.00	3.60

CAR / DRIVER / SPONSOR	MINT	NRMT
120 Joe Nemechek Bell South	6.00	2.70
121 Kevin Schwantz Ryder	6.00	2.70
122 Robert Pressley Kingsford	6.00	2.70
123 Bill Elliott McDonald's	8.00	3.60
124 Mark Martin Valvoline	8.00	3.60
125 Michael Waltrip Citgo	6.00	2.70
126 Dick Trickle Heilig-Meyers	6.00	2.70
127 Ted Musgrave Primestar	6.00	2.70
128 Michael Waltrip Citgo	6.00	2.70
129 Bobby Hamilton Kodak	6.00	2.70
130 Bill Elliott McDonald's	8.00	3.60
131 Terry Labonte Kellogg's	8.00	3.60
132 Rick Mast Remington Gold	8.00	3.60
133 Robert Pressley Kingsford	6.00	2.70
134 Michael Waltrip Citgo	6.00	2.70
135 Ken Schrader Petree Gold	8.00	3.60
136 Mark Martin Valvoline	8.00	3.60
137 Jeff Burton Track Gear	6.00	2.70
138 Bill Elliott McDonald's	8.00	3.60
139 Terry Labonte Kellogg's Corny	8.00	3.60
140 Rick Mast Remington	6.00	2.70
141 Terry Labonte Blasted Fruit Loops	8.00	3.60
142 Michael Waltrip Citgo Gold	8.00	3.60
143 Terry Labonte Kellogg's Gold	20.00	9.00

1998 Racing Champions Stock Rods Reflections of Gold 1:64

These 1:64 scale cars are replicas of vintage stock rods with NASCAR paint schemes and gold plating. Cars are listed by issue number instead of car number.

CAR / DRIVER / SPONSOR	MINT	NRMT
1 Terry Labonte Kellogg's	30.00	13.50
2 Jerry Nadeau First Plus	15.00	6.75
3 Bobby Hamilton Kodak	15.00	6.75
4 Todd Bodine Tabasco	15.00	6.75
5 Mark Martin Valvoline	30.00	13.50
6 Bill Elliott McDonald's	30.00	13.50
7 Ted Musgrave Primestar	15.00	6.75
8 Jeff Burton Exide	20.00	9.00

1998 Racing Champions Toys 'R Us Gold 1:64

This is a special series produced by Racing Champions to celebrate NASCAR's 50th anniversary. Each car is a limited edition of 19,998. Each car is also plated in gold chrome. These cars were distributed in Toys 'R Us stores.

CAR / DRIVER / SPONSOR	MINT	NRMT
5 Terry Labonte Blasted Fruit Loops	15.00	6.75
5 Terry Labonte Kellogg's Corny	15.00	6.75
6 Joe Bessey Power Team	8.00	3.60
6 Mark Martin Eagle One	15.00	6.75
6 Mark Martin Valvoline	15.00	6.75
9 Jerry Nadeau Zombie Island	8.00	3.60
9 Lake Speed Birthday Cake	8.00	3.60
10 Phil Parsons Duralube	6.00	2.70
10 Ricky Rudd Give Kids The World	6.00	2.70
11 Brett Bodine Paychex	6.00	2.70
13 Jerry Nadeau First Plus	6.00	2.70
17 Matt Kenseth Lycos	12.00	5.50
17 Darrell Waltrip Builders' Square	8.00	3.60
19 Tony Raines Yellow	6.00	2.70
20 Blaise Alexander Rescue Engine	6.00	2.70
21 Michael Waltrip Goodwill Games	6.00	2.70
23 Lance Hooper WCW	6.00	2.70
26 Johnny Benson Betty Crocker	6.00	2.70
26 Johnny Benson Cheerios	6.00	2.70
33 Tim Fedewa Kleenex	6.00	2.70
33 Ken Schrader Petree	6.00	2.70
35 Todd Bodine Tabasco	8.00	3.60
36 Ernie Irvan Wildberry Skittles	12.00	5.50
42 Joe Nemechek Bell South	6.00	2.70
50 NDA Dr. Pepper	6.00	2.70
60 Mark Martin Winn Dixie	15.00	6.75
63 Tracy Leslie Lysol	6.00	2.70
64 Dick Trickle Scheinder	6.00	2.70
74 Randy Lajoie Fina	6.00	2.70
77 Robert Pressley Jasper	6.00	2.70
87 Joe Nemechek Bell South	6.00	2.70
94 Bill Elliott Happy Meal	15.00	6.75
98 Greg Sacks Thorn Apple Valley	6.00	2.70
99 Jeff Burton Exide	8.00	3.60
300 Darrell Waltrip Flock Special	8.00	3.60

1998 Racing Champions SuperTrucks 1:64

Racing Champions continued their line of 1:64 SuperTrucks in 1998. This series features many of the circuit's first-time drivers and Winston Cup regulars.

Car / Driver / Sponsor	MINT	NRMT
2 Mike Bliss Team ASE	4.00	1.80
6 Rick Carelli Remax	4.00	1.80
18 No Driver Association Dana	4.00	1.80
19 Tony Raines Pennzoil	4.00	1.80
29 Bob Keselowski Mopar	4.00	1.80
31 Tony Roper Concor Tools	4.00	1.80
35 Ron Barfield Ortho	4.00	1.80
44 Boris Said Federated	4.00	1.80
52 Mike Wallace Pure One	4.00	1.80
66 Bryan Refner Carlin	4.00	1.80
75 Kevin Harvick Spears	4.00	1.80
84 Wayne Anderson Porter Cable	4.00	1.80
86 Stacy Compton RC Cola	4.00	1.80
87 Joe Nemechek BellSouth	4.00	1.80
90 Lance Norick National Hockey League	4.00	1.80
94 Bill Elliott Team ASE	4.00	1.80

1998 Racing Champions SuperTrucks Gold 1:64

This is a special series produced by Racing Champions to celebrate NASCAR's 50th anniversary. It parallels the regular 1998 1:24 scale series. Each truck is a limited edition of 5,000. Each truck is also plated in gold chrome and contains a serial number on its chassis.

Car / Driver / Sponsor	MINT	NRMT
2 Mike Bliss Team ASE	20.00	9.00
6 Rick Carelli Remax	20.00	9.00
29 Bob Keselowski Mopar	20.00	9.00
66 Bryan Refner Carlin	20.00	9.00
84 Wayne Anderson Porter Cable	20.00	9.00
86 Stacy Compton RC Cola	20.00	9.00

1999 Racing Champions 1:64

The 1:64 scale cars that appear in this series are replicas of many of the cars that ran in the 1998 season, but also many replicas are of the cars slated to appear in the 1999 season. The cars in this series are packaged in special blister packs that display the Racing Champions 10th anniversary logo.

	MINT	NRMT
4 Bobby Hamilton Kodak	4.00	1.80

	MINT	NRMT
4 Bobby Hamilton Kodak Advantix	4.00	1.80

	MINT	NRMT
5 Terry Labonte Kellogg's	4.00	1.80

	MINT	NRMT
6 Mark Martin Valvoline	4.00	1.80
6 Mark Martin Zerex	10.00	4.50
7 Michael Waltrip Philips	4.00	1.80
9 Jerry Nadeau Dextor's laboratory	4.00	1.80
9 Jerry Nadeau Goldberg	8.00	3.60

	MINT	NRMT
10 Ricky Rudd Tide Peroxide	4.00	1.80

	MINT	NRMT
10 Ricky Rudd Tide	4.00	1.80

	MINT	NRMT
86 Stacy Compton RC Cola ST	4.00	1.80

	MINT	NRMT
11 Brett Bodine Paychex	4.00	1.80
12 Jeremy Mayfield Mobil 1	4.00	1.80
14 Rick Crawford Circle Bar Super Truck	4.00	1.80
15 Ken Schrader Oakwood Homes	4.00	1.80

	MINT	NRMT
26 Johnny Benson Cheerios	4.00	1.80
30 Derrike Cope Bryan Foods	4.00	1.80
32 Jeff Green Kleenex	4.00	1.80
33 Ken Schrader Petree	4.00	1.80
34 Mike McGlaughlin Goulds Pumps	4.00	1.80
36 Ernie Irvan M&M's	4.00	1.80
38 Glen Allen Barbersol	4.00	1.80

	MINT	NRMT
94 Bill Elliott McDonald's	4.00	1.80
94 Bill Elliott QPC	8.00	3.60

	MINT	NRMT
97 Chad Little John Deere	4.00	1.80

	MINT	NRMT
16 Kevin Lepage Primestar	4.00	1.80
16 Kevin LePage TV Guide	4.00	1.80
17 Matt Kenseth DeWalt	8.00	3.60
21 Elliott Sadler Citgo	4.00	1.80
23 Jimmy Spencer TCE	4.00	1.80
23 Jimmy Spencer TCE Lights	4.00	1.80
24 Jack Sprague GMAC Super Truck	4.00	1.80
25 Wally Dallenbach Budweiser	4.00	1.80

	MINT	NRMT
40 Sterling Marlin John Wayne	4.00	1.80
40 Sterling Marlin Brooks & Dunn	4.00	1.80
42 Joe Nemechek BellSouth	4.00	1.80
43 John Andretti STP	4.00	1.80
45 Adam Petty Spree	8.00	3.60
50 Mark Green Dr. Pepper	4.00	1.80
55 Kenny Wallace Square D	4.00	1.80
59 Mike Dillion Kingsford	4.00	1.80
60 Mark Martin Winn Dixie	4.00	1.80
66 Darrell Waltrip Big K	4.00	1.80
75 Ted Musgrave Remington	4.00	1.80
77 Robert Pressley Jasper	4.00	1.80

	MINT	NRMT
99 Jeff Burton Exide	4.00	1.80

Car / Driver / Sponsor	MINT	NRMT
99 Jeff Burton Exide Bruce Lee	4.00	1.80
00 Buckshot Jones Crown Fiber	4.00	1.80
0 Larry Pearson Cheez-It	4.00	1.80

1999 Racing Champions Chrome Chase 1:64

This car featured chrome paint, special packaging and a low production run.

Car / Driver / Sponsor	MINT	NRMT
5 Terry Labonte Kellogg's	15.00	6.75
6 Mark Martin Valvoline	15.00	6.75
6 Mark Martin Zerex	20.00	9.00
9 Jerry Nadeau Dexter's laboratory	12.00	5.50
12 Jeremy Mayfield Mobil 1	12.00	5.50
15 Ken Schrader Oakwood Homes	12.00	5.50
16 Kevin LePage Primestar	12.00	5.50
17 Matt Kenseth DeWalt	15.00	6.75
21 Elliott Sadler Citgo	12.00	5.50
23 Jimmy Spencer TCE	12.00	5.50
25 Wally Dallenbach Hendrick	12.00	5.50
30 Derrike Cope Bryan	12.00	5.50

Car / Driver / Sponsor	MINT	NRMT
32 Jeff Green Kleenex	12.00	5.50

Car / Driver / Sponsor	MINT	NRMT
36 Ernie Irvan M&M's	20.00	9.00
43 John Andretti STP	15.00	6.75
59 Mike Dillion Kingsford	12.00	5.50
60 Mark Martin Winn Dixie	20.00	9.00
94 Bill Elliott Drive Thru	15.00	6.75
0 Larry Pearson Cheez-it	12.00	5.50

1999 Racing Champions Chrome Signature Series 1:64

This car featured chrome paint, special packaging, low production run and a simulated driver signature on the base of the car.

Car / Driver / Sponsor	MINT	NRMT
4 Bobby Hamilton Kodak	15.00	6.75
6 Mark Martin Valvoline	30.00	13.50
6 Mark Martin Zerex	30.00	13.50
9 Jerry Nadeau Dexter's laboratory	20.00	9.00
12 Jeremy Mayfield Mobil 1	15.00	6.75
16 Kevin LePage Primestar	15.00	6.75
23 Jimmy Spencer TCE	15.00	6.75
25 Wally Dallenbach Hendrick	15.00	6.75
36 Ernie Irvan M&M's	15.00	6.75
77 Robert Pressley Jasper	15.00	6.75
94 Bill Elliott Drive Thru	30.00	13.50

1999 Racing Champions Gold with Medallion 1:64

This is a special series produced by Racing Champions to celebrate their 10th anniversary. Each car is also plated in gold chrome.

Car / Driver / Sponsor	MINT	NRMT
4 Bobby Hamilton Kodak	12.00	5.50
4 Bobby Hamilton Kodak Advantix	12.00	5.50

Car / Driver / Sponsor	MINT	NRMT
5 Terry Labonte Kellogg's	30.00	13.50
6 Mark Martin Valvoline	30.00	13.50
6 Joe Bessey Power Team	12.00	5.50
9 Jerry Nadeau Dexter's laboratory	12.00	5.50
10 Ricky Rudd Tide	12.00	5.50
10 Phil Parsons Alltel	12.00	5.50
11 Brett Bodine Paychex	12.00	5.50
12 Jeremy Mayfield Mobil 1	12.00	5.50
15 Ken Schrader Oakwood Homes	12.00	5.50
16 Kevin LePage Primestar	12.00	5.50
23 Jimmy Spencer TCE	12.00	5.50
25 Wally Dallenbach Hendrick	12.00	5.50
26 Johnny Benson Cheerios	12.00	5.50
30 Derrike Cope Jimmy Dean	12.00	5.50
32 Jeff Green Kleenex	12.00	5.50
33 Ken Schrader Petree	12.00	5.50
36 Ernie Irvan M&M's	20.00	9.00
55 Kenny Wallace Square D	12.00	5.50
60 Mark Martin Winn Dixie	30.00	13.50
66 Darrell Waltrip Big K	20.00	9.00
77 Robert Pressley Jasper	12.00	5.50
78 Garry Bradberry Pilot	12.00	5.50
94 Bill Elliott Drive Thru	30.00	13.50
97 Chad Little John Deere	12.00	5.50
99 Jeff Burton Exide	15.00	6.75

1999 Racing Champions NASCAR RULES 1:64

Packaged with a display stand and collector card that explains some of the technical rules that govern NASCAR, these 1:64 scale replicas have an opening hood with detailed engine, opening trunk with fuel cell, and a replica NASCAR template.

Car / Driver / Sponsor	MINT	NRMT
6 Mark Martin Valvoline	20.00	9.00

CAR / DRIVER / SPONSOR	MINT	NRMT
6 Mark Martin Eagle One	20.00	9.00
6 Mark Martin Zerex	20.00	9.00
9 Jerry Nadeau WCW nWo	12.00	5.50
9 Jjeff Burton Track Gear	12.00	5.50

10 Ricky Rudd Tide	12.00	5.50

12 Jeremy Mayfield Mobil 1	15.00	6.75
16 Kevin LePage Primestar	12.00	5.50
21 Elliott Sadler Citgo	12.00	5.50

23 Jimmy Spencer TCE	12.00	5.50
26 Johnny Benson Cheerios	12.00	5.50
43 John Andretti STP	20.00	9.00

CAR / DRIVER / SPONSOR	MINT	NRMT

60 Mark Martin Winn Dixie	20.00	9.00
66 Darrell Waltrip Big K	12.00	5.50

94 Bill Elliott Drive Thru	15.00	6.75

97 Chad Little John Deere	15.00	6.75
99 Jeff Burton Exide	20.00	9.00

CAR / DRIVER / SPONSOR	MINT	NRMT

99 Jeff Burton Bruce Lee	20.00	9.00

1999 Racing Champions Platinum 1:64

This is a special series produced by Racing Champions to celebrate their 10th anniversary. It parallels the regular 1999 1:24 scale series. Each car is a limited edition of 9,999. Each car is also plated in platinum chrome and contains a serial number on its chassis.

4 Bobby Hamilton Kodak	12.00	5.50
5 Terry Labonte Kellogg's	20.00	9.00
6 Joe Bessey Power Team	12.00	5.50
6 Mark Martin Valvoine	20.00	9.00
9 Jerry Nadeau Dexter's laboratory	12.00	5.50
9 Jeff Burton Track Gear	12.00	5.50
10 Ricky Rudd Tide	12.00	5.50
10 Ricky Rudd Tide Happy Holiday	12.00	5.50
11 Brett Bodine Paychex	12.00	5.50
16 Kevin LePage Primestar	12.00	5.50
25 Wally Dallenbach Hendrick	12.00	5.50
26 Johnny Benson Cheerios	12.00	5.50
32 Jeff Green Kleenex	12.00	5.50
33 Ken Schrader Petree	12.00	5.50
36 Ernie Irvan M&M's	15.00	6.75
42 Joe Nemechek BellSouth	12.00	5.50
55 Kenny Wallace Square D	12.00	5.50
77 Robert Pressley Jasper	12.00	5.50
94 Bill Elliott Drive Thru	20.00	9.00
97 Chad Little John Deere	12.00	5.50
99 Jeff Burton Exide	12.00	5.50

1999 Racing Champions Platinum Stock Rods 1:64

CAR / DRIVER / SPONSOR	MINT	NRMT
1P Bobby Hamilton Valvoline	10.00	4.50
2P Terry Labonte Kellogg's	10.00	4.50
3P Mark Martin Valvoline	10.00	4.50
4P Ricky Rudd Tide	10.00	4.50
5P Bill Elliott Drive Thru	10.00	4.50
6P Ernie Irvan M&M's	10.00	4.50

1999 Racing Champions Press Pass Series 1:64

These 1:64 scale cars come packaged with a Press Pass card and feature opening hood and two piece tires.

CAR / DRIVER / SPONSOR	MINT	NRMT
4 Bobby Hamilton Kodak	6.00	2.70
4 Bobby Hamilton Advantix	6.00	2.70
5 Terry Labonte Kellogg's	6.00	2.70
6 Mark Martin Valvoline	6.00	2.70
6 Joe Bessy Power Team	6.00	2.70
7 Michael Waltrip Philips	6.00	2.70
9 Jeff Burton Track Gear	6.00	2.70
9 Jerry Nadeau Dexter's laboratory	6.00	2.70
10 Ricky Rudd Tide	6.00	2.70
11 Brett Bodine Paychex	6.00	2.70
15 Ken Schrader Oakwood Homes	6.00	2.70
16 Kevin LePage Primestar	6.00	2.70
21 Elliott Sadler Citgo	6.00	2.70
25 Wally Dallenbach Hendrick	6.00	2.70
26 Johnny Benson Cheerios	6.00	2.70
30 Derrike Cope Bryan Foods	6.00	2.70
32 Jeff Green Kleenex	6.00	2.70
33 Ken Schrader Petree	6.00	2.70
33 Elton Sawyer Lysol	6.00	2.70
33 Ken Schrader APR Blue	6.00	2.70
34 Mike McGlaughlin Goulds Pumps	6.00	2.70

CAR / DRIVER / SPONSOR	MINT	NRMT
36 Ernie Irvan M&M's	6.00	2.70
40 Sterling Marlin John Wayne	6.00	2.70
42 Joe Nemechek BellSouth	6.00	2.70
55 Kenny Wallace Square D	6.00	2.70
60 Geoffery Bodine Power Team	6.00	2.70
66 Darrell Waltrip Big K	6.00	2.70
66 Todd Bodine Phillips 66	6.00	2.70

CAR / DRIVER / SPONSOR	MINT	NRMT
72 Hermie Sadler MGM Brakes	6.00	2.70
77 Robert Pressley Jasper	6.00	2.70
78 Gary Bradberry Pilot	6.00	2.70
94 Bill Elliott Drive Thru	6.00	2.70
97 Chad Little John Deere	6.00	2.70
99 Jeff Burton Exide	6.00	2.70
00 Buckshot Jones Crown Fiber	6.00	2.70

1999 Racing Champions Radio Controled Die Cast 1:64

These cars are touted as the smallest RC cars available.

CAR / DRIVER / SPONSOR	MINT	NRMT
6 Mark Martin Valvoline	30.00	13.50
12 Jeremy Mayfield Mobil 1	30.00	13.50
36 Ernie Irvan M&M's	40.00	18.00
43 John Andretti STP	40.00	18.00
94 Bill Elliott Drive Thru	30.00	13.50

1999 Racing Champions Signature Series 1:64

This is a special series produced by Racing Champions to celebrate their 10th anniversary. It parallels the regular 1999 1:64 scale series. Each car is a packaged in a decorative box with the driver's facsimile autograph on the front.

CAR / DRIVER / SPONSOR	MINT	NRMT
4 Bobby Hamilton Kodak	6.00	2.70
4 Jeff Pervis Lance Snacks	6.00	2.70
5 Terry Labonte Kellogg's	6.00	2.70
6 Mark Martin Valvoline	6.00	2.70
6 Joe Bessey Power Team	6.00	2.70
7 Michael Waltrip Philips	6.00	2.70
9 Jerry Nadeau Dexter's laboratory	6.00	2.70
10 Ricky Rudd Tide	6.00	2.70
11 Brett Bodine Paychex	6.00	2.70
12 Jeremy Mayfield Mobil 1	6.00	2.70
16 Kevin LePage Primestar	6.00	2.70
17 Matt Kenseth DeWalt	6.00	2.70
23 Jimmy Spencer TCE	6.00	2.70
25 Wally Dallenbach Hendrick	6.00	2.70
26 Johnny Benson Cheerios	6.00	2.70
32 Jeff Green Kleenex	6.00	2.70

CAR / DRIVER / SPONSOR	MINT	NRMT
34 Mike McLaughlin Goulds Pump	6.00	2.70
36 Ernie Irvan M&M's	6.00	2.70

CAR / DRIVER / SPONSOR	MINT	NRMT
40 Sterling Marlin John Wayne	6.00	2.70
60 Mark Martin Winn-Dixie	6.00	2.70
77 Robert Pressley Jasper	6.00	2.70
94 Bill Elliott Drive Thru	6.00	2.70
99 Jeff Burton Exide	6.00	2.70
00 Buckshot Jones Crown Fiber	6.00	2.70

1999 Racing Champions Stock Rods 1:64

These 1:64 scale cars are replicas of vintage stock rods with NASCAR paint schemes. Cars are listed by issue number instead of car number.

CAR / DRIVER / SPONSOR	MINT	NRMT
144 Terry Labonte Kellogg's Iron Man	8.00	3.60
145 Rick Mast Remington	6.00	2.70
146 Terry Labonte Kellogg's	8.00	3.60
147 Ricky Rudd Tide	6.00	2.70
148 Kevin Lepage Primestar	6.00	2.70
149 Terry Labonte Kellogg's Corny	8.00	3.60
150 Terry Labonte Iron Man Gold	8.00	3.60
151 Ricky Rudd Tide Gold	8.00	3.60
152 Bobby Hamilton Kodak	6.00	2.70
153 Terry Labonte Kellogg's Iron Man	8.00	3.60
154 Mark Martin Valvoline	8.00	3.60
155 Ricky Rudd Tide	6.00	2.70
156 Kevin LePage Primestar	6.00	2.70
157 Jeff Burton Exide	6.00	2.70
158 Jeff Burton Exide Gold	15.00	6.75
159 Bobby Hamilton Kodak	6.00	2.70
160 Wally Dallenbach Hendrick	6.00	2.70
161 Wally Dallenbach Hendrick Gold	8.00	3.60
162 Ernie Irvan M&M's	8.00	3.60
163 Ernie Irvan M&M's Gold	12.00	5.50
164 Bobby Hamilton Kodak	6.00	2.70
165 Brett Bodine Paychex	6.00	2.70
166 Brett Bodine Paychex	6.00	2.70
167 Ken Schrader Petree	6.00	2.70
168 Ken Schrader Petree Gold	8.00	3.60
169 Bill Elliott Drive Thru	8.00	3.60
170 Bill Elliott Drive Thru Gold	15.00	6.75
171 Jerry Nadeau Dexter's Lab	8.00	3.60
172 Brett Bodine Paychex	6.00	2.70
173 Brett Bodine Paychex Gold	8.00	3.60

CAR / DRIVER / SPONSOR	MINT	NRMT
174 Wally Dallenbach Hendrick	6.00	2.70
175 Ernie Irvan M&M's	6.00	2.70
176 Kenny Wallace Square D	6.00	2.70
177 Kenny Wallace Square D Gold	8.00	3.60
178 Robert Pressley Jasper	6.00	2.70
179 Sterling Marlin John Wayne	8.00	3.60
180 Sterling Marlin John Wayne Gold	15.00	6.75
181 Bobby Hamilton Kodak	6.00	2.70
182 Ricky Rudd Tide	8.00	3.60
183 Jimmy Spencer TCE	6.00	2.70
184 Jerry Nadeau Dextor's Lab	6.00	2.70
185 Robert Pressly Jasper	6.00	2.70
186 Mark Martin Valvoline	8.00	3.60
187 Derrike Cope Bryan	8.00	3.60
188 Ken Schrader APR Blue	6.00	2.70
189 Sterling Marlin Sabco	6.00	2.70
190 Darrell Waltrip Big K	8.00	3.60
191 Jeff Burton Exide	8.00	3.60
192 Darrell Waltrip Big K Gold	15.00	6.75
193 Ken Schrader APR Maroon	6.00	2.70
194 Wally Dallenbach Hendrick	6.00	2.70
195 Ernie Irvan M&M's	8.00	3.60
196 Sterling Marlin John Wayne	8.00	3.60
197 Darrell Waltrip Big K	8.00	3.60

1999 Racing Champions Toy's R Us Chrome Chase 1:64

These Chrome plated cars were only available at Toy's R Us.

CAR / DRIVER / SPONSOR	MINT	NRMT
4 Bobby Hamilton Kodak	4.00	1.80
5 Terry Labonte Kellogg's	8.00	3.60
6 Mark Martin Valvoline	8.00	3.60
9 Jerry Nadeau Dexter	6.00	2.70
10 Ricky Rudd Tide	4.00	1.80
11 Brett Bodine Paychex	4.00	1.80
25 Wally Dallenbach Hendrick	4.00	1.80
33 Ken Schrader Petree	4.00	1.80
36 Ernie Irvan M&M's	8.00	3.60
55 Kenny Wallace Square D	4.00	1.80
94 Bill Elliott Drive Thru	8.00	3.60
99 Jeff Burton Exide	6.00	2.70

1999 Racing Champions Trackside 1:64

These 1:64 cars were only available at the track.

CAR / DRIVER / SPONSOR	MINT	NRMT
9 Jerry Nadeau Dexter	25.00	11.00
9 Jerry Nadeau WCW/nWo	25.00	11.00

CAR / DRIVER / SPONSOR	MINT	NRMT
23 Jimmy Spencer Winston	30.00	13.50
43 John Andretti STP	25.00	11.00
45 Adam Petty Spree	35.00	16.00
94 Bill Elliott Drive Thru	30.00	13.50

1999 Racing Champions Under the Lights 1:64

These 1:64 scale cars feature special anodized paint to give that under the lights appearance.

CAR / DRIVER / SPONSOR	MINT	NRMT
4 Bobby Hamilton Kodak	8.00	3.60
5 Terry Labonte Kellogg's	12.00	5.50
6 Mark Martin Valvoline	12.00	5.50

CAR / DRIVER / SPONSOR	MINT	NRMT
10 Ricky Rudd Tide	8.00	3.60
12 Jeremy Mayfield Mobil 1	8.00	3.60

Car / Driver / Sponsor	MINT	NRMT
21 Elliott Sadler, Citgo	8.00	3.60
94 Bill Elliott, Drive Thru	12.00	5.50
99 Jeff Burton, Exide	12.00	5.50

1999 Racing Champions 24K Gold 1:64

This is a special series produced by Racing Champions to celebrate their 10th anniversary. It parallels the regular 1998 1:64 scale series. Each car is a limited edition of 9,999. Each car is also plated in gold chrome and contains a serial number on its chassis.

Car / Driver / Sponsor	MINT	NRMT
4 Bobby Hamilton, Kodak	15.00	6.75
5 Terry Labonte, Kellog's	30.00	13.50
6 Joe Bessey, Power Team	15.00	6.75
6 Mark Martin, Valvoine	30.00	13.50
9 Jerry Nadeau, Dexter	15.00	6.75
9 Jeff Burton, Track Gear	15.00	6.75
10 Ricky Rudd, Tide Happy Holiday	15.00	6.75
10 Ricky Rudd, Tide	15.00	6.75
11 Brett Bodine, Paychex	15.00	6.75
16 Kevin LePage, Primestar	15.00	6.75
25 Wally Dallenbach, Hendrick	15.00	6.75
26 Johnny Benson, Cheerios	15.00	6.75
33 Ken Schrader, Petree	15.00	6.75
36 Ernie Irvan, M&M's	20.00	9.00
42 Joe Nemechek, BellSouth	15.00	6.75
77 Robert Pressley, Jasper	15.00	6.75
97 Chad Little, John Deere	15.00	6.75
99 Jeff Burton, Exide	15.00	6.75

1999 Racing Champions 24K Gold Stock Rods 1:64

Car / Driver / Sponsor	MINT	NRMT
1G Bobby Hamilton, Kodak	8.00	3.60
2G Terry Labonte, Kelloggs	15.00	6.75
3G Mark Martin, Valvoline	15.00	6.75
4G Ricky Rudd, Tide	15.00	6.75
5G Bill Elliott, Drive Thru	15.00	6.75
6G Ernie Irvan, M&M's	15.00	6.75

1999 Racing Champions 3-D Originals 1:64

This set features a hood open car with a 3-D card.

Car / Driver / Sponsor	MINT	NRMT
5 Terry Labonte, Kellogg's	15.00	6.75
6 Mark Martin, Valvoline	15.00	6.75
12 Jeremy Mayfield, Mobil 1	8.00	3.60
94 Bill Elliott, Drive Thru	15.00	6.75

2000 Racing Champions Premier Preview 1:64

These cars feature opening hood, two piece wheels, and a car tarp.

Car / Driver / Sponsor	MINT	NRMT
6 Mark Martin, Valvoline	10.00	4.50
14 Mike Bliss, Conseco	10.00	4.50
17 Matt Kenseth, DeWalt	10.00	4.50
22 Ward Burton, Caterpillar	10.00	4.50

	MINT	NRMT
99 Jeff Burton, Exide	10.00	4.50

2000 Racing Champions Pit Crew 1:64

The Pit Crew Scene is a unique look at what it can be like on NASCAR's pit row. A new addition to the Originals line, the Pit Crew Scene features a 1:64 scale Originals stock car with replica pit wagon and pit crew team figures all on a pit row base that simulates the sounds heard in the pits during a pit stop.

Car / Driver / Sponsor	MINT	NRMT
4 Bobby Hamilton, Kodak	12.00	5.50
6 Mark Martin, Valvoline	15.00	6.75
7 Michael Waltrip, Naions Rent	15.00	6.75
17 Matt Kenseth, DeWalt	15.00	6.75
97 Chad Little, John Deere	15.00	6.75

2000 Racing Champions Time Trial 2000 1:64

New for 2000, Racing Champions introduces a series that focuses on the testing and development of NASCAR stock cars rather than the final race-ready car - Time Trial stock car replicas. Sporting just a coat of gray primer and the team number. These cars feature opening hoods and two piece tires.

Car / Driver / Sponsor	MINT	NRMT
6 Mark Martin, Valvoline	10.00	4.50
17 Matt Kenseth, DeWalt	10.00	4.50
99 Jeff Burton, Exide	10.00	4.50

1997 Revell Club 1:18

These 1:18 scale cars were from the same production run as the Collection cars. Each car distributed by the club has a serial number on the chassis. The boxes were uniquely colored to match the colors on the car.

Car / Driver / Sponsor	MINT	NRMT
1 NDA, Coca Cola 600	110.00	50.00
5 Terry Labonte, Spooky Loops	150.00	70.00
5 Terry Labonte, Tony the Tiger	200.00	90.00
23 Jimmy Spencer, Camel	150.00	70.00
33 Ken Schrader, Skoal	150.00	70.00
46 Wally Dallenbach, Woody	120.00	55.00
88 Dale Jarrett, Quality Care	120.00	55.00
97 Chad Little, John Deere	150.00	70.00

1997 Revell Collection 1:18

This series marks Revell's first attempt to produce a 1:18 scale car. It was distributed to hobby dealers as part of Revell's Collection line.

Car / Driver / Sponsor	MINT	NRMT
1 No Driver Association, Coca Cola 600	75.00	34.00
2 Rusty Wallace, Miller Lite	100.00	45.00
3 Dale Earnhardt, Wheaties	160.00	70.00
4 Sterling Marlin, Kodak	80.00	36.00
5 Terry Labonte, Kellogg's	100.00	45.00
5 Terry Labonte, Spooky Loops	110.00	50.00
5 Terry Labonte, Tony the Tiger	120.00	55.00
6 Mark Martin, Valvoline	80.00	36.00
10 Ricky Rudd, Tide	80.00	36.00
18 Bobby Labonte, Interstate Batteries	80.00	36.00
21 Michael Waltrip, Citgo Top Dog paint scheme	75.00	34.00
23 Jimmy Spencer, Camel	160.00	70.00
24 Jeff Gordon, Lost World	160.00	70.00
25 Ricky Craven, Bud Lizard	100.00	45.00
28 Ernie Irvan, Havoline 10th Anniversary paint scheme	100.00	45.00
29 Jeff Green, Scooby-Doo	80.00	36.00
29 Jeff Green, Tom & Jerry	80.00	36.00

CAR / DRIVER / SPONSOR	MINT	NRMT
29 Steve Grissom Flintstones	80.00	36.00
33 Ken Schrader Skoal	90.00	40.00
35 Todd Bodine Tabasco	80.00	36.00
37 Jeremy Mayfield Kmart	80.00	36.00
40 Robby Gordon Coors Light	75.00	34.00
41 Steve Grissom Kodiak	80.00	36.00
43 Bobby Hamilton STP Goody's	80.00	36.00
46 Wally Dallenbach Woody Woodpecker	80.00	36.00
60 Mark Martin Winn Dixie	90.00	40.00
88 Dale Jarrett Ford Credit	90.00	40.00
94 Bill Elliott McDonald's	90.00	40.00
94 Bill Elliott Mac Tonight	90.00	40.00
97 Chad Little John Deere Autographed box	90.00	40.00
97 No Driver Association Texas Motor Speedway	75.00	34.00

1998 Revell Club 1:18

These 1:18 scale cars were from the same production run as the Collection cars. Each car distributed by the club has a serial number on the chassis. The boxes were uniquely colored to match the colors on the car.

CAR / DRIVER / SPONSOR	MINT	NRMT
1 Dale Earnhardt Jr. Coke	150.00	70.00
1 Steve Park Pennzoil	200.00	90.00
1 Steve Park Pennzoil Indy	150.00	70.00
2 Rusty Wallace Adventures of Rusty	175.00	80.00
2 Rusty Wallace Miller Lite Elvis	150.00	70.00
3 Dale Earnhardt Coke	150.00	70.00
3 Dale Earnhardt Goodwrench Plus	175.00	80.00
3 Dale Earnhardt Goodwrench Plus Bass Pro	200.00	90.00
3 Dale Earnhardt Goodwrench Plus Daytona	200.00	90.00
3 Dale Earnhardt Jr. AC Delco	300.00	135.00
5 Terry Labonte Blasted Fruit Loops	150.00	70.00
5 Terry Labonte Kellogg's Corny	175.00	80.00
9 Lake Speed Birthday Cake	150.00	70.00
9 Lake Speed Huckleberry Hound	150.00	70.00
18 Bobby Labonte Interstate Batteries Hot Rod	150.00	70.00
18 Bobby Labonte Interstate Batteries Small Soldiers	150.00	70.00
23 Jimmy Spencer No Bull	200.00	90.00
24 Jeff Gordon DuPont	175.00	80.00
24 Jeff Gordon DuPont Chromalusion	225.00	100.00
28 Kenny Irwin Havoline	150.00	70.00

CAR / DRIVER / SPONSOR	MINT	NRMT
28 Kenny Irwin Havoline Joker	175.00	80.00
31 Mike Skinner Lowe's	150.00	70.00
35 Todd Bodine Tabasco	150.00	70.00
36 Ernie Irvan M&M's	200.00	90.00
36 Ernie Irvan Wildberry Skittles	150.00	70.00
44 Tony Stewart Shell	150.00	70.00
44 Tony Stewart Shell Small Soldiers	150.00	70.00
50 Ricky Craven Budweiser	150.00	70.00
81 Kenny Wallace Square D Lightning	150.00	70.00
88 Dale Jarrett Quality Care	150.00	70.00
88 Dale Jarrett Quality Care Batman	175.00	80.00

1998 Revell Collection 1:18

This series marks Revell's second year producing a 1:18 scale car. It was distributed to hobby dealers as part of Revell's Collection line.

CAR / DRIVER / SPONSOR	MINT	NRMT
1 Dale Earnhardt Jr. Coke	100.00	45.00
1 Steve Park Pennzoil	120.00	55.00
2 Rusty Wallace Adventures of Rusty	100.00	45.00
2 Rusty Wallace Miller Lite	100.00	45.00
2 Rusty Wallace Miller Lite Elvis	100.00	45.00
2 Rusty Wallace Miller Lite TCB	100.00	45.00
3 Dale Earnhardt Coke	100.00	45.00
3 Dale Earnhardt Goodwrench Plus	120.00	55.00
3 Dale Earnhardt Goodwrench Plus Bass Pro	120.00	55.00
3 Dale Earnhardt Goodwrench Plus Brickyard Special	120.00	55.00
3 Dale Earnhardt Jr. AC Delco	120.00	55.00
5 Terry Labonte Blasted Fruit Loops	100.00	45.00
5 Terry Labonte Kellogg's Corny	100.00	45.00
9 Lake Speed Birthday Cake	80.00	36.00
9 Lake Speed Huckleberry Hound	80.00	36.00
18 Bobby Labonte Interstate Batteries Hot Rod	80.00	36.00
18 Bobby Labonte Interstate Batteries Small Soldiers	80.00	36.00
23 Jimmy Spencer No Bull	120.00	55.00
24 Jeff Gordon DuPont	120.00	55.00
24 Jeff Gordon DuPont Brickyard Special	100.00	45.00
24 Jeff Gordon DuPont Chromalusion	150.00	70.00
28 Kenny Irwin Havoline	100.00	45.00
31 Dale Earnhardt Jr. Wrangler	175.00	80.00
31 Mike Skinner Lowe's	80.00	36.00
35 Todd Bodine Tabasco	80.00	36.00

CAR / DRIVER / SPONSOR	MINT	NRMT
36 Ernie Irvan M&M's	100.00	45.00
36 Ernie Irvan Wildberry Skittles	80.00	36.00
44 Tony Stewart Shell	80.00	36.00
46 Jeff Green First Union Devil Rays	80.00	36.00
50 Ricky Craven Budweiser	90.00	40.00
50 No Driver Association Bud Louie	100.00	45.00
81 Kenny Wallace Sqaure D Lightning	80.00	36.00
88 Dale Jarrett Quality Care	100.00	45.00

1999 Revell Club 1:18

These 1:18 scale cars were produced in very small numbers and were only available through the club.

CAR / DRIVER / SPONSOR	MINT	NRMT
3 Dale Earnhardt Goodwrench	175.00	80.00
23 Jimmy Spencer No Bull	150.00	70.00
24 Jeff Gordon Pepsi	150.00	70.00
24 Jeff Gordon Superman	170.00	75.00
31 Dale Earnhardt Jr. Gargoyles	175.00	80.00

1999 Revell Collection 1:18

This series marks Revell's third year producing a 1:18 scale car. It was distributed to hobby dealers as part of Revell's Collection line.

CAR / DRIVER / SPONSOR	MINT	NRMT
2 Rusty Wallace Miller Lite	80.00	36.00
3 Dale Earnhardt Goodwrench	100.00	45.00
3 Dale Earnhardt Wrangler	150.00	70.00
8 Dale Earnhardt Jr. Budweiser	150.00	70.00
12 Jeremy Mayfield Kentucky Derby	150.00	70.00
20 Tony Stewart Home Depot	175.00	80.00
23 Jimmy Spencer Winston Lights	100.00	45.00
24 Jeff Gordon DuPont	125.00	55.00
24 Jeff Gordon Pepsi	125.00	55.00
24 Jeff Gordon Star Wars	125.00	55.00
31 Dale Earnhardt Jr. Gargoyles	125.00	55.00
31 Dale Earnhardt Jr. Sikkens White 1997 Monte Carlo	125.00	55.00
40 Sterling Marlin John Wayne	80.00	36.00
40 Sterling Marlin Coors Brooks & Dunn	80.00	36.00
40 NDA Coca-Cola	80.00	36.00

1993-95 Revell 1:24

This set features many NASCAR's top drivers. Many of the pieces were issued through retail outlets but some were distributed through the drivers souvenir trailers.

CAR / DRIVER / SPONSOR	MINT	NRMT
1 Jeff Gordon	400.00	180.00
Baby Ruth produced for RCI		
3 Dale Earnhardt	30.00	13.50
Goodwrench Kellogg's Promo		
3 Dale Earnhardt	25.00	11.00
Goodwrench Black Wheels Sports Image car		
3 Dale Earnhardt	16.00	7.25
Goodwrench Silver Wheels		
3 Dale Earnhardt	25.00	11.00
Goodwrench 1994 Sports Image		
3 Dale Earnhardt	30.00	13.50
Goodwrench 6-Time Champion		
4 Rick Wilson	25.00	11.00
Kodak produced for GMP		
6 Mark Martin	18.00	8.00
Valvoline		
7 Harry Gant	60.00	27.00
Mac Tools produced by RCI		
7 Harry Gant	40.00	18.00
Morema		
8 Dick Trickle	18.00	8.00
Snickers		
8 1/2 No Driver Association	15.00	6.75
Racing For Kids		
10 Derrike Cope	20.00	9.00
Purolator		
15 Geoff Bodine	35.00	16.00
Ford Motorsports		
17 Darrell Waltrip	16.00	7.25
Western Auto		
18 Dale Jarrett	18.00	8.00
Interstate Batteries		
21 Morgan Shepherd	25.00	11.00
Cheerwine		
21 Morgan Shepherd	20.00	9.00
Citgo		
22 Sterling Marlin	20.00	9.00
Maxwell House		
26 Brett Bodine	18.00	8.00
Quaker State		
28 Davey Allison	30.00	13.50
Havoline		
28 Davey Allison	50.00	22.00
Mac Tools		
28 Ernie Irvan	40.00	18.00
Mac Tools		
30 Michael Waltrip	18.00	8.00
Pennzoil		
32 Dale Jarrett	35.00	16.00
Mac Tools		
33 Harry Gant	30.00	13.50
No Sponsor Farewell Tour		
42 Kyle Petty	16.00	7.25
Mello Yello		
52 Ken Schrader	30.00	13.50
No Sponsor Morema		
57 No Driver Association	18.00	8.00
Heinz 57		
59 Robert Pressley	55.00	25.00
Alliance produced RCI		
60 Mark Martin	40.00	18.00
Winn Dixie produced for GMP		
66 No Driver Association	18.00	8.00
Phillips 66 TropArtic		
66 Dick Trickle	40.00	18.00
Phillips 66 TropArtic		
68 Bobby Hamilton	18.00	8.00
Country Time		
75 Joe Ruttman	18.00	8.00
Dinner Bell		
83 Lake Speed	25.00	11.00
Purex produced for GMP		
90 Bobby Hillin Jr.	25.00	11.00
Heilig-Meyers		
94 Terry Labonte	18.00	8.00
Sunoco		

1994 Revell Hobby 1:24

These pieces were distributed through hobby outlets. Each piece came in a black and yellow box and had a few colors that matched the car. There were also a few promo cars done in this series.

CAR / DRIVER / SPONSOR	MINT	NRMT
4 Sterling Marlin	20.00	9.00
Kodak		
5 Terry Labonte	20.00	9.00
Kellogg's		
7 Geoff Bodine	20.00	9.00
Exide		
15 Lake Speed	20.00	9.00
Quality Care		
24 Jeff Gordon	50.00	22.00
DuPont		
31 Ward Burton	25.00	11.00
Hardee's		
41 Joe Nemechek	20.00	9.00
Meineke		
43 Wally Dallenbach Jr.	20.00	9.00
STP		

1995 Revell 1:24

These pieces were also a part of the continued growth of Revell's presence in the die cast market. The pieces were at the time updated with driver and sponsor changes. The boxes were uniquely colored to match the colors on the car.

CAR / DRIVER / SPONSOR	MINT	NRMT
4 Sterling Marlin	20.00	9.00
Kodak		
6 Mark Martin	20.00	9.00
Valvoline		
7 Geoff Bodine	20.00	9.00
Exide Promo		
15 Dick Trickle	20.00	9.00
Ford Quality Care		
16 Ted Musgrave	20.00	9.00
Family Channel		
18 Bobby Labonte	20.00	9.00
Interstate Batteries		
21 Morgan Shepherd	20.00	9.00
Citgo		
23 Chad Little	20.00	9.00
Bayer		
24 Jeff Gordon	50.00	22.00
DuPont		
25 Ken Schrader	20.00	9.00
Budweiser		
26 Steve Kinser	20.00	9.00
Quaker State		
31 Ward Burton	20.00	9.00
Hardee's Promo		
32 Dale Jarrett	20.00	9.00
Mac Tools Promo by American Miniatures		
44 David Green	20.00	9.00
Slim Jim		
71 Kevin Lepage	20.00	9.00
Vermont Teddy Bear		
71 Dave Marcis	40.00	18.00
Olive Garden Promo		
75 Todd Bodine	20.00	9.00
Factory Stores of America		
87 Joe Nemechek	24.00	11.00
Burger King		

1996 Revell 1:24

This series was distributed in retail outlets. These cars were packaged in colored boxes that matched the color schemes of the cars.

CAR / DRIVER / SPONSOR	MINT	NRMT
2 Rusty Wallace	20.00	9.00
Penske Motorsports		

CAR / DRIVER / SPONSOR	MINT	NRMT
3 Dale Earnhardt	30.00	13.50
Goodwrench		
3 Dale Earnhardt	30.00	13.50
Olympic car		
4 Sterling Marlin	20.00	9.00
Kodak		
5 Terry Labonte	25.00	11.00
Kellogg's		
6 Mark Martin	20.00	9.00
Valvoline		
10 Ricky Rudd	20.00	9.00
Tide		
11 Brett Bodine	20.00	9.00
Lowe's		
16 Ron Hornaday	50.00	22.00
Smith Wesson		
16 Ted Musgrave	20.00	9.00
Family Channel Primestar		
17 Darrell Waltrip	20.00	9.00
Parts America		
18 Bobby Labonte	20.00	9.00
Interstate Batteries		
21 Michael Waltrip	20.00	9.00
Citgo		
24 Jeff Gordon	25.00	11.00
DuPont		
28 Ernie Irvan	20.00	9.00
Havoline		
37 John Andretti	20.00	9.00
K-Mart		
75 Morgan Shepherd	22.00	10.00
Remington		
75 Morgan Shepherd	25.00	11.00
Remington Camouflage		
75 Morgan Shepherd	22.00	10.00
Stren		
77 Bobby Hillin Jr.	25.00	11.00
Jasper Engines		
87 Joe Nemechek	20.00	9.00
Burger King		
88 Dale Jarrett	22.00	10.00
Quality Care		
99 Jeff Burton	20.00	9.00
Exide		

1996 Revell Collection 1:24

This series was produced for and distributed in hobby outlets. These cars have significant upgrades in comparision to the standard Revell 1:24 1996 pieces. Each car is packaged with a mounting base. The Terry Labonte Honey Crunch car has been the subject of market manipulation due to the sale of a large portion of the production run to the general public before they were distributed to hobby distributors.

CAR / DRIVER / SPONSOR	MINT	NRMT
2 Rusty Wallace	45.00	20.00
MGD Silver		
2 Rusty Wallace	35.00	16.00
Penske		
3 Dale Earnhardt	40.00	18.00
Olympic		
4 Sterling Marlin	35.00	16.00
Kodak		
5 Terry Labonte	400.00	180.00
Honey Crunch		
5 Terry Labonte	80.00	36.00
Kellogg's		
5 Terry Labonte	90.00	40.00
Kellogg's Silver		
6 Mark Martin	35.00	16.00
Valvoline		
8 Kenny Wallace	40.00	18.00
Red Dog		
10 Ricky Rudd	40.00	18.00
Tide		

CAR / DRIVER / SPONSOR	MINT	NRMT
11 Brett Bodine	35.00	16.00
Lowe's 50th Anniversary		
16 Ted Musgrave	35.00	16.00
Primestar		
17 Darrell Waltrip	35.00	16.00
Parts America		
18 Bobby Labonte	35.00	16.00
Interstate Batteries		
22 Rusty Wallace	40.00	18.00
Miller Genuine Draft SuperTruck		
22 Rusty Wallace	50.00	22.00
Miller Genuine Draft Silver SuperTruck		
23 Chad Little	60.00	27.00
John Deere		
23 Chad Little	90.00	40.00
John Deere Autographed		
23 Chad Little	70.00	32.00
John Deere Bank		
23 Chad Little	100.00	45.00
John Deere Bank Autographed		
24 Jeff Gordon	50.00	22.00
DuPont		
24 Jack Sprague	35.00	16.00
Quaker State		
25 Ken Schrader	35.00	16.00
Budweiser		
25 Ken Schrader	35.00	16.00
Budweiser Olympic car		
28 Ernie Irvan	35.00	16.00
Havoline		
30 Johnny Benson	35.00	16.00
Pennzoil		
37 Jeremy Mayfield	35.00	16.00
K-Mart		
52 Jack Sprague	35.00	16.00
Pedigree		
75 Morgan Shepherd	35.00	16.00
Remington		
75 Morgan Shepherd	50.00	22.00
Remington Camouflage		
75 Morgan Shepherd	35.00	16.00
Stren		
76 David Green	35.00	16.00
Smith and Wesson		
77 Bobby Hillin Jr.	35.00	16.00
Jasper Engines		
87 Joe Nemechek	35.00	16.00
Burger King		
88 Dale Jarrett	35.00	16.00
Quality Care		
99 Jeff Burton	35.00	16.00
Exide		

1997 Revell Club 1:24

These pieces were also a part of the continued growth of Revell's presence in the die cast market. In the last quarter of 1997, Revell formed a collector's club to which they distributed cars in this series. The actual cars themselves were from the same production run as the Collection cars and banks. Each car distributed by the club has a serial number on the chassis. The boxes were uniquely colored to match the colors on the car.

	MINT	NRMT
1 NDA	80.00	36.00
Coca Cola 600		
1 No Driver Association	40.00	18.00
Revell Club		
2 Rusty Wallace	100.00	45.00
Miller Lite		
5 Terry Labonte	100.00	45.00
Kellogg's		
5 Terry Labonte	200.00	90.00
Spooky Loops		
5 Terry Labonte	225.00	100.00
Spooky Loops Bank		

CAR / DRIVER / SPONSOR	MINT	NRMT
5 Terry Labonte	175.00	80.00
Tony the Tiger		
5 Terry Labonte	200.00	90.00
Tony the Tiger Bank		
18 Bobby Labonte	150.00	70.00
Interstate Batteries		
Texas Motor Speedway		
21 Michael Waltrip	90.00	40.00
Citgo Top Dog paint scheme		
23 Jimmy Spencer	175.00	80.00
Camel		
23 Jimmy Spencer	350.00	160.00
No Bull		
28 Ernie Irvan	110.00	50.00
Havoline		
28 Ernie Irvan	150.00	70.00
Havoline		
10th Anniversary paint scheme.		
28 Ernie Irvan	175.00	80.00
Havoline Bank		
10th Anniversary paint scheme		
33 Ken Schrader	100.00	45.00
Skoal		
37 Jeremy Mayfield	90.00	40.00
K-Mart		
40 Robby Gordon	90.00	40.00
Coors Light		
43 Bobby Hamilton	90.00	40.00
STP Goody's		
43 Jimmy Hensley	90.00	40.00
Cummins Super Truck		
46 Wally Dallenbach	90.00	40.00
Woody		
75 Rick Mast	90.00	40.00
Remington		
96 David Green	90.00	40.00
Caterpillar		
97 Chad Little	100.00	45.00
John Deere		
97 Chad Little	100.00	45.00
John Deere 160th Anniversary		

1997 Revell Collection 1:24

This series is the continuation of the 1996 series. It signals Revell's expansion into the diecast market by its sheer number of cars in the series.

	MINT	NRMT
2 Rusty Wallace	75.00	34.00
Miller Suzuka		
2 Rusty Wallace	50.00	22.00
Miller Lite		
2 Rusty Wallace	50.00	22.00
Miller Lite Japan		
2 Rusty Wallace	65.00	29.00
Miller Lite Texas Motor Speedway		
4 Sterling Marlin	45.00	20.00
Kodak		
5 Terry Labonte	65.00	29.00
Kellogg's		
5 Terry Labonte	80.00	36.00
Kellogg's 1996 Champion		
5 Terry Labonte	80.00	36.00
Kellogg's		
distributed by Mac Tools		
5 Terry Labonte	120.00	55.00
Kellogg's Texas Motor Speedway		
5 Terry Labonte	150.00	70.00
Spooky Loops		
5 Terry Labonte	150.00	70.00
Tony the Tiger		
6 Mark Martin	50.00	22.00
Valvoline		
7 Geoff Bodine	45.00	20.00
QVC		
8 Hut Stricklin	45.00	20.00
Circuit City		
10 Ricky Rudd	45.00	20.00
Tide		

CAR / DRIVER / SPONSOR	MINT	NRMT
11 Brett Bodine	45.00	20.00
Close Call		
15 Mike Colabacci	45.00	20.00
VISA		
16 Ted Musgrave	45.00	20.00
Primestar		
17 Rich Bickle	45.00	20.00
Die Hard Super Truck		
17 Darrell Waltrip	45.00	20.00
Parts America		
18 Bobby Labonte	45.00	20.00
Interstate Batteries		
18 Bobby Labonte	100.00	45.00
Interstate Batteries		
Texas Motor Speedway		
19 Tony Raines	45.00	20.00
Pennoil Super Truck		
21 Michael Waltrip	45.00	20.00
Citgo		
Pearson paint scheme		
21 Michael Waltrip	45.00	20.00
Citgo		
Top Dog paint scheme		
23 Jimmy Spencer	100.00	45.00
Camel		
23 Jimmy Spencer	350.00	160.00
No Bull		
25 Ricky Craven	50.00	22.00
Budwesier		
28 Ernie Irvan	50.00	22.00
Havoline		
28 Ernie Irvan	90.00	40.00
Havoline		
10th Anniversary paint scheme		
29 Jeff Green	40.00	18.00
Scooby-Doo		
29 Steve Grissom	40.00	18.00
Flintstones		
29 Robert Pressley	40.00	18.00
Tom & Jerry		
30 Johnny Benson	45.00	20.00
Pennzoil		
32 Dale Jarrett	40.00	18.00
White Rain		
33 Ken Schrader	55.00	25.00
Skoal		
35 Todd Bodine	40.00	18.00
Tabasco		
36 Todd Bodine	40.00	18.00
Stanley		
36 Derrike Cope	40.00	18.00
Skittles		
37 David and Jeff Green	40.00	18.00
Red Man Super Truck		
37 Mark Green	40.00	18.00
Timber Wolf		
37 Jeremy Mayfield	45.00	20.00
Kmart		
Kids Against Drugs		
37 Jeremy Mayfield	45.00	20.00
K-Mart Lady Luck		
37 Jeremy Mayfield	45.00	20.00
K-Mart RC Cola		
40 Robby Gordon	40.00	18.00
Coors Light		
41 Steve Grissom	40.00	18.00
Kodiak		
42 Joe Nemechek	45.00	20.00
BellSouth		
43 Bobby Hamilton	40.00	18.00
STP Goody's		
43 Jimmy Hensley	40.00	18.00
Cummins Super Truck		
46 Wally Dallenbach	45.00	20.00
Woody Woodpecker		
55 Michael Waltrip	45.00	20.00
Sealy		
60 Mark Martin	50.00	22.00
Winn Dixie		

CAR / DRIVER / SPONSOR	MINT	NRMT
75 Rick Mast Remington	45.00	20.00
90 Dick Trickle Heilig-Meyers	45.00	20.00
91 Mike Wallace SPAM	45.00	20.00
94 Ron Barfield New Holland	40.00	18.00
94 Bill Elliott McDonald's	45.00	20.00
94 Bill Elliott Mac Tonight	50.00	22.00
96 David Green Caterpillar	45.00	20.00
97 Chad Little John Deere Autographed box	60.00	27.00
97 Chad Little John Deere 160th Anniversary paint scheme	70.00	32.00
97 No Driver Association California 500	40.00	18.00
97 No Driver Association Texas Motor Speedway	40.00	18.00
98 John Andretti RCA	45.00	20.00
99 Jeff Burton Exide	45.00	20.00
99 Jeff Burton Exide Texas Motor Speedway	60.00	27.00
99 C.Bown/Exide ST	40.00	18.00

1997 Revell Hobby 1:24

This series, Revell Select, was produced to appease those collectors who wanted a upgraded production diecast without the upgrade price. The cars themselves appear to have similar production qualities as the Collection cars, but are lower priced and are packaged in black window boxes.

CAR / DRIVER / SPONSOR	MINT	NRMT
2 Rusty Wallace Miller Lite	40.00	18.00
4 Sterling Marlin Kodak	35.00	16.00
5 Terry Labonte Kellogg's	35.00	16.00
5 Terry Labonte Kellogg's Texas Motor Speedway	35.00	16.00
5 Terry Labonte Spooky Loops	60.00	27.00
5 Terry Labonte Tony the Tiger	40.00	18.00
6 Mark Martin Valvoline	35.00	16.00
10 Ricky Rudd Tide	35.00	16.00
17 Darrell Waltrip Parts America	35.00	16.00
18 Bobby Labonte Interstate Batteries	30.00	13.50
18 Bobby Labonte Interstate Batteries Texas Motor Speedway	70.00	32.00
21 Michael Waltrip Citgo Top Dog paint scheme	35.00	16.00
25 Ricky Craven Budwiser Lizard	40.00	18.00
28 Ernie Irvan Havoline	35.00	16.00
28 Ernie Irvan Havoline 10th Anniversary paint scheme	40.00	18.00
29 Robert Pressley Scooby-Doo	30.00	13.50
29 Robert Pressley Tom & Jerry	30.00	13.50
33 Ken Schrader Skoal	40.00	18.00

CAR / DRIVER / SPONSOR	MINT	NRMT
36 Derrike Cope Skittles	35.00	16.00
37 Jeremy Mayfield Kmart Kids Against Drugs	35.00	16.00
40 Robby Gordon Coors Light	35.00	16.00
42 Joe Nemechek Bell South	35.00	16.00
46 Wally Dallenbach First Union Bank	50.00	22.00
46 Wally Dallenbach Woody Woodpecker	30.00	13.50
75 Rick Mast Remington	35.00	16.00
91 Mike Wallace Spam	35.00	16.00
94 Bill Elliott McDonald's	35.00	16.00
94 Bill Elliott Mac Tonight	35.00	16.00
97 Chad Little John Deere 160th Anniversary paint scheme	35.00	16.00
97 No Driver Association Texas Motor Speedway	30.00	13.50
99 Jeff Burton Exide	35.00	16.00

1997 Revell Retail 1:24

This series, Revell Racing, was produced for and distributed in the mass-market.

CAR / DRIVER / SPONSOR	MINT	NRMT
1 No Driver Association Coca Cola 600	20.00	9.00
1 No Driver Association Mac Tools packaged in collectible tin	75.00	34.00
2 Rusty Wallace Penske	25.00	11.00
4 Sterling Marlin Kodak	30.00	13.50
5 Terry Labonte Kellogg's Texas Motor Speedway	25.00	11.00
5 Terry Labonte Spooky Loops	30.00	13.50
5 Terry Labonte Tony The Tiger packaged in Food City box	30.00	13.50
6 Mark Martin Valvoline	25.00	11.00
10 Ricky Rudd Tide	30.00	13.50
16 Ted Musgrave Primestar	30.00	13.50
17 Darrell Waltrip Parts America	20.00	9.00
17 Darrell Waltrip Parts America 6 Car set	200.00	90.00
21 Michael Waltrip Citgo Top Dog paint scheme	30.00	13.50
28 Ernie Irvan Havoline 10th Anniversary paint scheme	25.00	11.00
29 Robert Pressley Flintstones	20.00	9.00
29 Robert Pressley Scooby-Doo	20.00	9.00
29 Robert Pressley Tom & Jerry	20.00	9.00
37 Jeremy Mayfield Kmart	25.00	11.00
37 Jeremy Mayfield Kmart Kids Against Drugs	25.00	11.00
88 Dale Jarrett Quality Care	25.00	11.00

CAR / DRIVER / SPONSOR	MINT	NRMT
91 Mike Wallace Spam	30.00	13.50
97 No Driver Association California 500	20.00	9.00
97 No Driver Association Texas Motor Speedway	20.00	9.00
99 Jeff Burton Exide	25.00	11.00

1998 Revell Club 1:24

These 1:24 scale cars were the from the same production run as the Collection cars. Each car distributed by the club has a serial number on the chassis. The boxes were uniquely colored to match the colors on the car.

CAR / DRIVER / SPONSOR	MINT	NRMT
1 Dale Earnhardt Jr. Coke	125.00	55.00
1 Steve Park Pennzoil	200.00	90.00
1 Steve Park Pennzoil Indy	125.00	55.00
2 Rusty Wallace Miller Lite	120.00	55.00
2 Rusty Wallace Adventures of Rusty	150.00	70.00
2 Rusty Wallace Miller Lite Elvis	120.00	55.00
2 Rusty Wallace Miller Lite TCB Bank	125.00	55.00
3 Dale Earnhardt Coke	125.00	55.00
3 Dale Earnhardt Goodwrench Plus	150.00	70.00
3 Dale Earnhardt Goodwrench Plus Bass Pro	150.00	70.00
3 Dale Earnhardt Goodwrench Plus Daytona	150.00	70.00
3 Dale Earnhardt Jr. AC Delco	250.00	110.00
4 Bobby Hamilton Kodak	100.00	45.00
5 Terry Labonte Blasted Fruit Loops	125.00	55.00
5 Terry Labonte Kellogg's	100.00	45.00
5 Terry Labonte Kellogg's Corny	125.00	55.00
5 Terry Labonte Kellogg's Corny Bank	150.00	70.00
5 Terry Labonte Kellogg's Ironman Bank	150.00	70.00
12 Jeremy Mayfield Mobil 1	120.00	55.00
18 Bobby Labonte Interstate Batteries Hot Rod	120.00	55.00
18 Bobby Labonte Interstate Batteries Small Soldiers	100.00	45.00
21 Michael Waltrip Citgo	100.00	45.00
23 Jimmy Spencer No Bull	200.00	90.00
24 Jeff Gordon DuPont Chromalusion	200.00	90.00
24 Jeff Gordon DuPont	150.00	70.00
25 John Andretti Budweiser	100.00	45.00
28 Kenny Irwin Havoline	100.00	45.00
31 Mike Skinner Lowe's	100.00	45.00
31 Mike Skinner Lowe's Special Olympics	100.00	45.00
33 Ken Schrader Skoal	110.00	50.00
35 Todd Bodine Tabasco	125.00	55.00

CAR / DRIVER / SPONSOR	MINT	NRMT
36 Ernie Irvan / M&M's	125.00	55.00
36 Ernie Irvan / Wildberry Skittles	120.00	55.00
40 Sterling Marlin / Coors Light	120.00	55.00
41 Steve Grissom / Kodiak	100.00	45.00
42 Joe Nemechek / Bell South	100.00	45.00
44 Tony Stewart / Shell	150.00	70.00
44 Tony Stewart / Shell Small Soldiers	100.00	45.00
46 Wally Dallenbach / First Union	100.00	45.00
46 Jeff Green / First Union Devil Rays	100.00	45.00
50 Ricky Craven / Budweiser	125.00	55.00
50 No Driver Association / Bud Louie	125.00	55.00
74 Randy Lajoie / Fina	100.00	45.00
75 Rick Mast / Remington	100.00	45.00
81 Kenny Wallace / Square D Lightning	110.00	50.00
88 Dale Jarrett / Quality Care	120.00	55.00
88 Dale Jarrett / Quality Care Batman	120.00	55.00
90 Dick Trickle / Heilig-Meyers	100.00	45.00
96 David Green / Caterpillar	100.00	45.00
98 Greg Sacks / Thorn Apple Valley	100.00	45.00

1998 Revell Collection 1:24

This series was produced for and distributed in hobby outlets.

CAR / DRIVER / SPONSOR	MINT	NRMT
1 Dale Earnhardt Jr. / Coke	75.00	34.00
1 Steve Park / Pennzoil	65.00	29.00
2 Rusty Wallace / Adventures of Rusty	60.00	27.00
2 Rusty Wallace / Miller Lite	60.00	27.00
2 Rusty Wallace / Miller Lite Elvis	60.00	27.00
2 Rusty Wallace / Miller Lite TCB	60.00	27.00
3 Dale Earnhardt / Coke	75.00	34.00
3 Dale Earnhardt / Goodwrench Plus	70.00	32.00
3 Dale Earnhardt / Goodwrench Plus Bass Pro	90.00	40.00
3 Dale Earnhardt / Goodwrench Plus Brickyard Special	65.00	29.00
3 Dale Earnhardt Jr. / AC Delco Dealer Issued	125.00	55.00
3 Dale Earnhardt Jr. / AC Delco Trackside Issued	125.00	55.00
4 Bobby Hamilton / Kodak	40.00	18.00
5 Terry Labonte / Blasted Fruit Loops	65.00	29.00
5 Terry Labonte / Kellogg's	70.00	32.00
5 Terry Labonte / Kellogg's Corny	80.00	36.00
8 Hut Stricklin / Circuit City	40.00	18.00
9 Lake Speed / Birthday Cake	40.00	18.00
9 Lake Speed / Huckleberry Hound	40.00	18.00
12 Jeremy Mayfield / Mobil 1	65.00	29.00
18 Bobby Labonte / Interstate Batteries	50.00	22.00
18 Bobby Labonte / Interstate Batteries Hot Rod	80.00	36.00
18 Bobby Labonte / Interstate Batteries Small Soldiers	60.00	27.00
21 Michael Waltrip / Citgo	40.00	18.00
24 Jeff Gordon / DuPont	70.00	32.00
24 Jeff Gordon / DuPont Brickyard Special	65.00	29.00
24 Jeff Gordon / DuPont Chromalusion	110.00	50.00
25 John Andretti / Budweiser	40.00	18.00
28 Kenny Irwin / Havoline	60.00	27.00
28 Kenny Irwin / Havoline Joker	65.00	29.00
31 Dale Earnhardt Jr. / Wrangler	225.00	100.00
31 Mike Skinner / Lowe's	40.00	18.00
33 Ken Schrader / Skoal	50.00	22.00
35 Todd Bodine / Tabasco	40.00	18.00
36 Ernie Irvan / M&M's	100.00	45.00
36 Ernie Irvan / Wildberry Skittles	60.00	27.00
40 Sterling Marlin / Coors Light	60.00	27.00
41 Steve Grissom / Kodiak	40.00	18.00
42 Joe Nemechek / Bell South	40.00	18.00
44 Tony Stewart / Shell	65.00	29.00
44 Tony Stewart / Shell Small Soldiers	40.00	18.00
46 Wally Dallenbach / First Union	40.00	18.00
46 Jeff Green / First Union Devil Rays	40.00	18.00
50 Ricky Craven / Budweiser	60.00	27.00
50 No Driver Association / Bud Louie	65.00	29.00
74 Randy Lajoie / Fina	40.00	18.00
81 Kenny Wallace / Square D Lightning	50.00	22.00
88 Dale Jarrett / Quality Care	60.00	27.00
88 Dale Jarrett / Quality Care Batman	60.00	27.00
90 Dick Trickle / Heilig-Meyers	40.00	18.00
98 Greg Sacks / Thorn Apple Valley	40.00	18.00

1998 Revell Hobby 1:24

This series, Revell Select, was produced to appease those collectors who wanted a upgraded production diecast without the upgrade price. The cars themselves appear to have similar production qualities as the Collection cars, but are lower priced and are packaged in black window boxes.

CAR / DRIVER / SPONSOR	MINT	NRMT
1 Steve Park / Pennzoil	45.00	20.00
2 Rusty Wallace / Adventures of Rusty	35.00	16.00
2 Rusty Wallace / Miller Lite Elvis	35.00	16.00
3 Dale Earnhardt / Goodwrench Plus	40.00	18.00
3 Dale Earnhardt / Goodwrench Plus Bass Pro	45.00	20.00
3 Dale Earnhardt Jr. / AC Delco	50.00	22.00
4 Bobby Hamilton / Kodak	30.00	13.50
5 Terry Labonte / Kellogg's	35.00	16.00
5 Terry Labonte / Kellogg's Corny	40.00	18.00
8 Hut Stricklin / Circuit City	30.00	13.50
9 Lake Speed / Birthday Cake	30.00	13.50
9 Lake Speed / Hucklerberry Hound	30.00	13.50
18 Bobby Labonte / Interstate Batteries	30.00	13.50
18 Bobby Labonte / Interstate Batteries Hot Rod	30.00	13.50
21 Michael Waltrip / Citgo	30.00	13.50
23 Jimmy Spencer / No Bull	45.00	20.00
24 Jeff Gordon / DuPont	40.00	18.00
28 Kenny Irwin / Havoline	35.00	16.00
31 Mike Skinner / Lowe's	30.00	13.50
33 Ken Schrader / Skoal	35.00	16.00
35 Todd Bodine / Tabasco	30.00	13.50
36 Ernie Irvan / M&M's	40.00	18.00
36 Ernie Irvan / Wildberry Skittles	30.00	13.50
44 Tony Stewart / Shell	30.00	13.50
50 Ricky Craven / Budweiser	40.00	18.00
50 NDA / Bud Louie	30.00	13.50
77 Robert Pressley / Jasper	30.00	13.50
81 Kenny Wallace / Square D Lightning	30.00	13.50
88 Dale Jarrett / Quality Care	35.00	16.00

1999 Revell Club 1:24

These 1:24 scale cars were produced in very small numbers and were only available through the club.

CAR / DRIVER / SPONSOR	MINT	NRMT
2 Rusty Wallace / Miller Lite	100.00	45.00
2 Rusty Wallace / Harley-Davidson	120.00	55.00
3 Dale Earnhardt / Goodwrench	150.00	70.00
3 Dale Earnhardt / GM Goodwrench Sign	125.00	55.00
3 Dale Earnhardt / Wrangler	125.00	55.00
3 Dale Earnhardt Jr. / Superman	150.00	70.00
4 B.Hamilton/Advantix	100.00	45.00
5 Terry Labonte / Rice Krispy	125.00	55.00
5 Terry Labonte / K-Sentials	125.00	55.00

CAR / DRIVER / SPONSOR	MINT	NRMT
8 Dale Earnhardt Jr. Budweiser	150.00	70.00
9 Jerry Nadeau Dextor's laboratory	100.00	45.00
9 Jerry Nadeau Jetsons	100.00	45.00
10 Ricky Rudd Tide	100.00	45.00
12 Jeremy Mayfield Mobil 1	100.00	45.00
12 Jeremy Mayfield Kentucky Derby	120.00	55.00
17 Matt Kenseth DeWalt	150.00	70.00
18 Bobby Labonte Interstate Batteries	125.00	55.00
20 Tony Stewart Home Depot	175.00	80.00
20 Tony Stewart Habitat for Humanity	125.00	55.00
23 Jimmy Spencer Winston Lights	100.00	45.00
23 Jimmy Spencer No Bull	100.00	45.00
24 Jeff Gordon DuPont	100.00	45.00
24 Jeff Gordon DuPont Daytona	150.00	70.00
24 Jeff Gordon Superman	175.00	80.00
24 Jeff Gordon Pepsi	100.00	45.00
24 Jeff Gordon Star Wars	150.00	70.00
27 C.Atwood/Castrol	150.00	70.00
28 K.Irwin/Havoline	100.00	45.00
31 Dale Earnhardt Jr. Gargoyles 1997 Monty Carlo	100.00	45.00
31 Dale Earnhardt Jr. Sikkens Blue	100.00	45.00
31 Dale Earnhardt Jr. Sikkens White 1997 Monte Carlo	100.00	45.00
33 Ken Schrader Skoal Blue	150.00	70.00
36 Ernie Irvan M&M's	100.00	45.00
36 Ernie Irvan Pedagree	100.00	45.00
36 Ernie Irvan Crispy M&M's	125.00	55.00
40 Sterling Marlin Coors Brooks & Dunn	100.00	45.00
40 Sterling Marlin John Wayne	100.00	45.00
55 Kenny Wallace Square D	100.00	45.00
66 Darrell Waltrip Big K	100.00	45.00
88 Dale Jarrett Quality Care	100.00	45.00
88 Dale Jarrett Quality Care White	100.00	45.00

1999 Revell Collection 1:24

This series was produced for and distributed in hobby outlets.

CAR / DRIVER / SPONSOR	MINT	NRMT
1 Steve Park Pennzoil	70.00	32.00
2 Rusty Wallace Miller Lite	70.00	32.00
2 Rusty Wallace Harley-Davidson	75.00	34.00
3 Dale Earnhardt Goodwrench	70.00	32.00
3 Dale Earnhardt Goodwrench 25th	70.00	32.00
3 Dale Earnhardt Wrangler	90.00	40.00

CAR / DRIVER / SPONSOR	MINT	NRMT
4 Bobby Hamilton Advantix	70.00	32.00
5 Terry Labonte Kellogg's	70.00	32.00
5 Terry Labonte Rice Krispies	90.00	40.00
8 Dale Earnhardt Jr. Budweiser	70.00	32.00
9 Jerry Nadeau Dexter's Lab	70.00	32.00
9 Jerry Nadeau Jetsons	70.00	32.00
10 Ricky Rudd Tide	70.00	32.00
11 Dale Jarrett Rayovac	70.00	32.00
11 Dale Jarrett Green Bay Packers	70.00	32.00
12 Jeremy Mayfield Mobil 1	70.00	32.00
12 Jeremy Mayfield Mobil 1 Kentucky Derby	70.00	32.00
18 Bobby Labonte Interstate Batteries	70.00	32.00
20 Tony Stewart Home Depot	175.00	80.00
20 Tony Stewart Habitat for Humanity	125.00	55.00
22 Ward Burton Caterpillar	70.00	32.00
23 Jimmy Spencer No Bull	70.00	32.00
23 Jimmy Spencer Winston Lights	70.00	32.00
24 Jeff Gordon DuPont	70.00	32.00
24 Jjeff Gordon Superman	100.00	45.00
24 Jeff Gordon DuPont Daytona	90.00	40.00
24 Jeff Gordon Pepsi	90.00	40.00
24 Jeff Gordon Star Wars	90.00	40.00
25 Wally Dallenbach Budweiser	70.00	32.00
28 Kenny Irwin Havoline	70.00	32.00
30 Derrike Cope Jimmy Dean	70.00	32.00
31 Dale Earnhardt Jr. Gargoyles 1997 Monte Carlo	70.00	32.00
31 Dale Earnhardt Jr. Sikkens Blue	70.00	32.00
31 Dale Earnhardt Jr. Sikkens White 1997 Monte Carlo	70.00	32.00
31 Mike Skinner Lowe's	70.00	32.00
33 Ken Schrader Skoal Blue	70.00	32.00
36 Ernie Irvan M&M's	75.00	34.00
36 Ernie Irvan Pedigree	75.00	34.00
36 Ernie Irvan Crunchy M&M's	90.00	40.00
40 Sterling Marlin John Wayne	70.00	32.00
40 Sterling Marlin Coors Brooks & Dunn	70.00	32.00
40 Kerry Earnhardt Channelock	70.00	32.00
55 Kenny Wallace Square D	70.00	32.00
66 Darrell Waltrip Big K	70.00	32.00
88 Dale Jarrett Quality Care	70.00	32.00
88 Dale Jarrett QC White	70.00	32.00

CAR / DRIVER / SPONSOR	MINT	NRMT
99 Kevin LePage Red Man	70.00	32.00
00 Buckshot Jones Crown Fiber	70.00	32.00
0 Larry Pearson Cheez-it	70.00	32.00

1997 Revell Collection Banks 1:24

This series marks Revell's first attempt to produce a 1:24 scale car bank. It was distributed to hobby dealers are part of Revell's Collection line.

CAR / DRIVER / SPONSOR	MINT	NRMT
5 Terry Labonte Tony the Tiger	175.00	80.00
18 Bobby Labonte Interstate Batteries Texas Motor Speedway	150.00	70.00
28 Ernie Irvan Havoline	80.00	36.00
28 Ernie Irvan Havoline 10th Anniversary paint scheme	110.00	50.00
29 Jeff Green Scooby-Doo	80.00	36.00
35 Todd Bodine Tabasco	80.00	36.00
46 Wally Dallenbach First Union	70.00	32.00
46 Wally Dallenbach Woody Woodpecker	80.00	36.00
91 Mike Wallace Spam	80.00	36.00
97 Chad Little John Deere Autographed box	70.00	32.00
97 Chad Little John Deere Autographed box 160th Anniversary paint scheme	80.00	36.00
97 No Driver Association California 500	75.00	34.00

1998 Revell Collection Banks 1:24

This series marks Revell's second attempt to produce a 1:24 scale car bank. It was distributed to hobby dealers as part of Revell's Collection line.

CAR / DRIVER / SPONSOR	MINT	NRMT
1 Dale Earnhardt Jr. Coke	100.00	45.00
2 Rusty Wallace Miller Lite	100.00	45.00
3 Dale Earnhardt Coke	100.00	45.00
5 Terry Labonte Kellogg's	100.00	45.00
5 Terry Labonte Kellogg's Corny	100.00	45.00
9 Lake Speed Hucklerberry Hound	80.00	36.00
31 Dale Earnhardt Jr. Wrangler	250.00	110.00
88 Dale Jarrett Quality Care Batman	100.00	45.00

1999 Revell Collection Banks 1:24

This series was produced for and distributed in hobby outlets.

CAR / DRIVER / SPONSOR	MINT	NRMT
8 Dale Earnhardt Jr. Budweiser	120.00	55.00
9 Jerry Nadeau Dextor's Lab	100.00	45.00

CAR / DRIVER / SPONSOR	MINT	NRMT
12 Jeremy Mayfield Mobil 1	100.00	45.00
20 Tony Stewart Habitat for Humanity	120.00	55.00

2000 Revell Collection 1:24

These come in a plastic display with the car mounted to the base.

	MINT	NRMT
3 Dale Earnhardt Test Car	150.00	70.00
8 Dale Earnhardt Jr. Budweiser	75.00	34.00
8 Dale Earnhardt Jr. Test Car	150.00	70.00
20 Tony Stewart Home Depot ROTY	75.00	34.00
24 Jeff Gordon Test Car	150.00	70.00

1997 Revell Collection 1:43

This series marks Revell's first attempt to produce a 1:43 scale car. It was distributed to hobby dealers are part of Revell's Collection line.

	MINT	NRMT
1 No Driver Association Coca-Cola 600	30.00	13.50
2 Rusty Wallace Miller Lite	35.00	16.00
5 Terry Labonte Spooky Loops	35.00	16.00
5 Terry Labonte Tony The Tiger	35.00	16.00
6 Mark Martin Valvoline	30.00	13.50
21 Michael Waltrip Citgo	25.00	11.00
21 Michael Waltrip Citgo Top Dog paint scheme	25.00	11.00
23 Jimmy Spencer Camel	35.00	16.00
25 Ricky Craven Budweiser	30.00	13.50
28 Ernie Irvan Havoline	30.00	13.50
28 Ernie Irvan Texaco 10th Anniversary paint scheme	35.00	16.00
29 Jeff Green Tom & Jerry	25.00	11.00
29 Robert Pressley Flintstones	25.00	11.00
29 Robert Pressley Scooby-Doo	25.00	11.00
30 Johnny Benson Pennzoil	30.00	13.50
33 Ken Schrader Skoal	30.00	13.50
36 Derrike Cope Skittles	30.00	13.50
37 Jeremy Mayfield Kmart Kids Against Drugs	30.00	13.50
41 Steve Grissom Kodiak	30.00	13.50
43 Bobby Hamilton STP	30.00	13.50
46 Wally Dallenbach Woody Woodpecker	30.00	13.50
88 Dale Jarrett Ford Credit	35.00	16.00
94 Bill Elliott Mac Tonight	35.00	16.00
96 David Green Caterpillar	30.00	13.50

CAR / DRIVER / SPONSOR	MINT	NRMT
97 Chad Little John Deere 160th Anniversary paint scheme	35.00	16.00
99 Jeff Burton Exide	30.00	13.50

1998 Revell Collection 1:43

This series marks Revell's second attempt to produce a 1:43 scale car. It was distributed to hobby dealers are part of Revell's Collection line.

	MINT	NRMT
1 Dale Earnhardt Jr. Coke	30.00	13.50
1 Steve Park Pennzoil	30.00	13.50
1 Steve Park Pennzoil Indy	30.00	13.50
2 Rusty Wallace Adventures of Rusty	30.00	13.50
2 Rusty Wallace Miller Lite Elvis	30.00	13.50
3 Dale Earnhardt Coke	30.00	13.50
3 Dale Earnhardt Goodwrench Plus	40.00	18.00
3 Dale Earnhardt Goodwrench Plus Bass Pro	40.00	18.00
5 Terry Labonte Blasted Fruit Loops	30.00	13.50
5 Terry Labonte Kellogg's	30.00	13.50
5 Terry Labonte Kellogg's Corny	30.00	13.50
5 Terry Labonte Kellogg's Ironman	30.00	13.50
12 Jeremy Mayfield Mobil 1	30.00	13.50
18 Bobby Labonte Interstate Batteries	30.00	13.50
18 Bobby Labonte Interstate Batteries Hot Rod	30.00	13.50
18 Bobby Labonte Interstate Batteries Small Soldiers	30.00	13.50
23 Jimmy Spencer No Bull	40.00	18.00
24 Jeff Gordon DuPont	40.00	18.00
24 Jeff Gordon DuPont Chromalusion	50.00	22.00
28 Kenny Irwin Havoline	30.00	13.50
28 Kenny Irwin Havoline Joker	30.00	13.50
31 Dale Earnhardt Jr. Wrangler	60.00	27.00
31 Mike Skinner Lowe's	30.00	13.50
31 Mike Skinner Lowe's Special Olympics	30.00	13.50
33 Ken Schrader Skoal	30.00	13.50
36 Ernie Irvan M&M's	30.00	13.50
36 Ernie Irvan Wildberry Skittles	30.00	13.50
41 Steve Grissom Kodiak	30.00	13.50
44 Tony Stewart Shell Small Soldiers	30.00	13.50
50 Ricky Craven Budweiser	35.00	16.00
50 No Driver Association Bud Louie	35.00	16.00
81 Kenny Wallace Square D	30.00	13.50
81 Kenny Wallace Square D Lightning	30.00	13.50

CAR / DRIVER / SPONSOR	MINT	NRMT
88 Dale Jarrett Quality Care	30.00	13.50
88 Dale Jarrett Quality Care Batman	30.00	13.50

1999 Revell Collection 1:43

This series was produced for and distributed in hobby outlets.

	MINT	NRMT
2 Rusty Wallace Miller Lite Harley Davidson	30.00	13.50
3 Dale Earnhardt Goodwrench	30.00	13.50
3 Dale Earnhardt Jr. AC Delco	30.00	13.50
3 Dale Earnhardt Wrangler	30.00	13.50
8 Dale Earnhardt Jr. Budweiser	30.00	13.50
23 Jimmy Spencer No Bull	30.00	13.50
23 Jimmy Spencer Winston Lights	30.00	13.50
24 Jeff Gordon Superman	35.00	16.00
24 Jeff Gordon DuPont	30.00	13.50
24 Jeff Gordon Pepsi	30.00	13.50
24 Jeff Gordon Star Wars	30.00	13.50

2000 Revell Collection 1:43

These cars come in a plastic display with the car mounted to the base.

	MINT	NRMT
3 Dale Earnhardt GM Goodwrench Taz	30.00	13.50

1996 Revell 1:64

This series was distributed in retail outlets. These cars were packaged in black blister packs.

	MINT	NRMT
2 Rusty Wallace Miller Genuine Draft Promo	10.00	4.50
2 Rusty Wallace Miller Genuine Draft Silver car	8.00	3.60
2 Rusty Wallace Penske Racing	8.00	3.60

	MINT	NRMT
3 Dale Earnhardt Goodwrench	8.00	3.60

	MINT	NRMT
3 Dale Earnhardt Olympic	8.00	3.60

	MINT	NRMT
3 Dale Earnhardt Olympic Small Box	10.00	4.50
4 Sterling Marlin Kodak	6.00	2.70
5 Terry Labonte Kellogg's	6.00	2.70
6 Mark Martin Valvoline	6.00	2.70
9 Lake Speed SPAM	6.00	2.70
10 Ricky Rudd Tide	6.00	2.70
11 Brett Bodine Lowe's	6.00	2.70
16 Ron Hornaday Smith and Wesson	8.00	3.60
17 Darrell Waltrip Parts America	6.00	2.70

	MINT	NRMT
18 Bobby Labonte Interstate Batteries	6.00	2.70
21 Michael Waltrip Citgo with Eagle on deck lid	10.00	4.50
21 Michael Waltrip Citgo	6.00	2.70

	MINT	NRMT
24 Jeff Gordon DuPont	6.00	2.70
24 Jack Sprague Quaker State	6.00	2.70

	MINT	NRMT
28 Ernie Irvan Havoline	6.00	2.70
37 Jeremy Mayfield K-Mart	6.00	2.70

	MINT	NRMT
71 Dave Marcis Olive Garden Promo	10.00	4.50
75 Morgan Shepherd Remington	6.00	2.70
75 Morgan Shepherd Remington Camouflage	8.00	3.60
77 Bobby Hillin Jr. Jasper Engines	6.00	2.70
87 Joe Nemechek Bell South	8.00	3.60
99 Jeff Burton Exide	6.00	2.70

1996 Revell Collection 1:64

This series was produced for and distributed in hobby outlets. These cars have significant upgrades in comparision to the standard Revell 1:64 1996 pieces. Each car is packaged in a box which has the same color scheme as the car.

	MINT	NRMT
2 Rusty Wallace Miller	15.00	6.75
2 Rusty Wallace Miller Genuine Draft Silver	15.00	6.75
2 Rusty Wallace Miller Genuine Draft 2 car set	25.00	11.00

	MINT	NRMT
3 Dale Earnhardt Olympic	12.00	5.50
4 Sterling Marlin Kodak	8.00	3.60

	MINT	NRMT
5 Terry Labonte Honey Crunch	50.00	22.00
5 Terry Labonte Kellogg's 2 car set	25.00	11.00
6 Mark Martin Valvoline	8.00	3.60
6 Mark Martin Valvoline Dura Blend	10.00	4.50
10 Ricky Rudd Tide	8.00	3.60
11 Brett Bodine Lowe's Gold	8.00	3.60
16 Ted Musgrave Family Channel	8.00	3.60
17 Darrell Waltrip Parts America	8.00	3.60
18 Bobby Labonte Interstate Batteries	10.00	4.50
23 Chad Little John Deere	10.00	4.50
25 Ken Schrader Budweiser	8.00	3.60

	MINT	NRMT
25 Ken Schrader Budweiser Olympic	8.00	3.60

CAR / DRIVER / SPONSOR	MINT	NRMT
28 Ernie Irvan Havoline	8.00	3.60
30 Johnny Benson Pennzoil	8.00	3.60
37 Jeremy Mayfield K-Mart	8.00	3.60
75 Morgan Shepherd Remington	8.00	3.60
75 Morgan Shepherd Remington Camouflage	10.00	4.50

75 Morgan Shepherd Stren	8.00	3.60
76 David Green Smith and Wesson Super Truck	8.00	3.60
87 Joe Nemechek Burger King	8.00	3.60
88 Dale Jarrett Quality Care	8.00	3.60
99 Jeff Burton Exide	8.00	3.60

1997 Revell Collection 1:64

This series is the continuation of the 1996 series. It signals Revell's expansion into the diecast market by its sheer number of cars in the series.

1 No Driver Association Coca Cola 600 HO	10.00	4.50

2 Rusty Wallace Miller Lite	12.00	5.50

2 Rusty Wallace Miller Lite Texas Special	12.00	5.50

CAR / DRIVER / SPONSOR	MINT	NRMT
5 Terry Labonte Kellogg's	12.00	5.50
5 Terry Labonte Kellogg's 1996 Champion	20.00	9.00

5 Terry Labonte Kellogg's Tony HO	15.00	6.75

5 Terry Labonte Spooky Loops	15.00	6.75
18-May Bobby and Terry Labonte Interstate Batteries and Kellogg's 2-car Tin Set	35.00	16.00
Jun-60 Mark Martin Valvoline/Winn Dixie 2 car set	35.00	16.00

16 Ted Musgrave Primestar	10.00	4.50

23 Jimmy Spencer Camel HO	15.00	6.75
23/97 Chad Little John Deere 2 car set Autogrpahed tin	30.00	13.50

28 Ernie Irvan Havoline 10 Years HO	15.00	6.75

CAR / DRIVER / SPONSOR	MINT	NRMT
28 Ernie Irvan Havoline 2 car set	30.00	13.50

30 Johnny Benson Pennzoil	10.00	4.50

33 Ken Schrader Skoal HO	15.00	6.75

36 Derrike Cope Skittles	10.00	4.50

37 Jeremy Mayfield K-Mart RC Cola	10.00	4.50

40 Robby Gordon Coors Light	10.00	4.50

41 Steve Grissom Kodiak HO	15.00	6.75

43 Bobby Hamilton STP Goody's HO	15.00	6.75

91 Mike Wallace SPAM	10.00	4.50

97 Chad Little John Deere	12.00	5.50
97 Chad Little John Deere 2 car set	30.00	13.50

97 No Driver Association California 500	10.00	4.50

1997 Revell Hobby 1:64

This series, Revell Select, was produced to appease those collectors who wanted a upgraded production diecast without the upgrade price. The cars themselves appear to have similar production qualities as the Collection cars, but are lower priced and are packaged in black window boxes.

2 Rusty Wallace Miller Lite	10.00	4.50

4 Sterling Marlin Kodak	8.00	3.60

5 Terry Labonte Kellogg's	8.00	3.60
5 Terry Labonte Spooky Loops	10.00	4.50

5 Terry Labonte Tony the Tiger	10.00	4.50

6 Mark Martin Valvoline	8.00	3.60

7 Geoff Bodine QVC	8.00	3.60

17 Darrell Waltrip Parts America	8.00	3.60
17 Darrell Waltrip Parts America 7 Car Set	30.00	13.50
18 Mike Dokken Dana Super Truck	8.00	3.60
18 Bobby Labonte Intertstate Batteries	8.00	3.60

18 Bobby Labonte Intertstate Batteries Texas Motor Speedway	8.00	3.60

21 Michael Waltrip Citgo Top Dog paint scheme	8.00	3.60
25 Ricky Craven Bud Louie	10.00	4.50

28 Ernie Irvan Havoline	8.00	3.60

28 Ernie Irvan Havoline 10th Anniversary paint scheme	8.00	3.60

29 Steve Grissom
   Flintstones   8.00   3.60

29 Robert Pressley   8.00   3.60
   Cartoon Network
29 Bob Keselowski   8.00   3.60
   Mopar

32 Dale Jarrett   8.00   3.60
   White Rain
33 Ken Schrader   8.00   3.60
   Skoal

35 Todd Bodine   8.00   3.60
   Tabasco
36 Derrike Cope   8.00   3.60
   Skittles

37 Jeremy Mayfield   8.00   3.60
   Kmart
   Kids Against Drugs

40 Robby Gordon   8.00   3.60
   Coors Silver Bullet

41 Steve Grissom   8.00   3.60
   Kodiak

42 Joe Nemechek   8.00   3.60
   Bell South

43 Bobby Hamilton   8.00   3.60
   STP Goody's

43 Jimmy Hensley   8.00   3.60
   Cummins

75 Rick Mast   8.00   3.60
   Remington

94 Bill Elliott   8.00   3.60
   McDonald's

97 Chad Little   8.00   3.60
   John Deere 160th

97 No Driver Association   8.00   3.60
   Texas Motor Speedway

1997 Revell Retail 1:64

This series, Revell Racing, was produced for and distributed in the mass-market.

1 No Driver Association	6.00	2.70
Coca Cola 600		
2 Rusty Wallace	6.00	2.70
Penske		
5 Terry Labonte	6.00	2.70
Kellogg's Texas Motor Speedway		
5 Terry Labonte	8.00	3.60
Spooky Loops		
16 Ted Musgrave	6.00	2.70
Primestar		
18 Bobby Labonte	6.00	2.70
Interstate Batteries		
18 Bobby Labonte	6.00	2.70
Interstate Batteries		
Texas Motor Speedway		
21 Michael Waltrip	6.00	2.70
Citgo Top Dog paint scheme		
29 Robert Pressley	6.00	2.70
Cartoon Network		
29 Robert Pressley	6.00	2.70
Tom & Jerry		
30 Johnny Benson	6.00	2.70
Pennzoil		
37 Jeremy Mayfield	6.00	2.70
Kmart		
Kids Against Drugs		
37 Jeremy Mayfield	6.00	2.70
Kmart		
42 Joe Nemechek	6.00	2.70
Bell South		
91 Mike Wallace	6.00	2.70
SPAM		

CAR / DRIVER / SPONSOR	MINT	NRMT
97 No Driver Association California 500	6.00	2.70
97 No Driver Association Texas Motor Speedway	6.00	2.70

1998 Revell Collection 1:64

ALL CARS HAVE OPEN HOODS

	MINT	NRMT
1 Dale Earnhardt Jr. Coke	20.00	9.00

	MINT	NRMT
1 Steve Park Pennzoil	18.00	8.00

	MINT	NRMT
1 Steve Park Pennzoil Indy	15.00	6.75

	MINT	NRMT
2 Rusty Wallace Adventures of Rusty	12.00	5.50

	MINT	NRMT
2 Rusty Wallace Miller Lite	12.00	5.50

	MINT	NRMT
2 Rusty Wallace Miller Lite Elvis	12.00	5.50

	MINT	NRMT
2 Rusty Wallace Miller Lite TCB	12.00	5.50
3 Dale Earnhardt Coke	20.00	9.00

	MINT	NRMT
3 Dale Earnhardt Goodwrench Plus	12.00	5.50

	MINT	NRMT
3 Dale Earnhardt Goodwrench Plus Bass Pro	18.00	8.00
3 Dale Earnhardt Goodwrench Plus Brickyard Special	12.00	5.50

	MINT	NRMT
3 Dale Earnhardt Jr. AC Delco	30.00	13.50

	MINT	NRMT
4 Bobby Hamilton Kodak	10.00	4.50

	MINT	NRMT
5 Terry Labonte Blasted Fruit Loops	15.00	6.75

	MINT	NRMT
5 Terry Labonte Kellogg's	12.00	5.50

	MINT	NRMT
5 Terry Labonte Kellogg's Corny	15.00	6.75

	MINT	NRMT
5 Terry Labonte Kellogg's Ironman	15.00	6.75
9 Lake Speed Birthday Cake	10.00	4.50

	MINT	NRMT
9 Lake Speed Huckleberry Hound	10.00	4.50

12 Jeremy Mayfield
Mobil 1   12.00   5.50

23 Jimmy Spencer
No Bull   15.00   6.75

28 Kenny Irwin
Havoline Joker   12.00   5.50

18 Bobby Labonte
Interstate Batteries   15.00   6.75

24 Jeff Gordon
DuPont   12.00   5.50

24 Jeff Gordon
DuPont Brickyard Special   12.00   5.50

31 Mike Skinner
Lowe's   10.00   4.50

18 Bobby Labonte
Interstate Batteries Hot Rod   15.00   6.75

24 Jeff Gordon
DuPont Chromalusion   40.00   18.00

31 Mike Skinner
Lowe's Special Olympics   10.00   4.50

18 Bobby Labonte
Interstate Batteries Small Soldiers   15.00   6.75

25 John Andretti
Budweiser   12.00   5.50

33 Ken Schrader
Skoal   12.00   5.50

21 Michael Waltrip
Citco   12.00   5.50

28 Kenny Irwin
Havoline   12.00   5.50

33 Ken Schrader
Skoal Shootout   12.00   5.50

36 Ernie Irvan
M&M's · 18.00 · 8.00

44 Tony Stewart
Shell Small Soldiers · 18.00 · 8.00

75 Rick Mast
Remington · 10.00 · 4.50

36 Ernie Irvan
Wildberry Skittles · 12.00 · 5.50

46 Wally Dallenbach
First Union · 10.00 · 4.50

81 Kenny Wallace
Square D Lightning · 10.00 · 4.50

40 Sterling Marlin
Coors · 12.00 · 5.50

41 Steve Grissom
Kodiak · 10.00 · 4.50

46 Jeff Green
First union Devil Rays · 10.00 · 4.50

88 Dale Jarrett
Quality Care · 15.00 · 6.75

42 Joe Nemechek
Bell South · 10.00 · 4.50

50 Ricky Craven
Budweiser · 12.00 · 5.50

88 Dale Jarrett
Quality Care Batman · 15.00 · 6.75

1998 Revell Hobby 1:64

This series, Revell Select, was produced to appease those collectors who wanted a upgraded production diecast without the upgrade price. The cars themselves appear to have similar production qualities as the Collection cars, but are lower priced and are packaged in black window boxes.

1 Steve Park Pennzoil	12.00	5.50
3 Dale Earnhardt Jr. AC Delco	20.00	9.00
4 Bobby Hamilton Kodak	8.00	3.60

44 Tony Stewart
Shell · 10.00 · 4.50

50 No Driver Association
Bud Louie · 12.00 · 5.50

CAR / DRIVER / SPONSOR	MINT	NRMT
5 Terry Labonte Kellogg's Corny	10.00	4.50
8 Hut Stricklin Circuit City	8.00	3.60
18 Bobby Labonte Interstate Batteries	8.00	3.60
23 Jimmy Spencer No Bull	12.00	5.50
24 Jeff Gordon DuPont	10.00	4.50
31 Mike Skinner Lowe's	8.00	3.60
33 Ken Schrader Skoal	10.00	4.50
36 Ernie Irvan M&M's	10.00	4.50
50 No Driver Association Bud Louie	10.00	4.50
77 Robert Pressley Jasper	8.00	3.60
81 Kenny Wallace Square D Lightning	8.00	3.60

1999 Revell Collection 1:64

This series was produced for and distributed in hobby outlets.

	MINT	NRMT
1 Steve Park Pennzoil	15.00	6.75
2 Rusty Wallace Miller Lite	15.00	6.75
2 Rusty Wallace Harley-Davidson	15.00	6.75
3 Dale Earnhardt Goodwrench	15.00	6.75
3 Dale Earnhardt Goodwrench 25th	15.00	6.75
3 Dale Earnhardt Wrangler	15.00	6.75
3 Dale Earnhardt Jr. AC Delco	15.00	6.75
3 Dale Earnhardt Jr. Superman	18.00	8.00
4 Bobby Hamilton Advantix	15.00	6.75
5 Terry Labonte Kellogg's	15.00	6.75
5 Terry Labonte K-Sentials	18.00	8.00
8 Dale Earnhardt Jr. Budweiser	18.00	8.00
9 Jerry Nadeau Dextor's Lab	15.00	6.75
9 Jerry Nadeau Jetsons	15.00	6.75
11 Dale Jarrett Green Bay Packers	18.00	8.00

	MINT	NRMT
12 Jeremy Mayfield Mobil 1	15.00	6.75
12 Jeremy Mayfield Kentucky Derby	15.00	6.75

	MINT	NRMT
18 Bobby Labonte Interstate Batteries	15.00	6.75

	MINT	NRMT
20 Tony Stewart Home Depot	40.00	18.00
20 Tony Stewart Habitat for Humanity	35.00	16.00
21 Elliott Sadler Citgo	15.00	6.75
23 Jimmy Spencer No Bull	18.00	8.00

	MINT	NRMT
23 Jimmy Spencer Winston Lights	18.00	8.00
24 Jeff Gordon DuPont	15.00	6.75
24 Jeff Gordon Superman	18.00	8.00
24 Jeff Gordon DuPont Daytona	15.00	6.75
24 Jeff Gordon Pepsi	15.00	6.75
24 Jeff Gordon Star Wars	18.00	8.00

	MINT	NRMT
28 Kenny Irwin Havoline	15.00	6.75

CAR / DRIVER / SPONSOR	MINT	NRMT
31 Dale Earnhardt Jr. Gargoyles	20.00	9.00
31 Dale Earnhardt Jr. Sikkens Blue	15.00	6.75
31 Dale Earnhardt Jr. Sikkens 1997 Monty Carlo	15.00	6.75
31 Mike Skinner Lowe's	15.00	6.75

	MINT	NRMT
36 Ernie Irvan M&M's	15.00	6.75
36 Ernie Irvan Pedigree	15.00	6.75
40 Sterling Marlin John Wayne	18.00	8.00
40 Sterling Marlin Coors Brooks & Dunn	15.00	6.75
40 Kenny Earnhardt Channellock	15.00	6.75
88 Dale Jarrett Quality Care	15.00	6.75

2000 Revell Collection 1:64

These 1:64 scale cars come in a plastic case with the car mounted to the base and have opening hoods.

	MINT	NRMT
3 Dale Earnhardt GM Goodwrench	15.00	6.75
8 Dale Earnhardt Jr. Budweiser	15.00	6.75
18 Bobby Labonte Interstate Batteries	12.00	5.50
24 Jeff Gordon DuPont	15.00	6.75

1999 Team Caliber 1:24

This marks Team Calibers inaugural year in the Die-Cast market.

	MINT	NRMT
1 Randy LaJoie Bob Evans	80.00	36.00
5 Terry Labonte Rice Krispy	125.00	55.00
5 Terry Labonte K-Sentials	125.00	55.00
5 Dick Trickle Schneider	90.00	40.00
6 Mark Martin Valvoline	125.00	55.00
6 Mark Martin Eagle One	150.00	70.00
7 Michael Waltrip Philips	90.00	40.00
10 Ricky Rudd Tide	90.00	40.00
12 Jeremy Mayfield Mobil 1	100.00	45.00

CAR / DRIVER / SPONSOR	MINT	NRMT
12 Jeremy Mayfield Mobil 25th Anniversary	125.00	55.00
12 Jimmy Spencer Chips Ahoy	125.00	55.00
17 Matt Kenseth DeWalt	150.00	70.00
23 Jimmy Spencer No Bull	100.00	45.00
23 Jimmy Spencer Winston Lights	125.00	55.00
25 Wally Dallenbach Budweiser	90.00	40.00
30 Derike Cope Jimmy Dean	90.00	40.00
30 Derrike Cope State Fair	90.00	40.00
40 Sterling Marlin John Wayne	100.00	45.00
42 Joe Nemechek BellSouth	90.00	40.00
43 John Andretti STP	125.00	55.00
55 Kenny Wallace Square D	90.00	40.00
60 Geoffery Bodine Power Team	90.00	40.00
75 Ted Musgrave Polaris	100.00	45.00
99 Jeff Burton Exide No Bull	100.00	45.00

1999 Team Caliber Banks 1:24

This marks Team Calibers inaugural year in the Die-Cast market.

CAR / DRIVER / SPONSOR	MINT	NRMT
1 Randy LaJoie Bob Evans	125.00	55.00
5 Terry Labonte K-Sentials	150.00	70.00
5 Terry Labonte Rice Krispy	150.00	70.00
10 Ricky Rudd Tide	125.00	55.00
12 Jeremy Mayfield Mobil 1	150.00	70.00
23 Jimmy Spencer No Bull	150.00	70.00
23 Jimmy Spencer Winston Lights	150.00	70.00
25 Wally Dallenbach Budweiser	125.00	55.00
40 Sterling Marlin John Wayne	150.00	70.00
43 John Andretti STP	150.00	70.00
55 Kenny Wallace Square D	125.00	55.00

1999 Team Caliber 1:64

This marks Team Calibers inaugural year in the Die-Cast market.

CAR / DRIVER / SPONSOR	MINT	NRMT
5 Terry Labonte K-Sentials	40.00	18.00
5 Terry Labonte Rice Krispy	40.00	18.00
6 Mark Martin Valvoline	40.00	18.00
6 Mark Martin Eagle One	40.00	18.00
7 Michael Waltrip Philips	20.00	9.00
10 Ricky Rudd Tide	20.00	9.00

CAR / DRIVER / SPONSOR	MINT	NRMT
12 Jeremy Mayfield Mobil 1 P	20.00	9.00
12 Jeremy Mayfield Mobil 1	20.00	9.00
12 Jeremy Mayfield Mobil 25th Anniversary	30.00	13.50
12 Jimmy Spencer Chips Ahoy	40.00	18.00
12 Jeremy Mayfield Mobil 25th Anniversary P	40.00	18.00
23 Jimmy Spencer No Bull	20.00	9.00
23 Jimmy Spencer Winston Lights	30.00	13.50
40 Sterling Marlin Coors John Wayne	20.00	9.00
40 Sterling Marlin Coors Brooks & Dunn	20.00	9.00
43 John Andretti STP	40.00	18.00
55 Kenny Wallace Square D	20.00	9.00
75 Ted Musgrave Polaris	20.00	9.00
97 Chad Little John Deere	20.00	9.00
99 Jeff Burton Exide	20.00	9.00

1997-98 Winner's Circle 1:24

This series marks the teaming of Action Performance and Hasbro. This line of cars was produced for and distributed in the mass-market. It is highlighted by the Jeff Gordon Lifetime Series and the Dale Earnhardt lifetime Series.

CAR / DRIVER / SPONSOR	MINT	NRMT
2 Rusty Wallace Penske Elvis	30.00	13.50
3 Dale Earnhardt Goodwrench	30.00	13.50
3 Dale Earnhardt Goodwrench Plus	30.00	13.50
3 Dale Earnhardt Goodwrench Plus Bass Pro	35.00	16.00
3 Dale Earnhardt Goodwrench Silver	40.00	18.00
3 Dale Earnhardt Wheaties	40.00	18.00
3 Dale Earnhardt AC Delco 1996 Monte Carlo	25.00	11.00
3 Jay Sauter Goodwrench Super Truck	25.00	11.00
3 Dale Earnhardt Jr. AC Delco	30.00	13.50
16 Ron Hornaday NAPA	25.00	11.00
18 Bobby Labonte Interstate Batteries	25.00	11.00
18 Bobby Labonte Interstate Batteries Small Soldiers	25.00	11.00
22 Ward Burton MBNA Gold	25.00	11.00
24 Jeff Gordon Dupont Million Dollar Date	35.00	16.00
24 Jeff Gordon DuPont	30.00	13.50
24 Jeff Gordon DuPont Premier	40.00	18.00
24 Jeff Gordon Lost World	40.00	18.00
28 Kenny Irwin Havolline	25.00	11.00
28 Kenny Irwin Havoline Joker	25.00	11.00
31 Mike Skinner Lowe's	25.00	11.00

CAR / DRIVER / SPONSOR	MINT	NRMT
44 Tony Stewart Shell	25.00	11.00
44 Tony Stewart Shell Small Soldiers	25.00	11.00
81 Kenny Wallace Square D	25.00	11.00
88 Dale Jarrett Quality Care	25.00	11.00

1999 Winner's Circle 1:24

This line is the result of an alliance between Action and Hasbro to bring exclusive license such as Gordon and Earnhardt to the mass market.

CAR / DRIVER / SPONSOR	MINT	NRMT
2 Rusty Wallace Rusty	20.00	9.00
3 Dale Earnhardt Jr. AC Delco	35.00	16.00
20 Tony Stewart Home Depot	40.00	18.00
22 Ward Burton Caterpillar	30.00	13.50
24 Jeff Gordon DuPont	35.00	16.00
24 Jeff Gordon DuPont No Bull	35.00	16.00
24 Jeff Gordon Pepsi	35.00	16.00
24 Jeff Gordon Star Wars	30.00	13.50
88 Dale Jarrett Quality Care	20.00	9.00

2000 Winner's Circle Preview 1:24

Winner's Circle takes on a new look for 2000.

CAR / DRIVER / SPONSOR	MINT	NRMT
3 Dale Earnhardt GM Goodwrench Sign	25.00	11.00
3 Dale Earnhardt Goodwrench Taz No Bull	25.00	11.00
18 Bobby Labonte Interstate Batteries	25.00	11.00
20 Tony Stewart Home Depot	25.00	11.00
24 Jeff Gordon DuPont	25.00	11.00

1998 Winner's Circle 1:43

This series marks the teaming of Action Performance and Hasbro. This line of cars was produced for and distributed in the mass-market.

CAR / DRIVER / SPONSOR	MINT	NRMT
1 Dale Earnhardt Jr. Coke	10.00	4.50
2 Rusty Wallace Miller Lite Elvis	15.00	6.75
3 Dale Earnhardt Goodwrench Plus	15.00	6.75
3 Dale Earnhardt Goodwrench Plus Bass Pro	20.00	9.00
3 Dale Earnhardt Coke	10.00	4.50
3 Dale Earnhardt Jr. AC Delco	20.00	9.00
12 Jeremy Mayfield Mobil 1	15.00	6.75
24 Jeff Gordon DuPont	15.00	6.75
24 Jeff Gordon DuPont MDD Win	15.00	6.75
28 Kenny Irwin Havoline	15.00	6.75

CAR / DRIVER / SPONSOR	MINT	NRMT
31 Dale Earnhardt Jr. Sikkens Blue	15.00	6.75
88 Dale Jarrett Quality Care Batman	10.00	4.50
88 Dale Jarrett Quality Care	15.00	6.75

1999 Winner's Circle 1:43

This line is the result of an alliance between Action and Hasbro to bring exclusive license such as Gordon and Earnhardt to the mass market.

3 Dale Earnhardt Goodwrench 25th Anniversary	20.00	9.00
3 Dale Earnhardt Jr. AC Delco Superman	30.00	13.50
20 Tony Stewart Home Depot	40.00	18.00
22 Ward Burton Caterpillar	20.00	9.00
24 Jeff Gordon DuPont Superman	25.00	11.00
24 Jeff Gordon Pepsi	20.00	9.00
88 Dale Jarrett Quality Care No Bull 5 Win	20.00	9.00

1999 Winner's Circle Select 1:43

This set features cars Dale Earnhardt drove in various Winston Select races.

3 D.Earnhardt Goowrench Silver '95	20.00	9.00
3 Dale Earnhardt Goodwrench Olympic '96	20.00	9.00
3 Dale Earnhardt Goodwrench Bass Pro '98	20.00	9.00
3 Dale Earnhardt Goodwrench Wrangler '99	20.00	9.00

1999 Winner's Circle Speedweeks 1:43

These cars are preview cars for the 1999 Daytona 500.

3 Dale Earnhardt Goodwrench	12.00	5.50
3 Dale Earnhardt Jr. AC Delco	12.00	5.50
18 Bobby Labonte Interstate Batteries	12.00	5.50
24 Jeff Gordon DuPont	12.00	5.50

2000 Winner's Circle Preview 1:43

Winner's Circle takes on a new look for 2000.

3 Dale Earnhardt Jr. Superman '99	12.00	5.50
18 Bobby Labonte Interstate Batteries	12.00	5.50
20 Tony Stewart Home Depot	12.00	5.50
24 Jeff Gordon DuPont	12.00	5.50

1997-98 Winner's Circle 1:64

This series marks the teaming of Action Performance and Hasbro. This line of cars was produced for and distributed in the mass-market.

CAR / DRIVER / SPONSOR	MINT	NRMT

It is highlighted by the Jeff Gordon Lifetime Series and the Dale Earnhardt lifetime Series.

1 Jeff Gordon Baby Ruth	20.00	9.00

1 Jeff Gordon Carolina Ford	12.00	5.50
1 Steve Park Pennzoil	10.00	4.50
2 Rusty Wallace Penske Elvis	8.00	3.60
K2 Dale Earnhardt Dayvault's	10.00	4.50
2 Mike Bliss Team ASE Super Truck	6.00	2.70
2 Dale Earnhardt Mike Curb 1980 Olds	20.00	9.00
2 Dale Earnhardt Wrangler 1981 Pontiac	20.00	9.00
3 Dale Earnhardt Jr. AC Delco GN Champ	20.00	9.00
3 Dale Earnhardt Wrangler 1984 Monte Carlo	20.00	9.00
3 Dale Earnhardt Wrangler 1985 Monte Carlo	25.00	11.00
3 Dale Earnhardt Wrangler 1986 Momte Carlo	20.00	9.00
3 Dale Earnhardt Wrangler 1987 Monte Carlo Fast Back	20.00	9.00
3 Dale Earnhardt Goodwrench '88 MC	25.00	11.00
3 Dale Earnhardt Goodwrench 1990 Lumina	20.00	9.00
3 Dale Earnhardt Goodwrench Camaro ASA	15.00	6.75
3 Dale Earnhardt Lowes Foods	10.00	4.50

CAR / DRIVER / SPONSOR	MINT	NRMT
3 Dale Earnhardt Goodwrench 1994 Lumina	8.00	3.60
3 Dale Earnhardt Goodwrench 1995 Monte Carlo	8.00	3.60

3 Dale Earnhardt Goodwrench Silver	30.00	13.50
3 Dale Earnhardt Wheaties	15.00	6.75
3 Dale Earnhardt AC Delco	70.00	32.00
3 Dale Earnhardt Goodwrench	12.00	5.50
3 Dale Earnhardt Goodwrench Plus	8.00	3.60
3 Dale Earnhardt Goodwrench Plus Daytona	8.00	3.60
3 Dale Earnhardt Bass Pro	10.00	4.50
3 Dale Earnhardt Coke	8.00	3.60
3 Dale Earnhardt Jr. AC Delco	15.00	6.75
3 Jay Sauter Goodwrench Super Truck	6.00	2.70
8 Dale Earnhardt 10,000 RPM 1975 Dodge	20.00	9.00
12 Jeremy Mayfield Mobil 1	6.00	2.70
15 Dale Earnhardt Wrangler 1982 TB	8.00	3.60
16 Jeff Gordon 1985 Pro Sprint	30.00	13.50

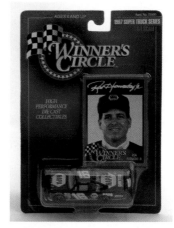

16 Ron Hornaday NAPA	8.00	3.60
18 Bobby Labonte Interstate Batteries	6.00	2.70

CAR / DRIVER / SPONSOR	MINT	NRMT
18 Bobby Labonte Interstates Batteries Small Soldiers	6.00	2.70
18 B.Labonte/IB Hot Rod '98	6.00	2.70
22 Ward Burton MBNA	6.00	2.70
22 Ward Burton MBNA Gold	6.00	2.70
24 Jeff Gordon DuPont 1993 Lumina	20.00	9.00

CAR / DRIVER / SPONSOR	MINT	NRMT
24 Jeff Gordon DuPont 1994 Lumina	15.00	6.75
24 Jeff Gordon DuPont	20.00	9.00
24 Jeff Gordon DuPont 1997 Champion Gordon on Roof of Car	20.00	9.00
24 Jeff Gordon DuPont ChromaPremier	25.00	11.00
24 Jeff Gordon Lost World	15.00	6.75
24 Jeff Gordon Dupont Million Dollar Date	10.00	4.50
24 Jeff Gordon DuPont 1998	10.00	4.50
24 Jeff Gordon DuPont No Bull Brickyard 1998	15.00	6.75
24 Jeff Gordon DuPont '98 Champ	10.00	4.50
27 Kenny Irwin Tonka	6.00	2.70
28 Kenny Irwin Havoline	6.00	2.70
31 Mike Skinner Lowe's	6.00	2.70
32 Dale Jarrett White Rain 1998	6.00	2.70
33 K.Schrader/APR '98	6.00	2.70

	MINT	NRMT
40 Jeff Gordon Challenger Sprint	40.00	18.00

CAR / DRIVER / SPONSOR	MINT	NRMT
44 Tony Stewart Shell	10.00	4.50
44 Tony Stewart Shell Small Soldiers	6.00	2.70
81 Kenny Wallace Square D	6.00	2.70
88 Dale Jarrett Quality Care 1997	6.00	2.70
88 Dale Jarrett Quality Care	6.00	2.70
98 Dale Earnhardt 1978 MC	30.00	13.50

1998 Winner's Circle Pit Row 1:64

This set displays the car on pit road being serviced by the crew.

	MINT	NRMT
1 Dale Earnhardt Jr. Coke	15.00	6.75
1 Steve Park Pennzoil	15.00	6.75
2 Rusty Wallace Rusty	15.00	6.75
2 Rusty Wallace Elvis	15.00	6.75
3 Dale Earnhardt Coke	15.00	6.75
3 Dale Earnhardt Bass Pro	15.00	6.75
3 Dale Earnhardt Goodwrench	15.00	6.75
3 Dale Earnhardt Jr. AC Delco	15.00	6.75
12 Jeremy Mayfield Mobil 1	15.00	6.75
18 Bobby Labonte Interstate Batteries	15.00	6.75
18 Bobby Labonte Small Soldiers	15.00	6.75
22 Ward Burton MBNA	15.00	6.75
24 Jeff Gordon DuPont	15.00	6.75
28 Kenny Irwin Havoline	15.00	6.75
28 Kenny Irwin Joker	15.00	6.75
31 Mike Skinner Lowe's	15.00	6.75
33 Ken Schrader Schrader	15.00	6.75
88 Dale Jarrett Batman	15.00	6.75
88 Dale Jarrett Quality Care	15.00	6.75

1999 Winner's Circle 1:64

This line is the result of an alliance between Action and Hasbro to bring exclusive license such as Gordon and Earnhardt to the mass market.

	MINT	NRMT
1 Dale Earnhardt Jr. Coke	15.00	6.75

CAR / DRIVER / SPONSOR	MINT	NRMT
2 Dale Earnhardt Crane Cams 1979 Monte Carlo	10.00	4.50
2 Rusty Wallace Rusty	6.00	2.70
3 Dale Earnhardt Goodwrench '89 Monte Carlo	10.00	4.50
3 Dale Earnhardt Goodwrench 1995 Brickyard Winner	10.00	4.50
3 Dale Earnhardt Coke	15.00	6.75
3 Dale Earnhardt Goodwrench	10.00	4.50
3 Dale Earnhardt Jr. AC Delco	10.00	4.50
7 Alan Kulwicki Hooters	10.00	4.50
8 Dale Earnhardt Goodwrench '88	10.00	4.50
12 Jeremy Mayfield Mobil 1	6.00	2.70
12 Jeremy Mayfield Mobil 1 Kentucky	8.00	3.60
16 Ron Hornaday NAPA '98 Champ	6.00	2.70
18 Bobby Labonte Interstate Batteries	10.00	4.50
19 Mike Skinner Yellow Freight	12.00	5.50
20 Tony Stewart Home Depot	30.00	13.50
20 Tony Stewart Home Depot with rookie stripe	20.00	9.00
22 Ward Burton Caterpillar	10.00	4.50
24 Jeff Gordon DuPont	10.00	4.50
24 Jeff Gordon Datona 500 Celebration	16.00	7.25
24 Jeff Gordon DuPont Datona Win	20.00	9.00
24 Jeff Gordon Superman	10.00	4.50
24 Jeff Gordon Pepsi	10.00	4.50
24 Jeff Gordon Star Wars	12.00	5.50
28 Kenny Irwin Havoilne	6.00	2.70
31 Dale Earnhardt Jr. Gargoyles	12.00	5.50
31 Dale Earnhardt Jr. Sikkens	10.00	4.50
31 Dale Earnhardt Jr. Wrangler	12.00	5.50
31 Mike Skinner Kolbalt	15.00	6.75
33 Ken Schrader APR	6.00	2.70
88 Dale Jarrett Quality Care	6.00	2.70

88 Dale Jarrett
Quality Care No Bull 5 Winner — 6.00 | 2.70

1999 Winner's Circle Fantasy Pack 1:64

This set includes the vehicles a plane, a boat, and a car all in same paint.

	MINT	NRMT
3 Dale Earnhardt Jr. AC Delco	12.00	5.50
3 Dale Earnhardt Goodwrench	12.00	5.50
3 Dale Earnhardt Wrangler	12.00	5.50
24 Jeff Gordon DuPont	12.00	5.50
24 Jeff Gordon Pepsi	12.00	5.50

1999 Winner's Circle Pit Row 1:64

These cars are set in a pit scene.

	MINT	NRMT
2 Rusty Wallace Rusty	15.00	6.75
3 Dale Earnhardt Goodwrench 25th	15.00	6.75
3 Dale Earnhardt Jr. Superman	15.00	6.75
20 Tony Stewart Home Depot	30.00	13.50
22 Ward Burton Caterpillar	15.00	6.75
24 Jeff Gordon Dupont No Bull 5 Winner	15.00	6.75
24 Jeff Gordon Superman	15.00	6.75
24 Jeff Gordon Pepsi	15.00	6.75
27 Casey Atwood Castrol	25.00	11.00

1999 Winner's Circle Speedweeks 1:64

These cars are preview cars for the 1999 Daytona 500.

	MINT	NRMT
2 Rusty Wallace Rusty	8.00	3.60
3 Dale Earnhardt Goodwrench	8.00	3.60
12 Jeremy Mayfield Mobil 1	8.00	3.60
18 Bobby Labonte Interstate Batteries	8.00	3.60
24 Jeff Gordon Dupont	8.00	3.60
28 Kenny Irwin Havoline	8.00	3.60
88 Dale Jarrett Quality Care	8.00	3.60

1999 Winner's Circle Tech Series 1:64

These 1:64 scale cars feature bodies that are removable from the chassis.

	MINT	NRMT
2 Rusty Wallace	8.00	3.60
3 Dale Earnhardt Goodwrench	15.00	6.75

3 Dale Earnhardt Jr.
AC Delco — 15.00 | 6.75

Jeremy Mayfield

	MINT	NRMT
12 Jeremy Mayfield Mobil 1	8.00	3.60
18 Bobby Labonte Interstate Batteries	20.00	9.00
24 Jeff Gordon DuPont	20.00	9.00

Kenny Irwin

	MINT	NRMT
28 Kenny Irwin Havoline	8.00	3.60

Dale Jarrett

	MINT	NRMT
88 Dale Jarrett Quality Care	8.00	3.60

1999 Winner's Circle Track Support Crew 1:64

This set features Support vehicles in the drivers colors.

	MINT	NRMT
3 Dale Earnhardt Goodwrench	16.00	7.25
3 Dale Earnhardt Jr. AC Delco	16.00	7.25
24 Jeff Gordon DuPont	16.00	7.25
24 Jeff Gordon Pepsi	16.00	7.25

1999 Winner's Circle 24K Gold 1:64

These cars are gold plated on a gold plated base.

	MINT	NRMT
3 Dale Earnhardt Goodwrench	20.00	9.00
3 Dale Earnhardt Jr. AC Delco	20.00	9.00
24 Jeff Gordon DuPont	20.00	9.00
24 Jeff Gordon Pepsi	20.00	9.00

2000 Winner's Circle Preview 1:64

Winner's Circle takes on a new look for 2000 with the car sitting at an angle not flat on the card back and a blue back ground.

	MINT	NRMT
3 Dale Earnhardt GM Goodwrench Sign	8.00	3.60
18 Bobby Labonte Interstate Batteries	8.00	3.60
20 Tony Stewart Home Depot First Win	8.00	3.60
24 Jeff Gordon DuPont	8.00	3.60
27 Casey Atwood Castrol New Stars of NASCAR	8.00	3.60
31 Mike Skinner Lowe's	8.00	3.60

2000 Winner's Circle Deluxe 1:64

These 1:64 scale cars come with a larger replica hood painted in the sponsors colors.

	MINT	NRMT
3 Dale Earnhardt Goodwrench	10.00	4.50
18 Bobby Labonte Interstate Batteries	10.00	4.50
20 Tony Stewart Home Depot	10.00	4.50
24 Jeff Gordon DuPont	10.00	4.50

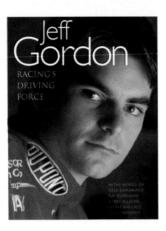
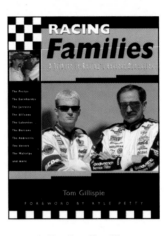
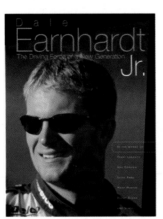